THE EMERGING PUBLIC REALM OF THE GREATER BAY AREA

Through illustrated case studies and conceptual re-framings, this volume showcases ongoing transformations in public space, and its relationship to the public realm more broadly in the world's most populous urban megaregion—the Greater Bay Area of southeastern China—projected to reach eighty million inhabitants by the year 2025.

This book assembles diverse approaches to interrogating the forms of public space and the public realm that are emerging in the context of this region's rapid urban development in the last forty years, bringing together authors from urbanism, architecture, planning, sociology, anthropology and politics to examine innovative ways of framing and conceptualizing public space in/of the Greater Bay Area. The blend of authors' first-hand practical experiences has created a unique cross-disciplinary book that employs public space to frame issues of planning, political control, social inclusion, participation, learning/education and appropriation in the production of everyday urbanism. In the context of the Greater Bay Area, such spaces and practices also present opportunities for reconfiguring design-driven urban practice beyond traditional interventions manifested by the design of physical objects and public amenities to the design of new social protocols, processes, infrastructures and capabilities.

This is a captivating new dimension of urbanism and critical urban practice and will be of interest to academics, students and practitioners interested in urbanization in China.

Miodrag Mitrašinović is professor of Urbanism and Architecture at Parsons School of Design, The New School. Miodrag is the co-editor of the *Public Space Reader* (Routledge 2021); editor of *Concurrent Urbanities: Designing Infrastructures of Inclusion* (Routledge 2016); co-editor of *Travel, Space, Architecture* (Routledge 2009); and author of *Total Landscape, Theme Parks, Public Space* (Routledge 2006). One of the foci of his scholarly work is infrastructural dimensions of public space, specifically at the intersections of urban and public design, socio-spatial justice and public policy.

Timothy Jachna is professor of Architecture and Dean of the School of Design, Architecture, Art, and Planning (DAAP) at the University of Cincinnati. His recent research and publications deal with the impact of digital technologies on urban public space, as well as the relationship between material/performative and psychological/sociological aspects of the planning, design, construction, inhabitation and critique of urban environments.

THE EMERGING PUBLIC REALM OF THE GREATER BAY AREA

Approaches to Public Space in a Chinese Megaregion

Edited by Miodrag Mitrašinović and Timothy Jachna

NEW YORK AND LONDON

First published 2021
by Routledge
605 Third Avenue, New York, NY 10158

and by Routledge
2 Park Square, Milton Park, Abingdon, Oxon, OX14 4RN

Routledge is an imprint of the Taylor & Francis Group, an informa business

© 2021 Taylor & Francis

The right of Miodrag Mitrašinović and Timothy Jachna to be identified as the authors of the editorial material, and of the authors for their individual chapters, has been asserted in accordance with sections 77 and 78 of the Copyright, Designs and Patents Act 1988.

All rights reserved. No part of this book may be reprinted or reproduced or utilised in any form or by any electronic, mechanical, or other means, now known or hereafter invented, including photocopying and recording, or in any information storage or retrieval system, without permission in writing from the publishers.

Trademark notice: Product or corporate names may be trademarks or registered trademarks, and are used only for identification and explanation without intent to infringe.

Library of Congress Cataloging-in-Publication Data
Names: Mitrašinović, Miodrag, 1965- editor. | Jachna, Timothy, editor.
Title: The emerging public realm of the Greater Bay Area : approaches to public space in a Chinese megaregion /edited by Miodrag Mitrašinović and Timothy Jachna.
Description: New York, NY : Routledge, 2021. | Includes bibliographical references and index.
Identifiers: LCCN 2021006263 (print) | LCCN 2021006264 (ebook) | ISBN 9780367367183 (hardback) | ISBN 9780367367176 (paperback) | ISBN 9780429350948 (ebook)
Subjects: LCSH: Regional planning—China—Guangdong Sheng. | Regional planning—China—Hong Kong. | Regional planning—China—Macau (Special Administrative Region)
Classification: LCC HT395.C552 G8354 2021 (print) | LCC HT395.C552 (ebook) | DDC 307.1/209512/7—dc23
LC record available at https://lccn.loc.gov/2021006263
LC ebook record available at https://lccn.loc.gov/2021006264

ISBN: 9780367367183 (hbk)
ISBN: 9780367367176 (pbk)
ISBN: 9780429350948 (ebk)

Typeset in Bembo
by Apex CoVantage, LLC

Publisher's Note
Chapter 4 has been prepared from camera-ready copy provided by the editors.

CONTENTS

List of Figures vii
List of Tables x
List of Contributors xi
Acknowledgments xvii
Glossary xix

    Introduction: Approaching the Public Space of the Greater Bay
    Area Megaregion   1
    Timothy Jachna

1 From the Pearl River Delta Estuary to the Greater Bay Area
    Megaregion: Producing the New Public Realm   9
    Miodrag Mitrašinović

2 Planning a Value Network of Exploding Infrastructures and
    Imploding Centers in Shenzhen   27
    Adrian Blackwell

3 Liquid Stories: Maritime Cultures in the Pearl River Delta   40
    Laurent Gutierrez and Valérie Portefaix

4 The Hyper-Collage City: Public Space in the Pearl River Delta   49
    Stefan Al

5 Gardens as Public Space: A Century of Continuity and Change in
    the Greater Bay Area, 1920–2020   62
    David Grahame Shane

6 Cross-Border and Transient Public Space in the Greater Bay Area   77
   Peter Hasdell

7 What Kind of Public Space Is the City of Shenzhen?   89
   Mary Ann O'Donnell

8 Interiorized urbanism in Macau: Model City for Post-Mao China   98
   Tim Simpson

9 A Comparative Study of Spatial Analysis and Residents' Perception of Accessibility to Public Open Space   109
   Yang Xiaochun, Shi Ji, Pei Xiaochen, Li Jingsheng, Zhang Li

10 Responsible, Remote Research and Design of the Public Realm in Shenzhen   120
   Georgeen Theodore

11 Soul of the City: Public Space and Urban Planning in Hong Kong   127
   Bo-sin Tang and Siu Wai Wong

12 Where 'City' Meets 'Village': Contesting Public Spaces During Shenzhen's Urban Renewal   136
   Juan Du

13 Three Genealogies: The Spatial Production of Social Publics in Tsuen Wan, Hong Kong   147
   Brian McGrath and Paul Chu Hoi Shan

14 Hong Kong's Civic Square: A Short History of a Public Space   158
   Mark W. Frazier

15 Reflections on Emerging Public Space Design Approaches in Hong Kong   168
   Hendrik Tieben and Chen Ying-Fen

16 Relearning the City and Public Space in the Greater Bay Area   180
   Merve Bedir and Jason Hilgefort

17 The GBA Public Realm and the Megaregional Dialectic: The Public Space of the Megaregion, Public Spaces in the Megaregion   192
   Miodrag Mitrašinović

Index   209

FIGURES

1.1	Urbanization of the Pearl River Delta between 1979 and 2020.	11
1.2	Border crossings. In clockwise order: Gong Bei border crossing between Macau and Zhuhai; The Venetian casino, Macau, line for the border bus; Hong Kong Port Passenger Clearance Building of the Hong Kong–Zhuhai–Macau Bridge; Hong Kong–Guangdong border at the Hong Kong–Zhuhai–Macau Bridge; Macau–Hong Kong Bridge Port Facility.	12
1.3	Manuel Castells' network diagram of the Pearl River Delta in 1996.	15
1.4	The Greater Bay Area Aggregate Rail Transit Network.	16
1.5	Lianhuashan Park, Shenzhen.	19
1.6	The Three Olds Regeneration Policy.	21
2.1	Shenzhen infrastructures and centers, 1980–2020.	28
2.2	The 1986 plan of Shenzhen SEZ.	32
2.3	The 1996–2010 plan of Shenzhen.	32
2.4	The Shenzhen urban design plan with major axis of development.	33
2.5	Investment intensity in Shenzhen, 1997–2018.	35
3.1	PRD on/off.	41
3.2	Disneyland reclamation in Lantau Island, 2002.	42
3.3	Amphibious living in the Pearl River Delta, Nansha area, 2004.	44
3.4	Man-made island serving as a geographic marker in Tolo Harbour, Hong Kong, 2013.	46
3.5	The amphibious creature Lo Ting walking out of the water at Chai Wan, 2017.	47
5.1	Heterotopic systems diagram.	63
5.2	Guangzhou city plan 1860: Enclaves, armatures, heterotopias.	65
5.3	PRD GZ-HK Machine City armature and enclave extensions.	68
5.4	Comparison of Futian CBD and Tianhe, Gangzhou.	70
5.5	Urbanus, Shenzhen Yuehai Community Culture and Sports Center (2020).	71
5.6	Litchi Gardens Liwan plan and photos.	72

6.1	Occupy central: Umbrella Movement Hong Kong, 29 September 2014.	78
6.2	Border ecologies, mapping cross-border eco-system operations on the Hong Kong-Shenzhen border, 2012.	79
6.3	Cross-border schoolchildren on the Hong Kong-Shenzhen border, 2014.	79
6.4	Cross-border schoolchildren diagram, 2014.	81
6.5	Hong Kong-Shenzhen cross-border logistics mapping.	83
6.6	Hong Kong-Shenzhen cross-border parallel trading mapping.	86
8.1	The Venetian Macao Resort, one of the world's largest buildings.	99
8.2	Simulated Lisbon cityscape and privatized public space enclosed under glass atrium in the MGM Macau Resort.	101
8.3	Interiorized urbanism in St. Mark's Square inside the Venetian Macao Resort.	104
8.4	Chinese tourists pack a suitcase with diapers and other everyday items purchased at shops in Macau.	105
8.5	Comportment of the quality tourist subject in the Venetian Macao Resort.	106
9.1	The distribution of the two types of residential buildings and their spatial relationships with POS.	112
9.2	Estimated population kernel density and spatial accessibility to POS within 10-minute walking distance (2015).	113
9.3	Comparison of spatial accessibility and residents' satisfaction by investigation area.	115
10.1	Detail of the "Clues" map.	124
10.2	The "Clues" map.	125
11.1	Public sitting-out area before and after upgrading in an old urban district.	129
11.2	New harbor-front promenade and public park network on Hong Kong Island.	131
11.3	Holistic planning in urban redevelopment for public space enhancement.	132
11.4	Reinvented public space at the Kwun Tong waterfront by Energizing Kowloon East Office.	133
11.5	Bottom-up reinvented public space at the Western District Public Cargo Working Area.	134
12.1	Shenzhen Civic Square.	137
12.2	Public space in Huanggang urban village, Shenzhen.	138
12.3	Futian CBD planning in 1984, and satellite image in 2003.	139
12.4	Locations of urban villages in the inner-city Shenzhen.	140
12.5	Operational strategy: Futian CBD phased planning and comparisons.	141
13.1	Map of the migration of Chu Hai University from its origins on the Pearl River in Guangzhou, to its temporary locations in Mong Kok and Tsuen Wan as Chu Hai College of Higher Education, to the new permanent campus of Chu Hai Hong Kong University in Tuen Mun.	148
13.2	Layered model of Tsuen Wan, from fishing village to satellite new town, to commercial node in the Greater Bay megaregion.	150
13.3	A field work "drawing machine"	155
14.1	Students enter Civic Square, Hong Kong, on 28 September 2014.	159
14.2	Hong Kong Civic Square on 18 October 2014.	159
14.3	Map of the Civic Square district.	160

15.1	Magic Carpet Community Re-Envisioning event in Sai Ying Pun at Moon Festival 2013 (Magic Carpet, 2013).	170
15.2	Public space prototyping and co-design of the MaD "Health Street Lab" at Sham Shui Po, Hong Kong, 2019.	172
15.3	"Morning exercise park" at Bishop Hill.	173
15.4	"Morning exercise park" at Bishop Hill.	174
15.5	"Morning exercise park" at Bishop Hill.	175
16.1	Discussion at Hubei metro stop during Shennan Avenue workshop on the public transportation infrastructure system of Shenzhen.	182
16.2	Gathering at an urban park in Shenzhen during an Aformal Academy workshop.	183
16.3	Collage made during the Melbourne University visiting-school workshop.	184
16.4	Shangmeilin Village workshop.	185
16.5	Baishizhou village workshop.	186
16.6	Maozhou River walk.	186
16.7	Wechat newspaper made during Mobile Spa + Tea House workshop.	187
16.8	"Maozhou River." Collage made during the Maozhou River workshop.	189
17.1	West Kowloon Station, Hong Kong.	194
17.2	The megaregional public space of Macau contrasted with exchange and negotiation in everyday public spaces of the old city.	197
17.3	Appropriations of GBA public spaces: singing in Central Park, Guangzhou; parallel traders at work in Macau; villain hitters of Causeway Bay, Hong Kong; and tai chi practice in Kowloon Park, Hong Kong.	201
17.4	Hong Kong Umbrella Revolution, October 2014.	202
17.5	Foreign domestic helpers gathering on Sunday morning in the entryway of the HSBC headquarters building.	203
17.6	Global Urban Studio books 2018 and 2019, Parsons School of Design.	204

TABLES

9.1 Questionnaire applied in this study. 114
9.2 Comparison of GRB and UVRB residents' perception of POS and spatial accessibility. 116
9.3 Residents' perception of accessible area of POS by investigation area. 116

CONTRIBUTORS

Stefan Al, PhD, is an architect, urban designer, researcher and TED resident. In addition to his professional work as a designer on high-profile projects across the world, he has published seven books and teaches at Virginia Tech and Columbia University. His latest research advocates for designing more resilient cities in the face of climate change, most notably in his new book *Adapting Cities to Sea Level Rise: Green and Gray Strategies* (Island Press 2018). His co-authored book, *Beyond Mobility: Planning Cities for People and Places* (Island Press 2017), won the National Urban Design Award. His book *Villages in the City* (Hong Kong University Press 2014) was selected by *Architectural Record* as "one of the best" books on informal urbanism.

Merve Bedir and Jason Hilgefort are co-founders of Land and Civilization Compositions (2012) and Aformal Academy (2015), based in the Pearl River Delta region. They approach design as a transdisciplinary, collective and multi-scalar act. Bedir is an adjunct assistant professor at Hong Kong University. She holds a PhD from Delft University of Technology, The Netherlands, and BArch from Middle East Technical University, Turkey. Merve's research focuses on the labor and ownership relations and organizational modes that produce public spaces and landscapes. Merve is also a founding member of the Kitchen Atelier and Center for Spatial Justice.

Adrian Blackwell's practice spans photography, video, sculpture, urban theory and design and responds to the political and economic forces inscribed in physical spaces. Blackwell's work has been exhibited at artist-run centers and public institutions across Canada; in the United States; and at the 2005 Shenzhen Biennale of Urbanism\Architecture, the 2011 Chengdu Biennial, the 2019 Toronto Biennial of Art and the 2019 Chicago Architecture Biennial. He has taught architecture and urbanism at universities in Chongqing, Michigan, Harvard and Toronto and is now an associate professor at the University of Waterloo. He is an editor and founder of the journal *Scapegoat: Architecture/Landscape/Political Economy*. With David Fortin, he is co-editing Issue 12—*c\a\n\a\d\a: Delineating a Capitalist Nations State*.

Juan Du is Dean of the University of Toronto's John H. Daniels Faculty of Architecture, Landscape and Design. Prior to joining University of Toronto, she taught architecture and urban design at the University of Hong Kong (HKU), the Massachusetts Institute of Technology and Peking University. Her research and design works have been published and exhibited in China, Europe and the United States. Her book *The Shenzhen Experiment: The Story of China's Instant City* was recently published by Harvard University Press. Dr. Du is a recognized scholar on China's rapid urbanization, and her works have been featured by international journals and media such as the *New York Times,* the *Wall Street Journal, Financial Times, Foreign Affairs, CNN, Wired* and *Nature.* Her research and design focus on the often-overlooked relationships between formal planning and informal developments. Through research activities and community design projects, she regularly collaborates with various stakeholders within the urbanization processes of mainland China and Hong Kong.

Chen Ying-Fen is a postdoctoral fellow at the Chinese University of Hong Kong and holds a PhD from the University of California Berkeley. She has participated in urban justice movements in Taiwan since 2006. Her academic interests include cinematic urbanism, filmic tourism, participatory planning and community design in Taiwan and Hong Kong.

Mark W. Frazier is professor of Politics at the New School for Social Research and Co-Director of the India China Institute at the New School. He has published articles on the 2019–20 Hong Kong protests for *Asia-Pacific Journal, Public Seminar,* and *The Washington Post Monkey Cage* blog. His book *The Power of Place: Contentious Politics in Twentieth Century Shanghai and Bombay* (Cambridge University Press 2019) examines long-term changes in political geographies and patterns of popular protest in the two cities. He is also the author of *Socialist Insecurity: Pensions and the Politics of Uneven Development in China* (Cornell University Press 2010) and *The Making of the Chinese Industrial Workplace* (Cambridge University Press 2002) and co-editor of the *SAGE Handbook of Contemporary China* (SAGE Publications 2018).

Laurent Gutierrez is a co-founder and co-principal of MAP Office, a multidisciplinary platform devised with Valérie Portefaix. This duo of artists/architects has been based in Hong Kong since 1996, working on physical and imaginary territories using varied means of expression including literary and theoretical texts. Gutierrez earned a PhD in architecture from RMIT. He is a professor at the School of Design, the Hong Kong Polytechnic University, where he leads the Master of Design program (MDes) and the MDes in design strategies, as well as the MDes in urban environment design.

Peter Hasdell is an academic, architect and urbanist. He is an associate professor in the Hong Kong Polytechnic University and Associate Dean of Academic Programmes at the School of Design. Peter is a former key research member of the renowned Chora Institute of Architecture and Urbanism, London and C.A.S.T., Manitoba, he founded the Architecture and Urban Research Lab (A+URL), Stockholm, Pneuma, Canada, and currently runs the In-situ Project (http://insitu-project.com) focusing on sustainable community development. His present research focuses on metabolic architecture on the scale of the city (city as a life form, urban ecology) and as architecture (interactive and responsive architectures). Recent publications include *Border Ecologies: Hong Kong's Mainland Frontier* (Birkhauser 2016).

Jason Hilgefort and Merve Bedir are co-founders of Land and Civilization Compositions (2012) and Aformal Academy (2015), based in the Pearl River Delta region. Their approach designs as a transdisciplinary, collective and multi-scalar act. Jason is a lecturer in urban design at Hong Kong University. His research focuses on how emerging infrastructure networks reframe the world that surrounds us.

Timothy Jachna is Dean of the School of Design, Architecture, Art, and Planning (DAAP) at the University of Cincinnati. He earned degrees from the University of Illinois at Chicago (BArch); the Architectural Association, London (AADip); and RMIT University, Melbourne (PhD). He has previously held academic and professional posts in architecture, design and urbanism in Hong Kong, Berlin and Chicago. His recent research and publications deal with psycho-sociological aspects of the planning, design, construction, inhabitation and critique of urban environments, spanning scales from the object to the regional plan. Jachna has presented and published in disciplines as diverse as urban theory, tourism, digital culture, social innovation, semiotics, participatory design, art, architecture, planning, cybernetics and human-computer interaction. His book *Wiring the Streets, Surfing the Square: Producing Public Space in the Mediated City* was published in 2021 by Springer.

Li Jingsheng is a professor in the Department of Urban Planning, College of Architecture and Urban Planning, Tongji University, China. He is mainly engaged in ecological urban design and rural planning research. His research on the background of Chongming Dongtan has made important contributions to eco-city theory and design research. Professor Li is the Chief Editor for the Chinese textbook *Principles of Rural Planning*. In 1991, he was a visiting scholar at the Bordeaux College of Architecture in France. In 1995, he received a PhD in regional planning and architecture from the College of Biological Resources, Nihon University. In 2004, was a visiting professor at the European Urban Research Center of the Weimar College of Architecture in Germany. Since 2015, he has served as an advisor to the Rural Planning and Construction Academic Committee of the Chinese Urban Planning Society.

Zhang Li is a postdoctoral researcher in the Department of Urban and Rural Planning, Shenzhen University. Doctor Zhang received his bachelor's degree in architecture from Harbin Institute of Technology; his master's degrees in architecture and building engineering from Tongji University and the University of Pavia, respectively; and his doctoral degree from the University of Kitakyushu, Japan.

Brian McGrath is professor of Urban Design and former Dean of the School of Constructed Environments, Parsons School of Design, the New School. McGrath served as a co-principal investigator in the Baltimore Ecosystem Study, where he led the Urban Design Working Group. His books and publications include: *Patch Atlas* (2019), *Urban Design Ecologies Reader* (2012), *Digital Modeling for Urban Design* (2008), *Transparent Cities* (1994), *Resilience in Ecology and Urban Design* (2012), *Growing Cities in a Shrinking World: The Challenges in India and China* (2010), *Sensing the 21st Century City* (2007) and *Cinemetrics: Architectural Drawing Today* (2007). McGrath also served as a Fulbright senior scholar in Thailand in 1998–99, India China Institute fellow in 2006–2008 and research director in the joint US-EU Transatlantic exchange program Urbanisms of Inclusion from 2010–2014. He has been an external advisor for the Chu Hai Department of Architecture since 2005. He received his MArch from Princeton University and BArch from Syracuse University.

Miodrag Mitrašinović is professor of Urbanism and Architecture at Parsons School of Design, the New School. Miodrag is the co-editor of *Public Space Reader* (Routledge 2021) and *Cooperative Cities (Journal of Design Strategies* Vol. 8, 2018); editor of *Concurrent Urbanities: Designing Infrastructures of Inclusion* (Routledge 2016); co-editor of *Travel, Space, Architecture* (Routledge 2009); and author of *Total Landscape, Theme Parks, Public Space* (Routledge 2006). Miodrag is has served in a variety of scholarly, professional and editorial roles, as well as various academic leadership roles. His professional and scholarly work has been published internationally. His scholarly work focuses on the role design plays as an agent of social and political change and as a catalyst for critical urban transformations. His research argues for the centrality of designing in the conceptualization, production and representation of democratic and participatory urban space. His work also focuses on the generative capacity and infrastructural dimensions of public space, specifically at the intersections of urban and public design, socio-spatial justice and public policy.

Mary Ann O'Donnell has sought alternative ways of inhabiting Shenzhen, the flagship of China's post-Mao economic reforms. As an artist-ethnographer, O'Donnell creates and contributes to projects that reconfigure and repurpose shared spaces where our worlds mingle and collide, sometimes collapse and often implode. Ongoing projects include her blog, "Shenzhen Noted," and Handshake 302, an art space that began in Baishizhou. In 2017, the University of Chicago Press published *Learning From Shenzhen: China's Post Mao Experiment From Special Zone to Model City*, which she co-edited with Winnie Wong and Jonathan Bach. Her research has been published in *positions: east asian cultures critique*, *TDR: The Drama Review* and the *Hong Kong Journal of Cultural Studies*. O'Donnell curated the "Migrations: Home and Elsewhere" exhibition at the P+V Gallery for the seventh edition of the Shenzhen-Hong Kong Bi-City Biennale of Urbanism\Architecture.

Valérie Portefaix is a co-founder and co-principal of MAP Office, a multidisciplinary platform devised with Laurent Gutierrez. This duo of artists/architects has been based in Hong Kong since 1996, working on physical and imaginary territories using varied means of expression including literary and theoretical texts. Portefaix is an artist and architect. After receiving a bachelor of fine art and a master of architecture, she earned a PhD in urbanism from the University Pierre Mendes, France. She is an adjunct professor at the Architecture Department, the Hong Kong University.

Paul Chu Hoi Shan is associate professor and Head of the Department of Architecture, Chu Hai College of Higher Education, Hong Kong. He received his BArch from the University of Hong Kong and his MSc in architecture and urban design from Columbia University, where he was Hong Kong Rotary Ambassadorial Scholar. Chu is a registered architect in both Hong Kong and PRC (Class 1). He is Fellow of the Hong Kong Institute of Architects and Founding Member of the Hong Kong Institute of Urban Design and was Convener of the Hong Kong Urban Design Alliance. Chu was awarded Contemporary Construction Expert of China, Hong Kong Young Architect Award, 21st Century Emerging Hong Kong Architect and Hong Kong 10 Outstanding Designers. His research interest in social and cultural sustainability expands architecture and urbanism discourse to sociological resilience. He was contributing editor for the books *Factory Towns of South China* (Hong Kong University Press 2012) and *Villages in the City* (Hong Kong University Press 2014), which revealed the spontaneity of planned urbanization in the Pearl River Delta of PRC.

David Grahame Shane is professor in the Urban Design program at Columbia University, Graduate School of Architecture, Planning and Preservation. He is the author of *Recombinant Urbanism: Conceptual Modeling in Architecture, Urban Design and City Theory* (Wiley 2005) and *Urban Design Since 1945: A Global Perspective* (Wiley 2011) and co-editor of *Sensing the 21st Century City: Close-up and Remote* (*Architectural Design* AD, 2005). He has published widely in architectural journals in Europe, the United States and Asia, including *Architectural Design, Lotus International, Artforum* and *Harvard Architectural Review*. He has also contributed to numerous edited volumes, including "Chinese Rapid Urbanization and the Megacity" in *Cities in Transition* (NAi, 2015) and "A Short History of Hong Kong Malls and Towers" in Stefan Al's (Ed) *Mall City: Hong Kong's Dreamworlds of Consumption* (2016).

Ji Shi is a registered urban and rural planner with a master's degree from Shenzhen University, 2018. She is currently working at the Transportation Development Planning Institute of Chengdu Urban Planning and Design Institute.

Tim Simpson is associate professor of Communication, Faculty of Social Sciences, University of Macau, where he has worked since 2001. He is the co-author (with photographer Roger Palmer) of the book *Macao Macau* (Black Dog Publishing 2015) and editor of the volume *Tourist Utopias: Offshore Islands, Enclave Spaces, and Mobile Imaginaries* (Amsterdam University Press 2017). He is currently completing a manuscript under contract with University of Minnesota Press entitled *Macau: Casino Capitalism and the Biopolitical City*.

Bo-sin Tang is a professor in the Department of Urban Planning and Design at the University of Hong Kong and the Programme Director of its MSc in Urban Planning program. Prior to joining University of Hong Kong, he was Professor and Associate Head of the Department of Building and Real Estate at the Hong Kong Polytechnic University. He received his PhD in urban and regional planning from the London School of Economics and Political Science. He is a fellow of the UK Academy of Social Sciences and holds professional memberships in the Royal Town Planning Institute, the Hong Kong Institute of Planners, the Royal Institution of Chartered Surveyors and the Hong Kong Institute of Surveyors. His research interests cover land use planning, property development and governance.

Hendrik Tieben is an associate professor at the Chinese University of Hong Kong, where he serves as Director of the MSc in Urban Design program and Assistant Director of the BSSc in Urban Studies program. His research focuses on public space, placemaking and community empowerment, and he has been published in a range of international journals. Since 2013, he developed the project series "Magic Carpet," which engages residents in the co-creation of community spaces.

Georgeen Theodore is an architect, urban designer and professor at the New Jersey Institute of Technology's College of Architecture and Design, where she is the Director of the

Master of Infrastructure Planning program. She received a BArch from Rice University and a MArch in urban design from Harvard University's Graduate School of Design, where she graduated with distinction. Theodore is Founding Partner and Principal of Interboro, a New York City-based architecture and planning research office. Since its founding in 2002, Interboro has worked with a variety of public, private and not-for-profit clients and has accumulated many awards for its innovative projects, including the Curry Stone Design Prize Social Design Circle (2017), the Rice Design Alliance Spotlight Award (2013), the Museum of Modern Art PS1's Young Architects Program (2011), the Architectural League's Emerging Voices Award (2011) and Young Architects Award (2005) and the AIA New York Chapter's New Practices Award (2006).

Siu Wai Wong is an assistant professor in the Department of Building and Real Estate at the Hong Kong Polytechnic University. She received her PhD in planning from the University of British Columbia, Canada. Her research interests are related to urbanization in China, urban planning and governance. She is the founder and convener of the China Innovative Urban-rural Governance Research Network (CIURG), which provides a platform to connect peers and stakeholders who are interested in intellectual debates, exchange of ideas and research collaboration about urbanization and local governance transformation in China. She is a registered estate surveyor specializing in land development planning and a member of both the Royal Institution of Chartered Surveyors (RICS) and the Hong Kong Institute of Surveyors (HKIS).

Pei Xiaochen is a registered urban and rural planner with a master's degree from Shenzhen University, 2016. He is currently working in Tsinghua Urban Planning, Design and Research Institute.

Yang Xiaochun is a professor of Urban Planning, Deputy Dean of the School of Architecture and Urban Planning and Head of Urban Planning Department at Shenzhen University, China. She is a registered urban and rural planner and chief planner of Shenzhen University Urban Planning and Design Institute. Professor Yang received a bachelor's degree in architecture and a master's degree in urban planning from Tsinghua University and her PhD from Tongji University. She used to work in the Shenzhen Urban Planning and Design Institute. She also serves as the Director of the Chinese Urban Planning Society and Vice Chairman of the Shenzhen Planning Association. Professor Yang focuses on sustainable urban design for high-density cities in the south, urban design management technology and development control and urban and rural heritage restoration.

ACKNOWLEDGMENTS

The first conversation about the personal and institutional collaboration that would eventually produce this book took place between the editors in 2015 in Hong Kong. Over the years, we organized a number of workshops which brought our students and colleagues together to investigate public spaces in Hong Kong and later also in Macau and Shenzhen. Our ongoing engagement with the rapid urbanization of the Pearl River Delta, and with the role public spaces and infrastructures have played in the formation of the new public realm of the Greater Bay Area megaregion, has also brought together an international network of colleagues whose intersecting scholarly and professional interests in the subject eventually converge in this volume.

As our relationships, both personal and institutional, became more robust and also formalized through scientific exchange agreements, we embarked on organizing two conferences on the subject in which we benefited from the support, advice and contributions of many individuals and our universities. Most of the authors contributing to this book were speakers at these conferences and have developed their respective chapters from their presentations and the discussions that emerged from these events.

The first of these conferences took place in 2016 at the Hong Kong Polytechnic University School of Design in Hong Kong. We would like to thank School of Design Dean Cees de Bont for supporting this event.

The second conference took place in 2017 at the New School in New York City. Parsons School of Design and the India China Institute (ICI) generously supported this event: we are grateful to ICI Director Ashok Gurung and Parsons Dean Joel Towers for making the conference a success. The New School Provost Office and Parsons School of Design Strategies generously supported the making of this book through multiple grants between 2016 and 2020.

We would like to most sincerely thank Anže Zadel, who helped with organizing both conferences, systematizing the recorded materials and assisting in preparing the book proposal in 2018 and also assisted with the first phase of work on this volume. Our sincere thanks also go to Sara Dević and Blake Roberts for creating diagrams and helping us prepare images for print. Special appreciation goes to Fu Na, who generously agreed to read the material and make sure the use of Chinese terms and phrases is standardized across the chapters and has developed the lexicon in order to facilitate easier understanding for readers not familiar with Chinese language, politics, policy and urbanization. We would also like to acknowledge Amy Dorta McIlwaine for her excellent copyediting work in Chapters 1 and 17.

Our appreciation goes to Kathryn Schell, our editor at Routledge, and editorial assistant Sean Spears, whose combination of professionalism and kindness made the production of this book an exceptional experience. We would also like to extend sincere thanks to the authors in this volume, particularly those who were with us since the first communication back in 2015: you have been wonderful and insightful collaborators in this process, and your unwavering commitment to this project has been truly inspiring.

The final eight months of work on this book have been particularly challenging—for us and for our colleagues who have contributed chapters—as we have lived and worked through the ongoing global pandemic. We would like to extend the deepest gratitude to our families for the incredible support we have received in the process of making this book: without your love, forbearance and encouragement, this would not have been feasible.

3 November 2020
Miodrag Mitrašinović and Timothy Jachna

GLOSSARY

BRI Belt and Road Initiative 一带一路 *Yidai Yilu*
CACHe Conservancy Association Centre for Heritage 长春社文化古迹资源中心 *Zhangchunshe Wenhua guji ziyuan zhongxin*
CAUPD China Academy of Urban Planning and Design 中国城市规划设计研究院 *Zhongguo Chengshi Guihua Sheji Yanjiuyuan*
CBD Central business district 中央商务区 *Zhongyang Shangwuqu*
CCP Chinese Communist Party 中国共产党 *Zhongguo Gongchandang*
COC Coastal Open Cities 沿海开放城市 *Yanhai kaifang Chengshi*
CGO Central Government Office 中央政府办公室 *Zhongyang Zhengfu Bangongshi*
CHU Chu Hai University 香港珠海大学 *Xianggang Zhuhai Daxue*
CHCHE Chu Hai College of Higher Education 香港珠海学院 *Xianggang Zhuhai Xueyuan*
CUPDI China Urban Planning and Design Institute 中国城市规划设计研究院 *Zhongguo Chengshi Guihua Sheji Yanjiuyuan*
CUHK Chinese University of Hong Kong 香港中文大学 *Xianggang Zhongwen Daxue*
DBPD Development Bureau and Planning Department 发展局和规划部 *Fazhanju he Guihuabu*
DIY Do It Yourself 自己动手做 *Ziji Dongshouzuo*
DISI Design Institute for Social Innovation 社会创新设计院 *Shehui Chuangxin Shejiyuan*
EKEO Energizing Kowloon East Office 起动九龙东办事处 *Qidong Jiulongdong Banshichu*
ETH Eidgenössische Technische Hochschule 慕尼黑工业大学 *Munihei Gongye Daxue*
GBA Greater Bay Area 大湾区 *Dawangqu*
GDP Gross domestic product 国内生产总值 *Guonei Shengchan Zongzhi*
GRB General residential buildings 普通住宅 *Putong Zhuzhai*
HKFS Hong Kong Federation of Students 香港学生总会 *Xianggang Xuesheng Zonghui*
HKPSI Hong Kong Public Space Initiative 拓展公共空间 *Tuozhan Gonggong Kongjian*

HKSAR Hong Kong Special Administrative Region 香港特别行政区 *Xianggang Tebie Xingzhengqu*
HKU Hong Kong University 香港大学 *Xianggang Daxue*
HSR High-speed railway 高速铁路 *Gaosu Tielu*
ICF International Financial Center 国际金融中心 *Guoji Jinrong Zhongxin*
ICR Intercity Commute Railway 城际通勤铁路 *Chengji Tongqin Tielu*
IDP International Design Program 国际设计专业 *Guoji Sheji Zhuanye*
IVS Individual visit scheme 自由行 *Ziyouxing*
KCRC Kowloon—Canton Railway Corporation 九广铁路公司 *Jiuguang Tielu Gongsi*
KMT Kuomintang 国民党 *Guomindang*
LegCo Legislative Council 立法委员会 *Lifa Weiyuanhui*
LSE London School of Economics 伦敦经济学院 *Lundun Jiangji Xueyuan*
MaD Make a Difference 创不同 *Chuangbutong*
MBEs Migrant Business Enterprises 移民企业 *Yimin Qiye*
MTR Mass Transit Railway 城市轨道交通系统 *Chengshi Guidao Jiaotong Xitong*
NGO Non-governmental organization 非政府组织 *Feizhengfu Zuzhi*
NJIT New Jersey Institute of Technology 新泽西理工学院 *Xinzexi Ligong Xueyuan*
NPO Non-profit organization 非盈利机构 *Feiyingli Jigou*
NSFC Natural Science Foundation of China 中国国家自然科学基金委员会 *Zhongguo Guojia Ziran Kexue Jijin Weiyuanhui*
OCC Open coastal city 沿海开放城市 *Yanhai Kaifang Chengshi*
OCT Overseas Chinese Town 华侨城 *Huaqiaocheng*
OCTS One Country Two Systems 一国两制 *Yiguo liangzhi*
POS Public open space 公共开放空间 *Gonggong Kaifang Kongjian*
PRD Pearl River Delta 珠江三角洲 *Zhujiang Sanjiaozhou*
PRC People's Republic of China 中华人民共和国 *Zhonghua Renmin Gongheguo*
PSMR Public spaces in the megaregion 大都会中的公共空间 *Dadouhui zhongde Gonggong Kongjian*
Public space 公共空间 *Gong gong kong jian*
ROU Reform and Opening-Up 改革开放 *Gaige Kaifang*
RMB Renminbi (Chinese currency) 人名币 *Renminbi*
SAR Special Administrative Region 特别行政区 *Tebie Xingzhengqu*
SARS Severe acute respiratory syndrome 严重急性呼吸系统综合症 *Yanzhong Jixing Huxi Xitong Zonghezheng*
SEZ Special Economic Zone 经济特区 *Jingji Tequ*
SMG Shenzhen municipal government 深圳市政府 *Shenzhenshi Zhengfu*
Shenzhen Institute of Urban Planning and Design 深圳市城市规划设计研究院 *Shenzhenshi Chengshi Guihua Sheji Yanjiuyuan*
SPSS Statistical Product and Service Solutions 统计产品和服务解决方案 *Tongji Chanpin he Fuwu Jiejue Fang'an*
SQ Sungang Qingshuihe 笋岗清水河 *Sungang Qingshuihe*
TMPS The Megaregional Public Space 大都会公共空间 *Dadouhui Gonggong Kongjian*
TOD Transport-oriented development 公共交通导向发展 *Gonggong Jiaotong Daoxiang Fazhan*
UABB Hong Kong/Shenzhen Bi-City Biennale of Urbanism/Architecture 双城双年展 *Shuangcheng Shuangnianzhan*

UN United Nations 联合国 *Lianheguo*
UPDIS Urban Planning and Design Institute of Shenzhen 深圳市城市规划设计院 *Shenzhenshi Chengshi Guihua Shejiyuan*
URA Urban Renewal Authority 市区重建局 *Shiqu Chongjianju*
UVRB Residential buildings as part of an urban village 城中村住宅 *Chengzhongcun Zhuzhai*
2SFCA Two-step floating catchment area 两步移动搜寻法 *Liangbu Yidong Souxunfa*

INTRODUCTION

Approaching the Public Space of the Greater Bay Area Megaregion

Timothy Jachna

The Greater Bay Area (GBA), in the southeast of China, comprising the eleven urban centers of Dongguan, Foshan, Guangzhou, Hong Kong, Huizhou, Jiangmen, Macau, Shenzhen, Zhaoqing, Zhongshan and Zhuhai, as well as the territory around and between them and the network of infrastructure that links them, has emerged as one of the world's most populous and economically productive urban megaregions. The GBA is defined by the confluence of several distinguishing characteristics that make it a very specific case in the discourse of public space in the contemporary era. As the locus at which China historically first opened contact with global systems of trade, and in the present day the site of the greatest concentration of manufacturing of consumer goods for global distribution, the historical development of the GBA has long been implicated in its embeddedness in international networks of economic and cultural exchange. The erstwhile colonies of Hong Kong and Macau, returned to Chinese rule in the 1990s but still existing as special cases within China's territory, are another element of specificity to this region. The exceptional states of these two Special Administrative Regions (SARs) and, to a lesser extent, of the Special Economic Zones (SEZs) of Shenzhen and Zhuhai, also within the GBA, are maintained by internal borders that divide the region into a patchwork of political, cultural and economic regimes, even as infrastructural and political programs seek their increasing integration into the megaregional network.

Notoriously, the GBA has experienced the most intensive and rapid urbanization of any area in the world in the past decades, leading to unique urban forms and situations and a fragmented urban fabric. This rapid and expansive urbanization, coupled with the vagaries of Chinese land tenure laws, has led to an immense concentration in this region of "villages in the city" (*chengzhongcun* 城中村; Al 2014; Du in this volume), formerly rural villages embedded in urbanized areas, leading to stark juxtapositions of different urban structures, ways of life and models of public space. These multiple dimensions of specificity highlight the public space of the GBA as a particular megaregional urban context worthy of concerted attention.

Nested Networks and Systems

The megaregion perspective implies, among other things, a network perspective on the analysis of the spatiality and relationality of urban regions, modeling complex constructs in terms of an understanding of the entities (nodes) and the interrelations between them by which they are organized into an integral whole. The network perspective implies a relational and situational understanding of the individual instances that are conceptualized as its nodes and connections, each being understood in terms of its relationships to other instances in the network. The specificities of each element in a network thus imply the existence of all of the network's other elements. Identity takes on a pronouncedly relational sense, in which each place, each city, each individual is defined by its connections and relationships with all others: by the influence that it has on other entities in the network and the influences that others have on it. The sociological facet of this framing is articulated in the guise of "network culture" (Wellman et al. 2006; Varnelis 2008).

Nodes in a network are the loci at which flows are gathered and entangled with one another. The network perspective applies to multiple scales and perspectives, such that cities can be seen as nodes in a megaregional mesh; public spaces as the constituent components of the network of urban space in a city; and individuals and objects of the built environment, and their interactions, as forming the network from which the public life of a given public spatial locality emerges. The public realm of a city is understood in terms of a network of physical urban spaces, infrastructures, artifacts and their interrelations and at the same time as a network of "urban agents" such as citizens, planners, governing bodies and private enterprises. The megaregional public space emerges from the patterns that manifest from the juxtaposition of tangible, embodied and located bodies, places and physical constructs with the flow of people, value, goods and influences through the networks in which these bodies are embedded (Farias and Bender 2010; Graham and Marvin 1996; Healey et al. 1995). The nodes in such a network are seen as "almost places" (Thrift 1993) characterized by different "stages of intensity" and by their ability to attract activities, people and investment.

Largely because of the technocratic and mechanistic implications that some readers may associate with the concept of a "system" and the discipline of systems theory when applied to cities, one hesitates to apply these terms too prominently to the ways in which the various contributors to this volume structure their approaches to investigating public space of the GBA. However, at its origin, general systems theory defines a system as a "way of seeing" any situation in terms of the components that make up that situation and the interactions between components (von Bertalanffy 1968). Notwithstanding the instrumentalization and canonization of systems approaches in certain realms of human inquiry and action, a system is first and foremost one of many possible descriptions of a situation intended to enable access to a way of knowing certain aspects of that situation and not an exclusive "definition" or definitive "explanation" of the situation.

While the chapters of this book do not explicitly adopt a systems theory approach in the canonical sense (nor would such a unified approach be appropriate to the ambition of the editors of this volume to bring together heterogeneous approaches to understanding and interrogating public space), each of the contributions can be understood as identifying and analyzing a system of urban public spatial practice at a particular scale and with a particular lens of analysis. The megaregion as a whole, and each of the increasingly narrowly circumscribed situations in the nested hierarchy of places, systems and communities of which it is composed, is understood as a "socio-materiality," in Simmel's (1975 [1903]) sense, in which the cultural, economic, social and spatial dimensions of public space are always co-defining. The ways in which such a perspective is framed—in terms of how broadly or narrowly the system/situation under investigation is geographically and temporally circumscribed; which components, actors and relationships are deemed relevant; which analytical tools and methods are applied; and within which intellectual tradition the analysis is undertaken—are the choices of the individual authors, and this volume is stronger for the diversity of the chapters in terms of these aspects.

Constructing This Volume

The journey of assembling this book has been a process of learning for all involved. The editors resolved, early on in the process, to take this project as an opportunity to probe the diversity of current approaches to understanding public space in the GBA, without predisposition towards either exclusively espousing nor categorically excluding any theoretical, ideological or methodological predilections (or lack thereof) that the individual contributors have found efficacious in revealing insights into the nature of the emerging public space in/of the GBA. This precarious but invigorating endeavor entailed soliciting contributions from a group of authors bringing a wide range of perspectives on public space, representing a broad swathe of intellectual traditions and practices. Chapter authors include Western scholars—many of them expatriates who have lived/worked or are living/working in the GBA—as well as Chinese academics from both Hong Kong and mainland China. Some have found the application of classical theorizations of public space fruitful in yielding insights; others adopt the spirit (if not the canonized methods) of "grounded theory" (Strauss and Corbin 1994) that seeks to "discover" a theorization implicit in a situation. We believe this has generated a work that both situates developments in the public space of this urban agglomeration within established discourses on public space and provides enticing insights into the specificities of this region and historical period.

The efforts of the editors, in the process of corresponding with the authors during the preparation of their chapters and intensively during the final stages of preparing this manuscript, have also necessarily involved an incremental parsing of the chapters in search of a way to give structure to a work subsuming the wide-ranging set of responses that our invitations for contributions elicited. A number of schemas annealed from this process of conversation. For instance, although not a theme in the original discussions among the editors and contributors to this work, the framing device of the megaregion, which will be explored in more depth in the next chapter (Mitrašinović in this volume), emerged, *post hoc*, as an apt (if not unproblematic) conceptual scaffolding on which to array the various contributions. Similarly, there has emerged a much more explicit focus on the notion of the *public realm* (Arendt 1998 [1958]; Fraser 1990; Habermas 1989 [1962]) as a concept than was originally envisioned, because of its utility in drawing together the multiple aspects of publicness (public goods, public life, public infrastructure, public policy, public action. . .) seen as crucial by the different chapter authors to elucidate the public space of the GBA. The public realm is not (only) spatial in its definition. It is also material, social, technological, cultural and temporal—a common project continuously produced through the sustained engagement and interaction of multiple public actors.

The Structure and Contents of This Volume

The ordering of the chapters in this book follows a loose sequence from the territorial scale to the hyper-localized, with a roughly parallel progression from "top-down" strategies of ordering and control to an increasing prevalence of "bottom-up" perspectives of individuals' and groups' performative tactics of appropriation of, and engagement with, specific public spaces. This is paralleled with a drift from broad historical narratives of the development of the megaregion's infrastructures and its systems of government, technology and commerce to tellings of hyperlocal contemporary experiences and acts of agency within specific public spatial "situations." This fluid sequencing acknowledges that such binary oppositions as top-down/bottom-up, formal/informal, local/global and state/public are not absolute, complete or mutually exclusive, nor are such distinctions sufficiently nuanced or fine-grained to articulate the dynamics at play in the production of public space, particularly in a context as complex as the GBA. Indeed, contemporary public space is a realm in which the hybridization and interpenetration of these aspects is on full view.

In Chapter 1, Miodrag Mitrašinović sets the stage for the historical and conceptual framework within which we contextualize the various chapters that follow. He begins with a chronology of the emergence of the GBA both as a physical network of cities and as a rhetorical device for designating the region as the object of development strategies. He continues with an exposition and critical review on the concept of a megaregion, the specific manifestation of this urban form in the GBA and the implications of the megaregional perspective on public space in theory and in practice.

Adrian Blackwell's Chapter 2 is based on the understanding of the megaregion as being constituted by networks, in which geographically dispersed nodes of cities are unified into a coherent whole by transportation infrastructure. He conceptualizes the public space of the GBA as suffusing both the urban nodes and the transport infrastructure that link them in a "spatialized economic strategy," in which the constant exchange of value affects the distribution of public space and public amenities throughout the system. The nomenclature of the "Greater Bay Area," to refer to the densely urbanized area of southeastern China that is the subject of this book, is a relatively new one (Mitrašinović in this volume). The much older moniker, "Pearl River Delta" (PRD), evokes the genesis of this region as a cohesive cultural landscape, transport network and interacting system of settlements linked by the lattice of waterways converging on the Pearl River and its mouth at the South China Sea between present-day Hong Kong and Macau. In Chapter 3, Laurent Gutierrez and Valérie Portefaix of MAP Office explore the history of this watery network as the seminal proto-megaregional-level public spatial continuum. In refocusing on this progenitor regional infrastructure, they propose a possible re-framing of the present and future of a public realm that unites the PRD/GBA.

With the subsequent two chapters in this book, the lens of analysis narrows to the types of urban units that are the recurrent building blocks of the urban spatial realm across the GBA megaregion; the organization schemas inherent in these components, reflecting and molding particular structures and practices of public life; and the combinatorial paradigms by which these units of public space come together. Stefan Al's Chapter 4 takes the form of a visual essay, applying collage techniques and shifting conventions of visual documentation and representation to interrogate the "hyper-collage" disjointed composition of disparate urban fragments that for him epitomize the assemblage of the urban environments of the GBA. An exterior public realm marked by jarring juxtapositions of different logics of public space of these fragments is compensated by the controlled, interiorized and commodified public spaces of malls and casinos. Applying his "metacity" analytical schema, in Chapter 5, David Grahame Shane undertakes an itinerant and diachronic investigation of the ways in which a particular typology of public space in the GBA—the urban garden—has evolved and been appropriated into different urban contexts and in the service of different strategies, as a structural element in urban morphology and an "information sorting" mechanism in regulating the dynamics of public life.

From these investigations of some of the "generic" components whose repetition and adaptation across time and space assemble the tangible mesh of urban instances that begin to give form and texture to the GBA conurbation, the subsequent Chapter 6 zeroes in on a specific instance of one such structuring element: the internal borders that delineate the divisions between administrative sub-entities of the megaregion. In this chapter, Peter Hasdell demonstrates that these geographical dividing lines, which delineate and enforce the distinctions that inhere on either side of them, are in themselves the focuses of idiosyncratic ecosystems of public life. Focusing on the controlled border between the Hong Kong SAR and the Shenzhen SEZ, he coaxes out a delineation of the choreography of an informal web of practices that emerge from individuals' circumvention and exploitation of the very restrictions and differentiations that the border embodies and enforces.

The "special cases" partitioned off from the rest of China's geographical expanse by internal borders have been characterized as laboratories for experimentation with alternative, even extreme, modes of urban assemblage (MAP Office 2000). Contributions to this volume indicate that they can be seen as incubators for the intentional prototyping of urban strategies under controlled and contained conditions and as metaphorical organs for the incubation of a new breed of urban public citizen. In Chapter 7, Mary Ann O'Donnell presents a chronology of the processes and policies by which the Shenzhen SEZ has served as a staging ground for an aspirational model of Chinese urban transformation, driven by strategic governmental programs of investment, development and communication. She frames the city as a system for the provision of public goods, also making excursions into how the public spaces of Shenzhen, and the practices that they support, link the SEZ, and by extension China, to global networks of consumption. Tim Simpson purports, in Chapter 8, that the heterotopic status of the SAR of Macau within China, as the only place in Chinese territory in which gambling is legal, enables it to become an instrument for the cultivation of a new model of Chinese citizen through the behaviors engendered, and the value systems modeled and reinforced, within the interiorized and commodified public spaces of its cavernous casino complexes.

A subsequent set of chapters concentrate on the analysis of networks of public space at the city or urban district level. These chapters tend to adopt a more normative tone than those already discussed, with authors applying different approaches to seek to assess the attunement of the affordances of these local networks to the populations they serve. While privileged urban actors such as planners and political figures are still considered, either implicitly or explicitly, the casts of characters involved shift markedly towards urban citizens, with a central role being played by figures who advocate on behalf of urban citizens as mediators between publics and urban power structures. Yang Xiaochun et al.'s Chapter 9 applies a structured quantitative approach to assess equity of access to public space in Shenzhen's Nanshan District, targeted at producing data and insights of an order and format that can inform governmental policy in achieving equity in availability of this public good to citizens across the full range of socio-economic strata.

Georgeen Theodore (Chapter 10) describes a complementary approach to the understanding of systems of public space in a city. This chapter marks the first appearance in this book of an investigation based on an explicitly *pedagogical* approach to public space, in which one of the driving intentions of the investigative exercise is to provide the conditions for a learning experience for students (and teachers) in the context of an educational program. Like the other pedagogical exercises presented in subsequent chapters, the work described in this chapter is structured less by a prescribed analytic framework and more by an open-ended search for "clues" that serve as pieces of evidence that are stitched together by students using a forensic approach to reveal subtle patterns of relationships. In a contribution that addresses the ways in which formal and informal forces intermix in the formation of a city's network of public spaces, in Chapter 11, Bo-sin Tang and Siu Wai Wong report on the current spectrum of public space provision practice in Hong Kong, from the SAR government's traditional pragmatic approach, to current experiments with increasing public consultation and involvement in defining public space initiatives, to the tolerance of informal appropriation of indeterminate spaces in the city as public-by-proxy places by the city's citizens and visitors.

The following chapters take a sharper focus on specific nexuses in the urban spatial continuums of the GBA's cities to elucidate these places as points of convergence of the elements and influences that give form to public space. Juan Du's Chapter 12 contrasts the expansive and stark formal urbanism of the "Grand Urban Living Room" of Shenzhen's Civic Square with the granular and lively informal urbanism of its urban villages and recounts the formulation of a planning proposal for the extension of the city's ceremonial central axis, which sought to mediate between these two public space paradigms.

The project examined in this chapter exemplifies processes of urban "tinkering" (Elmqvist et al. 2018), "post-planning" (Martraire and Weng 2014) or "metrofitting" (Fry 2017), characterized by intervention into existing urban fabrics and systems in ways that work with existing conditions and systems, drawing on insights into the shortcomings and potentials of these systems drawn from experiencing and analyzing them as ongoing living experiments. This is a particularly apt practice in a megaregional urban context such as the GBA, in which the speed of urban development has outstripped the capacity for consolidated planning, resulting in a disjointed, uneven urban fabric (Al in this volume). Such approaches can also be discerned as operating in other chapters of this book, such as the use of transport infrastructure to weave existing cities and other locations together to actualize the megaregional vision (Blackwell in this volume) and the tactics by which urban citizens appropriate and adapt urban spaces to their needs and desires (Tieben and Chen in this volume).

In Chapter 13, Brian McGrath and Paul Chu Hoi Shan use the trope of three intertwined "genealogies" of an educational institution (Chu Hai College), a new town in Hong Kong's New Territories (Tsuen Wan) and a program of pedagogical engagement with the city and its public spaces to speculate on the emergence of new "social publics" under contemporary social, political and technological realities of the early 21st-century GBA. Mark W. Frazier's contribution, in Chapter 14, brings a sharpened spatial and temporal focus to bear on the events that unfolded in Hong Kong's Civic Square during the 2019 protests against police brutality and a proposed extradition bill. This chapter most explicitly exemplifies the nature of public space as a contested realm and of hyperlocal public spaces as loci that often become flashpoints for tangible, visceral confrontation between different segments of the public or, as in the case at hand, between governmental control and citizens' desire for manifestation as a counterforce to regimes of command and control.

Having ventured, with the previous chapter, into "performative" (Wolfrum and Brandis 2015; Whybrow 2010) aspects of public space, centered on the situated actions of specific urban actors in the use and construction of public spaces, the subsequent two chapters delve into examples of initiatives in which individuals and communities have been empowered to cognitively and tangibly appropriate local public spaces. Such practices exemplify Arendt's notion of public space as the arena in which individuals are able to initiate—to "make a beginning" by asserting their right as active agents in the public realm. The role of the designer and the design educator in facilitating such initiatives is a prominent theme in these chapters.

Hendrik Tieben and Chen Ying-Fen's contribution in Chapter 15 examines three grassroots initiatives dealing with three neighborhood-level public spaces in Hong Kong, exploring the processes of negotiation between pragmatic governmental public space strategies and the situated, often improvisational, tactics of urban citizens in carving out literal and metaphorical spaces in the public realm requisite to the practices of their everyday lives. In their discussion of the pedagogical workshops addressing different public space sites in the GBA presented in Chapter 16, Merve Bedir and Jason Hilgefort demonstrate their "aformal" approach to analyzing public spaces, based on the conviction that the education of the next generation of designers in and of cities needs to be grounded in a conscious jettisoning of analytical categories to enable a "re-learning" of the city through embedded exploration.

In Chapter 17, the concluding chapter of the book, Miodrag Mitrašinović synthesizes the contents of the invited authors' contributions, venturing a broad theorization of the *emerging public realm of the GBA megaregion* rooted in a distinction between the perspective of *the megaregional public space* that facilitates a conceptualization of the public spatial realm at the megaregional scale and its links to global publics and flows, and that of *public spaces of the megaregion* that scrutinizes the specific instantiations of the public spatial realm as encountered by those whose day-to-day lives pass through these spaces and for whom these spaces are the arenas for acts of negotiation of public identities, rights and practices.

Conclusion

The reader of any of the chapters that follow this introduction will gain a deepened understanding of the dynamics of a particular aspect or instance of contemporary public space and public spatial practice in the GBA. However, the editors trust that engaging the work as a whole—subsuming a range of explorations with different points of incursion, scales of investigation and modes of analysis into the public space of the GBA megaregion—will reward the reader with an appreciation of the ways in which the embedded scales, diverse urban actors and elements are linked in the constitution of the public space and public realm of the megaregion, as members of the cast of urban actors, elements, relationships, processes and flows that constitute the GBA make appearances in different guises and roles across the seventeen chapters.

The contributions that constitute this book represent a series of *approaches* to understanding the public space of the Greater Bay Area. We choose the word "approaches" advisedly. An approach implies a strategy for beginning, for sizing up an object of analysis and mapping out a strategy for closing the distance between one's current position and one from which the object can be scrutinized in increasing detail. It is explicitly not the ambition of this book to arrive at a single definitive description or explanation of the dynamics at play in the context under study, nor to propose or predict future developments. Rather, we have found value in mobilizing a diverse set of minds to consider how one should frame one's inquiries into the still-emerging public space of this megaregion, and indeed of megaregions in general.

Accordingly, in crafting a set of approaches—ways of beginning—the diverse chapter authors, implicitly or explicitly, take on very fundamental questions in the pursuit of an understanding the public space of the megaregion: What does public space do? What is it made of? How is this public space produced? How is it perceived by its "stakeholders?" And what ways of perceiving could be applied to open up new insights into its patterns and rules that are not proffered by the frameworks offered by the standard canon of techniques? In pursuing such basic questions, the authors have collectively arrived at a manifold of insights into the public space of this urban context and have defined a panoply of trajectories for future research and action.

References

Al, S. (2014) *Villages in the city: A guide to South China's informal settlements.* University of Hawaii Press.

Arendt, H. (1998 [1958]) *The human condition* (2nd ed.). University of Chicago Press.

Elmqvist, T., Siri, J., Andersson, E., Anderson, P., Bai, X.M., Das, P.K., Gatere, T., Gonzalez, A., Goodness, J., Handel, S.N., Hermansson Török, E., Kavonic, J., Kronenberg, J., Lindgren, E., Maddox, D., Maher, R., Mbow, C., McPhearson, T., Mulligan, J., Nordenson, G., Spires, M., Stenkula, U., Takeuchi, K. and Vogel, C. (2018) "Urban tinkering." *Sustainability Science* 13. pp. 1549–1564.

Farias, I. and Bender, T. (Eds.) (2010) *Urban assemblages: How actor network theory changes urban studies.* Routledge.

Fraser, N. (1990) "Rethinking the public sphere: A contribution to the critique of actually existing democracy." *Social Text* 25 (26). pp. 56–80.

Fry, T. (2017) *Re-making cities: An introduction to urban metrofitting.* Bloomsbury Academic.

Graham, S. and Marvin, S. (1996) *Splintering urbanism: Networked infrastructures, technological mobilities and the urban condition.* Routledge.

Habermas, J. (1989 [1962]) *The structural transformation of the public sphere: An inquiry into a category of bourgeois society.* Polity.

Healey, P., Cameron, S., Davoudi, S., Graham, S. and Madanipour, A. (Eds.) (1995) *Managing cities: The new urban context.* Wiley.

MAP Office (2000) *Mapping HK.* MAP Book Publishers.

Martraire, M. and Weng, X.Y. (2014) *Hou Hanru (Interview transcript).* SFAQ International Art and Culture, 15 September. At: www.sfaq.us/2014/09/in-conversation-hou-hanru-with-marie-martraire-and-xiaoyu-weng/. Last accessed on 1 November 2020.

Simmel, G. (1975 [1903]) "The metropolis and mental life." In: Wolff, K.H. (Ed.) *The sociology of Georg Simmel.* Free Press.

Strauss, A. and Corbin, J. (1994) "Grounded theory methodology: An overview." In: Denzin, N.K. and Lincoln, Y.S. (Eds.) *Handbook of qualitative research.* Sage. pp. 273–285.

Thrift, N. (1993) "Inhuman geographies: Landscapes of speed, light and power." In: Cloke, P.J., Doel, M.A., Matless, D., Thrift, N. and Phillips, M. (Eds.) *Writing the rural: Five cultural geographies.* Sage.

Varnelis, K. (Ed.) (2008) *Networked publics.* Annenberg Center for Communication.

Von Bertalanffy, L. (1968) *General system theory.* George Braziller.

Wellman, B., Hogan, B., Berg, K., Boase, J., Carrasco, J., Côté, R., Kayahara, J., Kennedy, T. and Tran, P. (2006) "Connected lives: The project." In: Purcell, P. (Ed.) *Networked neighbourhoods: The connected community in context.* Springer. pp. 157–211.

Whybrow, N. (Ed.) (2010) *Performance and the contemporary city.* Palgrave Macmillan.

Wolfrum, S. and Frhr V. Brandis, N. (Eds.) (2015) *Performative urbanism: Generating and designing urban space.* Jovis.

1

FROM THE PEARL RIVER DELTA ESTUARY TO THE GREATER BAY AREA MEGAREGION: PRODUCING THE NEW PUBLIC REALM

Miodrag Mitrašinović

This book endeavors to make a timely yet historically situated contribution to the growing body of literature and scholarship on the rapid urbanization of the Pearl River Delta (PRD) and the role public spaces and infrastructures have played in the formation of the new public realm of the Greater Bay Area (GBA) megaregion. It is based in a pragmatic understanding that one can grasp this rapidly evolving process only episodically, by reflecting on a series of fragments that necessitate scholarly attention and reflection. This seems to be both an accurate and an ethical approach, as the totality of the process has reportedly escaped even its main protagonists: as Vlassenrood noted, "It is still unclear to both foreigners and Chinese how urban planning processes and decision-making are ultimately taking place" (2016: 8). Orff accurately employs the term "has becoming" to describe the ongoing contiguities of accomplishment and suspension (Orff 2001: 383) that epitomize the drama of frantic PRD urbanization. Each chapter in this book acts as analysis, a reflection and a theorem of public space as it *has becoming* in the PRD since 1978 and in the GBA megaregion since 2016. This chapter aims to contextualize the PRD→GBA transformation and to examine the relevance to the GBA of ongoing discourses of megaregionalism and practices of megaregionality. The new public realm, the megaregional public space and public spaces in the GBA megaregion will be briefly outlined here and then discussed in Chapter 17.

A Brief Chronology of the Transformation

Since the 1980 establishment of Shenzhen, Zhuhai and Shantou in the Guangdong province as the first Special Economic Zones (SEZs) on the heels of Deng Xiaoping's 1978 Open Door Policy and the subsequent establishment of Hong Kong and Macau as Special Administrative Regions (SARs) in 1997 and 1999,[1] the PRD has unquestionably been the testbed for the global geopolitical ambitions of the People's Republic of China (PRC). The rapid urbanization of the PRD, particularly since the 2016 launch of the Belt and Road Initiative (BRI)[2] global development strategy, must be understood as part of an assertive planetary urbanization, through which the Chinese government has massively urbanized mainland China while also investing directly in infrastructure development in over seventy countries around the world (Scissors 2020; Arnold 2014). The scale and intensity of this enterprise have been breathtaking.

Initiated and modeled by the fourteen SEZs (Bach, O'Donnell, and Wong 2017), the "de-Maofication" (Vogel 1989: 780) and economic modernization (i.e., decentralization and deregulation) of China have obliterated landscapes, towns and villages across the nation. Until Gordon Wu's 1994 Guangzhou-Shenzhen Expressway (Guangshen), Guangdong province boasted not a single mile of high-speed highway (Campanella 2008: 231). Typical of a river delta landform—a rural estuary supporting rice fields, farms and fishing villages—the region was among the most fertile in Asia (Du 2020). As the world's most rapidly urbanizing territory from 1978 to 2008, the PRD epitomized contradictions inherent in the economic reforms of the SEZs—incongruities that strongly challenged expectations regarding concordant political ideology, economic development, urbanization and social transformation and urban and architectural forms (Chung et al. 2001). The hurried development of large-scale transportation, production and communication corridors gave rise to an urbanism predicated on polarization and interregional competition and on *infrastructure* as the main ideological device for development of the PRD.

A comprehensive national urbanization strategy was first proposed in the Tenth Five-Year Plan (2001–2005) aimed to coordinate urbanization with economic development and environmental protection. Whereas the Eleventh Five-Year Plan (2006–2010) put forth *megaregion* as the main vector of the national urbanization strategy, it was the National New-Type Urbanization Plan (2014–2020) that has solidified the megaregional approach as key to China's national urbanization platform (Tan 2017). China's Thirteenth Five-Year Plan (2016–2020) put forth a *megaregional imaginary* that reframed the PRD estuary as a new geopolitical, geo-economic and spatial concept—the GBA—assembling four "core cities" (Guangzhou, Shenzhen SEZ, Hong Kong SAR and Macau SAR) and seven "key node cities" (Zhuhai SEZ, Foshan, Dongguan, Zhongshan, Jiangmen, Huizhou and Zhaoqing). The GBA is part of the national urban system of twenty-three megaregions categorized into three levels—national, national secondary and regional—each with an estimated 50 million inhabitants (Sua et al. 2017). All these plans gradually moved official rhetoric from the "quality of urbanization" to "humanized urbanization," indicating the orientation toward social equity and environmental sustainability in addition to economic development.

The Concept of Megaregion

The megaregion is not a Chinese invention—indeed, it often means "different things, to different people, in different contexts" (Harrison and Hoyler 2015: 237)—yet the concept has certainly developed into a "megaregionalism with Chinese characteristics." That is, megaregions have become the foremost geo-economic, geopolitical and spatial configurations for globalized wealth creation and accumulation and drivers of the post-national and post-metropolitan space of neoliberal economic competition (Sassen 2007, 2012; Florida et al. 2008; Ross 2009), forming an increasingly coherent and globally competitive urban space (Harrison and Hoyler 2015: 18). They represent spatial agglomerations of economic functions, characterized by large, global-oriented markets; significant economic capacity; innovative activities and processes; and a skilled, educated and creative labor force. A specific advantage of the megaregion is the scale on which it enables agglomerations of economic activity, far exceeding the capacity of any given metropolitan area (Sassen 2007); in fact, Richard Florida et al. claimed that megaregions relate to the global economy in ways analogous to a metropolitan region's relationship with national economies (Florida et al. 2008: 3). Unlike in Europe (Hall and Pain 2006; Pain and Van Hamme 2014) and the United States (RPA 2006; Hagler 2007; Ross 2009)—where megaregions are "assertive systemic units of the global economic and political system" (Scott 2011), largely independent from nation-states vis-à-vis their formation and development—megaregions in China are established and organized

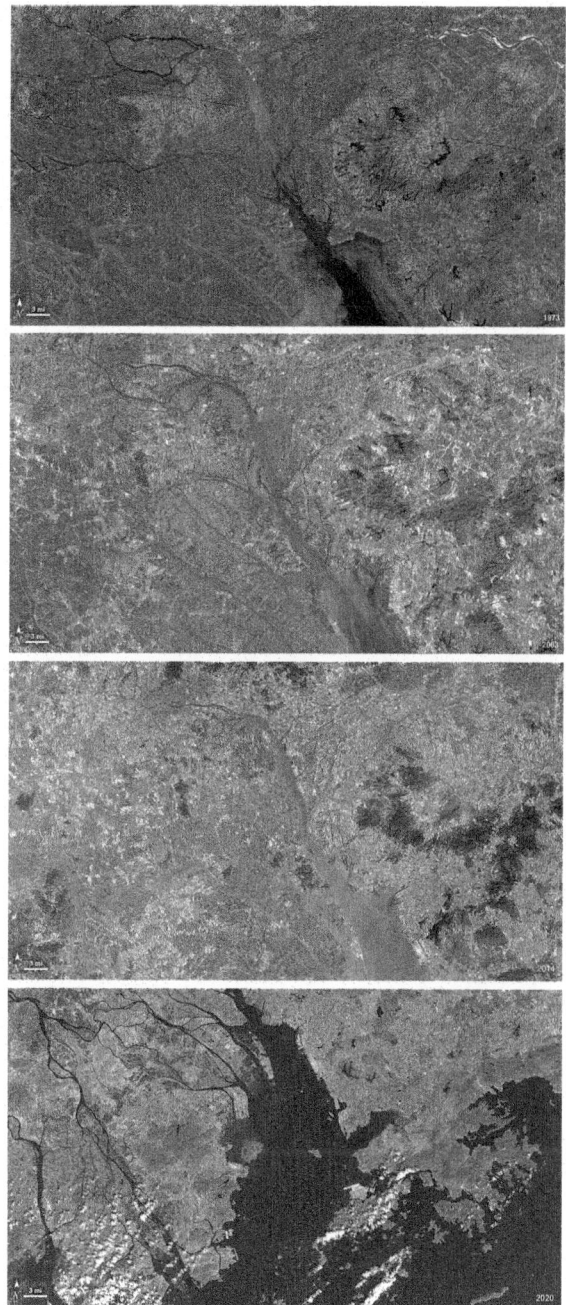

FIGURE 1.1 Urbanization of the Pearl River Delta between 1979 and 2020.

Source: Images by NASA and the U.S. Department of the Interior through the U.S. Geological Survey (USGS) and NASA Earth Observatory © Creative Commons BY-2.0.

These images of the Pearl River Delta were taken by Landsat 7 in 1979 and 2003 and Landsat 8 in 2014 and 2020. In 1979, the image depicts a largely rural region with agricultural grids and dense, plant-covered land. By 2003, the Pearl River Delta was a densely populated, polycentric urban region with several large cities, depicted in gray. By 2014, it assumed the spatial form of a megaregion populated by over 60 million people. Between 2014 and 2020, less urban expansion and more densification and "spillover" can be observed. The 2020 Landsat image focuses on the southern portion of the Pearl River Delta, with Hong Kong, Macau and Shenzhen in focus.

FIGURE 1.2 Border crossings. In clockwise order: Gong Bei border crossing between Macau and Zhuhai; The Venetian casino, Macau, line for the border bus; Hong Kong Port Passenger Clearance Building of the Hong Kong–Zhuhai–Macau Bridge; Hong Kong–Guangdong border at the Hong Kong–Zhuhai–Macau Bridge; and Macau–Hong Kong Bridge Port Facility.

Source: Author.

by the central state as a matter of national and regional policy. In geopolitical and geo-economic terms, this is a critical distinction, and it must be placed in proper historical context.

Arguing that the PRD economy's external-facing global orientation originated centuries ago, Zhang weaves its current development into a more complex historical narrative that recognizes the central state's key role in Chinese national and regional development and accordingly its function as the fundamental driver of the GBA megaregion today (2015: 193). Thus, in many ways, the GBA should be understood as a continuation of the place-specific historical processes that have produced the political geography of the PRD. In China, the megaregion is both a geographic and a policy concept, causing megaregional boundaries to correspond with existing administrative divisions and regional policies (Sua et al. 2017). To ease tensions between cities and municipalities, orient them toward the global market and re-establish a significant degree of political control, the Chinese government has since 2013 employed a regional planning strategy, particularly concerning the megaregions that incorporate SEZs and SARs.

Consequently, the GBA megaregion also symbolizes and materializes new alignments of economic, political and geographic systems—a coherent ideological narrative fabricated and promoted in order to achieve certain political outcomes (Harrison and Hoyler 2015: 10). Such re-alignments are also necessary at the global scale and must be supported by the politics and policies of supra-national organizations, including the World Trade Organization, the World Bank and UN-Habitat. Under the leadership of Dr. Joan Clos, UN-Habitat has not only promoted megaregions but also attempted to normalize them as "natural economic units that result from the growth, convergence and spatial spread of geographically linked metropolitan areas and other agglomerations" (UN-Habitat 2010a: 8). The 2010–2011 *State of the World's Cities* report claimed that while the planet's forty largest megaregions covered only a very small portion of its surface and housed less than 18% of its population, they accounted for 66% of economic activity and about 85% of technological and scientific innovation. In China, the five largest megaregions accounted for 50% of overall wealth the nation produced (UN-Habitat 2010a: ix).[3]

Megaregionalism of the GBA, Megaregionality in the GBA

In an attempt to develop a megaregional dialectic, Schafran proposes an analytical framework composed of "megaregional space," "spaces of the megaregion" and "tactical sub-regionalism" (2014: 597, 2015). This dialectical framework—together with Harrison and Hoyler's definitions of megaregionalism and megaregionality (2015)[4]—is adapted here for the GBA context and employed to argue for an understanding of: GBA *megaregionalism* as a national strategy focused on governance, economy, planning and urban policy and operationalized through production of the *megaregional space*; GBA *megaregionality* as an ongoing process of producing megaregional geographies operationalized through production of the *spaces in/of the megaregion*; and *tactical sub-regionalism*, understood for the purposes of this book as the collaborative civically and socially engaged practices that emerge at the intersections of infrastructure, networked governance and community organizing and that focus on the issues relevant in the specific public spaces in/of the megaregion. The synergetic workings of these three interrelated domains construct what we call *the emerging public realm of the GBA megaregion*. Accordingly, public spaces are the locations and spatial extensions in/of the GBA where these synergies are represented, materialized and contested. After all, such spaces are the loci for struggles over the constitution of the new publics (see Chapter 17).

Megaregional space is a rational, quantifiable, highly standardized spatial extension employed as the strategic and rhetorical medium of government agencies, global economic and political organizations, economic planners, engineers and urban planners and urban designers and architects. It is produced through multi-year national and regional plans, cartographic representations, statistical charts and network diagrams, masterplans, timetables and schedules and other technologies of power and representation that emphasize efficiency, speed, territory and communication (Mitrašinović 2006). The GBA megaregional space is principally characterized by strong, discursive framing; narrative coherence; political legitimacy; and implied economic validity of the megaregional concept (Harrison and Hoyler 2015). Its main objective is to ideologically and geographically align urban/spatial, economic and political systems toward the achievement of regional, national and global objectives.

Although megaregionalism renders the GBA as a totalizing, systemic artifact, spaces of the GBA megaregion are process oriented and dynamic, co-produced by alliances of local and regional municipalities, business and industry leaders, real estate developers and local and international investors, as well as by "social organizations" and community associations in the civil society space through varied modalities of "urban governmentality" (Appadurai 2001; Roy 2009). Often experienced as incoherent, fragmented, uneven and interstitial, these spaces are where denizens experience the impact of shifting GBA geographies. The porousness is particularly important to local actors engaged in tactical sub-regionalism, who are powerless to address megaregionalism as a totality; their perceived agency in the process of megaregionality is limited by their vantage points and their economic and political status. Spaces in/of the GBA megaregion are thus constructed as a nexus of evolving relationships between political projects, urban imaginaries and the material realities and outcomes of urbanization (Pain 2016). Together with megaregionalism's glossy images of national progress, and expanding upper and middle classes, urbanization in the GBA has produced uneven geographies characterized by the polarization of wealth creation and distribution, mass migration and dramatic demographic shifts and transformed social and physical mobilities. It has engendered inequitable access to public resources, education, housing, recreation and public sites for collectivization and social reproduction. The significant impact on local and regional ecosystems is compounded by mounting environmental problems related to air pollution and ever-expanding land cover across political boundaries and jurisdictions (Pickett and Zhou 2015; Barnett 2020).

The Spatial Form of Megaregion

The title of Harrison and Hoyler's 2014 book provocatively asks whether megaregions indeed symbolize "globalization's new urban form." Scholars invested in studying processes of global economic integration, the emergence of global information networks and flows of knowledge and capital concern themselves with the economic, political and governance forms (Harrison and Hoyler 2015: 10) that characterize the GBA megaregion. Urban, architectural and spatial planning scholarship focusing on urbanization in and from China—and, more specifically for this book, the GBA megaregion—has been dominated instead by an analytical focus on (and often concern with) rapid infrastructure-driven development (Blackwell in this volume; Barnett 2020); the genealogy and epistemology of urban spatial forms and morphology (Shane, Due, Blackwell, Al in this volume); urban sprawl (Yu and Zhou 2017); the immense growth of the built environment (Al in this volume; Chung et al. 2001); and the emergence (Hulshof and Roggeveen 2011), erasure and revitalization of urban villages (O'Donnell and Du in this volume).

Analysts and scholars across disciplines have employed various theoretical terms to define and demarcate the context for this study, often employing city- and region-centric terms interchangeably without qualifying their particularities and distinctions. In this volume, we too employ a variety of terms and concepts, including "megalopolis" (Blackwell); "metropolis," "megacity" and "megamachine" (Simpson); "metapolis" (Shane); "metacity" (McGrath and Chu; Shane); and "megaregion" (Mitrašinović). Yet their use here is neither inaccurate nor mutually exclusive, particularly because they are employed within different disciplinary epistemologies to frame and describe differentiated yet interrelated sets of urban, spatial and social phenomena.

In *The Rise of the Network Society* (2000), Castells calls PRD a "metropolitan region" (2000: xxxiv), a "mega-city" (2000: 434; see also Linden 1993; Perlman 2010; Lai 2016), a "metropolitan regional system" (2000: 436), an "urban region" (2000: 437) and the "southern China metropolis" (2000: 439). In the first (1996) edition of the book, Castells anticipates the PRD's destiny to "become the most representative urban face of the twenty-first century" (2000: 439) and argues that as a "metropolitan regional system," it would prefigure "the megapolitan future of China" (2000: xxxiv) and "be one of the pre-eminent industrial, business, and cultural centers of the twenty first century, without indulging in futurology" (2000: 436). The

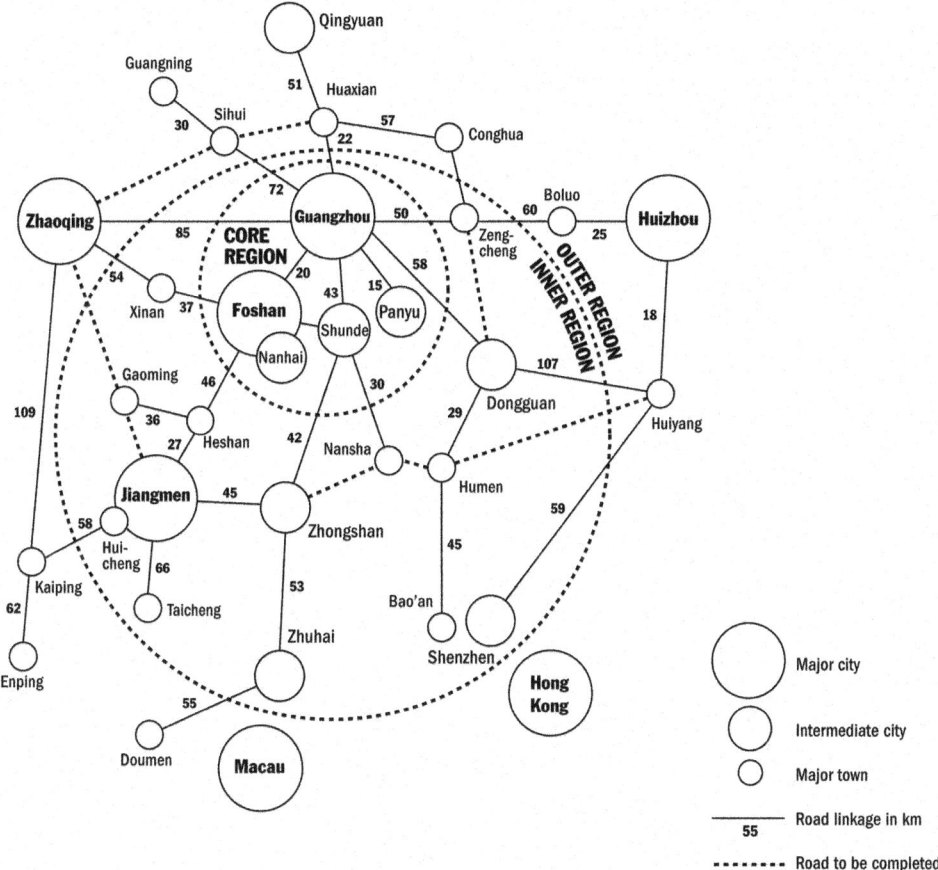

FIGURE 1.3 Manuel Castells' network diagram of the Pearl River Delta in 1996 (after Woo 1994). Original 1996 caption read: "Diagrammatic representation of major nodes and links in the urban region of the Pearl River Delta."

Source: Adapted from Castells 1996 by Sara Dević.

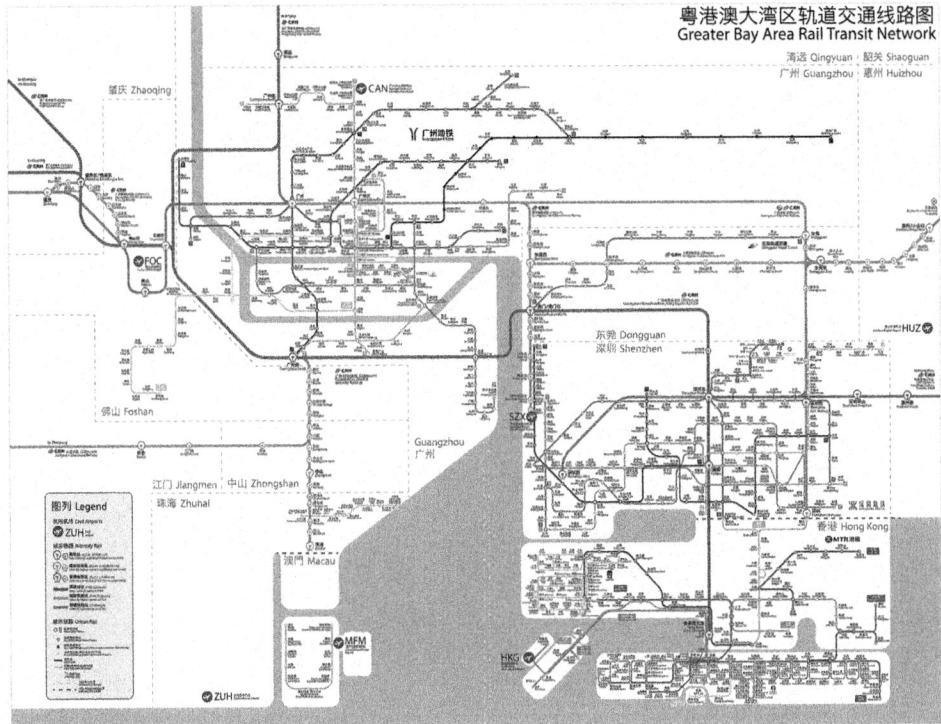

FIGURE 1.4 The Greater Bay Area Aggregate Rail Transit Network, including high-speed rail, intercity rail, metro, light rail and tram services.

Source: Adapted from the map created by Picrazy2. Wikimedia Commons © Creative Commons BY-SA 4.0.

key spatial feature of Castells' network society is the connections between the local and the global, embodied in the "new urban form" of mega-cities (2000: 436).

The main spatial form of the GBA megaregion is polycentric,[5] comprised of multiple, interrelated urban systems in the PRD estuary that are simultaneously increasingly interdependent with the global urban system.[6] The reality of the GBA's form is particularly important given the differentiated social and political systems, values and beliefs still present (as of this writing) across the PRD's SARs and SEZs. It is also timely in light of both assertive efforts by the PRC government toward territorial integration of the PRD—via the GBA megaregional imaginary—and the struggles of Hong Kong citizens to safeguard and defend that SAR's relative political autonomy through 2047 as originally agreed upon.[7]

Of China's twenty-three developing megaregions, the GBA has the most unequal distribution of agglomerations and clustering and a very low major polycentricity index of 0.27 (Yang et al. 2015: 5). The PRD's original core function zones—Hong Kong, Shenzhen and Guangzhou—highly developed and concentrated before 1990, saw urban clusters expanding outward by more than 60% from 1990 until 2010, when the overall urbanization level reached 82% (Tan 2017: 78). The 2000–2010 period was characterized by a spatio-temporal pattern of continued urban expansion, including peri-urban development and edge expansion, urban infilling and urban sprawl (Yu and Zhou 2017). After entering the "mature" (Altrock and Schoon 2014) stage of morphological development, the PRD has experienced an increasing "positive spillover effect," with urban development spreading from those original core function zones (Zhang et al. 2018).[8] Researchers identify these "spillovers" as important spaces of the megaregion: territories where urban designations and boundaries are negotiated and where true integration of distinct urban systems takes place (Schafran 2014: 592).[9]

The Emerging Public Realm of the GBA Megaregion

The emerging public realm of the GBA is forged by synergetic strategies, processes and mechanisms that produce megaregional space and spaces in/of the megaregion and tactical actions and coalitions in the domain of critical sub-regionalism. Megaregionalism and megaregionality have been explicitly at work since 2016, yet many of the urban/spatial processes that these forces amplify, realign, synergize and instrumentalize have been taking place for a very long time. Because the PRD estuary was historically perceived as a single homogeneous ecology, its trans-historical public realm has been more prominently water based than land based (Gutierrez and Portefaix in this volume)—organized around the delta waters and incorporating both *roots* and *routes* (Clifford 1997; McGee 1971, 2009; Traganou and Mitrašinović 2009) into a mnemonic infrastructure of historical and cultural specificities. The public realm of the delta has been configured by infrastructure and communication lines; the logic of rice fields and the logistics of agriculture and fishing; the built environment composed of villages, towns and cosmopolitan colonial and imperial cities; open spaces, parks and gardens; public spaces, market streets and passages; and "spaces of appearance" and exchange. The trans-historical syncretic processes that have formed PRD's complex ecologies and its public realm have been radically disrupted since 1978.[10]

The Land-Infrastructure Nexus

The transformation of land laws has been critical to urban and infrastructural explosion in the PRD. All land in mainland China was nationalized after the Chinese Revolution of

1949 and is owned by the state and by various workers' collectives. In 1987, when the first land-use reform was initiated in Guangdong province to enable incremental deregulation of land ownership in the SEZs, the rural population was permitted to collectively sell agricultural land-use rights to developers at very high prices (Du and O'Donnell in this volume). When China's Property Law codified "property rights" in 2007 (Clarke 2017), it radically changed questions of land zoning, parcellation, use and management, allowing the local land-administration authority or municipal government to grant land-use rights—or a "land contract"—to a land "user" for purposes of commercial development. A wave of real estate speculation followed and, combined with strong market forces in other sectors, gave rise to hyper-commodified, market-driven, often predatory urbanization predicated on the development of infrastructure. This process has been certainly most obvious in Shenzhen, as urbanization of the PRD from 1978 through 2016 lacked an integrated territorial approach across the region's urban systems.

With megaregionalism in full force since 2016, the process has expanded across the GBA and is driven in large part by the mass-transport industry.[11] Both the 2017 Framework Agreement (GBA 2017) and the 2019 Outline Development Plan (GBA 2019) propose to strengthen the megaregional spatial structure by connecting three development corridors—Hong Kong–Shenzhen, Guangzhou–Foshan and Macau–Zhuhai—and improving underdeveloped ones (Zhang et al. 2020) through expansion of the Intercity Commuter Railway (ICR) and the high-speed railway (HSR) system and additional highways, bridges and tunnels. This circular, polycentric mobility infrastructure is predicated on the construction of additional transit hubs in cities and airports to facilitate "hub-to-hub networking," encourage equitable regional competitiveness and cooperation (Yang et al. 2015: 6–7) and further integrate Hong Kong and Macau into the GBA megaregional grid. Together with the Wealth Management Connect financial plan announced in May 2020 (Yiu 2020) and the US$68 billion for the rail transit expansion approved in July 2020 (Zhang and Rui 2020), the previous plans attempt to further integrate GBA's urban systems and coordinate future development.

The Built Environment, Public Spaces, and Open Space Systems

The PRD conurbation was historically composed of distinct fragments of colonial urbanization in Hong Kong and Macau; towns and villages in the deep southern Chinese province of Guangdong; and the magnificent city of Guangzhou, once a major terminal on the maritime Silk Road. The Portuguese-Chinese urban-spatial configuration of Macau differed radically from that of British-designed Hong Kong (Kvan et al. 2013) in terms of not only urban and building traditions but also a divergence in the colonists' understanding of Chinese cultures and peoples. Ever since the Chinese imperial authority leased Macau to Portugal as a trading post in 1557 and ceded Hong Kong to the British Empire in 1842, multiplicity and hybridity have characterized the southern PRD hand in hand with colonization, expropriation and oppression.

In the rest of China, urban planning principles, theory and practice in the period between 1949 and 1978 originated principally in the Soviet Union. The first time mainland Chinese urban planning and design professionals had a chance to learn, apply and experiment with market-based models of urban development was in Shenzhen, a process led initially by the Central Urban Planning Institute in Beijing and after 1990 by the Shenzhen Urban Planning and Design Institute (Huang 2016: 19). From 1980 onward, planning has been clearly understood as a strategic instrument of economic growth (Blackwell in this volume, citing

FIGURE 1.5 Lianhuashan Park, Shenzhen. Facing Futian from the Lotus Peak in 1998 and in 2018.

Source: Adapted from the photos by wanghongliu (1998) and sparktour (2018). Wikimedia Commons © Creative Commons BY-SA 4.0.

Wu 2007), and in that respect, Shenzhen was built purely as a "growth machine" (Wu 2018). The mythology of this "instant city" (Du 2020; Blackwell and Du in this volume) came to epitomize megaregionalism and the explosive growth of the built environment in the GBA.

Both open space- and public space-making have a long tradition in the PRD, yet historic, normative public spaces have been overshadowed in the 21st century by both the totalizing scale of Shenzhen's Civic Square and the vulgar commodity of Macau's Cotai strip (Du and Simpson in this volume). Together, open-space systems and public spaces (discussed in the following chapters and summarized in Chapter 17) form a critical aspect of the public realm. Both are constituent parts of the megaregional space: the open-space system as the sum of all open, functionally integrated "surfaces" of the megaregion that offer a "possibility of general public access"—such as parks, gardens, forests, trails, streets, squares and waterfronts—and public space when it embodies and represents the totalizing megaregional narratives, rationality, commodification and efficiency. On the other hand (see Chapter 17 for a more nuanced delineation), public spaces in the megaregion are also spaces of everyday public encounter, environments of social exchange and reproduction where the potential for tactical sub-regionality emerges.

After the "first wave" of massive urbanization between 1980 and 2010, the GBA megaregion has arguably reached the point of "maturity" and consolidation (Altrock and Schoon 2014: 4), characterized by significant restructuring of the public realm. This process is evident in the retrofitting and renovation of abandoned buildings and city blocks, the consolidation of waterfronts, the renewal of community parks and the emergence of mega-transit hubs such as West Kowloon Station. Meanwhile, the Umbrella Movement in 2014 and the Hong Kong student protests in 2020 appropriated and occupied public spaces for the purposes of political contestation. It is through these types of synergies between participation, appropriation and contestation—which leverage the public realm in order to both construct and project new social and political imaginaries—that public space truly becomes the "geography of the public sphere" (Smith and Low 2006).

Megaregion's Weak Publics

Megaregionality is operationalized through the formation and solidification of links between municipal entities, incorporation of different jurisdictions and re-alignment of regulatory frameworks. Networked forms of governance—involving state units on many levels, municipal decision-makers, non-governmental organizations (NGOs) and other components of civil society, market-based organizations and community organizers—are not yet well developed and vary greatly across the GBA megaregion. Cross-boundary economic and policy integration of the PRD and Hong Kong, already evident in the early 1990s (Yang 2006), has advanced exponentially with the rise of globalization and megaregionality, shaping the GBA as a *de facto* regional network of municipalities across which state agencies coordinate regional planning and development of transportation infrastructure, the preservation of green corridors and economic and spatial restructuring (Ma 2014). This process also gave rise to forms of networked governance throughout the GBA, which became somewhat robust between 1990 and 2000 (Ren 2006). However, government regulations on "social organizations," NGOs and civil society have since 2011 undermined connections between urban development and participatory decision-making. A vibrant civil society in Hong Kong (and to a lesser extent Macau) has supported various forms of participation, appropriation, contestation, urban

FIGURE 1.6 The Three Olds Regeneration Policy. The Three Olds Regeneration Policy (*san jiu gaizao*) implemented in Guangzhou and Shenzhen in 2009 is the first comprehensive, integrated effort to revitalize old towns (*jiu cheng*), old villages (*jiu cun*) and old industry areas (*jiu chang*) (Schoon 2014), an effort which has sparked the creation of "urban regeneration" offices across the GBA. This process is evident in the retrofit and renovation of buildings and urban blocks abandoned during the period of rapid growth—such as "City of Design" in Shenzhen's Tianmian Village, Shekou's Nanhai Yiku bottom left image, Tai Kwun Centre for Heritage and Art in Hong Kong top image—as well as through the upgrade of existing infrastructure, improvement of parks and open green spaces, expansion of public spaces (Haide Square in Nanshan, Shenzhen, bottom right image and general attempts to improve qualitative aspects of urban living (Naughton 2015: 56). After all, the 2014 National New-type Urbanization Plan also puts forth a proposal for "humanized urbanization," which has been interpreted as an impetus for "social construction" initiatives meant to generate community organization and development, social support and solidarity networks and also improvement of public spaces at the neighborhood scale (Vlassenrood 2016: 93).

Source: Author.

pedagogy and urban education (all discussed in the following chapters and in Chapter 17). As will be argued in this volume, inclusive public spaces co-produced through varied forms of participation, cooperation and contestation are fundamental and critical for the emergence of a dynamic, diverse and inclusive public realm of the GBA.

Challenges With Analytical Work in the GBA

Despite the central government's commitment to megaregionalism, megaregionality as a process is not clearly understood in China and presents an evolving political and economic dilemma (Harrison and Gu 2019). This is manifested through "non-transparent territorial strategies" and practices of the PRC government which in turn result in a missing "conceptual and empirical link with urbanization as it actually unfolds" (Duan et al. 2017: 144). For urban scholars, this presents a serious analytical challenge because it is nearly impossible to establish workable causalities between intentions and outcomes. Even when such causalities can be established, standard international epistemologies and methodologies that underpin urban research and analysis do not always hold in China. Finally, what Banham calls the "gap of comparability" (Banham 1971: 5) is at work here through the lack of practical and theoretical models for a productive comparative analysis of the total artifact of the GBA. These challenges, when combined, often present an overwhelming obstacle for international researchers, analysts and urban scholars.

Recognizing the limitations that international scholars bring to their work in China, Zhang (2015: 176) critiques the implicit "Euro-American hegemony" in theoretical work on Chinese urbanization. Building on the work of Roy (2009), Zhang suggests that the naturalizing narrative of global cities, city-regions and megaregions has so far abrogated specific accounts from the rapidly urbanizing regions of "the global South," hence concealing their "heterogeneity and multiplicity" (Roy 2009: 821). Like other Chinese and international scholars working in China, we have struggled with these challenges. In this volume, we try to resolve them—often provisionally—so that new work can proceed in earnest.[12]

Notes

1. Pursuant to the Sino-British Joint Declaration of 1984 and the Sino-Portuguese Joint Declaration of 1987.
2. BRI was a rebranding of the One Belt One Road (OBOR) global development strategy (officially, the Silk Road Economic Belt and the 21st-century Maritime Silk Road Development Strategy) in place between 2013 and 2016.
3. The 2010 UN report recognized three major forms of urbanization particularly observable in "the global South": mega-regions, urban corridors and city-regions ("cities in clusters"). These spatial units are "territorially and functionally bound by economic, political, socio-cultural and ecological systems. [They] are becoming the new engines of both global and regional economies, and they reflect the emerging links between urban expansion and new patterns of economic activity" (UN-Habitat 2010a: ix).
4. For a valuable discussion of megaregions, also employed in Chapter 17, see Harrison and Hoyler (2015: 7–10); see also Pain's review (2016) of Harrison and Hoyler's book.
5. Polycentric spatial structure is the key underlying feature of spatial and theoretical models from Gottmann's "megalopolis" (1961) and Taylor's "world city network" (1995, 2004) to "megapolitan areas" (Castells 1996, 2000), "mega-city regions" (Hall and Pain 2006) and "global-city regions" (Sassen 1991, 2012). Significant debate focuses on the symbolic, macro-economic and geo-political origins of these theoretical urban models: whereas *metropolis* represents a monocentric, rational,

imperial and colonial model, *megalopolis* is a distributed, polycentric formation—a product of the North American, post-Fordist political-economic order exported around the world during the Cold War. The "megacity" (and its corollary "mega-city region" concept) is a post-colonial, polycentric, sprawling urban form common in the global South and particularly characteristic of southeast Asia (McGrath and Shane 2012; Hall 1999; Xu and Yeh 2011; Harrison and Hoyler 2015; see also McGrath et al. in this volume). UN-Habitat (2018) reports that of the world's thirty-three megacities (i.e., ten million inhabitants or more), twenty-seven are in the global South, including six in China and five in India.

6. In this context, Harrison and Hoyler's categorization (2015: 7–11) seems particularly pertinent. Whereas "megalopolis," "mega-city region," "metropolitan region" and "global-city region" refer to singular urban systems grounded in the city idiom, and "planetary urbanization" (Brenner 2014) as a process occurring across the entire planet is framed as the "global urban system," Harrison and Hoyler deem "megaregion" a spatial configuration composed of two or more urban systems.

7. The Basic Law of the Hong Kong SAR is a national law that serves as the constitution of Hong Kong enacted under the Constitution of China in order to implement the Sino-British Joint Declaration of 1984. It protects Hong Kong's relative economic and political autonomy for a period of fifty years, 1997–2047.

8. These findings support observations that urbanization through which (a) large ("global") cities generate sizable polycentric regions with multiple connections into the global economy and (b) "proximate cities" connect to construct megaregions are not mutually exclusive (Taylor and Pain 2007: 64–65). Schafran (2014: 592) suggests the concept of megaregionality as defined by these two parallel processes—(a) and (b)—ought to become "an operational foundation for megaregional research."

9. For proponents of megaregionalism, the working assumption is that agglomeration is a function of dispersal (Sassen 2012) and that the megaregion offers sufficient internal differentiation and diversity to provide for these spillover areas the benefits of "globalization, urbanization, and rapid social development."

10. MAP Office has done a remarkable job of mapping the transformations of the public realm in Hong Kong and across the PRD through a series of outstanding publications starting in 1999. A full list can be found here: www.map-office.com/publication/. Last accessed on 20 September 2020. See also Gutierrez and Portefaix in this volume.

11. For instance, GBA's railways are owned and operated by multiple actors: state-owned, public-private and some privately owned subsidiaries with headquarters in China and around the world. One major stakeholder is the Kowloon–Canton Railway Corporation (KCRC), owned by the Hong Kong government; it leased the high-speed Kowloon–Guangzhou line to the Mass Transit Railway Corporation (MTR) in 2007 under a 50-year service concession. MTR is itself a majority Hong Kong state-owned company listed on the Hong Kong Stock Exchange and a leading property developer and landlord not only in Hong Kong and the GBA but around the world. See also Blackwell in this volume.

12. Because my research is limited to works of Chinese and international scholars published in English and to original Chinese sources translated into English in publications available to me as a non-Chinese speaker and scholar working in the United States, it is right to acknowledge here my inherent bias. One significant limitation of the available English-language literature on Chinese urbanization is the unavoidable presence of the "foreign gaze." This chapter, despite my best intentions, is no exception in that regard.

References

Altrock, U. and Schoon, S. (Eds.) (2014) *Maturing megacities: The Pearl River Delta in progressive transformation*. Springer.

Appadurai, A. (2001) "Deep democracy: Urban governmentality and the horizon of politics." *Environment & Urbanization* 13 (2). pp. 23–43, October.

Arnold, F. (Ed.) (2014) "Chinese urbanism in Africa." *Urban China* 63 (3).

Bach, J., O'Donnell, M.A and Wong, W. (Eds.) (2017) *Learning from Shenzhen: China's post-Mao experiment from special zone to model city*. University of Chicago Press.

Banham, R. (1971) *Los Angeles: The architecture of four ecologies*. Harper and Row.
Barnett, J. (2020) *Designing the megaregion: Meeting urban challenges at a new scale*. Island Press.
Brenner, N. (Ed.) (2014) *Implosions/explosions: Towards a study of planetary urbanization*. Jovis.
Campanella, T. (2008) *The concrete dragon: China's urban revolution and what it means for the world*. Princeton Architectural Press.
Castells, M. (2000) *The rise of the network society: The information age: Economy, society and culture* (volume 1, 2nd ed.). Wiley-Blackwell.
Chung, C.J., Leong, S.T., Inaba, J. and Koolhaas, R. (Eds.) (2001) *Great leap forward*. Harvard Design School Project on the City, Taschen.
Clarke, D. (2017) "Has China restored private land ownership? The implications of Beijing's new policy." *Foreign Affairs*, 16 May. At: www.foreignaffairs.com/articles/china/2017-05-16/has-china-restored-private-land-ownership. Last accessed on 18 September 2020.
Clifford, J. (1997) *Routes: Travel and translation in the late twentieth century*. Harvard University Press.
Du, J. (2020) *The Shenzhen experiment: The story of China's instant city*. Harvard University Press.
Duan, X., Derudder, B., Ye, L. and Shen, W. (2017) "Hierarchical tendencies and functional patterns among mainland China's megaregions." *Eurasian Geography and Economics* 58 (2). pp. 143–168.
Florida, R., Gulden, T. and Mellander, C. (2008) "The rise of the mega-region." *Cambridge Journal of Regions, Economy and Society* 1 (3). pp. 459–476, November.
Gottmann, J. (1961) *Megalopolis: The urbanized northeastern seaboard of the United States*. Twentieth Century Fund.
Greater Bay Area (GBA) (2017) *Framework agreement on deepening Guangdong-Hong Kong-Macao cooperation in the development of the Greater Bay Area* [深化粵港澳合作 推進大灣區建設框架協議], 1 July. At: www.bayarea.gov.hk/en/outline/plan.html. Last accessed on 18 September 2020.
Greater Bay Area (GBA) (2019) *Greater Bay Area development: A national strategy. Outline development plan for the Guangdong-Hong Kong-Macao Greater Bay Area*, 18 February. At: www.bayarea.gov.hk/en/outline/plan.html. Last accessed on 18 September 2020.
Hagler, Y. (2007) *Defining U.S. megaregions*. Regional Planning Association, America 2050, November. At: https://rpa.org/uploads/pdfs/2050-Paper-Defining-US-Megaregions.pdf. Last accessed on 20 September 2020.
Hall, P. (1999) "Planning for the mega-city: A new Eastern Asian urban form?" In: Brotchie, J., Newton, P., Hall, P. and Dickey, J. (Eds.) *East-west perspectives on 21st century urban development: Sustainable Eastern and Western cities in the new millennium*. Ashgate. pp. 3–36.
Hall, P. and Pain, K. (Eds.) (2006) *The polycentric metropolis: Learning from mega-city regions in Europe*. Earthscan.
Harrison, J. and Gu, H. (2019) "Planning megaregional futures: Spatial imaginaries and megaregion formation in China." *Regional Studies*, November. At: https://doi.org/10.1080/00343404.2019.1679362. Last accessed on 20 September 2020.
Harrison, J. and Hoyler, M. (Eds.) (2015) *Megaregions: Globalization's new urban form?* Edward Elgar Publishing.
Huang, W. (2016) "The urban planning imaginary: Lessons from Shenzhen. Interview by Mary Ann O'Donnell." In: Vlassenrood, L. (Ed.) *Shenzhen: From factory of the world to world city*. International New Town Institute (INTI) and The Netherlands Architecture Institute (NAI). pp. 18–27.
Hulshof, M. and Roggeveen, D. (2011) *How the city moved to Mr. Sun: China's new megacities*. Sun.
Kvan, T., Shelton, B. and Karakiewicz, J. (2013) *The making of Hong Kong: From vertical to volumetric*. Routledge.
Lai, S. (2016) "The Pearl River Delta megacity." *Time Out Hong Kong*, 17 May. At: www.timeout.com/hong-kong/en-hongkong/the-pearl-river-delta-megacity-051716. Last accessed on 15 September 2020.
Linden, E. (1993) "Mega-cities." *Time Magazine* 141(2), 11 January.
Ma, X. (2014) "The influence of regional planning administration on local development." In: Altrock, U. and Schoon, S. (Eds.) *Maturing megacities: The Pearl River Delta in progressive transformation*. Springer. pp. 61–82.

McGee, T. (1971) *The urbanization process in the third world*. Bell and Sons.
McGee, T. (2009) *The spatiality of urbanization: The policy challenges of mega-urban and desakota regions of Southeast Asia*. UNU-IAS Working Paper #161. United Nations University Institute of Advanced Studies.
McGrath, B. and Shane, G.D. (2012) "Metropolis, megalopolis and metacity." In: Crysler, C.G., Cairns, S. and Heynen, H. (Eds.) *The Sage handbook of architectural theory*. Sage. pp. 641–656.
Mitrašinović, M. (2006) *Total landscape, theme parks, public space*. Routledge.
National New-Type Urbanization Plan (2014–2020). *Released in March 2014*. At: www.gov.cn/zhuanti/xxczh/. Last accessed on 20 September 2020.
Orff, K. (2001) "Landscape: Zhuhai." In: Chung, C.J., Leong, S.T., Inaba, J. and Koolhaas, R. (Eds.) *Great leap forward*. Harvard Design School Project on the City, Taschen. pp. 336–417.
Outline Development Plan for the Guangdong-Hong Kong-Macao Greater Bay Area (2019) At: www.bayarea.gov.hk/en/about/overview.html. Last accessed on 20 September 2020.
Pain, K. (2016) "Megaregions imaginaries: Excursions through a dialectical maze." *Geographical Review* 107 (3). pp. 536–550, July. First published on 7 March 2016.
Pain, K. and Van Hamme, G. (Eds.) (2014) *Changing urban and regional relations in a globalizing world: Europe as a global macro-region*. Edward Elgar.
Perlman, J. (2010) *Favela: Four decades of living on the edge in Rio de Janeiro*. Oxford University Press.
Pickett, S.T.A. and Zhou, W. (2015) "Global urbanization as a shifting context for applying ecological science toward the sustainable city." *Ecosystem Health and Sustainability* 1 (1). pp. 1–15.
Ren, Y. (2006) "Globalization and grassroots practices: Community development in contemporary urban China." In: Wu, F. (Ed.) *Globalization and the Chinese city*. Routledge. pp. 292–309.
Ross, C. (Ed.) (2009) *Megaregions: Planning for global competitiveness*. Island Press.
Roy, A. (2009) "The 21st-century metropolis: New geographies of theory." *Regional Studies* 43 (6). pp. 819–830.
RPA (2006) *America 2050: A prospectus*. Regional Planning Association, America 2050. At: https://rpa.org/work/reports/america-2050-prospectus. Last accessed on 20 September 2020.
Sassen, S. (1991) *The global city: New York, London, Tokyo*. Princeton University Press.
Sassen, S. (2007) "Megaregions: Benefits beyond sharing trains and parking lots." In: Goldfeld, K.S. (Ed.) *The economic geography of megaregions*. Policy Research Institute for the Region, Woodrow Wilson School of Public and International Affairs, Princeton University and the Regional Plan Association. pp. 59–84.
Sassen, S. (2012) "Novel spatial formats for urban inclusion: Megaregions and global cities." *Booksandideas.net*, 5 May. At: https://booksandideas.net/Novel-Spatial-Formats-For-Urban.html. Last accessed on 20 September 2020.
Schafran, A. (2014) "Rethinking mega-regions: Sub-regional politics in a fragmented metropolis." *Regional Studies* 48 (4). pp. 587–602.
Schafran, A. (2015) "Beyond globalization: A historical urban development approach to understanding megaregions." In: Harrison, J. and Hoyler, M. (Eds.) *Megaregions: Globalization's new urban form?* Edward Elgar Publishing. pp. 75–96.
Scissors, D. (2020) *China's global investment in 2019: Going out goes small*. American Enterprise Institute.
Scott, A.J. (2011) "A world in emergence: Notes toward a resynthesis of urban-economic geography for the 21st century." *Urban Geography* 32. pp. 845–870.
Smith, N. and Low, S. (Eds.) (2006) *The politics of public space*. Routledge.
Sua, S., Liua, Z., Xua, Y., Lib, J., Pia, J. and Weng, M. (2017) "China's megaregion policy: Performance evaluation framework, empirical findings and implications for spatial polycentric governance." *Land Use Policy* 63. pp. 1–19.
Tan, M. (2017) "Uneven growth of urban clusters in megaregions and its policy implications for new urbanization in China." *Land Use Policy* 66. pp. 72–79.
Taylor, P.J. (1995) "World cities and territorial states: The rise and fall of their mutuality." In: Knox, P.L. and Taylor, P.J. (Eds.) *World cities in a world-system*. Cambridge University Press. pp. 48–62.
Taylor, P.J. (2004) *World city network*. Routledge.

Taylor, P.J. and Pain, K. (2007) "Polycentric mega-city regions: Exploratory research from Western Europe." In: *The Healdsburg research seminar on megaregions: Discussion papers and summary*. Regional Plan Association and Lincoln Institute of Land Policy. pp. 59–66. At: https://rpa.org/uploads/pdfs/2050-The-Healdsburg-Research-Seminar-on-Megaregions-2007.pdf. Last accessed on 20 September 2020.

Thirteenth five-year plan for economic and social development of the people's Republic of China (2016–2020) (2016). *Central compilation & translation press*. At: https://en.ndrc.gov.cn/news release_8232/201612/P020191101481868235378.pdf.

Traganou, J. and Mitrašinović, M. (Eds.) (2009) *Travel, space, architecture*. Routledge.

UN-Habitat (2010a) *State of the world's cities 2010/2011: Bridging the urban divide*. United Nations Human Settlements Programme (UN-Habitat).

UN-Habitat (2010b) *Urban trends: Urban corridors—shape of things to come?* Press release, 13 March. United Nations Human Settlements Programme (UN-Habitat).

UN-Habitat (2018) *The world's cities in 2018: Data booklet*. United Nations Human Settlements Programme (UN-Habitat).

Vlassenrood, L. (Ed.) (2016) *Shenzhen: From factory of the world to world city*. International New Town Institute (INTI) and The Netherlands Architecture Institute (NAI).

Vogel, E.F. (1989) *One step ahead in China: Guangdong under reform*. Harvard University Press.

Wu, F. (2007) "Re-orientation of the city plan: Strategic planning and design competition in China." *Geoforum* 38 (2). pp. 379–392, 1 March.

Wu, F. (2018) "Planning centrality, market instruments: Governing Chinese urban transformation under state entrepreneurialism." *Urban Studies* 55 (7). pp. 1383–1399.

Xu, J. and Yeh, A.G.O. (Eds.) (2011) *Governance and planning of mega-city regions: An international comparative perspective*. Routledge.

Yang, C. (2006) "Cross-boundary integration of the Pearl River Delta and Hong Kong: An emerging global city-region in China." In: Wu, F. (Ed.) *Globalization and the Chinese city*. Routledge. pp. 125–146.

Yang, J., Sone, G. and Lian, J. (2015) "Measuring spatial structure of China's megaregions." *Journal of Urban Planning and Development* 141 (2). pp. 1–7.

Yiu, E. (2020) "China unveils financial plan for Hong Kong, Macau to spur tighter embrace of Greater Bay Area master plan." *South China Morning Post*, 15 May. At: www.scmp.com/business/banking-finance/article/3084576/china-unveils-financial-plan-hong-kong-macau-spur-tighter. Last accessed on 20 September 2020.

Yu, W. and Zhou, W. (2017) "The spatiotemporal pattern of urban expansion in China: A comparison study of three urban megaregions." *Journal of Remote Sensing* 9 (1). P. 45. At: www.mdpi.com/2072-4292/9/1/45. Last accessed on 20 September 2020.

Zhang, P. and Rui, G. (2020) "China's US$68 billion Greater Bay Area rail plan for faster, easier city links." *South China Morning Post*, 5 August. At: www.scmp.com/news/china/society/article/3096034/chinas-us68-billion-greater-bay-area-rail-plan-faster-easier. Last accessed on 20 September 2020.

Zhang, W., Fang, C., Zhou, L. and Zhu, J. (2020) "Measuring megaregional structure in the Pearl River Delta by mobile phone signaling data: A complex network approach." *Cities* 104, September. At: www.sciencedirect.com/journal/cities/vol/104/suppl/C. Last accessed on 20 September 2020.

Zhang, X. (2015) "Globalization and the megaregion: Investigating the evolution of the Pearl River Delta in a historical perspective." In: Harrison, J. and Hoyler, M. (Eds.) *Megaregions: Globalization's new urban form?* Edward Elgar Publishing. pp. 175–199.

Zhang, X., Guo, S., Guan, Y., Cai, D., Zhang, C., Fraedrich, K., Xiao, H. and Tian, Z. (2018) "Urbanization and spillover effect for three megaregions in China: Evidence from DMSP/OLS nighttime lights." *Remote Sensing* 10 (12), 27 November. At: www.mdpi.com/2072-4292/10/12/1888. Last accessed on 20 September 2020.

2
PLANNING A VALUE NETWORK OF EXPLODING INFRASTRUCTURES AND IMPLODING CENTERS IN SHENZHEN

Adrian Blackwell

This chapter focuses on the networks of value created through the dynamic interaction between two dominant forms of public space: (1) evolving urban infrastructures composed of expressways, railways and metro systems and (2) urban centers formed around the nodes and hubs in these transportation networks. The aggressive development of these urban networks is a key strategic dimension of Chinese urban planning. Though these two forms of space overlap and intersect, they appear opposed to one another in their respective tendencies: the first facilitating people's dispersion and the second drawing people together. Dominant metropoles of the 20th century like Paris and Beijing formed as centralized networks, with infrastructural lines radiating from their historic centers toward smaller nodes. However, since Jean Gottmann (1961) described the megalopolis of the eastern seaboard of the United States in the 1950s, theorists have remarked on the tendency toward poly-centric urban networks produced through the growth and interconnection of historic centers (Castells 2000; Sieverts 2003). The explosion of new urban spaces under globalized neoliberalism has been characterized by an intensified networking of modern urban space through the accelerated production of urban mobility infrastructures and multiplication of new high-value urban centers. Shenzhen is the key strategic node in the urban network of the Greater Bay Area, China's high-tech megalopolis. The internal development of its urban form over four decades has been exceptional in the rapid expansion of its infrastructural corridors and the succession of its central areas. This chapter will sketch a theory of dynamic networks of value, using the development of Shenzhen as a case study.

Urban Networks: Machines for Exacerbating Differences in Value

Sociologist Manuel Castells' 1996 *The Rise of the Network Society* proposed the contemporary reconfiguration of modern space and time as the "space of flows" and "timeless time" of abstract networks (Castells 2000: 407–499). Together these new dimensions of experience served to physically and temporally separate labor—which occupies clock time and physical places—from capital, which circulates instantaneously in both physical and informational networks (Castells 2000: 505–507). Networks separate their nodes from the surrounding spaces

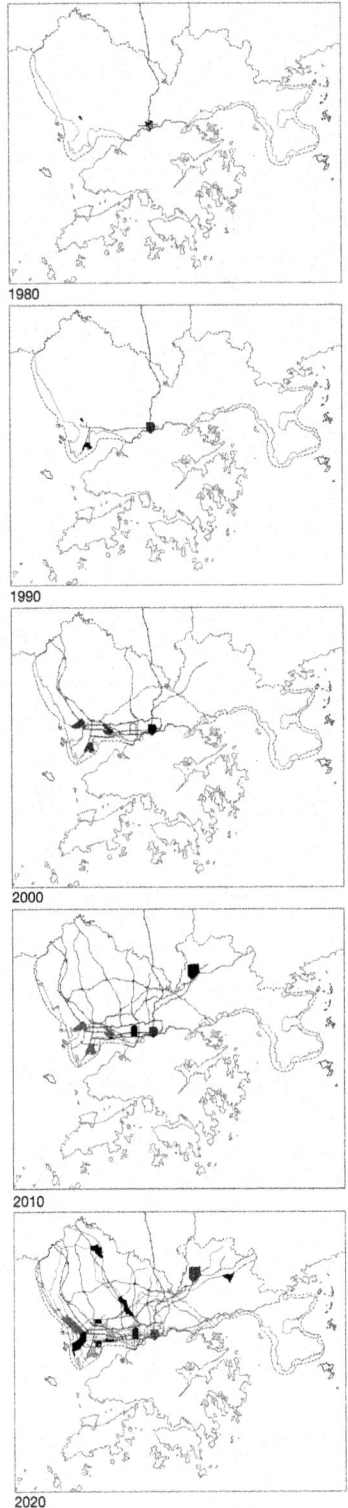

FIGURE 2.1 Shenzhen infrastructures and centers, 1980–2020.

Source: Adrian Blackwell and Sophie Fan.

they bypass. Castells explicitly addressed the emerging forms of networked urbanism in dominant capitalist spaces of North America and Europe before describing "third millennium urbanization" of "mega-cities" in the Pearl River Delta (PRD). At the conceptual center of Castells' description sat a provocative network drawing, a convincing visual representation of the idea that a new form of urban spatiality was emerging as a function of this networked society (2000: 437). This image was reproduced from a 1994 essay by Hong Kong geographer Edward Woo, who analyzed the emerging urban development of the PRD as a distributed regional economy (Woo 1994: 350) in relation to the "multiplication of urban centers, diversification of urban functions in major cities, and emergence of urban regions" (Woo 1994: 329–331). Woo in turn copied the image from a 1989 essay by Zhongshan geographer Zheng Tianxiang (1989: 99). There are two conceptual differences between the original and the copy. First, where Woo's drawing sized city-nodes by national administrative hierarchy, overstating the significance of Zhaoqing, Jiangmen, Foshan and Huizhou while diminishing the importance of Shenzhen and Guangzhou, Zheng more accurately sized them according to population. Second, Woo introduced a set of concentric circles, describing the core, inner and outer regions of the PRD emanating from Guangzhou. This hierarchy, biased toward the provincial capital, undermined the open network structure essential to Zheng's conceptualization of a "multi-nuclei, multi-tier urban system" with Guangzhou and Hong Kong as its dominant anchors (Zheng 1989: 97–98). Zheng describes the PRD's urban system in terms Castells would later popularize, focusing on the "manifold" of transport, computer, energy and trade "networks" that knit this space together, insisting that "[m]odern society is an information society," with "Hong Kong [as] one of the world's information centres," and finally describing the space itself through its "material flows," "flows of people," "monetary flows" and "information, technology and ideology flows." Zheng ends, "we believe that the emergence of this super special economic region is one of the most breath-taking phase[s] of development in China as well as the entire Asia-Pacific Rim" (1989: 101), a prediction echoed by Castells seven years later (2000: 439).

According to Zheng, Hong Kong geographers in the late 1980s understood the PRD as Hong Kong's hinterland (1989: 91). While this characterization was accurate at the time, provoking Hong Kong investment in the PRD, Zheng also accused Hong Kong geographers of failing to take seriously the disequilibrium state of urban configurations and the system's fast transformation. Socio-technical networks are constantly evolving according to a double logic of decentralization and recentralization, as new channels of connection are constructed, new strategic points of centrality emerge in the network acting to both reconfigure and re-scale urban space. Henri Lefebvre points out that the fundamental form of the urban is centrality itself, and yet the urban phenomenon is a dialectical process of implosion and explosion, a bidirectional movement that produces both centralization and decentralization. "The urban . . . is a form. Because of this, it tends toward 1. centrality [and] 2. polycentrality, omnicentrality" (2003: 119–120). Contemporary urban theory has embraced this Lefebvrian concept, examining the ways in which the planet is urbanized through the implosion-explosion dynamic (Brenner and Schmid 2015).

If the regional network of the PRD can be seen as the most typical 21st-century example of regional urbanization, linking many cities into an urban system, then Shenzhen itself can be seen as a representative example of an intra-municipal urban network. What has characterized its development over the past forty years is the rapid proliferation of urban infrastructures and the migration and multiplication of urban centralities. Shenzhen is structured as a *value network*, made up of connecting lines of public infrastructure and the dense points of agglomeration where they cross and intersect. This produces a dialectic of infrastructural expansion and the consequent migration of centers toward spaces of increased connectivity and economic value. Old centers are constantly being devalued, eclipsed by the value of newer ones, as new infrastructures propel real estate speculation toward new frontiers, and through this diastolic implosion and explosion of public spaces, the city is unevenly developed. In Shenzhen, this dynamic can be read through the succession of urban plans, with each proposing a new strategic network for growth and development. The Shenzhen Metro makes the clearest case study for the close relationship between land development and infrastructure construction, as its construction is funded by the sales of developments along its route.

Value networks sort and organize differential systems of value in four ways (Karatani 2014: 7, 97).[1] First, as Castells himself suggests, any network produces a difference in value between spaces it connects and those that lie outside it (2000: 500–509). Second, urban networks connect differences. Within a given network at any given scale, each node is sorted hierarchically. In a theoretical or electronic network, distances between nodes tend toward zero, but in physical networks such as urban space, certain nodes are better connected than others, and as a result, some nodes have lower transaction costs and better-defined property rights. Third, Castells adds that different networks are connected through "switches," which organize the varied movements of information between them.[2] Intermodal portals between specific networks modulate the exchange between differential networks of value within the overall urban system. Finally, Henri Lefebvre emphasizes the unstable and dynamic nature of urban networks: value networks are themselves always in formation through processes of centralization and decentralization, implosion and explosion; they expand and decrease in scale while internalizing and externalizing different costs of exchange and production. Through external difference, internal differentiation, network-to-network exchange and rescaling, value networks are dynamically constructed in urban space. The dynamic interiority of an urban network is designed to minimize transaction costs and establish and enforce exclusive property rights within it. The city's public–private network functions as a "super-firm," built to erase the frictions of market exchange.[3]

Planning as Spatialized Economic Strategy

In Chinese planning, there is a strong belief in the relationship between spatial organization and political-economic performance. This tradition has a long history in Chinese thought, which privileges strategic thinking in general and spatial strategy in particular. Sebastian Heilmann argues that the Chinese Communist Party has internalized a "guerrilla policy style," which evolved during the long period of revolutionary war during the second quarter of the 20th century (2018: 31–36). This "policy style . . . can be characterized as a change-oriented 'push-and-seize' style that contrasts with the stability-oriented 'anticipate-and-regulate' norm of modern constitutional governments and rule-of-law polities" (Heilmann 2018: 34). It shares much with the current fascination with the application of military strategy to business in North America but with two crucial differences: first, Chinese strategic thinking focuses more on secrecy in its approach, in contrast to the direct confrontation favored by the European thought, and second, in China, it is mobilized not only by private enterprise but also by the State for both political and economic objectives (Heilmann 2018: 32–34).

As geographer Wu Fulong has pointed out, urban planning has taken on a different role in reform China than in neoliberal North America and Europe: Chinese planners have been less conflicted because planning is clearly understood as a strategic engine of economic growth. Wu argues that this has occurred through the evolution of technocratic socialist planning within a developmentalist reform economy focused on rapid growth (2007). Shenzhen was a key experiment in this novel mutation of planning in China. Wu points to a new form of plan which emerged in the 2000s called the "strategic" or "concept" plan whose flexibility allows for maximum suggestion and minimum restriction (Zhao 2001); the roots of this form of planning can be seen in the 1982, 1986 and 1996 plans for Shenzhen, which were broadly influential across the country. The very concept of "planning" sometimes appears as a modernist and communist practice disempowered through neoliberalism's emphasis on the market, but it is important to also see planning as an essential element of any business strategy. Chinese reform and opening has been especially good at mobilizing the State not just toward market-like modes of action and evaluation (as it has been in the so-called market economies) but also as a hierarchical authoritative planner, a mode of governance typical within modern capitalist firms.[4]

The 1986 Shenzhen Masterplan was an impressive document whose authors deftly synthesized English, Scandinavian, Hong Kong, Chinese and Singaporean influences and won the "Nationwide Best Planning" award (Figure 2.2). In its diagram, three parallel roads connect six independent clusters in a linear sequence. Each cluster has one or two centers within it and is separated from the next by naturalized corridors, connecting the lakes and hills in the north to Shenzhen Bay, echoing green belts suggested independently by Eliel Saarinen and Sir Patrick Abercrombie in the mid-20th century.[5] This elegant linear clustered urban structure was also infrastructure efficient: clusters could be connected by one major street, highway or railway. As soon as more than one parallel line was complete, the system offered productive redundancy. The efficiency of the plan's linearity and resulting connectivity created a clear sense of concentrated decentralization and poly-centrality. Within this multiplicity, the plan gave precedence to Futian District as the new center of municipal government, displaced 6 kilometers west of the historic town of Luohu and organized as a formal axis running south from the peak of Lianhua Mountain in a direct reprise of Liang Sicheng's (1901–1972) and Chen Zhanxiang's (1916–2001) 1950 proposal for a new administrative center for Beijing.[6]

By 1996, the Shenzhen Special Economic Zone (SEZ) was largely built out, so the 1996 plan added three north-south axes to the original east-west belt extending through the city's outer districts (Figure 2.3). The SEZ was drawn with three growth centers: one in the west in Nanshan, a central node combining Futian new center and historic Luohu, a third, Yantian, in the east. Although not yet constructed, Futian's north-south axis was strongly reinforced as the symbolic, administrative and financial heart of the larger metropolis, illustrating the first planned migration of the city center westward. The diagram's three north-south axes connect beyond the SEZ through Shenzhen's suburbs: one running along the western coast, serviced by the 1994 Guangzhou-Shenzhen (Guangshen) expressway; another through the valley North of Luohu and Futian along the historic railway connection from Hong Kong to Guangzhou; and the third running northeast toward Huizhou though Longgang district, supporting a complex web of transportation designed to guide and instigate the development of regional centers beyond the SEZ at each of its intersections.

The 2010 Plan—Three Axes and Two Belt Structure—The City as a Meshwork

The concept diagram for the 2010–2020 plan led by Bing Zou at the Urban Planning and Design Institute of Shenzhen (UPDIS) was named the Three-Axis Two-Band Multi-Center (Figure 2.4). While its meshwork appears entirely different from the tree structure of the 1996 plan, it added just one conceptual element to the earlier diagram: an east-west band through the outer districts of Bao'an and Longgang which fell along the line of a highway

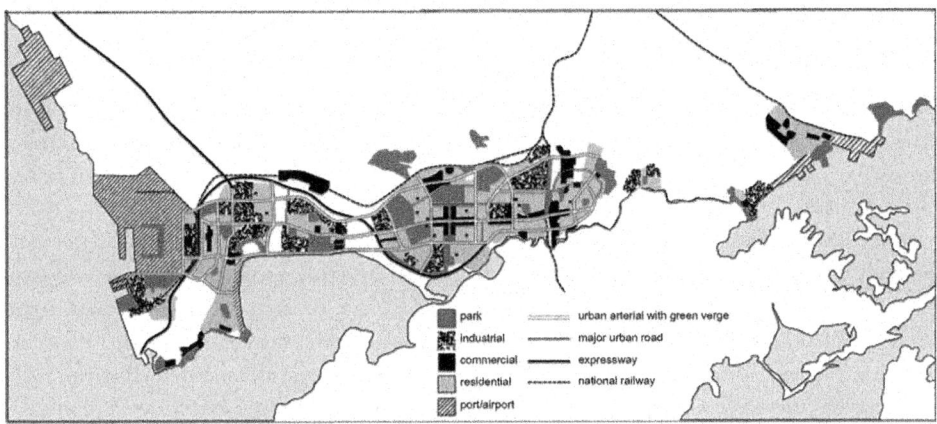

FIGURE 2.2 The 1986 plan of Shenzhen SEZ.

Source: Shenzhen Comprehensive Development Draft Plan, 2007–2020.

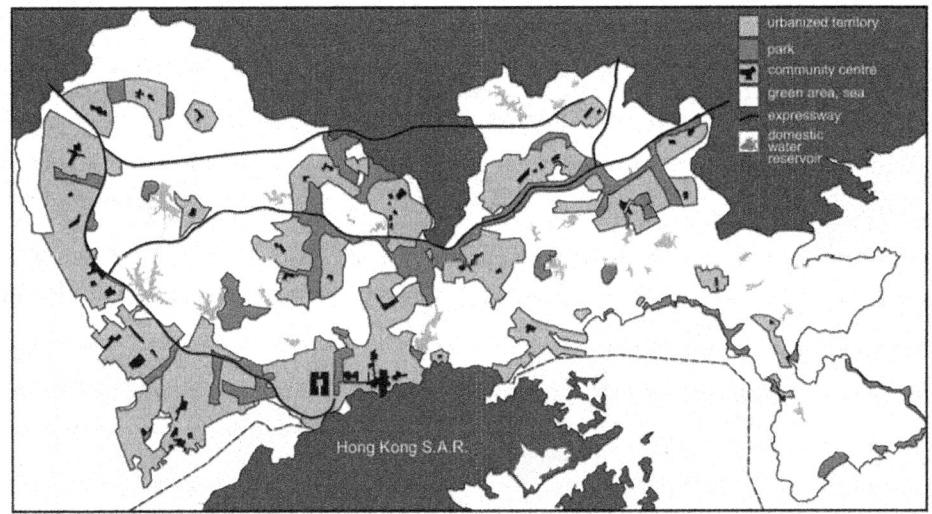

FIGURE 2.3 The 1996–2010 plan of Shenzhen.

Source: Adapted from the Shenzhen Urban Planning and Land Administration Bureau (2000). Shenzhen Comprehensive Plan, 1996–2010.

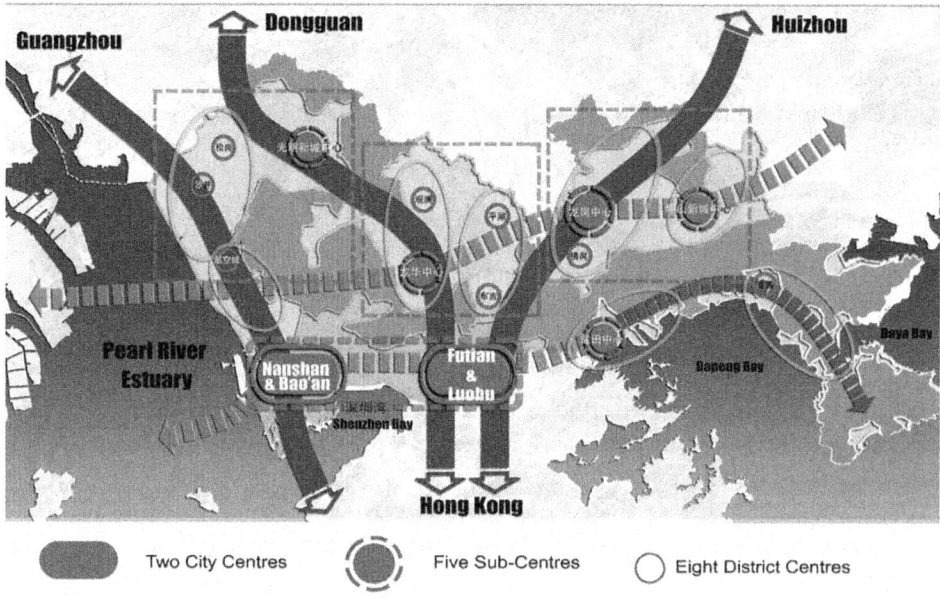

FIGURE 2.4 The Shenzhen urban design plan with major axis of development.

Source: Shenzhen Urban Planning and Land Administration Bureau (2007), Shenzhen Comprehensive Development Draft Plan, 2007–2020.

already proposed in 1996 and since built. However, in the 2010 plan, this new axis is strategically decisive, clearly connecting through the heart of the GBA across a tunnel and bridge to Zhongshan in the west and beyond the city's borders to cheap land resources in Huizhou and Shantou in the east. The 2010 plan makes it clear that Bao'an and Longang are reaching their development capacity as linear tendrils of nearly continuous sprawl, tightly enclosed by Shenzhen's 2004 Ecological Control Line.[7] The 2010 plan sees the city's hinterland beyond its municipal boundaries, so its network stretches west toward the PRD's less-developed coast and east toward its less-expensive outer ring cities to procure affordable land for economic expansion.

In 1986, the large bay at the western terminus of the city's axis was planned as a vast harbor for a planned chemical industry. It was later decided to move this industry eastward, first to Shenzhen's Dapeng peninsula and eventually even further east to Huizhou's Daya Bay.[8] As a result, in the 1996 plan, Shenzhen's western coast was reserved for future development.[9] In the 2010 plan, this site, made almost entirely of land reclaimed from the Pearl River estuary, was designated Qianhai, the city's future center. In an international competition whose results were announced in 2010, the US landscape architecture practice Field Operations was awarded the commission for the masterplan of this new zone of 1,800 hectares and 1.5 million people (Cilento 2010; JCFO 2010).

The 2010 plan also describes a vast network of rail transportation across the entire city. In 2004, the first two lines of the Metro had finally opened, but their planning stretched back through the earlier urban plans.[10] In 1995, a preliminary proposal for an ambitious system of nine lines was included in the preparatory work for the 1996 plan when the central government abruptly halted Metro construction in all but the country's three largest cities: Beijing, Shanghai and Guangzhou. With its ambitious plans on hold, the Shenzhen government leveraged the return of Hong Kong to argue for a short length of subway to connect the border crossings at Luohu and Huanggang to Luohu and Futian centers, and this minimal proposal was the sole fragment made public in the 1996 plan. Submitted for approval in 1997, construction finally began in 1999, and the east to west line from Luohu to the Window of the World theme park, and a south to north line with just four stops from Fumin to Shaoniangong (Children's Palace), were completed in 2004 (Wang 2010; Tang and Ju 2011). After an embarrassing period when construction proceeded at "earthworm speed" (Chao 2007), Mayor Xu Zongheng pushed forward with Phase II to expand the system to 177 km in time for the Universiade Games in 2011.

Phase II was based closely on the plans made in preparation for the 1996 One Band and Three Axes plan. So, the 2010 plan extended the Metro plan far beyond it, proposing a complex web of future phases organized into a hierarchy of three grades of rail connections: (1) inter-city and inner-city express trains, (2) trunk lines and (3) local lines (SZGOV 2010). The 2010 plan's far-reaching system has been closely followed in the rapid expansion of the Metro ever since. By August 2020, Shenzhen's system was 382 km long—sixth in the world and fourth in China by length—28.5 more kilometers are on track for completion in 2020, which would leap-frog Shenzhen to both the world's and China's fourth longest. The 2016–2030 Metro plan aspires to complete thirty-two lines totaling 1,142 km by the year 2030, twenty-four regular Metro lines and eight high-speed rail lines that will reach outward through adjacent municipalities while allowing for express commuting within Shenzhen.

If Phase I was clearly planned to string Shenzhen's centers together like "beads on a chain" (UPDIS 1999), subsequent phases have been led by an intensified logic of "rail plus property" through which profits from property development offset the costs of building transit. This development-led process of infrastructure provision reprises Gordon Wu's practice in the late 1980s when he secured valuable development land along the route of the Guangshen expressway as part of his compensation for its construction. In 2004, Shenzhen Metro signed an agreement with the Hong Kong Mass Transit Railway (MTR) to co-develop the expansion of the Longhua line, which runs directly north from Futian center into Longhua district.[11] Hong Kong had developed an innovative model for mass transit finance based on experiments in Japan and Singapore (Luan et al. 2014). Starting in the 1980s, the MTR used property development as a tool to help offset costs of the construction of its urban lines in Central and Kowloon, narrowly breaking even by the late 1980s. Learning from these early experiments, the MTR returned to property development at the end of the 1990s to help finance its airport line and in 2000 listed a quarter of its shares on the Hong Kong Stock Exchange, injecting a dose of market discipline to its management structure (Cervero and Murakami 2009). Since then, the MTR has been able to recoup substantial surpluses from property development, and it is this experience which Shenzhen Metro sought to leverage in their joint venture.

One characteristic of the development-led transit planning is that it is not intended to connect existing communities but to favor peripheral lands. Plans are based on low cost of construction and the super-profits produced through the change in land use and value. The Longhua line is a good example of this. In 2007, the Shenzhen government developed five criteria for evaluating the potential of different Metro lines: "urban traffic pressure (ridership),

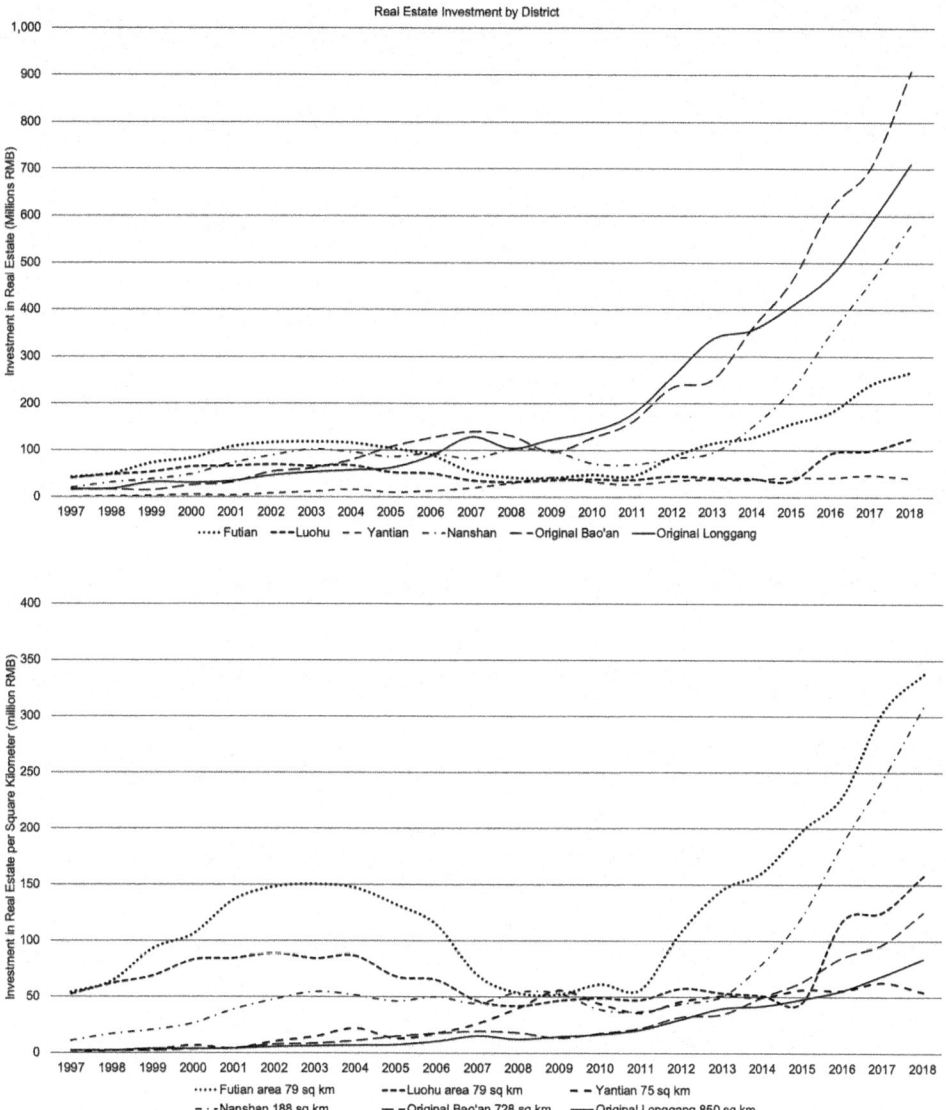

FIGURE 2.5 Investment intensity in Shenzhen, 1997–2018.

Source: Shenzhen Statistical Yearbook. Courtesy of the Shenzhen Statistical Yearbook.

network strategy (connectivity), urgency, coordination with urban development, operational revenue, and land-sector revenue" (Yang et al. 2016: 95). In a comparison with eight different Metro lines, the Longhua line ranked last overall and last in each category except land-sector revenue, and yet it was chosen to be developed first. The line's path deliberately passes through underdeveloped land and bypasses Longhua center, where residents currently need transit. Despite rapid residential development around the line, Longhua's new central area is still in the early stages of construction surrounding Shenzhen's North Train Station.

This land-development–led process of infrastructure provision has been instrumental in producing a consistent wave of new centers and attendant public spaces in formerly peripheral districts. Bao'an was the first densely developed center outside the SEZ because of its proximity to Nanshan and the fact that the Guangshen highway to Dongguan and Guangzhou runs through it. Longgang gained significant stimulus from the 2011 Universiade and the explosion of subway connectivity planned for it. The Universiade site is now a new center which will house the tallest tower in China, the Shimao Shenzhen-Hong Kong International Center (Shanghaiist 2018). The 2010 plan named the underdeveloped peripheral town of Guangming as a high-tech center, and further district planning has focused on building it as a low-carbon eco-city (Zacharias and Tang 2010; Cales 2014). In April 2019, the Shenzhen Municipal Government announced the Shenzhen National High-tech Zone Expansion Plan, with "one zone, two cores and multiple parks"; one of its two centers is in Nanshan, which is surrounded by new commercial centers in Qianhai, Houhai, Super-headquarters base and Liuxiandong, and the other is in Pingshan district and has been designated "the core of the future development of high-tech industries" with the smaller technology parks planned for Bao'an, Longgang and Longhua (SZGOV 2019).

Value Networks in Motion

Examining the change in the increase in real estate investment in different districts from 1997 to the present, a pattern emerges: investment rises sharply at a rate of 23% per year from 1997 to 2002 as the central government moved to mitigate the effects of the Asian economic crisis by creating policies to accelerate the commodification of housing (Wu 2016) (Figure 2.5). Growth plateaus in 2003, dips into the negative in the wake of the 2008 financial crisis, and then accelerates to grow at an average of 27% from 2011 to 2018 in response to RMB 4 trillion in government infrastructure investment (Wu 2018: 1391). This recent growth in real estate development is even more surprising given the slow deceleration of Chinese GDP growth over the same period, from 10.6% in 2010 to 6.6% in 2018 (Trading Economics 2018). These two growth spurts coincide with the release of the 1996 and 2010 urban plans, and the development of both plans was closely timed to economic crises, illustrating their strong stimulus toward urban growth and the way that different levels of the Chinese state have been using land development as a tool to offset financial crises by channeling investment into city building.

Each district has followed a different trajectory of development (Figure 2.5). The city began its development in Luohu, which dominated construction in the 1980s and early 1990s. By 1999, the planned new center in Futian overtook Luohu and remained the most intensive development center measured in investment per square kilometer until 2018, but in 2013, with the announcement of Qianhai, Nanshan District accelerated and is set to overtake Futian in the next few years. At the same time, most urban development is now happening in the new centers of the outer districts, even if it remains at a lower level of intensity than in the new centers within the SEZ.

This process illustrates the way planning is used as an entrepreneurial tool not only in competition between municipalities but also between districts within a single municipality. Like other countries, China's path toward neoliberalism has not focused on the displacement of State by market governmentality but in the transformation of both markets and the State toward more entrepreneurial and competitive behavior (Davies 2014). Chinese planning, undertaken under the direction of municipal planning bureaus and state-owned planning institutes at different levels, has been fully mobilized to build cities as growth machines in ways that far exceed the abilities and ambitions of planners in Europe, North America or Australasia (Wu 2018). The strategic and conceptual nature of Shenzhen's path-breaking planning techniques has allowed for municipalities to focus on the production of robust high-value urban networks while letting much of the city function independently through self-organized and informal networks of daily life and work. As Wang Fuhai, director of the 1996 plan argues, Shenzhen was the pioneer of dual-track urbanism,[12] now ubiquitous in China: the planned city is disciplined through its integration within the network, the unplanned city disciplined through the precarity of its labor and living conditions outside the network.

The history of Shenzhen illustrates the use of planning as a strategic tool to build the city's public spaces and its public realm as differential value networks composed of ever-expanding urban infrastructures—such as highways, roadways, rail and public transport lines—and migrating and multiplying urban centralities: downtowns, special zones and high-tech parks. These networks produce an urbanism of arbitrage in four distinct ways. First, the urban network has been overlaid on a marginal rural territory, creating high-value networked spaces superimposed over a low-value territory. Second, network planning involves both functional and hierarchical differentiation between network nodes, producing internal differentiation. Third, networks exist at different jurisdictional scales—villages, districts, municipalities, regions, nation, international—and legislative and infrastructural switches govern the movement of different factors of production between each of these distinct networks of value, because at each of these levels, there is competition (for the control of land, labor and capital markets) with other networks in adjacent jurisdictions as well as with adjacent levels above and below it in the same jurisdiction. Finally, the multiplication of infrastructural lines and the continual creation of new centers is a dynamic process that continually changes both the internal hierarchy, the number of nodes in the network and the switching techniques, drawing external nodes inside and jettisoning older ones. While in Shenzhen this dynamic is guided by planners, it is equally governed by unforeseen market exigencies and local insurgencies: it is simultaneously planned and unplanned.

Notes

1. The concept of "value networks" is derived from Kojin Karatani's argument that surplus value is produced through a form of arbitrage between different "systems of value." See Karatani (2014).
2. "The switchers are the power-holders. Since networks are multiple, the inter-operating codes and switches between networks become the fundamental sources in shaping, guiding, and misguiding societies" (Castells 2000: 502).
3. The thesis that value networks allow for the internalization of transaction costs is drawn from the work of Ronald Coase, which has been instrumental in the formation of global neoliberalism, and with the help of Steven N.S. Cheung, of Chinese neoliberalism through the concept of the super-firm applied by Cheung. See: (Coase 1937, 2013: 852; Cheung 1982: 39).
4. In *The Nature of the Firm*, Ronald Coase points out that the market economy is filled with hierarchical organizations called "firms." See Coase (1937).
5. According to Wang Fuhai, the leader of the 1996 plan, the 1986 plan was inspired by Eliel Saarinen's concept of "organic decentralization" (Wang, interview with the author, 2017). Chen Zhanxiang, co-author with Liang Sicheng of the Liang Chen 1950 plan for Beijing, worked as a senior planner at the China Academy of Urban Planning and Design (CAUPD) in the 1980s and was an advisor on the 1986 Shenzhen plan. Chen studied with Patrick Abercrombie (1879–1957) in the 1940s when Abercrombie worked on the Greater London Plan of 1944.

6. The Plan's chief planner, Zhou Ganzhi (1930–2014), was a student of Liang and Chen at Tsinghua University in the 1940s when they were working on the 1950 plan for Beijing. See: (Jun 2011: 92–172, 314; Zhou 1990).
7. The control line strictly prohibits most forms of urban development in almost 50% of the city's area. It was the first of these legislations in China, and it has since influenced policies across the nation (Wang, interview with the author 2017).
8. Zuo, interview with the author 2017.
9. Wang, Interview with the author 2017.
10. The 1986 plan had called for a single line of light rail transit along Shennan Avenue which was never built.
11. Until 2011, when it became a new district, Longhua was the name of a town in Bao'an district of Shenzhen.
12. Wang, interview with the author 2017.

References

Brenner, N. and Schmid, C. (2015) "Towards a new epistemology of the urban?" *City* 19 (2–3). pp. 151–182.

Cales, R. (2014) *Shenzhen low carbon city: A transformation of concept and planning process*. Unpublished MSc Thesis, University of Amsterdam. At: www.newtowninstitute.org/pdf/MasterthesisRuben Cales.pdf. Last accessed on 20 September 2020.

Castells, M. (2000) *The rise of the network society: The information age: Economy, society and culture* (volume 1, 2nd ed.). Wiley-Blackwell.

Cervero, R. and Murakami, J. (2009) "Rail and property development in Hong Kong: Experiences and extensions." *Urban Studies* 46 (10). pp. 2019–2043, 2025–2026, September.

Chao, H. (2007) "Metro construction 'earthworm speed'." *Nanfang Daily*, 19 January. At: http://news.sina.com.cn/o/2007-01-19/105811040167s.shtml. Last accessed on 20 September 2020.

Cheung, S.N.S. (1982) *Will China go capitalist? An economic analysis of property rights and institutional change*. Hobert Paper #94. The Institute of Economic Affairs.

Cilento, K. (2010) "James Corner field operations to design Qianhai." *Archdaily*, 1 July. At: www.archdaily.com/66650/james-corner-field-operations-to-design-qianhai. Last accessed on 20 September 2020.

Coase, R.H. (1937) "The nature of the firm." *Economica, New Series* 4 (16). pp. 386–405, November.

Coase, R.H. (2013) "The problem of social cost." *Journal of Law and Economics* 56 (4). pp. 837–877, November.

Davies, W. (2014) *The limits of neoliberalism: Authority, sovereignty, and the logic of competition*. Sage.

Gottmann, J. (1961) *Megalopolis: The urbanized northeastern seaboard of the United States*. Twentieth Century Fund.

Heilmann, S. (2018) *Red swan: How unorthodox policy making facilitated China's rise*. Chinese University Press. pp. 31–36.

JCFO (2010) *Qianhai water city, Shenzhen, China*. At: www.fieldoperations.net/project-details/project/qianhai-water-city.html. Last accessed on 20 September 2020.

Jun, W. (2011) *Beijing record: A physical and political history of planning modern Beijing*. World Scientific Publishing.

Karatani, K. (2014) *The structure of world history: From modes of production to modes of exchange*. Duke University Press.

Lefebvre, H. (2003) *The urban revolution* (trans. Robert Bononno). University of Minnesota Press.

Luan, X., Lin, X., McGuinness, E. and Yang, J. (2014) "Emerging public–private partnerships in China's rail mass transit: Case of Shenzhen." *Transportation Research Record* 2450 (1). pp. 127–135, 1 January.

Shanghaiist (2018) "Shenzhen breaks ground on China's future tallest building." *Medium.com*, 27 March. At: https://medium.com/shanghaiist/shenzhen-breaks-ground-on-chinas-future-tallest-building-6ab46488033d. Last accessed on 20 September 2020.

Sieverts, T. (2003) *Cities without cities: An interpretation of the Zwischenstadt*. Routledge.
SZGOV (2010) *Comprehensive plan for Shenzhen 1996–2010*. Shenzhen Municipal People's Government, posted online on 18 May 2018 (in Chinese, with English translation). At http://pnr.sz.gov.cn/ywzy/ghzs/ztgh/index.htm. Last accessed on 15 September 2020.
SZGOV (2019) *Notice of Shenzhen municipal people's government on issuing the expansion plan of Shenzhen national high-tech zone*. Shenzhen Municipal People's Government, 22 May (in Chinese). At: www.sz.gov.cn/zfgb/2019/gb1101/content/post_4984098.html. Last accessed on 20 September 2020.
Tang, J. and Ju, H. (2011) "We walked into the subway era like this: Planning Shenzhen metro network framework was basically finalized 15 years ago." *Shenzhen News*, 25 June. At: https://web.archive.org/web/20140914190026/http://sztqb.sznews.com/html/2011-06/25/content_1632195.htm. Last accessed on 15 September 2020.
Trading Economics (2018) *China GDP annual growth rate*. At: https://tradingeconomics.com/china/gdp-growth-annual. Last accessed on 15 September 2020.
UPDIS (1999) *Rail transit, carrying the urban spatial structure upwards, and driving urban comprehensive development downwards*. UPDIS 25th Anniversary Publication. At: www.upr.cn/years-book.htm. Last accessed on 15 September 2020.
Wang, X. (2010) "Shenzhen metro's 'ten years of pregnancy' finally come true." *Shenzhen News*, 14 April. At: https://web.archive.org/web/20160106183158/http://sztqb.sznews.com/html/2010-04/14/content_1035002.htm. Last accessed on 15 September 2020.
Woo, E.S.W. (1994) "Urban development." In: Yeung, Y.M., David, K. and Chu, Y. (Eds.) *Guangdong: Survey of a province undergoing rapid change*. The Chinese University Press.
Wu, F. (2007) "Re-orientation of the city plan: Strategic planning and design competition in China." *Geoforum* 38 (2). pp. 379–392, 1 March.
Wu, F. (2016) *Planning for growth: Urban and regional planning in China*. Lecture at Columbia University, 17 November. At: www.youtube.com/watch?v=IVGW49jijWs. Last accessed on 15 September 2020.
Wu, F. (2018) "Planning centrality, market instruments: Governing Chinese urban transformation under state entrepreneurialism." *Urban Studies* 55 (7). pp. 1383–1399, 1 May.
Yang, J., Chen, J., HuiLe, X. and Zhang, Q. (2016) "Density-oriented versus development-oriented transit investment: Decoding metro station location selection in Shenzhen." *Transport Policy* 51. pp. 93–102.
Zacharias, J. and Tang, Y. (2010) "Restructuring and repositioning Shenzhen, China's new mega city." *Progress in Planning* 73 (4). pp. 209–250.
Zhao, Y. (2001) "On the theoretical foundation and methodology of concept planning" ("探索新的范型：概念规划的理论与方法"). *City Planning Review* 25 (3). pp. 38–52 (in Chinese).
Zheng, T. (1989) "The spatial relationships among Hong Kong, Macau and the Pearl River Delta Area." *Asian Geographer* 8 (1–2). pp. 89–102.
Zhou, G. (1990) "Press forward to reach the contemporary state of the art of urban planning." In: *Shenzhen urban planning & design: A compilation for the first decade celebration of Shenzhen special economic zone*. Shenzhen Municipal Government, City of Shenzhen. pp. 3–14.

3

LIQUID STORIES: MARITIME CULTURES IN THE PEARL RIVER DELTA

Laurent Gutierrez and Valérie Portefaix

The Pearl River Delta (PRD) has recently been rebranded as the Greater Bay Area (GBA), giving a stronger power to the economic infrastructure than to the geography of the estuary. With the opening of the world's longest cross-sea bridge, a new runway and multiple land reclamations, the coastlines and the numerous islands are being solidified into one single mass of land, negating the water and related activities that used to unify the region.[1]

The politics of new infrastructures began in the mid-1980s, with reclamations and bridges and the planning of a continuous solidification of a region that had a most unique and complex liquid condition. After the development of the Shenzhen[2] Special Economic Zone (launched in 1980), the sea has resisted as well as the shrinking fishermen's culture which reminds us of the unique identity and development of Hong Kong and the delta since prehistoric times. Over the centuries, its body of water was inhabited by coastal and floating communities, such as fishermen and sea foragers. They have accumulated a precious knowledge and practiced alternative subsistence modes of living that need to be collected and evaluated today. Furthermore, their experience copes with a shift in the global economy and the looming threat of climate change with rising sea levels. The amphibious culture and infrastructure developed by the sea communities could serve to reformulate our present reality and imaginary of this territory. The various back-and-forth movements/conflicts between the land and the sea to control and exploit the delta served as a series of frameworks to narrate the construction of the PRD.

While the definition of public space has been heavily documented on land and solid territory,[3] one can simply refer to it as a place/zone of exchange (infrastructure and trade), encounter (culture and mythology) and conflict (wars and treaties). The aims of this chapter are to recollect the multiple stories in which the water body of the PRD offered multiple situations and functionalities of a public space and therefore produced an alternative view to its current geography as solid land.

Liquid Geography—Sediments, Sand and Other Fluid Grounds

The memory of the water, the one left in the hundreds of sand-dunes sites, of an early coastal route known as the "Canton Sea Route" illustrates the prosperity of Neolithic maritime

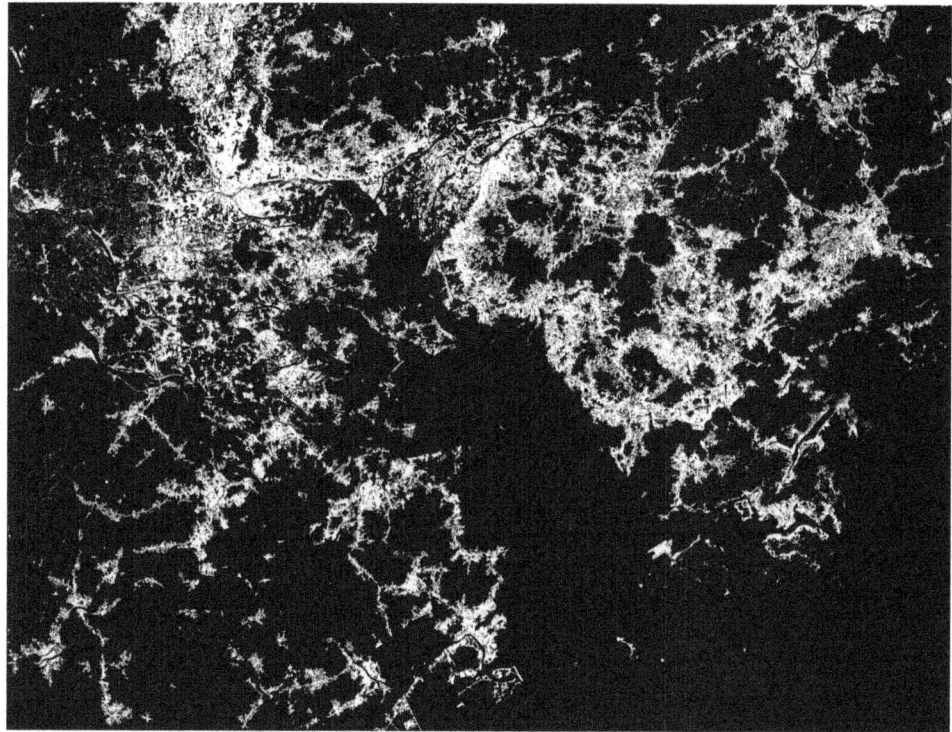

FIGURE 3.1 PRD on/off. Black-and-white print on transparency, 2007. Dimensions: 90 × 120 cm. Illustration of the built versus the non-built of the Pearl River Delta.
Source: MAP Office 2007.

cultures in the Pearl River Delta. The Pearl River or *Zhu Jiang* flows from Guangzhou to its mouth, forming a wide estuary with Macao on its west and Lantau, the largest island of Hong Kong, on the east. Along the multiple bays and coves, archeologists found a number of middens that contain rich ecological evidence, including not only shells and bones but also tools and artifacts showing a dynamic pattern of exchange in the South China Sea. Until the 1980s, the Delta was a large marine bay containing many islands, each with a specific function serving a complex network of economies and ecologies.

The Pearl River is China's third longest river and one of the world's twenty-five largest. Cartographic mapping and later satellite remote sensing have revealed that human activities engaged a continuous transformation of the bathymetry and the contours of the coastline. On British-made maps, the Pearl River has also been referred to as the River Tigris or Canton River. An extensive network of rivers flows into the main watercourse, together with many islands, playing significant roles in making the area into one complete system. The history of the subaqueous topography traces the lines of human activities, production and cultures in the estuary. The transport of sediments by the river to the ocean is a natural interface between land and sea. In the case of the Delta, hundreds of water lanes exponentially multiply this interaction. Hence, they play a major role in recording and archiving the anthropogenic environmental variations.

FIGURE 3.2 Disneyland reclamation in Lantau Island, 2002.
Source: MAP Office 2002.

From 1980 to 2002, unauthorized and massive sand excavation from 324 segments of the river network represents the volume of a century of sand deposition, or a total of 3.32 billion cubic meters. This action has not only impacted the water flow ratio, tides and routes but was also paired with more than 230 km^2 of reclamations from 1955 to 2010 (mostly after 1980). The demand for construction sand became voracious and also the main support of the unprecedented urban growth. Dredging impacted fishing at many levels: first by destroying fish breeding grounds and blocking the sunlight that sustains underwater vegetation, and later, from 2010, a new series of reclamation and navigation channels continued shaping the actual form of the Delta. Yet this new phase of sand extraction is causing massive damage to the infrastructure it is serving. In Hong Kong, the new reclamations around the airport are facing serious problems, with part of the infrastructure moving or sinking. Other reclamations around Victoria Harbour are showing alarming signs of sinking from "alert" to "action" level, and new excavation work has had to stop for an indefinite time (Cheng 2018).

When landing nowadays at the Hong Kong International Airport, built on reclaimed land on the island of Chek Lap Kok, one can observe the large group of islands forming the Wanshan Archipelago, most having been partly or entirely flattened down to sea level. Islands disappeared in order to either extend the existing ones or build new ones just a few kilometers away: a testimony that the liquid condition of the regional geography is now being pushed to dangerous limits. Today, the global shortage and restricted supply of sea sand is a new challenge for the development of new land reclamation (United Nations 2019). Yet the finitude of sand has not stopped the Hong Kong Task Force for Land Supply and the Lantau

Tomorrow Vision from planning the reclamation of 1,700 hectares of land from the sea to construct a new metropolis to the east of Lantau.[4] According to the Secretary of Development, the new land would stand at 6 meters above sea level, the same height as the Hong Kong International Airport, and be made of millions of tons of crushed construction waste instead of marine sand. Obviously, this controversial project would have a dreadful impact on the adjacent waters, with less flow and currents to flush out waste, causing oxygen depletion, red tides and therefore the death of all living species. It also represents a shift in the center of gravity of the territory towards the airport and the Hong Kong–Zhuhai–Macau bridge serving as a key political link to Xi Jinping's Greater Bay Area.

Island Network—A Timeline, Realities and Fictions

One of the purposes of this chapter is to characterize an amphibious region: a delta where the condition of land and water is neither neutral nor stable. The historic construction of an island network, connected by efficient communication and transportation infrastructure supporting a great number of public activities, shows a patchwork of interwoven realities and fictions serving both the politics and the culture of the territory (Harff et al. 2007). With no particular concern for spatial sequence or articulation, these extensive flow lines constituted an effective strategy for colonization, transforming the landscape into a series of polynuclear construction systems, therefore reinforcing the hybrid condition of the territory and its living cultures.

The Delta's extensive network of rivers, used as much for irrigation as for transportation, simultaneously stimulated the development of agriculture, aquaculture and trade. This freshwater ecosystem, for example, included dike-carp ponds bounded by mulberry trees for silkworms, setting up an early example of a combined ecology and economy. Living in simple wooden structures on land or above water, famers dug and moved the soil to make an intricate chessboard of farmland and fishponds.

Archeologists have also identified evidence of an active maritime exchange between the mainland coast of the Pearl River Delta and the neighboring islands such as Qi'ao, Sanzao, Hengqin, Dong'ao, Gaolan, Hebao islands of Zhuhai; Dachan and Neilingdin islands of Shenzhen; Dayu and Chilajiao islands of Hong Kong; and Jiu'ao island of Macao. Interaction across the trans-border coast of the South China Sea is found in the remnants of subsistence activities, fishing, hunting and foraging. Shell middens have preserved wild boar and deer teeth but most importantly species of fish such as rays and sharks, indicating that fishermen had mastered the art of offshore fishing.

The Pearl River Delta is probably one of the earliest areas massively transformed from fishing to a major trade base. During this evolution, the fluctuating depth and width of the water strategically distributed the role of the complex network of islands that serve as filters to control boats, collect taxes, accommodate foreigners and include their burial grounds. Rocky islands served as fortified gates. The wide and open waters allowed the mooring of boats. The upper part of the estuary depended on tidal flow and created a high-energy environment for the transportation system. The governance of the coastal and inter-island network first attracted Arab and Persian traders, then Europeans, who had been exporting material from Southern China since the Tang Dynasty. Finally, the colonization of Macau was a later important step to transform the region into a collection of economic enclaves, giving as much importance to the land as to the sea.

FIGURE 3.3 Amphibious living in the Pearl River Delta, Nansha area, 2004.

Source: MAP Office 2004.

Guangzhou Islands

Located at the tip of the estuary about 150 km inland, Guangzhou has been established since 214 BC as the major settlement in South China. The dense waterway system explains why the city remained on the same site, protected from pirates by shallow water and the many islands used to control navigation and trade. During the Ming Dynasty, Guangzhou became the largest port in China, if not Asia, and most importantly the only one that authorized trade with foreign merchant ships. At that time, products including precious silk and ceramics were carried by sea around Asia or to the Persian Gulf, the Middle East and Europe. The unstable condition of the coastline in a delta is difficult to map, especially when people of different ethnicities from various regions come to inhabit this fertile liquid land. Along the shoreline, rich merchants built large warehouses, while mobile floating communities would make stilt houses to live from fishing and farming.

The study of ethnicities shows that "commercial networks around Shunde and Panyu consisted of small clusters of straw huts controlling dikes and agricultural plots sustaining the community. Organically growing along man-made reclamation they present unique examples of a 'constantly reconfigured social ecology'" (Siu and Liu 2006). As merchants and controllers developed the accumulation of wealth and power, they organized the ethnic hierarchy and lineage in the various communities. During both the Ming (1368–1644) and Qing (1644–1912) periods, the extensive reclamation process and manipulation of the water flow and land reinforced the influence of the new settlers.

One extraordinary testimony of the diverse roles of fishermen, boat masters and river merchants can be seen in the different types of boats that use to cross the river (Lucarelli 2016). The first British ambassador to China, Lord George Macartney (1737–1806), described that "the river of Canton is covered with boats and vessels of various sorts and sizes, all, even the very smallest, constantly and thickly inhabited" (Barrow 1807). Floating structures reproduced typologies found in the city and the countryside, such as warehouses, grocery shops, customs buildings, theatres, brothels and chicken farms, with other types of fishing and passenger boats of different sizes.

Whampoa Island/The Canton System (Guangzhou)

Chinese cities were planned with internal restricted borders separating areas serving different purposes. Ancient Whampoa Anchorage or Huangpu Port, located 20 kilometers south of Guangzhou, served as a strategic buffer zone between the city and the foreign world and accommodated up to 2,000 sailors for three months during winter. Developing what was called the "Canton system," Chinese authorities invented a liquid geography of control with boats and islands used in specific steps.

In a first step, boats were registered in Macao before being escorted up the river at Whampoa. Merchandise was later moved towards and from the Canton market on local sampans and junks with exclusively Chinese crew. The most prominent features of the Whampoa anchorage were a nine-story pagoda and the various Christian and Muslim burial grounds: a peaceful bay where two cultures met in an environment of reciprocal exchange. Regulations and trade developed steadily through the 18th century, showing that restrictions such as taxes did not compromise profitable business. It is interesting to note that foreigners were living in buildings called "factories," a term used from the ancient English word "factor," denoting a commercial agent. The island locality grew under the name of "Thirteen Factories" with the arrival of the British followed by the Austrians, Danish, Dutch, French, Spanish, Swedish and Americans. This unique model of trade infrastructure was burned with several destructive fires and was later moved to the inner part of the city, at Shamian Island.

Lintin Island/Nei Lingding (Shenzhen)

Guangzhou became the flourishing port of China during the 18th century, making great profit from the sale of tea, porcelain and silk wares, yet foreign merchants had much difficulty selling their cargoes of cotton and woolen goods. A key location to secure the entrance of the Delta, Lintin Island became a strategic open-sea anchorage for foreign ships sailing to and from Guangzhou. Avoiding heavy taxes first and prohibition later, in 1820, British merchants began to sell opium grown in India from Lintin island. Remote from the Portuguese and under the protection of the British Chamber of Commerce, British ships found a safe and speedy place to control their business. The island quickly became the official trading port for contraband and played a major role during the Opium Wars of 1839 to 1842 and 1856 to 1860. The island was later disputed between Zhuhai and Shenzhen and was administratively part of the former before being handed over to the latter in 2009.

Fluid Mythology—New Archaeological Finding of Lo Tin in Lantau

Concentrating all the energy of the River Tigris, the island of Lantau remains the epicenter of the Pearl River Delta where mythologies and stories flow along the centuries for a better articulation of the natural and human forces in place. Today, Lantau is the center of gravity of Hong Kong's future development and further integration to the Greater Bay Area. The project Lantau Tomorrow Vision 2030, launched in 2018 by the Hong Kong chief executive, consists of a massive land reclamation of 1,700 hectares located to the east of Lantau. This includes the construction of four artificial islands with a new central business district and a gateway to the Greater Bay Area. The trillion-Hong Kong-dollar project envisions a technological future of a smart and connected territory, against the voices of all local fishermen and anxious ecologists.

Lantau Island is also the locus of Hong Kong's mythological origin. Surfaced from the sea, the fabulous figure of the Lo Ting[5] appears as the foundational myth of Hong Kong. Half-man, half-fish, the Lo Ting emerged in the mythological age around the bays of Lantau, and, as a form of punishment and/or revenge from gods, those creatures flourished in their amphibious life until 1197. The story of Lo Ting re-emerged symbolically 800 years later[6] in 1997 in a series of exhibitions curated by Oscar H. Ho based on new archeological finds on the island (Ho et al., 1997; Ho 1998, 1999).

While the Neolithic account of Hong Kong's origins should not be ignored, the revival of the Lo Ting is more than symbolic. The various narratives exposed by Oscar Ho and the invited artists as part of three consecutive shows questioned the sense of origin of Hong Kong as a territory impregnated by its surrounding waters. Besides the surreal figure of an inverted mermaid and the *mise-en-scène* of "pretended" archaeological artifacts, the question of identity

FIGURE 3.4 Man-made island serving as a geographic marker in Tolo Harbour, Hong Kong, 2013.

Source: MAP Office 2013.

Liquid Stories 47

and distance from the Han dominating ethnicity was the main motivation of the various narratives. In opposition to the official story of returning to the Motherland, the Lo Ting appeared as a key feature in the search for a post-colonial identity towards the definition of a new amphibious way of life and of a new species as a sense of origin. Here again, the opposition between the land and the sea served to balance the authorized storytelling and advocated for the re-definition of territories, one based on geographical apparatus rather than imposed constructed narratives to solidify the main power in place.

Ho's advocacies resonate with the controversial writing of Carl Schmitt's *Land and Sea*, in which the author recalls the tension between the two biomes and the prevalence of the sea: "In people's deepest and often unconscious memories, water and the sea are the mysterious and primordial source of all life" (1942: 2). More than anything else, the construction of mythologies and stories appears within the background of the human environment. Similar to the Greek mythology located in the Aegean Sea, the one in Hong Kong is situated in the water of the Delta. The complex network of islands, the free movement of fishing boats, the various modes of trade taking place offshore or the retroactive formulation of origin with the Lo Ting are some of the many attempts to construct those narratives and to define the PRD as a place, a location, an origin. With the question of beginning and mythology envisioned from the sea's perspective, Schmitt proposes a new subject matter and suggests, as a form of conclusion, the possibility to transform space from a traditional surface dimension

FIGURE 3.5 The amphibious creature Lo Ting walking out of the water at Chai Wan, 2017.
Source: MAP Office 2017.

into one in which "space has become the field of man's energy," adding at the end that "it is not the world that is in space, but rather it is the space that is in the world" (1942: 58).

In the context of the Delta, the periphery of the triangle (the coastline and the land) has become a more dominant spatial dimension in which the various agencies, the state and the corporates, extract their sources of profit and property (private): the surface (the sea) eventually disappears, engulfing with it all living and non-living forms of existence, including its main quality as a common, a free sea. This is what Carl Schmitt (1942: 59) names in conclusion the "spatial revolution."

Notes

1. For the anthropologist James C. Scott (2017), drainage and irrigation are the necessary transformations for the state to claim control and domesticate the land and the population.
2. The literal meaning of Shenzhen is translated as "deep drainage," referring to the trenches (*zhen*) between the rice fields.
3. This refers to the idea of the common and the private property.
4. Lantau Tomorrow Vision was announced in the Hong Kong chief executive's policy address in 2018 as a "solid foundation for a sustainable future for Hong Kong" and to strategically position the territory as a cornerstone of the GBA.
5. "A long time ago there was a fish called Lo living around the Lantau island area. After absorbing spiritual energy of the universe, they became human. The sea god envied their success and they were cursed to live forever a rootless life. They remained half human half fish until the famous monk Pei Tao (*Beidu Chanshi*) positioned many spiritual rocks all over the region to release them from the curse during the early part of the 4th century. They became fully human on the condition that they should never go beyond their own territory" (Shih 2007: 158).
6. According to the story, the Lo Ting were massacred in 1197 by Song Dynasty soldiers as a way to take over salt production.

References

Barrow, J. (1807) *Some account of the public life, and a selection from the unpublished writings of the Earl Macartney*. T. Cadell and W. Davies.
Cheng, K. (2018) *MTRC halts excavation work at new station in Wanchai after reports of sinking*. Hong Kong Free Press, 10 August 2018.
Harff, J., Hay, W.W. and Tetzlaff, D.M. (2007) *Coastline changes: Interrelation of climate and geological processes*. Geological Society of America.
Ho, H.O. (1998) *Hong Kong reincarnated: New Lo Ting archaeological find*. Hong Kong Arts Centre.
Ho, H.O. (1999) *Lo Ting: New discovery on 1197 massacre*. Hong Kong Arts Centre.
Ho, H.O., Hung, H., Leung, M. and Tung, K. (1997) *Museum 97: History, community, individual*. Hong Kong Arts Centre.
Lucarelli, F. (2016) "Boats of the Pearl River Delta." *Socks*. At: http://socks-studio.com/2016/11/13/boats-of-the-pearl-river-1800–1820/. Last accessed on 20 August 2020.
Schmitt, C. (1942) *Land and sea: A world-historical meditation*. Plutarch Press.
Scott, J.C. (2017) *Against the grain. A deep history of the earliest states*. Yale University Press.
Shih, S.M. (2007) *Visuality and identity: Sinophone articulations across the Pacific*. University of California Press.
Siu, H.F. and Liu, Z.W. (2006) *Empire at the margins: Culture, ethnicity, and frontier in early modern China*. University of California Press.
United Nations (2019) *The search for sustainable sand extraction is beginning*. At: www.unenviroment.org. Last accessed on 20 August 2020.

4

The Hyper-Collage City: Public Space in the Pearl River Delta

Stefan Al

In 1978, Colin Rowe and Fred Koetter rejected the grand overall visions of "total design" for a "collage city," with the city as an eclectic collective of coexisting utopias.
Coincidentally, that same year, Deng Xiaoping announced China's open-door policy, unleashing unprecedented urban growth in the Pearl River Delta, which transformed from a predominantly rural area to the world's largest megalopolis in the timespan of a single generation.

In this maelstrom of urbanization, the Pearl River Delta has become the hotbed of several recurring urban forms that together form a "hyper-collage city," a patchwork of utopias built at breakneck speed.

The evolution of these dominant urban forms trace the economic history of modern China. In places like the Shenzhen Special Economic Zone, thousands of factory towns accommodated millions of manufacturing workers. As the industry attracted migrants looking for affordable housing, farmers became landlords by urbanizing their villages, creating hundreds of "urban villages" with apartment buildings so close to each other they are dubbed "handshake houses." As China's industrial economy evolved to domestic consumerism, numerous Hong Kong-style podium-mall tower developments were built all over the Pearl River Delta, while dozens of Las Vegas-style resorts transformed the Macau peninsula and Cotai.

The region has transformed almost beyond recognition, and it continues to evolve in a collage of contemporaneous yet contrasting types of urbanisms. But without the benefit of accumulated time, this "hyper-collage city" of the Pearl River Delta may lack the layers of history and heterogeneity that Rowe and Koetter aspired to.

Image Sources

Fig 1. Al, S. (Ed.) (2012) *Factory Towns of South China: An Illustrated Guidebook*. Hong Kong University Press.

Fig 2. Al, S. (Ed.) (2014) *Villages in the City: A Guide to South China's Informal Settlements*. University of Hawaii Press and Hong Kong University Press.

Figs 3 and 4. Al, S. (Ed.) (2016) *Mall City: Hong Kong's Dream Worlds of Consumption*. University of Hawaii Press and Hong Kong University Press.

Figs 5 and 6. Al, S. (Ed.) (2018) *Macau and the Casino Complex*. University of Nevada Press.

Reference

Rowe, C. and Koetter, F. (1978) *Collage City*. MIT Press.

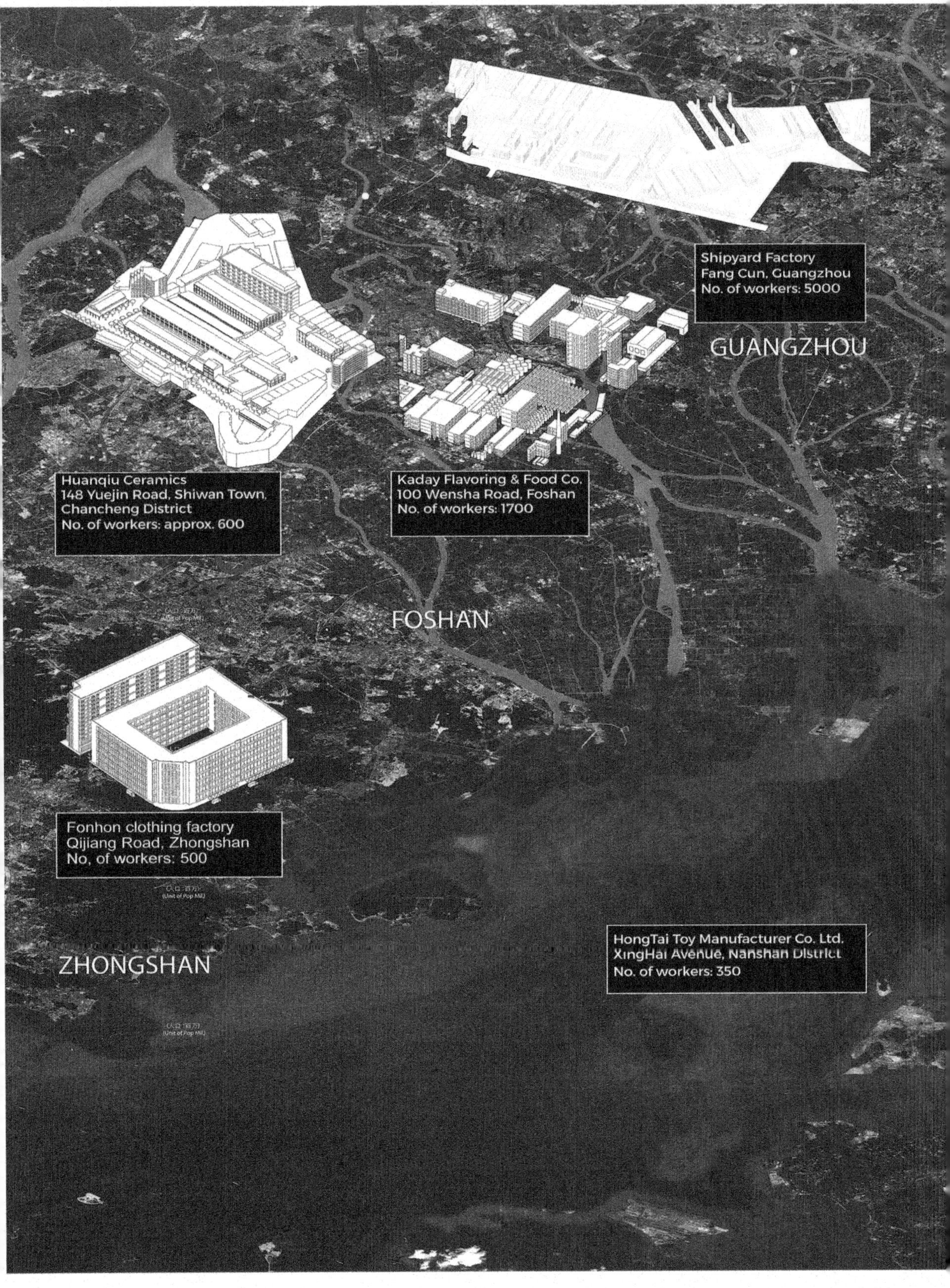

Shipyard Factory
Fang Cun, Guangzhou
No. of workers: 5000

GUANGZHOU

Huanqiu Ceramics
148 Yuejin Road, Shiwan Town,
Chancheng District
No. of workers: approx. 600

Kaday Flavoring & Food Co.
100 Wensha Road, Foshan
No. of workers: 1700

FOSHAN

Fonhon clothing factory
Qijiang Road, Zhongshan
No. of workers: 500

ZHONGSHAN

HongTai Toy Manufacturer Co. Ltd.
XingHai Avenue, Nanshan District
No. of workers: 350

SHENZHEN

DONGGUAN

Dongguan Ideal Autos
Guan Tai Road
No. of workers: 100

Weiga Electronics Limited
Baoshan Industrial District
No. of workers: approx. 900

Newcolor Optoelectronics Co., Ltd.
Yonghe Road, Shenzhen, China
No. of workers: 250 - 300

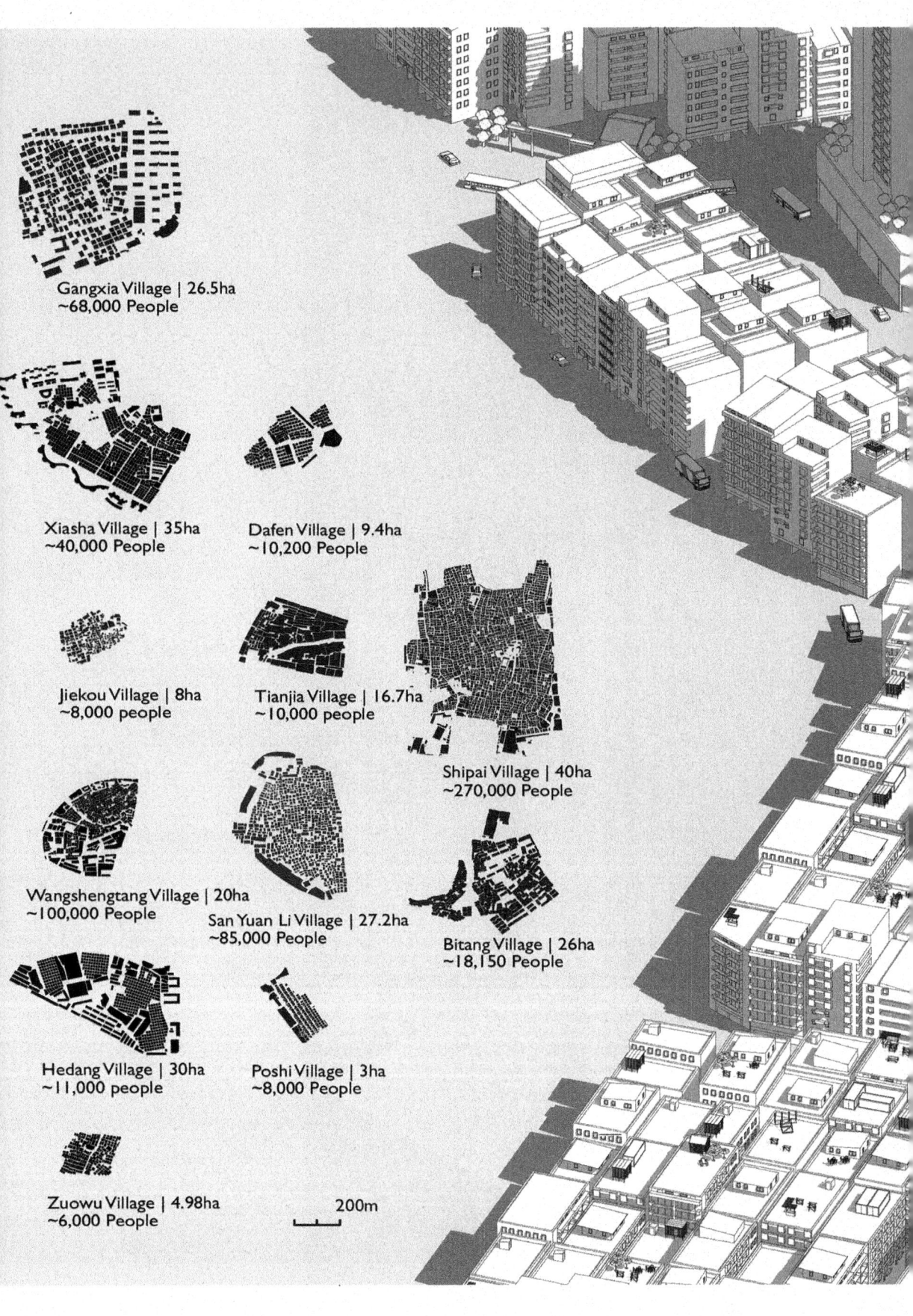

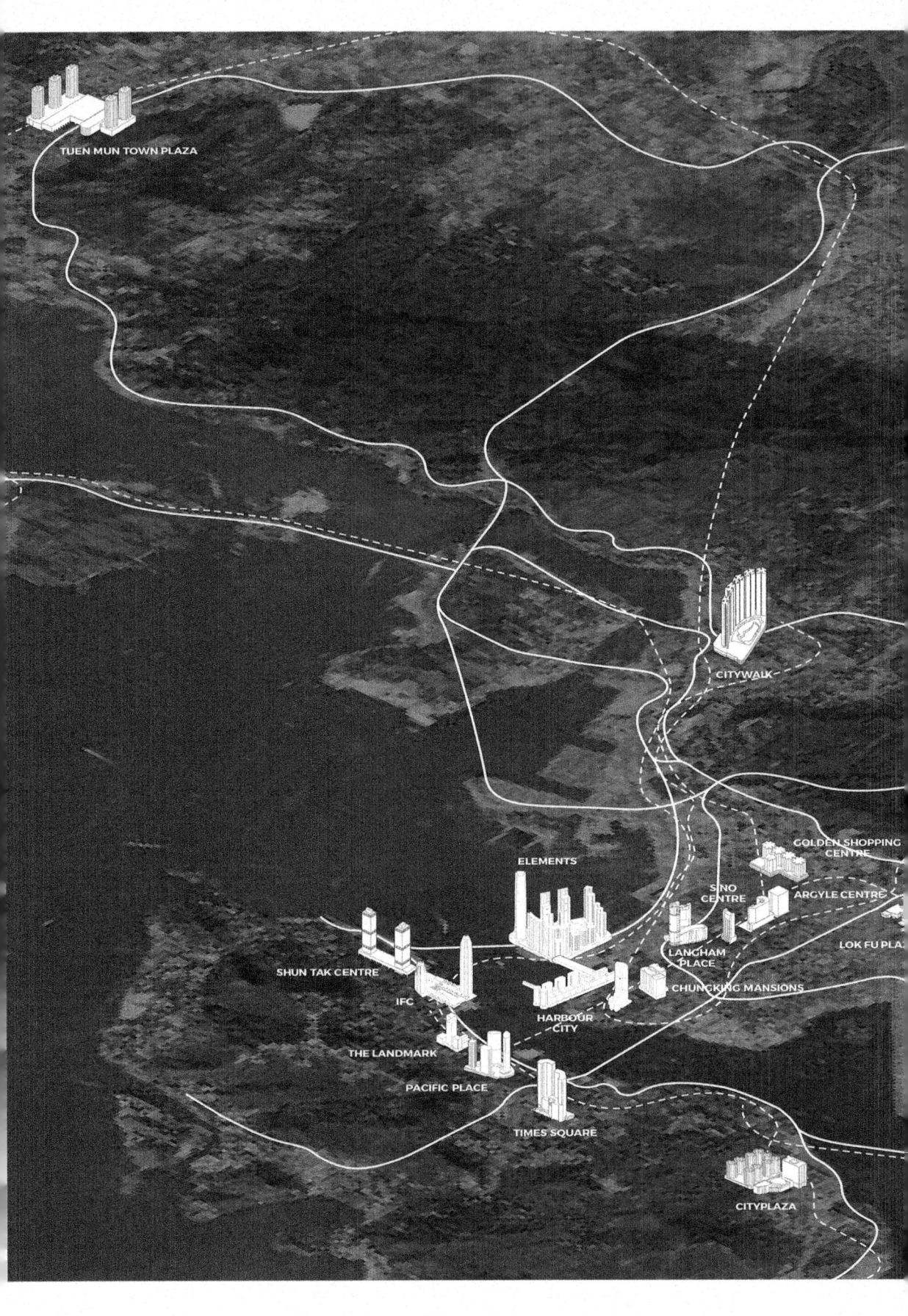

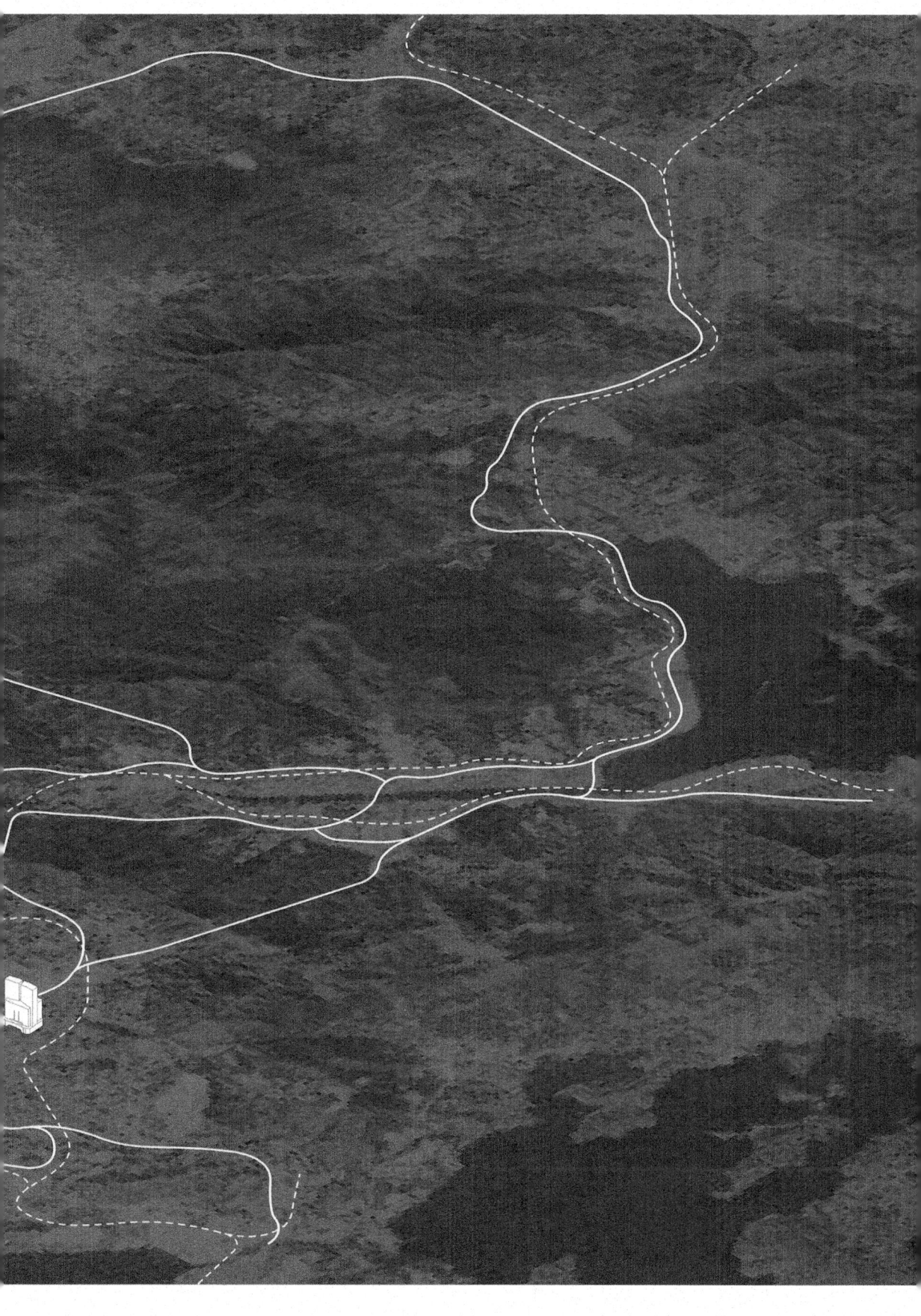

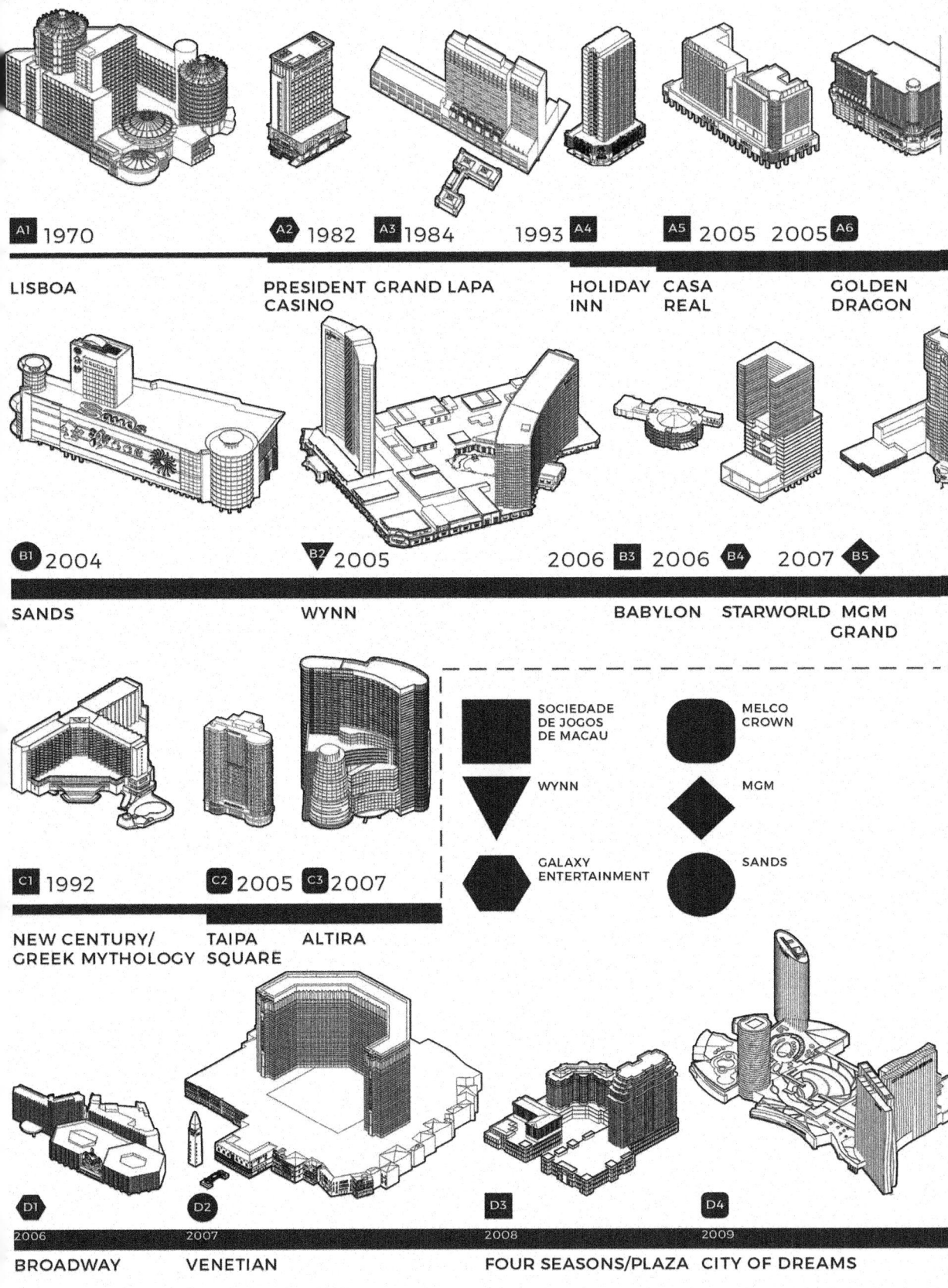

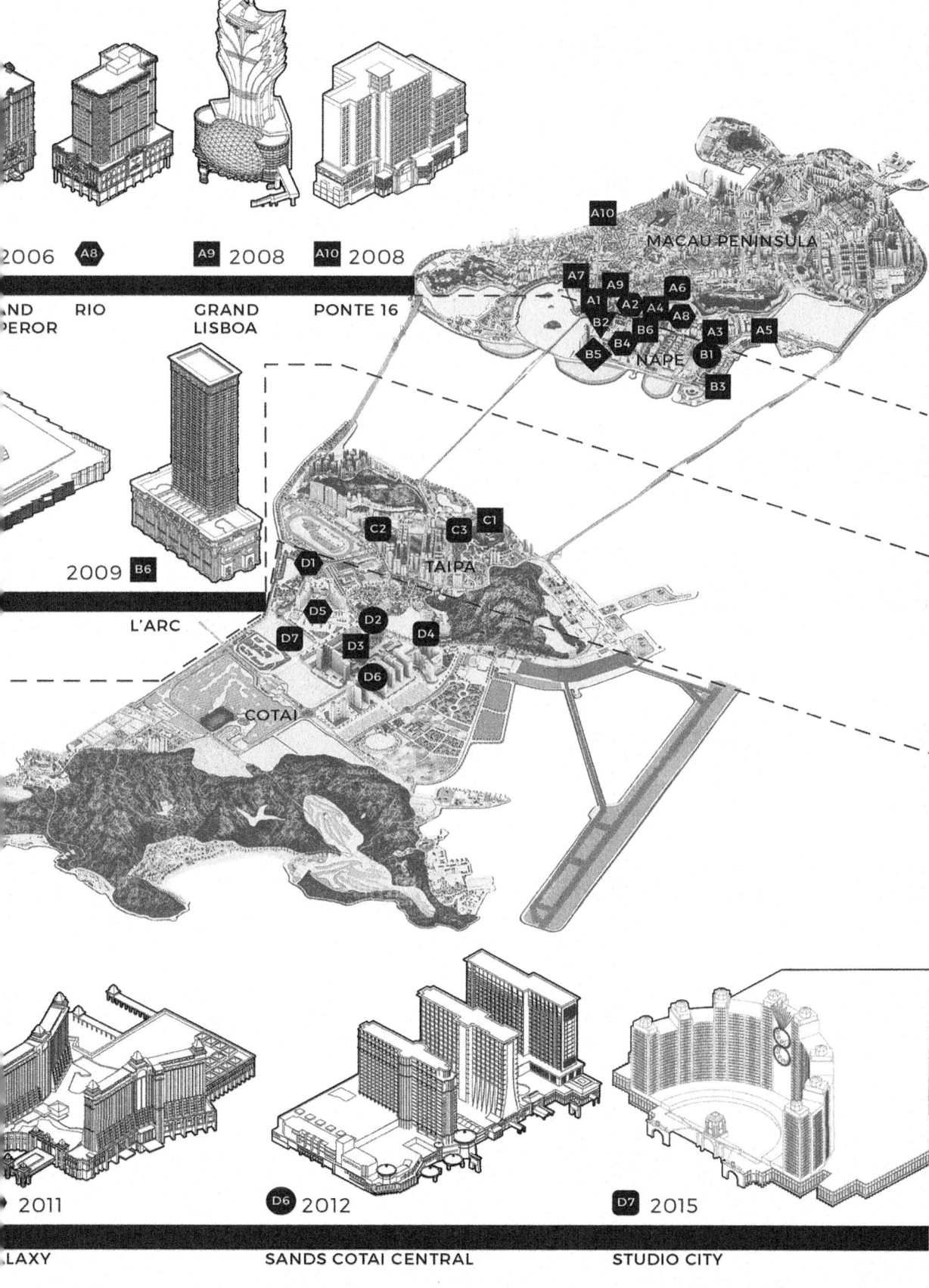

5

Gardens as Public Space: A Century of Continuity and Change in the Greater Bay Area, 1920–2020

David Grahame Shane

Cities have always included gardens and had a parasitic relationship with their surrounding countryside. Today, the hinterland of a city may extend across the countryside or even span a continent or an ocean thanks to planetary supply chains involving air transport and container logistics mapped in global information systems. The Greater Bay Area (GBA) was once one of the super-productive "rice bowls" of South Asia but now produces much of the world's electronics for Apple and Huawei, as well as hosting the headquarters of Tencent, one of the backbones of China's digital culture. This chapter explores whether landscape and garden traditions can prove a useful index to track urban changes in the subtropical climate of South China in the age of the Anthropocene and its associated informational culture.

Nature and culture have long provided a classical analytical binary in urban studies (Choay 1997). Scholars and designers have used this binary in changing normative urban models over time. With the industrialization of Europe in the 19th century, this binary became more potent as Romantics opposed gothic, medieval and feudal towns (Pugin 1836) to the Utilitarian Rationalism of Bentham's drive for a benevolent modernism with strict standards and rules enforced by disciplinary measures (Evans 1982; Rowe and Koetter 1975, 1978). Lynch (1981) described these two models as the "City of Faith" and the "City Machine," both of which are present in the GBA, implying very different relationships between these two archetypes and indeed between culture and nature. This binary also implies different sets of publics and urban actors, creating in the GBA very different public spaces.

Such fixed models have always provided a great hindrance to seeing how cities change. Their fixed and inflexible rules block a more methodical approach based on a system of urban elements that can be combined and recombined in different ways (Choay 1997). Lynch (1981) hoped for a third, "fuzzier" approach based on the 1970s "design with nature" concept (McHarg 1970), which layers ecological systems into a complex patchwork collage or matrix of the "ecocity." This term, a hybrid based on the nature/culture binary, was a "third space" (Soja 1989, 1996), breaking down the old binary, a heterotopia (Foucault 1967; Sohn 2008; Eldon 2016), or place of hybridity and change (Bhabha 2004), part of a recombinant system that facilitated or opposed shifts between models (Shane 2005). Such places exist in all urban systems and act as bridges (used by urban practitioners and participant stakeholders)

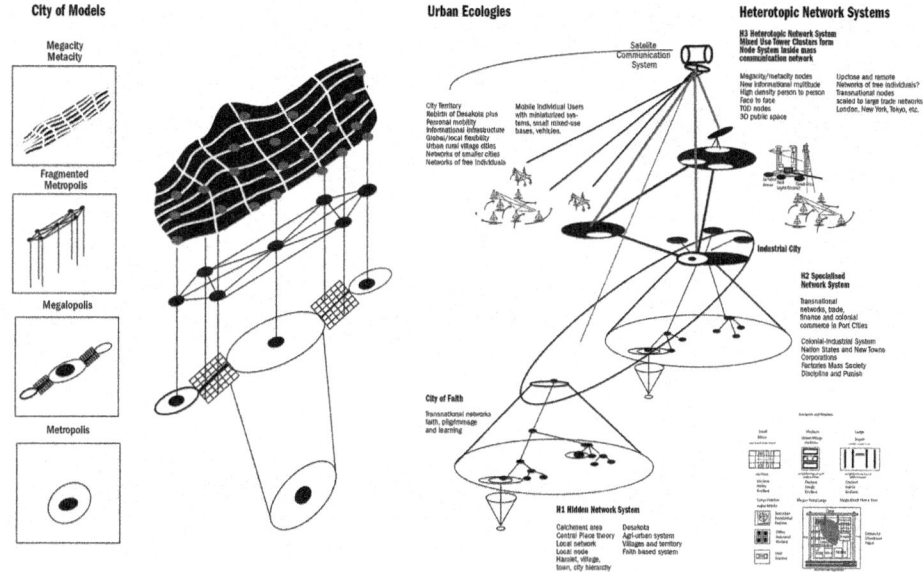

FIGURE 5.1 Heterotopic systems diagram.

Source: Author.

to advance, oppose or modify models in a discursive urban meta-space of information (Shane 2011).

The chapter builds upon the author's conceptual framework of the basic urban elements of the enclave, armature and heterotopia (Shane 2005, 2008), which can be understood as emerging in a historical succession. Enclaves set up a hierarchy of privileged positions close to a single symbolic, central position of power within controlled gates, as exemplified for Lynch (1981) by the "stasis" of the Forbidden City in Imperial Beijing. Armatures, as linear sequencing and spatial devices, question the concept of static enclaves and in conjunction with modern science provide an alternative, process-oriented mode of urban organization, thus forming "directional space" (Venturi et al. 1972) or "paths" (Lynch 1960, 1981). Heterotopias form the experimental mixing places between these systems, creating places that facilitate or block change. This chapter attempts to illustrate the shifting roles of the garden and information in creating landscape and territory in the cultural and political shifts of the GBA in the past century.

Public Spaces in the Imperial City of Faith

Old photographs and prints of Guangzhou show a large floating village of small *sampans* in front of a city that roughly followed a nine-square grid plan based on the Chinese imperial model but with significant variations. The Guangzhou hierarchy of nested enclaves and axial approach armatures conformed to the classical model of the City of Faith (Lynch 1981), but the Imperial Treasury and its garden enclave replaced the Forbidden Palace as the central terminus of the ceremonial north-south armature that led through honorific feudal clan portals from the waterfront. The Lieutenant Governor's Palace and gardens guarded the Treasury in the north and west, setting up a Mogul garden city quarter for the administrative class with its own temples, as in the northwest of Beijing. In the 1700s, the governor had a semaphore signal system that could send information to Beijing in a day (Farris 2007).

The substitution of the Treasury for the Forbidden City marked Guangzhou as a commercial hub attached to the ancient trade route to India and beyond (Abu-Lughod 1991). The Governor's Palace (with its bamboo garden) and tax collector's office were in the lower southern dense commercial sector of the city by the waterfront. Here, the smaller local grids of canal streets, markets, merchant shophouses, courtyard and alleyway morphologies were more flexible and contextual, working with the local topography and water courses (Whitehand et al. 2011). The floating village (Tanka clan, removed 1949) on the Guangzhou waterfront constituted the "third space" of this archipelago interface, ferrying village products to the merchants and silk, tea and porcelain out to the larger junks for international trade (Farris 2007).

In the Canton System (1757–1842), foreign traders were only allowed in China at the thirteen "factories" (Hongs, 行) in Guangzhou. They were restricted to a small enclave located slightly to the south and west of the lower commercial section of the city wall, owned by thirteen Chinese merchant families (including that of the famous merchant Wu Bingjian or Howqua, 1769–1843) and rented out under license from the emperor. Acting as the agents and bankers of these foreign traders, guaranteeing their tax payments and commercial debts, these thirteen families became enormously wealthy (Farris 2007). They created a series of gardens in Liwan to entertain their foreign guests, who otherwise were restricted to their Hong compound (Richard 2015; Wittkower 1969). The imperial restrictions created a hyperdense hybrid, three-dimensional, all-male example of Foucault's "heterotopia of deviance" (Foucault 1967). This was a prison-like City Machine for foreign traders with a fenced front garden (Foucault 1975). Chinese spectators could look through railings into the waterfront square, where foreign merchants strolled in the garden under a few trees and flagpoles (Farris 2007).

The thirteen Hongs were a compressed, linear informational sorting machine, based on thin strips of land stretching back from a waterfront square, each fronted by a European house with multi-story timber courtyard warehouse typologies behind. Three small interior street armatures allowed the Chinese and foreign males to trade, with one street of bars reserved for sailors''port leave. This hyper-compressed informational device provided legal and translation services, directing the logistics of international trading companies. In the east of the city, the Imperial Examination Halls (demolished in 1922) provided a similar informational sorting device for the imperial administration in a garden space of armatures with rows of cellular desks. In this heterotopia of deviance, the all-male competitors worked day and night, were forbidden to leave their desks and were often caught cheating, writing Confucian verses with fine calligraphy. Success in this competitive exam could lead to great wealth and social elevation as an imperial tax collector (Clunas 2004).

After the demolition of the thirteen Hongs, Shamian Island (1859), created on a sandbar, became the new international informational sorting device. A gated new town centered on a wide, tree-lined park armature, it tightly restricted access for Chinese citizens. Fireproof brick warehouses moved south into separate company enclaves in Liwan. Another modern City Machine riverfront armature of offices and a post office, modeled on the Shanghai Bund, replaced the ruins of the thirteen Hongs and connected to the railway from Hong Kong

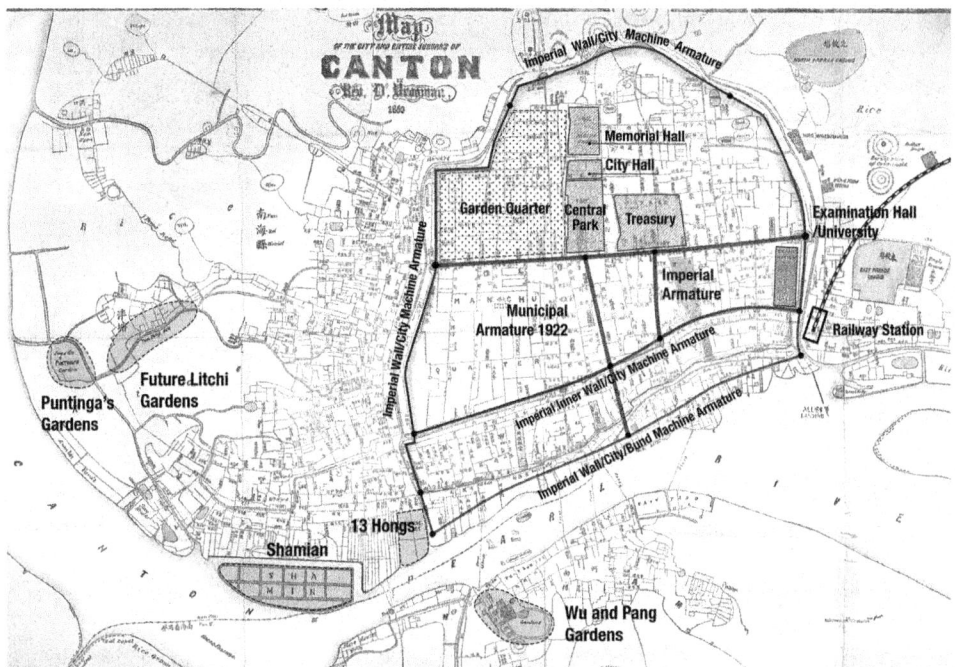

FIGURE 5.2 Guangzhou city plan 1860: Enclaves, armatures, heterotopias.
Source: Author.

(completed 1911) crossing the still-porous border at Luohu (Bolchover and Hasdell 2016; O'Donnell 2019; Sun 2019).

In stark contrast to the constricted enclosure of the Hongs, the ruins of the Imperial Liwan summer garden district extended beyond the city wall to the west of the Lieutenant Governor's Palace garden district. Built behind an early imperial embankment, successive administrators established a man-made miniature archipelago of canals, fishponds, rice paddies and lychee orchards, modeling in miniature the Pearl River Delta (PRD) and turning its agricultural function to leisure and pleasure (Feng and Chen 2019). Initially a "third space" created for the upper administrators, then for wealthy merchants and their guests, these gardens and their pavilions formed a heterotopia of illusion (Foucault 1967; Shane 2005, 2008) where leisure and pleasure replaced work. It was here that the competitors for imperial exams went for luck to the Sai Kwan Literary Pavilion (Feng and Chen 2019).

Public Space in the PRD City Machine

The appearance of the Guangzhou-Kowloon railway station on the waterfront in Kowloon, beside the Star Ferry terminal to Hong Kong Island, marked the extension and acceleration of the armature in the City Machine (Lynch 1981). By 1900, Hong Kong as a refuge for colonial expatriates had the appearance of a Garden City (Howard 1898 [2009]), perched on the slope of Victoria Peak facing north to the deep-water port, thus reversing imperial Feng Shui (风水) code where a city faced south from the mountain to the water. A cross-section of the harbor from the station corresponded to the well-known "valley section" of Geddes (1909) (Welter 2003), with fragmented patches of development linked to the local ecology and terrain, mixing heterotopias of deviance and illusion up the shaded northern face of the mountain. The Peak Funicular (1888) carried passengers from the hot and humid ferry terminal at the new central business district (CBD) on Chater Street and Statue Square (1898; Shane 2016), up the valley past the Governor's Mansion and Botanical Gardens (1864) to the villas on terraces of the Mid-Levels and finally to the exclusive 300 grand mansions in the cooler private gardens at the Peak, restricted to Europeans.

The Central Statue Square garden, where Chinese were also not admitted, was modeled on the waterfronts of central London and Liverpool. These centers controlled informational and logistical flows, like the Hongs, but with an electrical supply and telegraph and later tickertape, offices, banks, law courts and hotels, including a small public square (also a cricket ground and social club; Shane 2016). In Guangzhou, after the demolition of the city walls (1922), a similar CBD emerged along the riverfront Samian Island and the Bund. A similar valley section developed based on a new municipal axis, following Feng Shui principles, headed north from the waterfront to a new Central Park (1922, designed by Yang Xizong) and Municipal Building (1931) on the former grounds of the Lieutenant Governor's Palace. This axis continued further uphill after Sun Yat Sen's (1866–1925) death to his Memorial Hall (1929–31, designed by Lu Yanzhi) beside the mountain forests. Sun Yat Sen mourned the death of Lenin in the Republican public space of the Central Park that contained bourgeois leisure facilities like public tennis courts, a bandstand, an assembly hall, tea pavilion, lawns, flower gardens, winding paths and a large modern fountain, as well as a shooting gallery and the municipal radio station and its tower (Cody 1996), presenting a heterotopia of illusion.

A long section of the Guangzhou-to-Hong Kong corridor in the 1950s and 60s would reveal enormous differences in the public space at each pole. In the New China Land Reform, the consolidation of villages altered the historic rice cultivation patterns in the delta, proliferating small factory *danwei* (单位) or work units in villages in what Terry McGee (McGee 1971; McGee et al. 2007) termed the hybrid *desakota* (city-village) rural-urban pattern typical of Asian modernization. The public ownership of land facilitated Soviet-style planning on a territorial scale, with public spaces in huge public works for irrigation, hydraulic power and heavy industry, initially in three enormous, heterotopic *danwei* factory new town enclaves in southern Liwan; a steel mill; and two shipbuilding yards (1950s). These Soviet-style factory enclaves (city-within-the-city planned neighborhood units) included communal eating facilities, cinemas, clinics, children's schools and recreation fields (Bray 2005) as the urban population of China increased from 10% in the 1950s to 20% by 1980 (Shane 2015). The Soviet-style mass-produced concrete panel housing units all faced south, aligned following Feng Shui principles. Guangzhou still played an important role as an international trading center with its annual trade fair and its first modern hotel, the White Swan (1983) on Shamian Island.

At the other end of the Machine City corridor, Patrick Abercrombie's 1948 *Hong Kong: Preliminary Planning Report* amended Patrick Geddes' valley section into a ring-radial formula of the Garden City spread across the New Territories using the mountain ridges as green belts and proposing new town developments beside the walled Hakka clan villages as at Sha Tin (1973) (Lai 1999). The Stockholm Hötorget CBD, which integrated "third spaces" into a heterotopia of illusion for shopping and leisure (also including the municipal theater and library) in its multi-story, mixed-use section (1951), provided the model for the new Statue

Square garden with a City Hall (1956), now open to Chinese (Shane 2011, 2016). Gardens filled the compressed urban section, from the waterside square to interior shopping mall podium atria like the Landmark, developed by the Hong Kong Land property investment group (1970–83), to podium roofs and tower terraces and onto open rooftop restaurants and bars (Frampton et al. 2012). The Landmark scheme further compressed and amplified this heterotopic dimension, coinciding with the Mass Transit Railway's (MTR) commuter rail connection between the city and the first new town of Tsuen Wan (1961). There, high-density housing towers, flatted factory buildings and industrial districts connected to the early Kwai Chung Container Port (1970), create a dense, export-focused transport-oriented development (TOD; HK New Territories Development Department 1981; Shane 2016).

In stark contrast to the compression in Hong Kong, expansive gardens acted as "third space" heterotopias of illusion and leisure in New China. In Guangzhou's Liwan District, 6,000 volunteers dug lakes to create Litchi Park (1958), where wandering paths and bridges connected a miniature archipelago of small, wooded islands, with irregular ponds, boats, pavilions, restaurants and performance spaces, creating new public spaces for local workers' leisure and pleasure. Surrounding canals were covered for sewers, and small *danwei* factories with housing units were built, filling in wetlands and hiding the Sai Kwan literary pagoda but leaving the historic village of Pun Tong intact (2019).

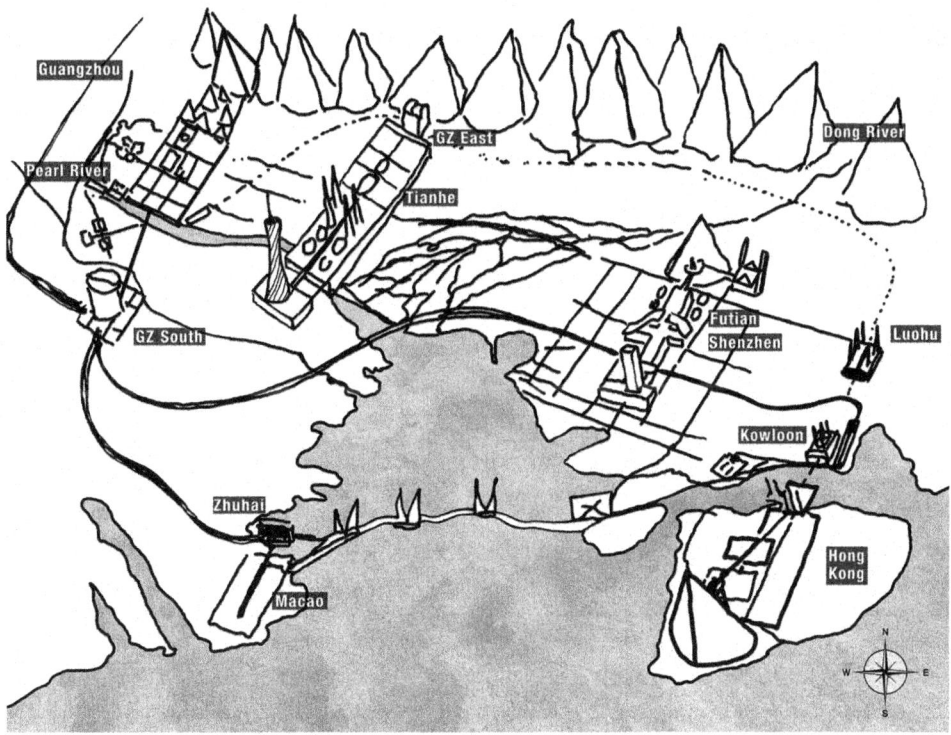

FIGURE 5.3 PRD GZ-HK Machine City armature and enclave extensions.

Source: Author.

Public Space in the Greater Bay Project: Metacity Heterotopic Systems

The arrival of high-speed trains in West Kowloon Station in 2018, close to the memorial to the 1910 terminal, marked a further shrinking of the space-time geography of the Pearl River archipelago (Farrell and Partners 1996). The extended armature from Hong Kong to Guangzhou contained a corridor of 44 million inhabitants by 2020, with an additional 10 million or more across the river and in outlying areas (Lai 2016). This classic linear Asian megalopolis formation (Gottmann 1961; Gottmann and Harper 1990), recognized by Koolhaas et al. (Chung et al. 2001) as a polycentric city archipelago, was declared a megacity by the United Nations (UN; 2008, 2014). This extended territory depended for coherence on the informational metacity (MVRDV 1999; Shane and McGrath 2012) and handheld apps on mobile phones, providing wayfinding tools, train timetables, booking facilities for travel, hotels, entertainment, food, banking, digital payments, social media, digital communities, meta-objects and quasi-objects in the augmented reality of the metacity (Castells 1989; Graham and Marvin 2001; Benkler 2006; Eldon 2013; Serres 2013, 2014; Shane 2014b; Carta 2019). The big data assembled by companies and the state from handheld phones and mobile tablet computers in the metacity allowed the megacity coordination and planning of a vast city-country territory on a macro scale and at a level of detail (micro-urbanisms) never possible before. This information was easily monitored by the central state (Greenwald 2015) and commercial interests (Pasquinelli 2009, 2014). During the SARS (2003) and COVID (2019) pandemics, informational algorithms derived from this big data were essential to local attempts to control disease, tracking the population's health and mobility (Hessler 2020; O'Donnell 2020).

Travel time between Kowloon and Shenzhen (Futian) new town became 10 minutes, while it takes 47 minutes to reach the gigantic new Guangzhou South (2010) rail hub, 17 kilometers south of the old city center (Chen and Wei 2013). This hub connected to Beijing and unified the Greater Bay Project, as travel time from Hong Kong to Zhuhai via the Hong Kong-Macao bridge was also reduced to one hour (Lai 2016). In Hong Kong, the West Kowloon station merged into a cross-harbor network at the service of international capital, with spectacular "third space" vertical malls, towers and rooftop gardens as at the International Financial Center mall (IFC 1998) and the podium rooftop park at the Elements mall (2007; Shane 2011, 2015; Al 2016). These connected directly to the new international airport by Norman Foster (1998), near the Disneyland theme park (2005) and the planned "grand theater urbanism" of the Kowloon Cultural District (2010), a heterotopia of illusion (Xue 2019). Across the Greater Bay bridge, Macao offered even more spectacular heterotopias, like the Grand Canal Mall in the Venetian Casino (2007) or the Tropical Forest in the Sands Casino (Simpson 2019).

Following Reform (Arrighi 2007; Harvey 1990, 2005) and the designation of Shenzhen as the first fenced Special Economic Zone (SEZ 1979; O'Donnell 2019), the balance of the *desakota* model shifted as new CBDs and Garden City industrial districts proliferated, creating a "horizontal metropolis" (McGee et al. 2007; McGee 2009; Viganò et al. 2018) along the corridor whose infrastructure could sometimes be used for protests in Hong Kong (Lin 2014). The Chinese Singaporean architect Meng Ta Cheang designed the Shenzhen Overseas Chinese Town (OCT 1993) factory district that preserved much of the hilly landscape, anchored by the success of three heterotopic theme parks (Sun 2019). The Ecocity mega-model established here was followed in the planning of the Shanghai Expo (Zhang et al. 2014) and the 2012 Shenzhen Qianhai Eco City designed by Field Operations (Corner and Field Operations 2010) with multiple CBDs. In Qianhai, Corner's landscape urbanism concept of "performative urbanism" (studying the past uses of the site, taking into consideration the remediation of polluted soil and the creation of a new "thick," well-serviced, flexible and informed platform as a "performance space" available to a wide variety of stakeholders and communities) proved a winning concept (Corner 2007; Shane 2007). In Liwan, old Soviet-style neighborhoods were demolished to be replaced by housing towers and shopping malls in megablock estates (Shane 2014a) as the urban population of China grew from 20% in 1980 to 50% in 2010. Huge new factory complexes, as in Taiwan-based Foxconn's gated Longhua "iPhone city" factory in Shenzhen (2010), housed many of their workers in a new town with their own private and public realms (Al 2012; Freeman 2013; O'Donnell 2019).

In the Futian CBD (1993), Shenzhen did have a new monumental public space descended from Guangzhou's Central Park. Following Feng Shui principles, Chinese planners with British consultants had created a new, nearly 2-km-long monumental raised concrete public armature extending north through the colorful city hall with its wave-like roof (designed by John M.Y. Lee and Michael Timchula, opened 2004) to a statue of Deng at Lianhua Mountain. "Grand theater urbanism" competitions later added museums, a library and a concert hall (Sun 2019). In 1993, the American planner Carol Thomas' winning design for the Tianhe, Gangzhou New Town competition projected a similar 2-km-long monumental public armature from the nearly 600-m-high Canton media tower (2010), symbol of the metacity, across the river north through the CBD skyscrapers to the old Guangzhou East Station and mountains. The public armature, also following Feng Shui, was extensively landscaped with shaded walks above and shopping malls below but surrounded by a similar "grand theater urbanism" public program, including ramps to Zaha Hadid's Guangzhou Opera House (2010; Ding 2019).

In contrast to this metacity monumentality, the Litchi Gardens restoration project in Liwan (2010) demonstrated the power of strategic micro-urbanism in the "horizontal metropolis," where citizens were empowered by handheld devices. The project uncovered the canals leading to the park, re-engineered the water flow through the ponds of the 1958 design and opened up the public plaza around the Sai Kwan Literary Pagoda Tower, moving the antique stores from the canal street into a converted *danwei* factory building but leaving the housing intact. Across the canal, a new low-rise mall beside a clan memorial hall was built, linked to Pun Tong Village, while local performative communal dragon boat festivals returned to the open canals, much loved on social media (Feng and Chen 2019). The success of the factory-to-loft "village" micro-urbanism conversions in OCT by the Shenzhen-based architectural firm Urbanus (都市实践; 2003–2012) led to the heterotopic grafting-on of the Shum Yip Upper Hill Lofts (2018) mixed-use development, also by Urbanus, on the roof of a mall connected to the Lianhua Park, creating a new horizontal and vertical landscaped hybrid "urban village" (城中村; Urbanus 2006, 2010, 2018; Al 2014; Crawford and Wu 2014; O'Donnell 2020). The public spaces threaded up along giant escalators at the Yuehai Community Culture and Sports Center (2020) pushed this logic to an extreme to save the surrounding parkland and gardens. Learning from the design of Hong Kong malls, this public sequence of giant escalators started from a civic plaza and underground car park, ascending to local community offices, a black box theater, a public library, a public viewing terrace, sports halls, swimming pools and finally a children's playground on two rooftop terraces (Barandy 2020; Urbanus 2020).

Futian looking south to CBD

Tianhe looking south to Olympic Tower

Futian looking north to park and Deng Statue.

Tianhe looking north to Guangzhou East station

Futian looking south to civic center.

Tianhe looking north through civic center.

FIGURE 5.4 Comparison of Futian CBD and Tianhe, Gangzhou.
Source: Author.

Third Space and Gardens: Public Space in the Metacity

This account of the arrival of the metacity in the Greater Bay project has used the fundamental morphological concepts of enclave, armature and heterotopia to explore successive steps that led to the idealization of the city-territory as a quasi-object, with an enormous

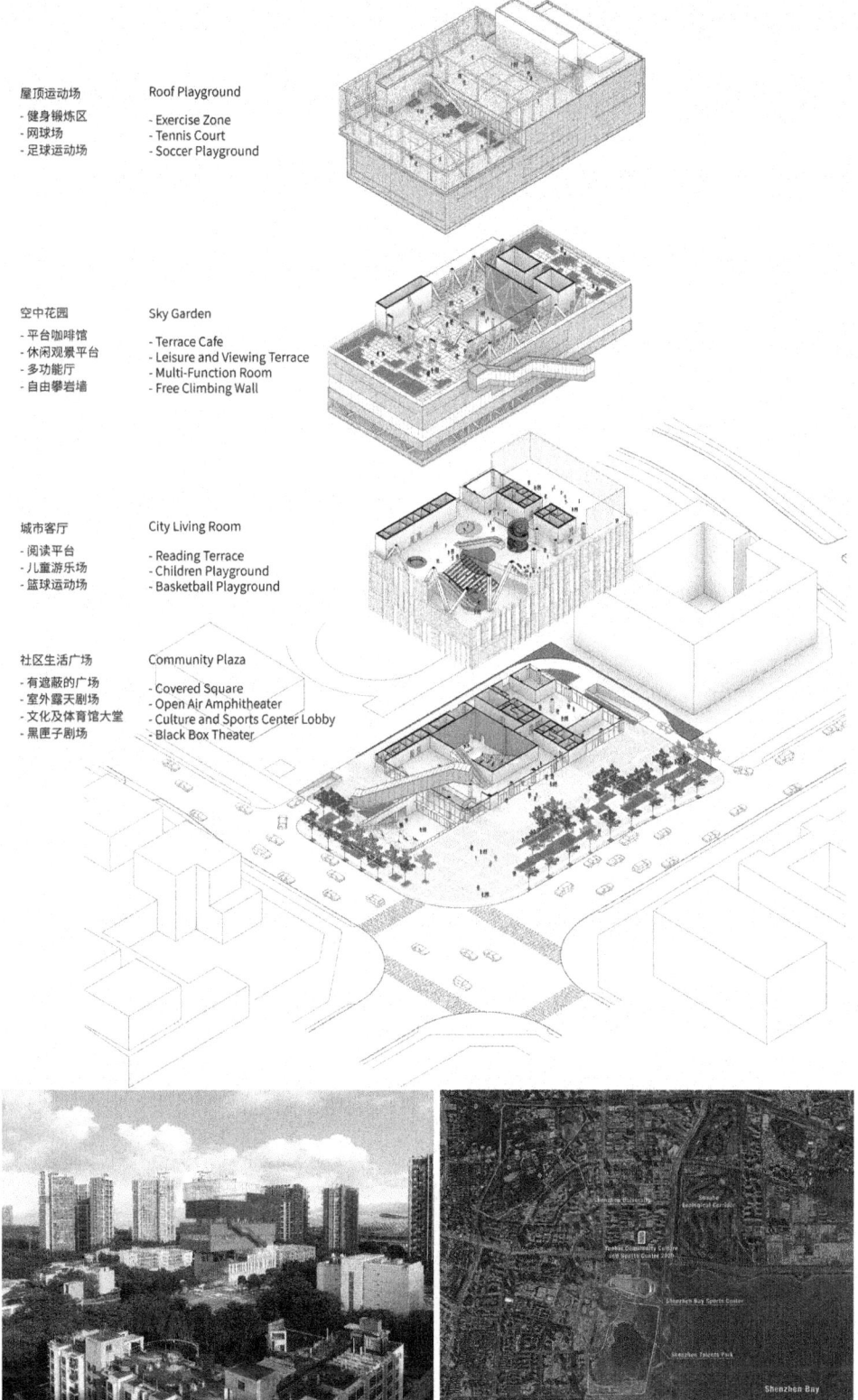

FIGURE 5.5 Urbanus, Shenzhen Yuehai Community Culture and Sports Center (2020). Extreme enclave and armature compression.

Source: Courtesy of Urbanus.

informational base and local strategic interventions. The place of gardens as an urban element throughout this historical development provided some insight in this account, especially the Litchi Park history and micro-urbanism project. There emerges a schema of island enclaves patched together with bridges and boats in a miniature model of the entire archipelago system that has been consistently instructive at each stage of the metacity/megacity development narrative. In the Imperial Age, enclaves dominated; in the Machine City period, canals were covered and armatures dominated. In the recent renovation, the two were brought into a new ecological balance, serving the local community and having a megacity, performative urbanism potential.

It is worth examining the role of each of the urban elements and their shifting morphology in more detail in evaluating this metacity approach. Clearly, in the Imperial Age contextual, hierarchical system enclaves dominated, aligned with Feng Shui principles. In this enclave narrative, the hyper-compression of the heterotopia of the thirteen Hongs takes on great importance, leading to Hong Kong's tradition of enclave compression at Statue Square, with the later addition of subways and three-dimensional megamalls, all of which promoted tiny landscape simulacra in atria and on rooftops. In the metacity, the enclave also expanded to provide an industrial database far larger than the earlier *danwei* in megablock housing tower clusters in new towns along the Hong Kong-to-Guangzhou armature and later across the Greater Bay.

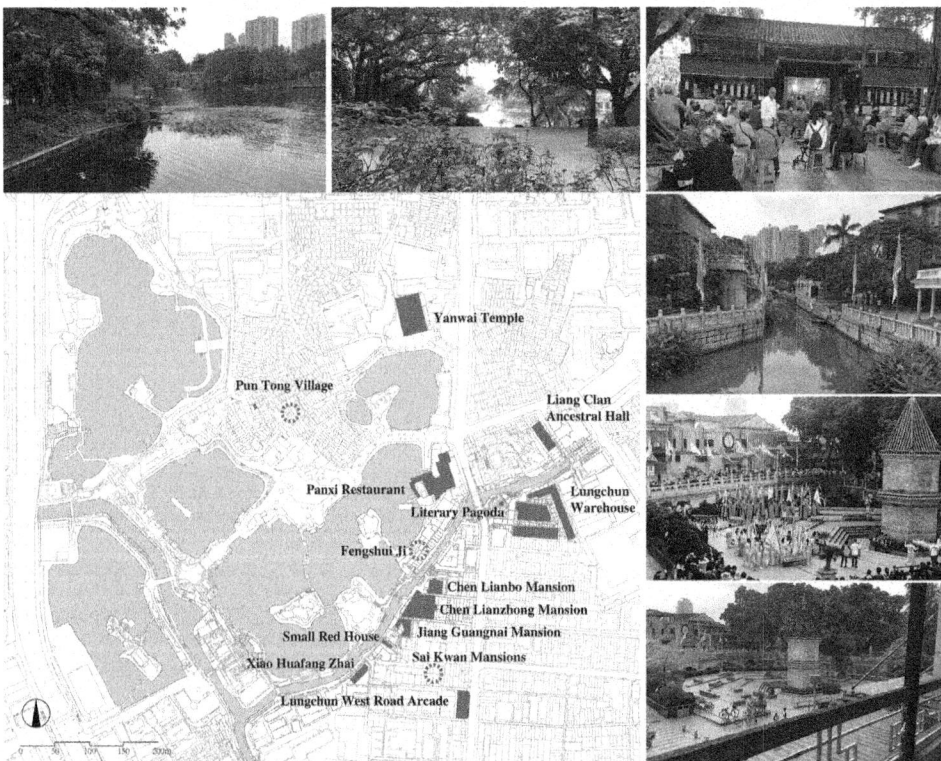

FIGURE 5.6 Litchi Gardens Liwan plan and photos.

Source: Feng, J. and Chen, K. plan and photo, and author photos.

The armature played an important role in breaking apart the imperial system, cutting through or bypassing the spatial structures of this regime entirely, as in the enormous Guangzhou South high-speed rail hub. The extended Machine City armature infrastructures opened up the possibility of the Garden City, and the Greater Bay Area displays a mixture of Chinese Imperial, British, Japanese, Soviet, New China and overseas Chinese versions on display as patches in the archipelago city territory. In the metacity, the monumental public spaces, skyscrapers and 600-meter-tall Canton Tower are the most visible evidence of this transformation. The garden became landscape: another contextual layer of information in the quasi-object big data model of the region, including its vulnerabilities to the Anthropocene and disease when its potential for capsular/enclave isolation proved of great value.

Heterotopia indicated code shifts and reversals from prior urban models, as when the Treasury replaced the Forbidden City or armatures replaced the enclave city walls. Hybrid armature and enclave layouts abound, like Guangzhou's Central Park or Futian and Tianhe with extended public armatures and gardens. Compressed armatures stacked around vertical atria, descended from the thirteen Hongs, lead to the public-private malls of Hong Kong with scarcely any gardens. Finally, the miniature heterotopia of the Litchi Garden archipelago demonstrates a powerful example in which the garden could give depth to the arrival of the metacity and focus the concept in a material realm of man-made islands, botanical planting, lakes, false mountains, grottos, pavilions and boats. Here, gardens formed a powerful element in the heterotopic systems that constitute the metacity: a quasi-object of the ecological, informational matrix reflecting the new structure of the Greater Bay Area.

References

Abercrombie, P. (1948) *Hong Kong: Preliminary planning report*. Great Britain's Colonial Office in Hong Kong. Ye Olde Printerie.
Abu-Lughod, J. (1991) *Before European hegemony: The world system A.D. 1250–1350*. Oxford University Press.
Al, S. (Ed.) (2012) *Factory towns of south China: An illustrated guide*. University of Hong Kong Press.
Al, S. (Ed.) (2014) *Villages in the city: A guide to south China's informal settlements*. University of Hong Kong Press.
Al, S. (Ed.) (2016) *Mall city: Hong Kong's dreamworlds of consumption*. University of Hawaii Press.
Arrighi, G. (2007) *Adam Smith in Beijing; lineages of the twenty-first century*. Verso.
Barandy, K. (2020) "Public plazas permeate through Shenzhen's Yuehai community center by Urbanus." *Designboom*. At: www.designboom.com/architecture/urbanus-yuehai-sport-cultural-center-shenzhen-china-09-13-19/. Last accessed on 20 September 2020.
Benkler, Y. (2006) *The wealth of networks: How social production transforms markets and freedom*. At: http://benkler.org/Benkler_Wealth_Of_Networks.pdf. Last accessed on 20 September 2020.
Bhabha, H.K. (2004) *The location of culture*. Routledge.
Bolchover, J. and Hasdell, P. (2016) *Border ecologies: Hong Kong's mainland frontier*. Birkhäuser.
Bray, D. (2005) *Social space and governance in urban China: The danwei system from origins to reform*. Stanford University Press.
Carta, M. (2019) *The augmented city: A paradigm shift*. ListLab.
Castells, M. (1989) *The informational city: Information technology, economic restructuring, and the urban regional process*. Blackwell.
Chen, C.L. and Wei, B. (2013) "High-speed rail and urban transformation in China: The case of Hangzhou East Rail Station." *Built Environment* 39 (3). pp. 385–398.
Choay, F. (1997) *The rule and the model: On the theory of architecture and urbanism*. MIT Press.

Chung, C.H.J., Inaba, J., Koolhaas, R. and Leong, S.T. (Eds.) (2001) *Project on the city I: Great leap forward*. Taschen.

Clunas, C. (2004) *Fruitful sites: Garden culture in Ming Dynasty China*. Reaktion Books.

Cody, J.W. (1996) "American planning in republican China, 1911–1937." *Planning Perspectives* 11. pp. 339–377.

Corner, J. (2007) "Terra fluxus." In: Waldheim, C. (Ed.) *The landscape urbanism reader*. Princeton Architectural Press.

Corner, J. and Field Operations (2010) *Qianhai water city*. At: www.fieldoperations.net/project-details/project/qianhai-water-city.html. Last accessed on 20 September 2020.

Crawford, M. and Wu, J. (2014) "The beginning of the end: Planning the destruction of Guangzhou's urban villages." In: Al, S. (Ed.) *Villages in the city: A guide to South China's informal settlements*. Hong Kong University Press. pp. 255–267.

Ding, G. (2019) "Guangzhou opera house: Building a gated public space." In: Xue, C.Q. (Ed.) *Grand theater urbanism: Chinese cities in the 21st century*. Springer.

Eldon, S. (2013) *The birth of territory*. University of Chicago Press.

Eldon, S. (2016) *Foucault's last decade*. Polity Press.

Evans, R. (1982) *The fabrication of virtue: English prison architecture, 1750–1840*. Cambridge University Press.

Farrell, T. and Partners (1996) *West Kowloon cultural district*. At: https://farrells.com/project/west-kowloon-cultural-district. Last accessed on 20 September 2020.

Farris, J. (2007) "Thirteen factories of Canton: An architecture of Sino-Western collaboration and confrontation." *Buildings & Landscapes: Journal of the Vernacular Architecture Forum* 14. pp. 66–83, Fall.

Feng, J. and Chen, K. (2019) "Cooperative historic landscape rejuvenation in China: The Litchi Bay project in Guangzhou." *Built Heritage*. At: https://built-heritage.springeropen.com/articles/10.1186/BF03545737. Last accessed on 20 September 2020.

Foucault, M. (1967) *Of other space: Heterotopias*. At: https://foucault.info/doc/documents/heterotopia/foucault-heterotopia-en-html. Last accessed on 20 September 2020.

Foucault, M. (1975) *Discipline and punish: The birth of the prison*. Vintage Books.

Frampton, A., Solomon, J. and Wong, C. (2012) *Cities without ground: A guide to Hong Kong*. Oro Editions.

Freeman, J.B. (2013) "Giant factories." *Labour/Le Travail* 72. pp. 177–203, Fall. At: https://muse.jhu.edu/article/528381. Last accessed on 20 September 2020.

Gottmann, J. (1961) *Megalopolis: The urbanized northeastern seaboard of the United States*. Twentieth Century Fund.

Gottmann, J. and Harper, R.A. (1990) *Since megalopolis: The urban writings of Jean Gottmann*. Johns Hopkins University Press.

Graham, S. and Marvin, S. (2001) *Splintering urbanism: Networked infrastructures, technological mobilities and the urban condition*. Routledge.

Greenwald, G. (2015) *No place to hide: Edward Snowden, the NSA, and the US surveillance state*. Metropolitan Books.

Harvey, D. (1990) *The condition of postmodernity: An enquiry into the origins of cultural change*. Blackwell.

Harvey, D. (2005) *A brief history of neo-liberalism*. Oxford University Press.

Hessler, P. (2020) "Letter from Chengdu: Life on lockdown: Forty-five days avoiding the coronavirus." *New Yorker*, 23 March.

HK New Territories Development Department (1981) *Hong Kong's new towns: Tsuen Wan, Hong Kong*. Works Department Hong Kong.

Howard, E. (1898 [2009]) *Garden cities of tomorrow: A peaceful path to real reform*. Routledge.

Lai, S. (2016) "The Pearl River Delta megacity." *Time Out Hong Kong*, May. At: www.timeout.com/hong-kong/en-hongkong/the-pearl-river-delta-megacity-051716. Last accessed on 20 September 2020.

Lai, W.C.L. (1999) "Reflections on the Abercrombie report 1948: A strategic plan for colonial Hong Kong." *Town Planning Review* 7 (1). pp. 61–87.

Lin, J. (2014) "Umbrella urbanism: Hong Kong protests." *The Architectural Review*, 28 October. At: www.architectural-review.com/essays/umbrella-urbanism-hong-kong-protests. Last accessed on 20 September 2020.
Lynch, K. (1960) *The image of the city*. MIT Press.
Lynch, K. (1981) *Good city form*. MIT Press.
McGee, T. (1971) *The urbanization process in the third world*. Bell and Sons.
McGee, T. (2009) *The spatiality of urbanization: The policy challenges of mega-urban and desakota regions of Southeast Asia*. UNU-IAS Working Paper #161. United Nations University Institute of Advanced Studies.
McGee, T., Lin, G.C.S., Marton, A.M., Wang, M.Y.L. and Wu, J. (2007) *China's urban space: Development under market socialism*. Routledge.
McHarg, I. (1970) *Design with nature*. American Museum of Natural History.
MVRDV (1999) *Metacity/datatown*. MVRDV/010 Publishers.
O'Donnell, M.A. (2019) "From bamboo curtain to the Silicon Valley of hardware." *e-flux: Software as infrastructure*. At: www.e-flux.com/architecture/software/337686/from-bamboo-curtain-to-the-silicon-valley-of-hardware/. Last accessed on 20 September 2020.
O'Donnell, M.A. (2020) "Are we all living in Xinjiang?" *Shenzhen Noted*, 13 February. At: https://shenzhennoted.com/2020/02/13/are-we-all-living-in-xinjiang/. Last accessed on 20 September 2020.
Pasquinelli, M. (2009) "Google's pagerank algorithm: A diagram of cognitive capitalism and the rentier of the common intellect." In: Becker, K. and Stalder, F. (Eds.) *Deep search: The politics of search beyond Google*. Transaction Publishers. At: www.academia.edu/Documents/in/Algorithms?swp=tc-ri-1992027. Last accessed on 10 October 2020.
Pasquinelli, M. (2014) "The labour of abstraction: Seven transitional theses on Marxism and accelerationism." *Fillip* 19. P. 107, Spring.
Pugin, A.W. (1836) *Contrasts: Or, a parallel between the noble edifices of the middle ages, and similar buildings of the present day*. John Grant.
Richard, J. (2015) "Uncovering the garden of the richest man on earth in nineteenth century Canton: Howqwa's gardens in Homan China." *Garden History* 43 (2). pp. 168–181.
Rowe, C. and Koetter, F. (1975) "Collage city." *Architectural Review* 158 (942). pp. 66–90.
Rowe, C. and Koetter, F. (1978) *Collage city*. MIT Press.
Serres, M. (2013) "Nouvelles technologies." *YouTube Video* (in French). At: www.youtube.com/watch?v=S-qIzalLof0. Last accessed on 20 September 2020.
Serres, M. (2014) *Thumbelina: The culture and technology of Millennials*. Rowman and Littlefield.
Shane, D.G. (2005) *Recombinant urbanism: Conceptual modeling in architecture, urban design and city theory*. Wiley.
Shane, D.G. (2007) "The emergence of landscape urbanism." In: Waldheim, C. (Ed.) *The landscape urbanism reader*. Princeton Architectural Press. pp. 55–69.
Shane, D.G. (2008) "Heterotopias of illusion: From Beaubourg to Bilbao and beyond." In: Dehaene, M. and De Cauter, L. (Eds.) *Heterotopia and the city: Public space in the postcivil society*. Routledge. pp. 259–272.
Shane, D.G. (2011) *Urban design since 1945: A global perspective*. Wiley.
Shane, D.G. (2014a) "Block, super block and megablock: A short history." *Arcduecitta*. At: www.arcduecitta.it/2014/01/block-superblock-and-megablock-una-breve-storia-gavid-grahame-shane/. Last accessed on 20 September 2020.
Shane, D.G. (2014b) "Metacity: Origins and implications." In: Contin, A. and Salerno, R. (Eds.) *Innovative technologies in urban mapping*. Springer. pp. 59–72.
Shane, D.G. (2015) "Chinese rapid urbanization and the metacity." In: Ding, W., Graafland, A. and Lu, A. (Eds.) *Cities in transition: Power, environment, society*. Nai010 Publishers. pp. 411–437.
Shane, D.G. (2016) "A short history of Hong Kong malls and towers." In: Al, S. (Ed) *Mall city: Hong Kong's dreamworlds of consumption*. University of Hawaii Press. pp. 35–53.
Shane, D.G. and McGrath, B. (2012) "Metropolis, megalopolis and the megacity." In: Crysler, C.G., Cairns, S. and Heynen, H. (Eds.) *The Sage handbook of architectural theory*. Sage. pp. 641–656.

Simpson, T. (2019) "Post-colonial Macau and post-socialist Chinese tourists." In: Simpson, T. (Ed) *Tourist utopias: Offshore islands, enclave spaces, and mobile imaginaries.* Amsterdam University Press. pp. 13–43.

Sohn, H. (2008) "Heterotopia: The *amenesis* of a medical term." In: Dehaene, M. and De Cauter, L. (Eds.) *Heterotopia and the city: Public space in the postcivil society.* Routledge. pp. 41–50.

Soja, E. (1989) *Postmodern geographies: The reassertion of space in critical social theory.* Verso.

Soja, E. (1996) *Third space: Journeys to Los Angeles and other real and imagined places.* Blackwell.

Sun, C. (2019) "City and cultural center shift: Performance space in Shenzhen." In: Xue, C.Q. (Ed.) *Grand theater urbanism: Chinese cities in the 21st century.* Springer. pp. 75–105.

UN (2008) *Megacities: The case of the Pearl River Delta.* At: www.un.org/en/development/desa/population/events/pdf/expert/13/P15_Ng.pdf. Last accessed on 10 October 2020.

UN (2014) *World's population increasingly urban with more than half living in urban areas.* At: www.un.org/en/development/desa/news/population/world-urbanization-prospects-2014.html. Last accessed on 20 September 2020.

Urbanus (2003–2012) *OCT loft renovation 2012.* At: www.urbanus.com.cn/projects/oct-loft/?lang=en. Last accessed on 20 September 2020.

Urbanus (2006) *Village/city city/village* (Bilingual, Chinese/English). China Power Press.

Urbanus (2010) *A village by the SEZ: The Dafen sample of China's urbanization.* Special Publication Brochure Collection for Shanghai World Expo 2010, Shanghai, and Shenzhen Pavilion Shanghai EXPO. At: www.urbanus.com.cn/projects/2010expo-szcp/. Last accessed on 20 September 2020.

Urbanus (2018) *Shum Yip Upperhills Loft 2018.* At: www.urbanus.com.cn/projects/shum-yip-upperhills-loft/?lang=en. Last accessed on 20 September 2020.

Urbanus (2020) *Yuehai Community Culture and Sports Center 2020.* At: www.urbanus.com.cn/projects/yuehaijiedao/?lang=en. Last accessed on 20 September 2020.

Venturi, R., Scott-Brown, D. and Isenour, J. (1972) *Learning from Las Vegas.* MIT Press.

Viganò, P., Cavalieri, C. and Barcelloni Corte, M. (2018) *The horizontal metropolis between urbanism and urbanization.* Springer.

Welter, V.M. (2003) *Biopolis: Patrick Geddes and the city of life.* MIT Press.

Whitehand, J.W.R., Gu, K., Whitehand, S.M. and Zhang, J. (2011) "Urban morphology and conservation in China." *Cities* 28. pp. 171–185.

Wittkower, R. (1969) "English neo-palladianism, the landscape garden, China and the enlightenment." *L'Arte* 5 (8). pp. 18–35.

Xue, C.Q. (2019) "From colonial to global: Performing art space in Hong Kong." In: Xue, C.Q. (Ed.) *Grand theater urbanism: Chinese cities in the 21st century.* Springer. pp. 231–253.

Zhang, Y., Yan, J. and Wei, W. (2014) "How I built a new China: A talk with Expo 2010 planner Siegfried Zhiqiang Wu." *ArchDaily.* At: www.archdaily.com/561083/how-i-built-a-new-china-a-talk-with-expo-2010-planner-siegfried-zhiqiang-wu/. Last accessed on 20 September 2020.

6

CROSS-BORDER AND TRANSIENT PUBLIC SPACE IN THE GREATER BAY AREA

Peter Hasdell

In the dense environs of Hong Kong, where land is a highly commodified resource, public space is notably limited and has a complex relationship to its civic functions. In planning terms, provision of public space in Hong Kong broadly falls into two distinct realms. One is the formal manifestation embodying governance and its symbolic representations, often as residues of colonial rule, as can be seen in Statue Square, for example. More recent examples can be found in the neo-liberal commercial developments which tend to offset increased densities with token public space amenity—evident in Hong Kong's Times Square development (1994), for example—resulting in highly regulated corporate public spaces. On the contrary, public space for citizens throughout Hong Kong's history has often been left to the informal, manifested as numerous market streets, transactional spaces doubling as public gathering spaces. In such market streets, the dense overlaying of temporal and changing functions—at one moment a goods market and later in the same day a cooked food or performance street—enact spatial choreographies. Across the border in Shenzhen, albeit for different developmental, governmental and regulatory reasons, public space provisions fall into a similar rubric, with the Futian government axis symbolizing state power versus former urban villages in which the street becomes a barometer of vibrant civic function and public space.

Although often contested, the transactional and therefore transient spaces of the street rely on difference to enable their lively nature. This is evident in the recent civic unrest periods in Hong Kong in which streets have been occupied (the Umbrella Movement of 2014, for instance) but equally in many everyday instances in the city that take advantage of unique spatial conditions. The nature of these differences—be they cultural, social, political or economic—gives rise to a conception of transient public space clearly exacerbated by the differences afforded by cross-border conditions arising at the Hong Kong-Shenzhen border. The border itself can therefore be posited as an integral part of a public space—a threshold condition—that generates issues that are played out in a series of micro- and macro-scale transient public spaces on both sides of the border.

78 Peter Hasdell

FIGURE 6.1 Occupy central: Umbrella Movement Hong Kong, 29 September 2014. *Images by Pasu Au Yeung.*

Source: Wikimedia Commons © Creative Commons BY-SA 2.0.

Exogenous Border Conditions

The Hong Kong-Shenzhen border in its current state intersects several complex registers that highlight systemic differentiation. These occur across a range of socio-cultural-economic factors and vary in scope from the official to the illicit. Even in its earlier manifestations, since its inception as a hard international border at the end of the Korean War (1950–53) and throughout its history, it has given rise to complex cross-border interactions that ebb and flow. Since then, tactical machinations of those on either side circumvent the border, leading variously to illegal immigration, refugee trafficking, piracy, money laundering, contraband smuggling, profiteering, petrol smuggling and many other localized adaptations. Under its post-1997 guise, the border has operated as an internal national boundary

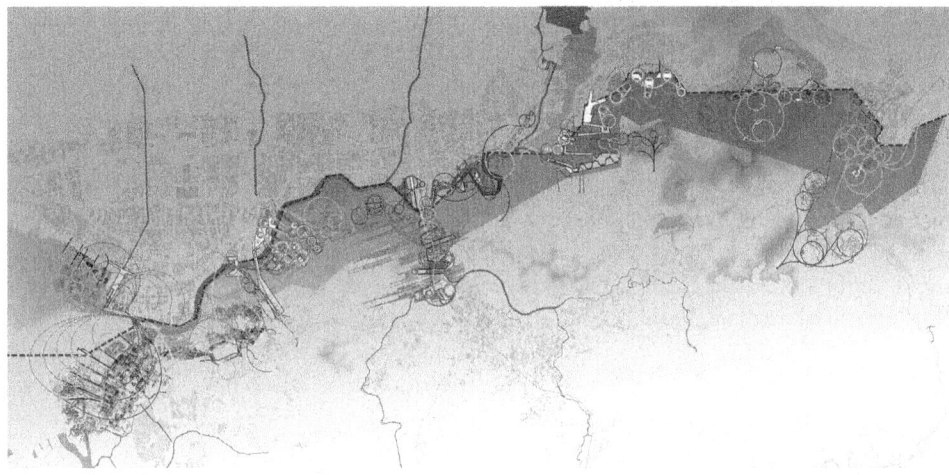

FIGURE 6.2 Border ecologies, mapping cross-border eco-system operations on the Hong Kong-Shenzhen border, 2012.

Source: Author.

FIGURE 6.3 Cross-border schoolchildren on the Hong Kong–Shenzhen border, 2014.

Source: Matthew Hung.

governed by the complex policies of the One Country Two Systems (一国两制) policy that has allowed the post-colonial Special Administrative Regions (SARs) of Hong Kong and Macau to maintain governmental, legal and economic systems that diverge from those of the People's Republic of China (PRC) in general, which in turn was planned to regulate Hong Kong's existence until 2047 as outlined in the Sino-British Joint Agreement of 1984. However, the chain of events in 2019–2020 triggered by a proposed extradition arrangement between Hong Kong and mainland China, the subsequent nine months of civil unrest and the implementing in July 2020 of the national security bill imposed by Beijing have significantly eroded this agreement and have led some to claim that One Country Two Systems is no longer applicable or in operation. The border, however, remains operational at the time of writing. While many quasi-illicit activities still span the border today, the increased porosity of the border has led to a myriad of everyday actions, involving cross-border school children and cross-border workers, as well as family and kinship ties between people on the two sides.

The border clearly delineates Hong Kong and is integral to the city's *entrepôt* status as an extraterritorial enclave. Although differences in governance, land ownership and legal systems impose obstacles to eventual 2047 integration, the projected date of dissolution of the One Country Two Systems policy will coincide with the erasure of the border itself and the dismantling of Hong Kong's status as an SAR, not to mention the termination of the UK-derived Basic Law, international finance center operations and the business-oriented proto-democratic system that have characterized Hong Kong, as well as the society's special semi-autonomous rights and privileges. However this plays out, the border will remain a contested territory in which the magnification of differences and contradictions will be exacerbated: remaining a highly complex space in which geopolitical ambitions, ideological polarities, national disagreements and cultural clashes can be found, in which struggles between individual aspirations and collective dreams *contra* state-driven agendas will continue to erupt in the public domain as forms of transient public space.

It is important to contextualize the border within the framework of the Greater Bay Area (GBA) ambitions that seek to combine eleven regional cities, including Hong Kong, Shenzhen, Guangzhou, Dongguan, Zhuhai, Macau and Fuoshan, into an urban agglomeration of over 70 million inhabitants. These measures were initiated under the Study on the Action Plan for the Bay Area of the Pearl River Estuary (2011), the National New-Type Urbanization Plan (2014–2020) outlining how urban agglomeration is to be the main spatial vehicle for urbanization in the coming decade and formally endorsed in China's 2016–2020 Five-Year Plan. It can be said, however, that aspects of this integration have been occurring unofficially since the 1997 Handover, perhaps more by stealth and policy relaxations than through overt plans, with the increased flexibility of visiting and visa rights and increased access to Hong Kong's property and investment sectors for mainland Chinese citizens, not to mention the later planning and implementation of large-scale connective tissues and infrastructures that include new border crossings (Nanshan 2007; Liantang 2018), the Hong Kong-Zhuhai-Macau Bridge (2019) and the high-speed rail connection between Hong Kong and the mainland (2018), which raised questions about the border control facilities from the mainland in Hong Kong territory. It remains unclear how the GBA ambitions will modify the border with respect to Hong Kong's autonomy. Clearly the political incentives to integrate are high. In other words, there are significant exogenous and cross-border factors that continue to impact urban development and its manifestations and controls on public space in Hong Kong.

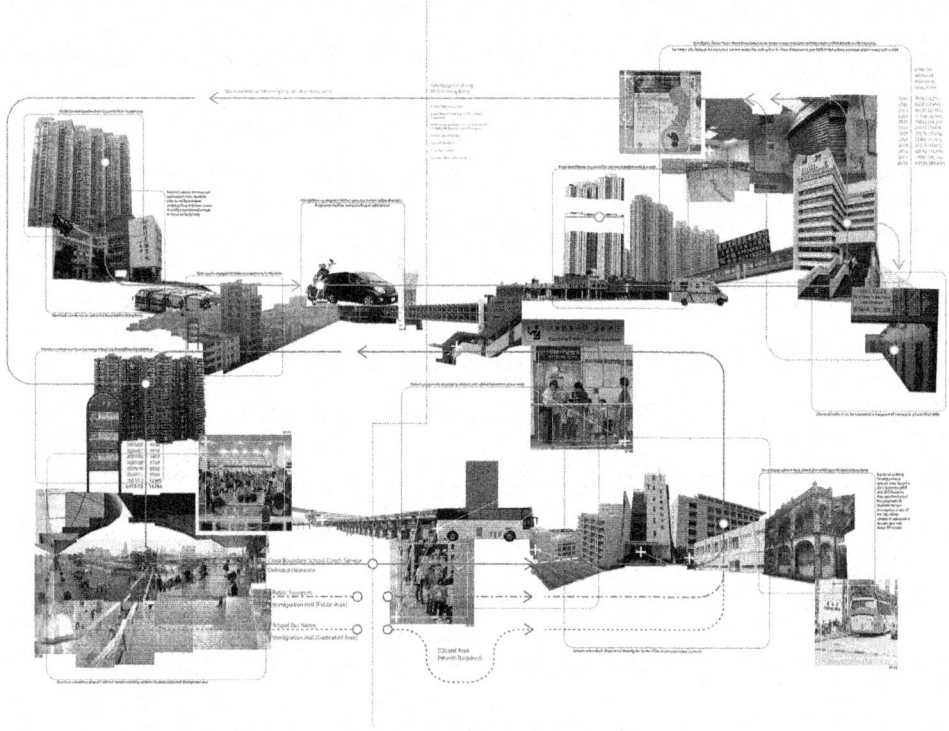

FIGURE 6.4 Cross-border schoolchildren diagram, 2014.
Source: Matthew Hung.

Broadly understood, the rise of borders and enclaves lead inevitably to exclusions, divisions and contestations. Similarly, their disincorporation may also lead to disruptions of pre-existing spatial, social and economic orders. Useful parallels can be drawn from other rapidly urbanized border regions as well as their current roll-backs in some cases. Globalization and neo-liberal policies have disconnected specific cities and regions from their territorial hinterlands during the past thirty years. As theorized by Sassen (2016), Castells (2010), Easterling (2012) and Brenner (2013), among others, this process can occur in order to connect cities and regions to global trade networks. Outcomes from this include increased migration, the proliferation of free trade zones and trade liberalization policies, coupled with the activation of cross-border networks in global systems (Sassen 2001). Border regions reveal this in the encroachment of massive informal urban settlements and subsequent rapid transformations into complex cross-border conurbation zones through logistics centers, infrastructure development and exogenous investment. This has led to some border regions expanding at unstable urban growth rates, such as Singapore-Johore, Dongxing-Mon Cai or Blagoveshchesnk-Heihe. For instance, the Tijuana-San Diego border zone has grown to become a cross-border region of well over 5 million inhabitants.

Each of these regions is complex in operation; the dynamics of these places; their identities; and their economic, social and cultural relations are inextricable from their shared border and singular in their unique cultural, geographic and spatial constituents. These border cities in turn are no longer peripheral to nation states but instead define new complex regional hubs, gateways and critical nodes in an increasingly globalized context of supply chains, import-export zones and low-wage assembly areas. This results in the unfolding of complex new cross-border issues and spatial conditions that cannot be comprehended by looking at cities as singular bounded entities. City-wide planning and governance tools are not able to deal with the complexities of cross-border phenomena. As Cruz (2014) argues, the very discontinuity, tension and conflict of border zones give rise to new paradigms of planning. As Davis (2000) pointed out, the effects of the urbanization of border areas have led to "second" and "third borders," in which social, economic, cultural and political discontinuities become evident in settlements across borders or even at some distance removed from border regions themselves, whereby fragments and partial manifestations of the border and populations give rise to "third space"–type conditions in which, for example, a small part of Tijuana may appear in a South Los Angeles suburb as a new cultural hybrid enclave.

Clearly, border regions contain a variety of spatial conditions and give rise to a proliferation of spatial hybrids and anomalies. Be they legal loopholes, grey zones where illicit activities or black economies may occur, tolerated exceptions such as tax- and duty-free zones, cultural enclaves or ghettos, they all cultivate exceptional urban conditions. Easterling (2005) expands upon this in the context of transnational globalization, classifying the concept of exclusion zones as

> spatial products that incubate in several species of zone-outlaw enclave formations [focused] on the instrumentality of duplicity, the preference for manipulating both state and non-state sovereignties-for alternately releasing and laundering power and identity to create the most advantageous political or economic climate. . . . Various enclave forms with various legal parameters, merge and hybridize to create new legal habitats. . . . They are the aggregate unit of many new global conurbations and the mechanism for a mongrel form of exception.

Such exceptions and loopholes have particular relationships with how a border permits or prohibits and is permeable or impermeable to the various entities on both sides of it. The co-dependencies arising from this are normally established in relation to changing conditions and factors on each side and may be able to bypass levels of control and regulation effectively. These regulatory frameworks include cross-border policies that aim to restrict mobility or migration; differing legal, political and security frameworks; and different economic or legal systems. In fact, they create possibilities for bypassing or seeking loopholes that enable exchange and value creation from the "exacerbated differences" (Chung et al. 2001: 704) the border establishes. These can become drivers for informal activities that operate outside the norm, despite the border laws in operation.

As Mar (2002) outlines, planning in Hong Kong has been "haphazard." Drawing a conception of a city that is more corporeal in operation than a structured socio-spatial one, he cites Cuthbert (cited in Mar 2002: 48), who articulates Hong Kong's urban condition in terms of four eroding ecologies (after Banham's 1971 seminal work on Los Angeles). Cuthbert outlines the contested relations between the Merchant City, the Industrial City, the Financial City and the Capital City as the roots of the current monopoly of development and the government-regulated mechanisms of land control. These have reached a critical juncture in the past four to five years after decades of under-development in specific sectors.

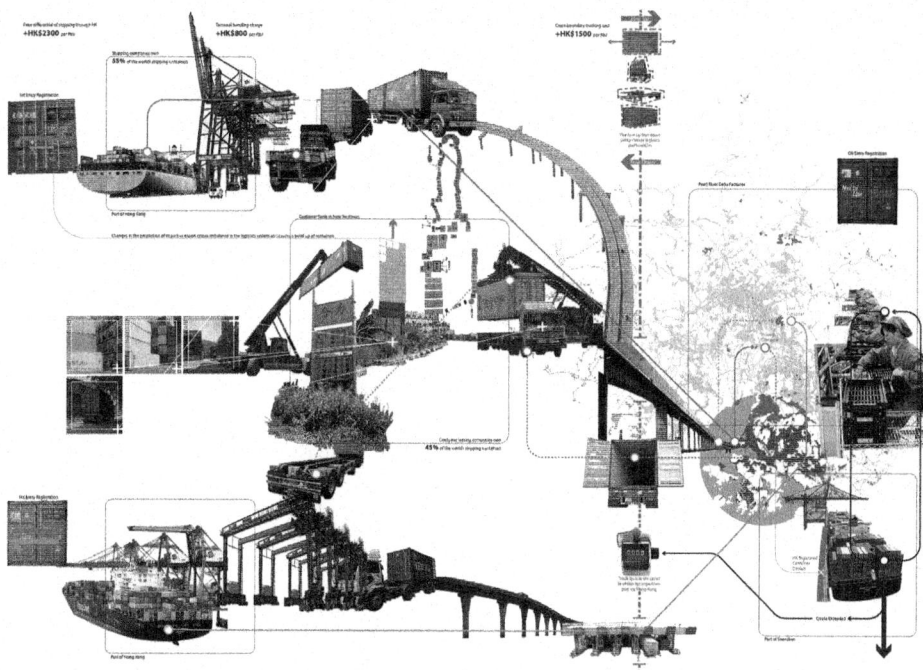

FIGURE 6.5 Hong Kong–Shenzhen cross-border logistics mapping.
Source: Matthew Hung.

Elsewhere, Cuthbert (1987, 1997, 1998) suggests that market-driven imperatives run counter to a citizen-centered approach. Similarly, Ng (1986) outlines how Hong Kong's planning systems have been inconsistent and fragmented since their inception, resulting in a patchwork of urban fabrics that are more opportunistic than strategic. This evinces an overemphasis of capital and value that reveals how the dominant planning model remains "derivative rather than creative": a clear oversight, in effect supporting an argument that the social finds its alignment not in social norms or socio-spatial models but through incorporation into economic frameworks of value and speculative development, leading to an under-investment in civic engagement and in public amenity provision. These have inexorably led to increasing inequality, as seen by rises in Gini coefficients, and are recognized as contributing factors to social unrest in recent years. When one considers that significant policies in Hong Kong have always been planned from afar in capitals distant from the city itself, be it London or Beijing, it becomes clear that the issues of Hong Kong's development cannot be disconnected from the border and the One Country Two Systems policy. Recent events show this to be an ongoing issue.

Transient Public Space, a Conceptualization

Notably, many of the differences structured by the Hong Kong-Shenzhen border remain capable of eliciting a crisis, be it an influx of refugees, outsourcing of industry or a fear of pandemics. As a critical inflection point, the year 2047 represents a systemic crisis for Hong Kong across many levels that will likely affect the city's identity, urban systems, modes of political and civic governance, social and cultural constitution and economic independence. Castells (2010) outlined four types of crisis: crisis of efficiency, crisis of legitimacy, crisis of identity and crisis of equity, stating that "[t]he growing gap between the space where the issues arise (global) and the space where the issues are managed (the nation-state) is at the source of four distinct, but interrelated, political crises that affect the institutions of governance." These various types of crises are becoming evident in the recent rise of anti-extradition and universal suffrage protests by Hong Kong citizens who target the growing encroachment of Beijing's policies. Ackbar Abbas (1998), on the eve of the 1997 Handover, wrote that Hong Kong and Shenzhen are "two peoples separated by a common ethnicity," although their differences are deeper. Clearly, the emerging internal contradictions of the crises are manifold and ongoing. Of note, but not outlined here, key urban and spatial developments on both sides of the border have historically been either responses to crises—with cultural, territorial and economic consequences—or have elicited crises, such as the recent high-speed rail link to Hong Kong and the debate concerning the border control points for passengers that disrupt the One Country Two Systems policy.

Weizman (2006) notes that "sovereign borders are linear and fixed, frontiers are deep, fragmented and elastic." As the Hong Kong-Shenzhen border has undergone a transition from a hard international border to a national frontier—an internal boundary rather than a border subject to frequent changes of policy for both material goods and human traffic—it continues to act as a "petri dish" for many of the wider issues that arise. As a frontier, any negotiation of its territories and overlaps is inherently tactical for border crossers from either side. The patterns and narratives of adaptation of border crossers to changing border conditions can be seen as responses to complex macro policies and are often counter to the interests of public and civic domains on both sides. Within the context of cross-border conditions, civic engagement in transient public spaces becomes a form of tactical enactment or even transaction in a paradoxically geopolitically localized space.

The massive number of border traversals by daily users and the skein of connections they make construct new kinds of reticules on either side. Intersections between these reticules manifest as interactions between the border crossers and the host city itself, at times defining proto-types of public space. We can therefore hypothesize that forms of transient public space arise or emerge from such encounters. These are inherently temporal in manifestation. Thus, for transient public space, it is clear that a spatio-temporal understanding is necessary to comprehend their aleatory nature as a relational heuristic. Such a new understanding requires a hybrid socio-spatial framework: one that draws from an urban sociological perspective (Wirth 1938; Lefebvre 1991; Castells 2010) and from the fields of cultural geography (Bhabha 1994; Soja 1996; Abbas 1998), as well as from planning and urban theory. This perspective seeks to understand both the spatial differences of places affected by borders and the temporal factors initiated by the mobilities of people, goods and value systems that give rise to their emergence.

Within this context, border crossers develop behaviors contributing to, and in some cases forming, new "border ecologies" through emerging social and cultural "border conditions" and as transitional and anomalous spaces (Bolchover and Hasdell 2016). Border ecologies research contributes to an understanding that borders give rise to kinds of eco-systems that seek to balance the differences established by the border. This can be understood when considering cross-border workers who remit money back to their families, for instance. Such processes employ a range of informal and formal mechanisms that exploit, feed off or circumvent borders, generating alternative "spatial practices" (De Certeau 1984) and liminal or hybrid existences (Bhabha 1994) contingent on changing macro-exigencies. They also generate complex sets of cross-border actors and tactics operating between macro-policies and micro-conditions. Put simply, on a tactical level, actors seeking to utilize differences make use of the disparities or differences between value systems on opposing sides of the border. As well, exogenous issues from across the border may agitate actors to initiate actions on the other side. These actions, which are causally linked to the border, in turn activate spaces in the public domain, often at a distance from the border itself. They generate non-sanctioned, or at least unrecognized, forms of public space that are "proto-urban" in nature (Bunschoten et al. 2001), to be institutionalized at a later time. Further, these tactical operations, when considered as a citywide urban system, can construct a new layer of disruptive tissue to an urban condition, resulting in the emergence of contested territories and eruptions of civic discontent, as evident in Hong Kong's 2014 and 2019 civic unrest.

Cross-Border Loopholes and Liminal Bodies

Cross-border operators include state actors as well as other liminal operators that include cross-border school children, smugglers, divided families, dislocated communities, cross-border commuters and parallel traders. Clearly, many of these actors operate in a variety of transient contexts, both disruptive but also redefining public amenity and use of space. Three examples drawn from the Hong Kong side are outlined in the following.

Sha Tau Kok enfolds a complexity of adjustments between two systems that wily operators once exploited for economic gain, citizenship rights or access to education within transient public space. Their tactical behaviors enable "within the transition zone, cultural, linguistic and social hybridity [resulting in] the formation of transnational, transboundary spaces with the emergence of new hybrid regional identities" (Bhabha 1994). The only urbanized part of the Hong Kong side of the border, Sha Tau Kok, has a complex relationship with Shataujiao, situated opposite it on the mainland side. This occurs through the shared Chung Ying Street Market (Chung referring to China and Ying to Britain), which occupies the shared border. During the Closed Period of the 1960s and 1970s, the market was a key point where the PRC and the external world could transact: over 90% of the shops were gold sellers, and access to hard currency was available. During the Opening Up period from 1980, it was a place where people could purchase Western-made products, consumer electronics, music and videos.

Additionally, differing legal jurisdictions led to smugglers evading police by crossing the border through the marketplace, whilst large groups of traders would rush the border control, having pre-ordained who was to be caught. Other ruses included pretending to deliver to shops in the market but using the maze of laneways to avoid detection. Traders also threw goods over unpoliced border fences or made devices with which goods could be lifted up to high-rise residential apartments. The fire station was also until recently a place where women from Shenzhen would come in the final stages of pregnancy in order to give birth in Hong Kong, giving their children the right of abode and access to education in Hong Kong. Such tactics also extended to smugglers during this time, with the nearby Starling Inlet being one of the major routes. Only after the Handover of Hong Kong to China in 1997, and China's joining the WTO in 2001, did the Chung Ying Street Market decline.

86 Peter Hasdell

The second example is informal, or parallel, trading in Hong Kong, a phenomenon in which traders from Hong Kong and the mainland exploit legal loopholes given by changes in the multiple-entry visa policy after 2012. The rise of this aligns with a twenty-fold increase in cross-border visitors, from 3 million in 1997 to over 60 million by 2015. Although sometimes acting in organized syndicates, goods are usually packed into shopping trolleys and taken by individuals across the border to be sold to take advantage of differing tax regimes. These goods are often displayed near transport interchanges or adjacent to shopping areas, but these practices are unregulated and illegal. An ongoing issue, it is most prevalent in Hong Kong's New Territory towns of Sheung Shui, Fanling and Yuen Long, in close proximity to cross-border transport networks. These practices have disrupted local markets and shops, decimating local shop-owners, and have led to almost a decade of escalating tensions and protests by Hong Kong traders and market places, as well as affecting the shops and types of products taken back over the border for sale on their return to the mainland. These include Western-made pharmaceuticals and milk powder for infants, which became a sought-after commodity in China in 2014 when Chinese-made milk powder contaminated with melamine became a food security issue. To an extent, this mirrors earlier parallel trading of Hong Kong goods in Shenzhen in the earlier years of the Opening Up period.

Finally, after the 2018 closure of a street market in Hong Kong's Mongkok District, well known for singing and performing, Chinese women known as "big mothers" or *damas*

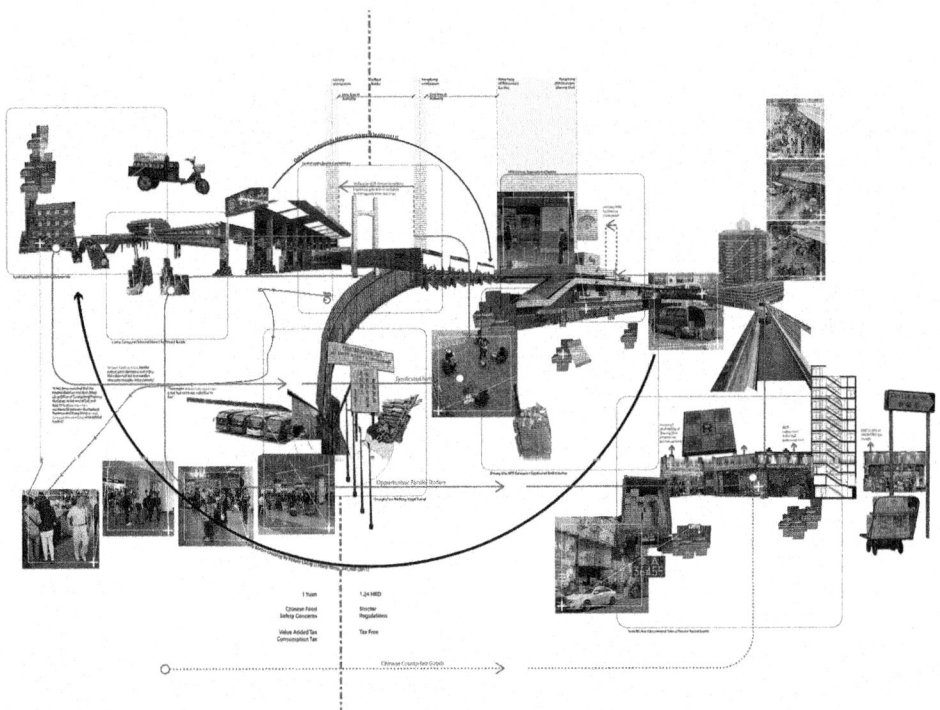

FIGURE 6.6 Hong Kong-Shenzhen cross-border parallel trading mapping.

Source: Matthew Hung.

relocated their activities to Tuen Mun Park, a dense residential area in the New Territories which had set aside performing areas in 2006. In part, the singing and dancing has been a foil for soft prostitution, which happens in temporary tents set up in the park for the dancers. The singers were reported to use large public address systems and block public access pathways. The existence of an organizational infrastructure for these daily events indicates that some syndication of these "damas" is happening. The performers are often paid with red pockets—money in red envelopes that are traditionally given on special occasions in Chinese society—by elderly men, leading to numerous complaints and protests from local residents, as well as creating a public nuisance and excessive noise, as police permits were generally not held. These resulted in a series of protests during 2019, closely allied to the other antigovernment protests in that year.

The unofficial tactical maneuvering and cross-border manifestations of individuals on either side of the border are driven by the seeking of opportunities to take advantage of the increasing porosity of the border itself. Such informal actions and the diverse actors are on the rise and are continually redefining the territories, identities and landscapes on either side. Their actions become manifested in transient public spaces as issues that highlight the differences between the opposite sides of the border. These are contingent on a myriad of multi-scalar and interwoven factors, including changes in macro governmental policy; public opinion; perceived economic stability; easing of travel restrictions for mainlanders to Hong Kong; burgeoning opportunities; increasing economic wealth; social and physical mobility; the attractions of an open society; and informal factors, including the black economy and money flows, smuggling, illegal immigration, increasing surveillance and heightened security provisions. As Simmel (1997) has written, "The boundary is not a spatial fact with sociological consequences, but a sociological fact that forms itself spatially." These very factors are sharply highlighted by the recent events of the 2019 Hong Kong protests and the 2020 coronavirus outbreak that bring to light the complex contradictions that the border masks yet which irrupt and find expression in transient public spaces.

References

Abbas, A. (1998) *Hong Kong: Culture and the politics of disappearance*. Hong Kong University Press.
Banham, R. (1971) *Los Angeles: The architecture of four ecologies*. Harper & Row.
Bhabha, H. (1994) *The location of culture*. Routledge.
Bolchover, J. and Hasdell, P. (2016) *Border ecologies, Hong Kong's mainland frontier*. Birkhäuser.
Brenner, N. (2013) "Global cities, glocal states: Global city formation and state territorial restructuring." *Journal of Economic Literature* 41. pp. 1–37.
Bunschoten, R., Binet, H. and Hoshino, T. (2001) *Urban flotsam: Stirring the city*. Chora Institute of Architecture and Urbanism. 010 Publishers.
Castells, M. (2010) "The new public sphere: Global civil society, communication networks and global governance." In: Thussu, D.K. (Ed.) *International communication: A reader*. Routledge. pp. 36–47.
Chung, C.H.J., Inaba, J., Koolhaas, R. and Leong, S.T. (Eds.) (2001) *Project on the city I: Great leap forward*. Taschen.
Cruz, T. (2014) *Mapping non-conformity: Post-bubble urban strategies*. At: https://hemisphericinstitute.org/en/emisferica-71/7-1-essays/mapping-non-conformity-post-bubble-urban-strategies.html. Last accessed on 20 September 2020.
Cuthbert, A. (1987) "Hong Kong 1997: The transition to socialism: Ideology, discourse, and urban spatial structure." *Environment and Planning D: Society and Space* 5 (2). pp. 123–150.

Cuthbert, A. (1997) "Ambiguous space, ambiguous rights: Corporate power and social control in Hong Kong." *Cities* 14 (5). pp. 295–311.

Cuthbert, A. (1998) "Genesis of land-use planning and urban development." In: Dimitrou, H.T. and Cook, A.H.S. (Eds.) *Land-use/transport planning in Hong Kong—the end of an era: A review of principles and practices.* Ashgate, Routledge.

Davis, M. (2000) *Magical urbanism: Latinos reinvent the US city.* Verso.

De Certeau, M. (1984) *The practice of everyday life.* University of California Press.

Easterling, K. (2005) *Enduring innocence: Global architecture and its political masquerades.* MIT Press.

Easterling, K. (2012) "Zone: The spatial softwares of extrastatecraft." *Places Journal,* June. At: https://placesjournal.org/article/zone-the-spatial-softwares-of-extrastatecraft/. Last accessed on 20 September 2020.

Lefebvre, H. (1991) *The production of space.* Blackwell.

Mar, P. (2002) *Hong Kong: A spatial story.* Unpublished doctoral dissertation, University of Sydney. At: http://ses.library.usyd.edu.au/bitstream/2123/1209/3/03chapter2.pdf. Last accessed on 20 September 2020.

Ng, M.K. (1986) *Urban planning in Hong Kong, a case study of the central district.* Master of Science thesis, Urban Planning, University of Hong Kong.

Sassen, S. (2001) *The global city: New York, London, Tokyo* (2nd ed.). Princeton University Press.

Sassen, S. (2016) *Expulsion: Brutality and complexity in the global economy.* At: http://saskiasassen.com/PDFs/ASA%20Expul%20Trajectories%20Spring%202016.pdf. Last accessed on 20 September 2020.

Simmel, G. (1997) "The sociology of space." In: Frisby, F. and Featherstone, M. (Eds.) and Ritter, M. and Frisby, D. (Trans.) *Simmel on culture: Selected writings.* Sage. pp. 137–169.

Soja, E.W. (1996) *Thirdspace: Journeys to Los Angeles and other real-and-imagined places.* Basil Blackwell Press.

Study on the Action Plan for the Bay Area of the Pearl River Estuary (2011). At: www.hkip.org.hk/en-position-papers/2017/10/29/study-on-the-action-plan-for-the-bay-area-of-the-pearl-river-estuary-april-2011. Last accessed on 20 September 2020.

Weizman, E. (2006) "Principles of frontier geography." In: Misselwitz, P. and Rienierts, T. (Eds.) *City of collision: Jerusalem and the principles of conflict urbanism.* Birkhäuser.

Wirth, L. (1938) "Urbanism as a way of life." *American Journal of Sociology* 44 (1). pp. 1–24, July.

7
WHAT KIND OF PUBLIC SPACE IS THE CITY OF SHENZHEN?

Mary Ann O'Donnell

North Americans have been slow to acknowledge our intimacies with Shenzhen. If you received a Cabbage Patch Kid during the early 1980s, a small piece of your childhood was fabricated in Shenzhen. If you blasted LL Cool J on a boombox in the 1990s or began personal computing in the early 2000s, some portion of your identity was assembled in Shenzhen. If you've listened to music on a Sony Walkman or watched movies on a tablet, your taste was miniaturized in Shenzhen. And, although the production chains that link Shenzhen to North American holidays, hip hop, and hacking as well as to fast fashion, cloning, animation and commercial drones have been significantly transformed since the city initiated top-down deindustrialization in 2005, nevertheless there's every chance that if you have resided in North America for the past thirty years, then many—if not all—of your cell phones have been produced in Shenzhen. Yet most North Americans have only become aware of Shenzhen since the 2010s, when the city emerged as the "Silicon Valley of hardware," attracting young, mostly male hackers to Huaqiangbei via Rotterdam, Berlin and San Francisco (Lindtner et al. 2015).

At first glance, the story of why North Americans missed Shenzhen's industrial revolution is straight-forwardly Marxian—commodity fetishism. In Marx's reading, industrial capitalism disappears the human cost of producing objects. The separation between spheres of production and consumption enable our collective misrecognition of the interconnection between how things are produced and how they are consumed because we take for granted that the economy is organized into places of production and consumption, where "[t]hat which was created in one sphere is used—ultimately used up, destroyed—in the other" (Graeber 2011: 492).

This chapter tracks the Cold War roots of Shenzhen, focusing on how the city has become a model of successful urbanization both within China and outside. In this model of development, the entire city is considered an effect of 'public policy,' while 'the public' is defined as a population that is formed (or potentially formed) through government actions with explicit (and usually measurable) outcomes. In this model, a city is the vehicle through which public goods are delivered via urban organization which is increasingly regulated to meet policy goals. This categorization of the city as 'public' resonates with its use in expressions such as 'public welfare,' 'public education,' 'public building' and 'public health.' At stake in this use of 'public' are the presumed responsibilities of a government and the spatial means by which these responsibilities are fulfilled. Of course, the catch to this (well-intentioned?) master planning is that not all goods are delivered equally, everywhere and at the same time. What's more, the place of a city in a global value chain has visceral effects on urban form.

Nets-to-Riches: Even Boat Dwellers Have Access to Public Goods in Shenzhen

In 1979, China followed the East Asian blueprint of using activist public policies to jumpstart modernization in Shenzhen, Zhuhai, Shantou and Xiamen Special Economic Zones (SEZ; Phillips and Yeh 1983). In Shenzhen, for example, China deployed the corps of engineers to implement the Five Connections One Leveling (五通一平) policy, which provisioned water, electricity, roads, telecommunications and sewage, in addition to flattening the land to facilitate industrial urbanization. The epicenter of this first round of state investment was Luohu and its immediate neighbor, Shangbu Management Area. Luohu was the location of the historical Shenzhen Market, which became the name of both the new city and its special economic zone. Shangbu was the location of its adjacent 'new town' and location of its restructured government. The national government relocated Third Front enterprises to the Shangbu and Bagualing Industrial Parks, which were located in Shangbu Management Area, bringing some of the country's top engineers to Shenzhen as well as trained workforces. In 1994, the World Bank published a policy working paper titled *China's Economic Reforms: Pointers for Other Economies in Transition?* which argued the country's experience might provide "pointers for other capital scarce economies in transition from strategies geared to heavy industry to a more balanced profile of development" even as it overlooked the extent to which only socialist states had 'readymade' manufacturing complexes that could be relocated to accommodate the needs of global logistics. The key point here is the level of state involvement and national restructuring that has predicated post-Japanese modernization.

Constructing Shenzhen's built environment makes salient the tension between the city as a spatial means for allocating public goods and the city as being composed of public spaces. The city's early infrastructure, for example, was provided by the corps of engineers for the use of all companies and residents in the SEZ. However, in practice, the distribution of these resources was sequential and geographic, resulting in some companies, people and urban spaces receiving first access. Luohu-Shangbu companies and residents had access to municipal water and electrical lines, roads, sewage and telecommunications before companies and residents in other parts of the city. Local Luohu and Shangbu villagers had immediate access to these new urban goods because of where they were born, while Third Front enterprises received them through their status within the state apparatus. Migrants obtained access to public goods by leaving their homes and moving to Luohu-Shangbu. Indeed, the concentration of public infrastructure and opportunities to use public goods to create private wealth in Luohu-Shangbu meant that for the first two decades, residents of the SEZ and its suburbs referred to Luohu-Shangbu as 'Shenzhen' or 'downtown.'

Early Chinese descriptions of Shenzhen emphasized the construction of an urban built environment that would (eventually) enable all Chinese people to enjoy modern infrastructure—the city as an instrument of public policy. As narrated in *The Secret of the Shenzhen Sphinx*, for example, Deng Xiaoping arrived in Shenzhen on 24 January 1984 to tour the nascent SEZ. "On the road, Deng Xiaoping opened the curtain several times to look at the busy construction sites and rising towers" (Chen et al. 1991: 95). The implied contrast was with the rice polders, fishponds and lychee orchards that still dominated the local landscape. On the second day of his trip, Deng visited a fishing collective which had built each of its thirty-two families a two-and-one-half–story house on land reclaimed from the Shenzhen River.

The village that Deng visited was called Fishing Village (渔民村), a reference to the historic livelihood of villagers who, before they were given land on which to build homes, had lived on boats and fished for a living. Sometimes called 'boat people,' 'boat dwellers,' or the pejorative Tanka (蛋家), southern Chinese fishing families historically organized in small groups of families that lived on their boats, trading with land-based villages (Ward 1985; Anderson 1972). In the early 1950s as part of a larger land reform initiative, the Chinese Communist Party (CCP) forced coastal villages in Bao'an County to provide small fishing groups with homestead land. The village that Deng Xiaoping visited, for example, had been established on land that historically belonged to Caiwuwei Village. Consequently, throughout Shenzhen, there are two kinds of fishing villages: land-based villages that operated fishing boats and fishing villages that were formally created in the early 1950s. These second types of villages, like Fishing Village in Luohu, include the character "to fish" (渔) in their name. Historically, boat dwellers were denied access to land settlements, making them some of the poorest communities along the Guangdong coast. Consequently, when the head of Luohu's Fishing Village proudly showed off sofas and chairs, a television and refrigerator, shelves filled with alcohol and cigarettes and a clean kitchen and bathroom to Deng, the images showed the realization of the city as successfully providing public goods to some of the poorest people in the country.

Images of Deng's visit to Fishing Village uncannily reproduced the visual rhetoric of *Life* magazine photo-essays from forty years earlier, which had presented consumption and home ownership as important elements of the American way of life (Webb 2012). As in the *Life* scenarios from the 1930s and 40s, photographs of Fishing Village were simultaneously nationalistic and aspirational, linking active consumption to nation-building, class status and gendered standards of success. Moreover, like the *Life* consumption scenarios, the visualization of Fishing Village occurred during a time of social upheaval, "bridging the gap between the demands of a Calvinistic (socialist) producer ethic with its emphasis on hard work, self-denial, and the new, increasing demands of a hedonistic consumer ethic: spend, enjoy, use up" (Susman 2003: 123). In the case of Fishing Village, the images showed how reforming the planned economy was a better strategy for delivering public goods to all Chinese people. Under the national plan, the State appropriated productive surpluses, which it then allocated to meet development goals. Under this regime, any kind of personal consumption was considered selfish at best and often illegal. Where the American images had framed citizenship and nation-building as the result of individual efforts (Webb 2012), the Chinese images functioned within a project to secure CCP hegemony in the immediate post-Mao era and before reforms were generalized more broadly in 1984 (O'Donnell 2017a). More generally, where the *Life* pictures presented the American way of life as an alternative to communism, the pictures of Fishing Village presented this way of life as the result of correct policy decisions made by an interventionist state.

The immediate backdrop for Deng's visit to Fishing Village was the Central State's promulgation of *On Rural Work* in 1984, which emphasized that "on the basis of stabilizing and perfecting the household responsibility system, [the goal is to] improve production, smooth distribution, and develop commodities" (CCP Central Committee 1984). The household responsibility system had been promulgated in 1979 and made local cadres responsible for the profits and losses of their respective communes and brigades. Under the household responsibility system, farmers could produce surplus crops and sell their goods at market. In just three years from

1979 to 1982, for example, the thirty-two families of Fishing Village had reached the 10,000 *yuan* annual income milestone by selling fish in both Shenzhen and neighboring Hong Kong. At the time, professionals in cities such as Beijing and Shanghai were earning less than 100 *yuan* a month; Fishing Village villagers not only had access to consumer goods but also could afford to purchase them. Thus, when the village head brought Deng (and by extension the millions of readers of *People's Daily*) into his home, he was not simply displaying his prowess as a local leader but was instead showing how new policies were in fact benefiting ordinary people. The polemic of the images was clear: if Reform and Opening policies could transform a marginalized village into a new neighborhood where the standard of living rivaled that of Beijing, then they would clearly benefit the rest of the country. In fact, Chinese news reports downplayed the local status of Fishing Village and the unruly fact that fishing villages had been set up in all of Bao'an County's coastal communes. Instead, Fishing Village came to stand for the generalized position of farmers in the Chinese state system, such that "fishing village" functioned as a rhetorical placeholder for rural lack in particular and the country's poverty in general.

In 1993, World Bank researchers argued that "activist public policy" rather than culture or geographic location explained how East Asian countries effectively transformed their economies through industrial urbanization by "getting the basics right"—managing private domestic investment and growing human capital to create wealth (World Bank 1993: 5). Roughly twenty-five years later, UN-Habitat made Shenzhen an exemplar of urbanization, publishing *The Story of Shenzhen* (UN-Habitat 2019) in Nairobi and offering the city as a model for equitable development in Africa. Both the World Bank and UN-Habitat have focused on Shenzhen's ability to provide infrastructure, housing and jobs to its residents; public policy has made the city a primary vehicle for sharing material resources.

Shenzhen's "nets-to-riches" tale frames the public good in terms of access to modern infrastructure, which is provided via governmental action—activist public policy. Chinese news reports used *Life*-like scenarios to demonstrate the effectiveness of these policies. Indeed, throughout the Cold War (roughly 1945–1990), American public policy deployed family consumption as an important element of its Cold War ideology, "vivid proof that the American way of life was superior to that of Soviet Communism" (Samuel 2014: 17). During the 1950s and 1960s, the United States not only promoted middle-class consumption as the most democratic form of modern living, it also invested heavily in Western Europe and East Asia in order to create middle-class homes where public goods could be privately consumed. By the time China initiated its reform and opening up policy at the end of 1978, this lifestyle had already become the presumed goal of modernization worldwide. Indeed, a few snapshots of middle-class fishing villagers were enough to help sell the idea of extending reforms to other Chinese cities as well as to convince foreign governments that China was serious about market reforms. The subtext of the images was: if private spaces of modern consumption exist, then the complementary spaces of production and public infrastructure that are necessary to sustain this lifestyle also exist.

Shekou: The Need for Critical Public Spaces

In contrast to Fishing Village, the establishment of the Shekou Industrial Zone illuminates how the spatial distribution of public infrastructure as well as state control over this infrastructure creates the necessity for watchdog institutions to ensure that public policies reach all residents rather than a selected few. To this end, UN-Habitat (2012) made public space central to its recommendations for improving cities. Public space, it argues, can be harnessed "to enhance safety and security, create economic opportunity, improve public health, create diverse public environments, and build democracy." In this reading, public spaces are spatial means for promoting the equitable distribution of public goods that cannot be simply distributed through the city as such (an end result which is assumed through aggressive public policies). Thus, a tension between the idea of the city's built environment being public as such and the city's built environment as requiring alternative public spaces vex World Bank and UN-Habitat reports. On the one hand, the city's built environment is tasked with delivering public goods—education, safety, sanitation and so forth—to large populations. This means that the city is implicitly understood as being a shared—and hence public—space. On the other hand, the lack of equitable access to urban resources worldwide requires the designation of critical public spaces, where social goods can be more equitably redistributed.

On 20 July 1979, China Merchants fired the 'first shot' of China's reform and opening up by detonating a section of Sixth Bay and enlarging the natural harbor to begin construction of the Shekou Industrial Zone. Shekou was selected because it was located near the Port of Hong Kong as well as China Merchants' Hong Kong offices. The Industrial Zone's earliest industries were related to shipping and ship repair and included light industry, catering and tourism services, as well as manufacturing for export. As the Shenzhen government did in Luohu-Shangbu, the Shekou Industrial Zone also studied the experience of foreign free trade and export processing zones, making infrastructure construction and employee recruitment top policy priorities. This level of coordination meant that the Industrial Zone's Management Committee operated as a *de facto* government of Shekou independent of Shenzhen. Consequently, Shekou's experience has come to represent an alternative origin for Shenzhen. In 1981, for example, at the entrance to the Shekou Ferry Terminal where the 'first shot' had been fired, the Shekou Industrial Zone erected a billboard that read, "Time is money, efficiency is life" (时间是金钱，效率是生命). The slogan was immediately controversial because it not only celebrated earning money but also framed earning money as a moral virtue, begging the question: When Shekou's charismatic leader, Yuan Geng, erected the sign was he 'selling out' the Chinese Revolution? Or was something else at stake?

The circulation of news creates an alternative 'public' by linking markets, ports, salons and offices via newspapers that report on information of use to ordinary people rather than the government; the 'public' that reads newspapers is not exactly the same 'public' that is the object of state policies. Habermas (1991) has identified the emergence of the bourgeois public sphere with the rise of the traffic in news that supported the traffic in commodities as the modern world system grew. In this reading, 'public opinion' is an organized attempt to understand the spatial (and spatializing) consequences of global value chains from a non-governmental perspective. Sometimes this perspective can be identified with a specific geographic entity (like a city, for example), but more often than not, it is identified with a particular set of users, whose interests necessarily cross geographic boundaries. The creation of a local public sphere is a critical effort to locate a city within and against other places on co-created value chains. And here, suddenly, abruptly, the slogan 'time is money' blurs the distance between Philadelphia 1748 (at the start of the second industrial revolution) and Shekou 1981 (when late developers such as China began mass modernization). Under Benjamin Franklin's editorship, *The Pennsylvania Gazette* became the most popular newspaper in the American colonies, while under Yuan's leadership, Shekou's small, local newspaper, the *Shekou Bulletin* (蛇口通讯报), cultivated a national subscription with stories that revealed the ways in which factories, leaders and other institutions abused public trust (Xu and Pan 2012). Both newspapers were 'watchdogs,' monitoring how well public institutions served the public.

Of course, the appeal of Fishing Village's nets-to-riches story is its simplicity: if we build a city according to certain standards, it will create a desirable lifestyle for all residents within a proscribed territory. The appeal of Shekou's story of watchdog institutions is in allowing a space for critical reflection on how well a city serves its resident population (i.e. public). The historical distance between Philadelphia and Shekou reminds us, however, to pay attention to how urbanization increasingly relies on centralized state action. Early developers, such as England and the United States; middle developers, such as Germany and France; late developers, such as the original East Asian tigers; and late, late developers such as China, have all required different levels of social organization in order to urbanize. Each successive generation of developers has not only required greater inputs of capital, investment goals, training programs and engineering but also access to larger hinterlands and markets in order to urbanize. Late developers have also required stronger government organizations to manage this social transition, including unequal access to the benefits of these policies, which have tended to be concentrated in national capitols and designated cities. The East Asian Tigers first grew their national hinterlands and then expanded via foreign policy into neighboring countries. In contrast, circa 1979 when the People's Republic of China (PRC) first used manufacturing for export to develop Shenzhen, the Chinese state controlled the third-largest national territory on the planet, providing it with both a vast hinterland and potential markets. What's more, the resources of this territory had already been organized within the Chinese state, facilitating the spatial reorganization from Third Front development of the hinterland to the development of coastal ports, begging the question of just how portable the Shenzhen model actually is.

Huaqiangbei, Chimerica: Hacking Global Value Chains?

Perhaps the most widely circulated example of North American 'first contact' with Shenzhen was written by Canadian author and illustrator Guy Delisle. Published in 2000, Delisle's *Shenzhen* sarcastically chronicled the narrator's encounters with "the smells, the noise, the crowds, the dirt everywhere" of the city, circa 1997 (Delisle 2006 [2000]: 7). Delisle went to Shenzhen to supervise animation, production layout and edge smoothing work for a French studio. His job embodied contemporary hierarchies of global cultural production, with 'creative work' located in Europe and North America and 'non-creative work' first located in Korea and Taiwan and then in the PRC. Readers imagined Delisle as experiencing

> the usual maladies of the long-term boarder: cultural and linguistic alienation, boredom, and cravings for Western food and real coffee [in] the hideously expanding 'Special Economic Zone of Guangdong Province,' a tariff-free city north of Hong Kong where the employers are foreign and the Cantonese locals are hungry
>
> *(Rall 2004: 72)*

Delisle's charcoal sketches evoke the stereotypical grime—material and spiritual—that English speakers have associated with industrial urbanization since Dickens and other Victorian reformers (Flanders 2012): cramped and repetitive work, unidentifiable and derivative spaces and an environment that is relentlessly, oppressively instrumental—one works until exhaustion for money that is insufficient to purchase objects of individualized desire. *Shenzhen* also took gendered hierarchies at face value, with young Chinese women translating for and otherwise facilitating the work of a hapless white male manager. Emphasizing the existential anxieties of living in capitalism's grim frontier, *Shenzhen*'s cover shows a solitary white man in a mass of Chinese figures.

English-language media, including *The Guardian*, *Time*, and the *New York Times* wrote positive reviews of *Shenzhen*, and the popular book review website *Goodreads* gave it 4.5 stars. Readers have raved about the quality of the book's illustrations while praising the text precisely because Delisle refused any meaningful engagement with Shenzhen, its residents and its national aspirations in order to better gripe about how horrible it is for a Westerner to live at "the grim frontiers of free trade" (Rall 2004: 72). One reviewer even asserted, "Delisle's keen awareness of how and why he can't connect to the city makes for a rarity: a thoroughly engaging memoir of being bored to distraction" (Wolk 2006). None questioned the book's description of Shenzhen's urban environment nor showed even passing interest in the inequalities of globalization which were so naturalized as to be invisible to its beneficiaries. In these reviews, Shenzhen didn't suffer from a lack of public spaces but rather from a lack of spaces for dedicated consumption; the Fishing Village model of urbanization was the assumed standard, with gendered translation service and access to recognizable commodities as expected as public infrastructure and noticeable only in their absence. At this moment of entitled blindness, we see precisely how commodity fetishism conflates with Shenzhen's nets-to-riches myth, where the city exists in and through consumption that is organized through the urban built environment.

It is notable that Delisle's French account of Shenzhen as capitalism's grim frontier was published in 2000, several years after companies located in the Shangbu Industrial Park had begun transitioning to produce mobile phones for China's domestic market, including *shanzhai* brands (Yang 2016), and the English account was published in 2006, when Shenzhen was de-industrializing its urban core by moving manufacturing to its outer districts and repurposing industrial parks for creative industries, including graphic design, architecture and tech innovation. The point, of course, is that Shenzhen's early factories produced consumer goods rather than intermediate products (such as turbines) that would be used by other industries. Consequently, much of the environmental pollution that Delisle experienced while in Shenzhen could have been attributed to urban construction rather than to heavy industry discharge and runoff, highlighting just how thoroughly Delisle and his readers conflated consumption and urban lifestyles and ignored (or didn't recognize) varieties of industrial manufacturing.

In the 2010s, North Americans were reintroduced to Shenzhen via Huaqiangbei, a rebranded section of the Shangbu Industrial Park. The British-produced WIRED documentary, *Shenzhen: The Silicon Valley of Hardware* (WIRED 2016), for example, used the area's narrow streets and crowded markets to illustrate a story in which creativity, hard work and free markets create new economic possibilities for individual makers who just happen to be predominantly male, English speaking and able to pursue their dreams wherever they take them. They were particularly pleased with the speed at which prototyping, production and shipping can be achieved in Huaqiangbei. After all, WIRED's *Shenzhen*, like Delisle's *Shenzhen*, presupposed a global manufacturing hierarchy in which unemployed North American and European inventors could obtain Chinese visas on the strength of their creativity and realize their dreams on Chinese assembly lines. What the documentary missed, however, is the relationship between access to public infrastructure and social organization. And this perspective—the city as a vehicle through which public goods are distributed—is precisely how Shenzhen has understood the rise of Huaqiangbei. Produced by Dushi (都市), a Shenzhen-based company, the documentary, *Decoding Shenzhen: The Huaqiangbei Backstory* (Dushi 2015) tells the story of Shenzhen's success as a story of successful public policy. The filmmakers point to Huaqiangbei as the spatial nexus where design, prototyping and manufacturing companies come together to produce new products for the market. Indeed, the Shenzhen filmmakers use 'Huaqiangbei' to emphasize the need for nimble institutions within the state apparatus.

As a globalized public space, Huaqiangbei redistributes resources that are critical to global value chains: spaces for design, components manufacturing and prototyping as well as links to factories and logics networks that will deliver finished goods to target markets. These resources are now considered 'public' in the sense that governments are held responsible for providing these resources to geographically bounded populations who can take advantage of them. As with the emergence of Luohu-Shangbu, the ability of the Shenzhen government to provide such a space is taken as a sign of its good public policies. However, it is also clear that this iteration and valuation of urban space—like the Fishing Village and *Shenzhen* narratives—hinges on consumption; Western makers praise Huaqiangbei because it allows them to purchase what they need to invent new gadgets, while Chinese businesses praise it for the policies that allow this kind of market to survive. What's missing from both these stories is the necessity of an alternative public *à la* Philadelphia and Shekou where once upon a time public opinion was thought to improve society through salons and a watchdog press. In this sense, it is telling that the success of Huaqiangbei has been the area's intensive support of open access goods (Lindtner et al. 2015). The success of Huaqiangbei cannot simply be attributed to its components markets or its formidable logistics network, but rather Huaqiangbei has succeeded because open access norms have constituted an alternative public.

Thus, in lieu of a conclusion, I'd like to posit that for both North Americans and Chinese people, Shenzhen's Fishing Village, repurposed factories and public infrastructure allow us to imagine our histories as cobbled together through material objects, even as we use these objects to tell stories that necessarily conjure diverse and possibly incompatible emotional experiences and intellectual understandings. In English, we might call this condition "Chimerica," a felicitous turn of phrase that not only combines China and America but also conjures the word 'chimera.' Simultaneously geopolitical and inter-cultural, innovative and oppressive, adaptable, whimsical, provisional, scary and global in its pretensions and reach, Chimerica comprises piracy, colonial expansion, international socialism, the Cold War, the rise of the East Asian Tigers and the era of Reform and Opening. Chimerica is also excruciatingly banal, suffusing everyday life and ordinary minds with a sense that suddenly, abruptly and even unexpectedly, we're all living intercultural lives but not the same intercultural lives and certainly not lives with the same values or, if with the same values, with different understandings of how to express those values in everyday life. We've been blindsided by globalization, and although Shenzhen's insertion into global manufacturing chains has been critical to what has happened in the postwar era and where we, as a planet, are headed, nevertheless we haven't reached agreement on what that means. In this sense, the Shenzhen experience not only echoes debates that have occurred and reoccurred since the Second Industrial Revolution began in the late 18th century but also shows up conflicting desires of industrial modernization. We want our cities to be truly public spaces, but we end up settling for limited public spaces and imagining that they are the solution to what remains a political problem—how do we create equitable lives for mass populations in the 21st century?

Acknowledgments

In addition to Nick Smith, who reminded me that it is always useful to return to Habermas when thinking through the tensions that vex the meanings of 'public,' I would especially like to thank the volume's editors, Miodrag Mitrašinović and Timothy Jachna, for their helpful responses to my original manuscript; this chapter is better for their input.

References

Anderson, E.N. (1972) *Essays on South China's boat people*. Orient Cultural Service.
CCP Central Committee (1984) *On rural work in 1984 (Guanyu 1984 nian nongcun gongzuo tongzhi)*. CCP Central Committee, 1 January.
Chen, B., Hu, G. and Liang, Z. (1991) *The secret of the Shenzhen sphynx (Shenzhen de sifenkesi zhi mi)*. Haitian Press.
Delisle, G. (2006 [2000]) *Shenzhen: A travelogue from China*. Drawn & Quarterly Press.
Deng, X. (1984) "Building a socialism with a specifically Chinese character." In: *Selected works of Deng Xiaoping, volume III (1982–1992)*. At: https://cpcchina.chinadaily.com.cn/2010-10/21/content_13918311.htm. Last accessed on 20 September 2020.
Dushi (2015) "Decoding Shenzhen: The Huaqiangbei backstory (Jiema Shenzhen: Huaqiangbei fengjing de beijing)." *YouTube Video*, Dushi, 1 April. At: www.youtube.com/watch?v=I2jRI76u5WE. Last accessed on 20 September 2020.
Flanders, J. (2012) *The Victorian city: Everyday life in Dickens' London*. Atlantic Books.
Graeber, D. (2011) "Consumption." *Current Anthropology* 52 (4). pp. 489–511.
Habermas, J. (1991) *The structural transformation of the public sphere: An inquiry into a category of bourgeois society*. MIT Press.
Lindtner, S., Greenspan, A. and Li, D. (2015) "Designed in Shenzhen: Shanzhai manufacturing and maker entrepreneurs." *Aarhus Series on Human Centered Computing*. At: www.researchgate.net/publication/280836923_Designed_in_Shenzhen_Shanzhai_Manufacturing_and_Maker_Entrepreneurs. Last accessed on 20 September 2020.
O'Donnell, M.A. (2017a) "Heroes of the special zone: Modeling reform and its limits." In: Bach, J., O'Donnell, M.A. and Wong, W. (Eds.) *Learning from Shenzhen: China's post-Mao experiment from special zone to model city*. University of Chicago Press. pp. 39–64.
Phillips, D.R. and Yeh, A.G.O. (1983) "China experiments with modernisation: The Shenzhen special economic zone." *Geography* 68 (4). pp. 289–300, October.
Rall, T. (2004) "Drawing behind the lines." *Foreign Policy* 142. pp. 72–76, May–June.
Samuel, L.R. (2014) *The American middle class: A cultural history*. Routledge.
Susman, W.I. (2003) *Culture as history: The transformation of American society in the twentieth century*. Smithsonian Institution Press.
UN-Habitat (2012) *Placemaking and the future of cities*. Draft, UN-Habitat and The Project for Public Spaces. At: www.pps.org/article/placemaking-and-the-future-of-cities. Last accessed on 20 September 2020.
UN-Habitat (2019) *The story of Shenzhen: Its economic, social and environmental transformation*. United Nations Human Settlements Programme (UN-Habitat).
Ward, B.N. (1985) *Through other eyes: Essays in understanding "conscious models"—mostly in Hong Kong*. Westview Press.
Webb, S. (2012) "The consumer-citizen: 'Life' magazine's construction of a middle-class lifestyle through consumption scenarios." *Studies in Popular Culture* 34 (2). pp. 23–47.
WIRED (2016) "Shenzhen: The Silicon Valley of hardware." *YouTube Video*, 5 July. At: www.youtube.com/watch?v=SGJ5cZnoodY. Last accessed on 20 September 2020.
Wolk, D. (2006) "Comics." *New York Times Sunday Book Review*, 3 December.
World Bank (1993) *The East Asian miracle: Economic growth and public policy*. World Bank Policy Research Report. At: https://documents.worldbank.org/en/publication/documents-reports/documentdetail/322361469672160172/summary. Last accessed on 20 September 2020.
Xu, L. and Pan, C. (Eds.) (2012) *Shekou subdistrict gazetteer (Shekou Jiedao Zhi)*. Haitian Publishers.
Yang, F. (2016) *Faked in China: National branding, counterfeit culture and globalization*. Indiana University Press.

8

INTERIORIZED URBANISM IN MACAU: MODEL CITY FOR POST-MAO CHINA

Tim Simpson

> In contemporary capitalism subjectivity is the product of a global mass industry.
> *(Maurizio Lazzarato 2014)*

In a seminar conducted in Brazil in 1984, the psychoanalyst and philosopher Felix Guattari spoke of the remarkable post-war transformation of the defeated and devastated Axis powers of Germany and Japan into two of the world's largest economies and most prosperous nations. Guattari noted that at the end of World War II, Japan was a completely destroyed society, both physically and psychically, but managed to emerge from that chaos to produce a genuine economic miracle. The success of Japan's post-war *political economy* was enabled by the country's emergent *subjective economy* and the production of a Japanese citizen appropriate to the new regime.

"They rebuilt a 'capital of subjectivity,'" Guattari said, and "invented a new type of subjectivity out of the devastation itself. The Japanese, in particular, recovered aspects of their archaic subjectivity, converting them into the most 'advanced' forms of social and material production" (quoted in Lazzarato 2014: 8).

The People's Republic of China (PRC) likewise emerged from its own period of post-war depredation to become a global economic powerhouse. In 1978, as the country emerged from the chaos of the Cultural Revolution, paramount leader Deng Xiaoping tentatively tested market reforms in the new Special Economic Zones (SEZs) of the Pearl River Delta region, which the central government has recently rebranded the "Greater Bay Area" (GBA).[1] These economic zones were designed to serve as *laboratories of capitalist production*, where China would experiment with a new capitalist regime (Chung et al. 2001). The explosive outcome of this experimental "market-socialist" economy, or what Deng called "socialism with Chinese characteristics," was a decade of sustained double-digit economic growth at the turn of the 21st century.

To achieve this result, China likewise reached back to recover formative elements of the country's Confucian culture which Mao Zedong had sought to eradicate, and combined them with socialist and capitalist components (Simpson 2018). For example, in *The Enigma of*

FIGURE 8.1 The Venetian Macao Resort, one of the world's largest buildings.
Source: Adam Lampton.

Capital, David Harvey suggests that both the Great Leap Forward and the Cultural Revolution inadvertently created new "mental conceptions" and underlying social conditions that ultimately played a part in China's subsequent economic revolution (Harvey 2010: 137). Today, China's reform-era political economy, like Japan's before it, is situated in a new *subjective economy* and relies on a nascent "post-socialist" Chinese consumer citizen who is poised to contribute to the country's economic development.

This chapter concerns the role of the former East Asian Portuguese colony of Macau in this process, and the formative function of the pseudo-public spaces of the city's new integrated casino megaresorts in China's subjective economy. The GBA region, in which Macau is located, is the engine of China's economic reforms, and Macau serves today as an experimental *laboratory of consumption* for market-socialism, a sort of mirror image of the productivist economic zones of Shenzhen and Zhuhai, located just across the border. To analyze this process, I will pay particular attention to Macau's Venetian Resort, which is one of the largest buildings in the world, and its role as an encapsulated and interiorized "model city" for China's reform economy (see Figure 8.1).

Chinese Tourists in Macau

To understand the function of Macau's megaresort spaces in processes of consumer subjection, we must start with the tourists themselves. The large majority of the nearly 40 million tourists who visited Macau in 2019 came from mainland China, making the tiny city one of the most popular destinations for Chinese travelers (Newsdesk 2020). Macau encompasses a peninsula and two small islands that are located on China's southern coast, approximately 40 kilometers from Hong Kong. Portugal returned Macau to the PRC in 1999 after nearly half a millennium of colonial administration, and, like Hong Kong, the city was designated a Special Administrative Region (SAR) under China's One Country Two Systems regime. Macau is the only site of legal casino gambling in the PRC, and tourism to Macau is driven primarily by the city's casino gaming attractions.

Macau's phenomenal popularity with Chinese travelers is in part the result of recent policies implemented at both the local and national scales, which have facilitated mainland tourist travel and enabled a significant influx of transnational capital, the investment of which has markedly transformed the post-colonial cityscape.

After the handover of Macau's sovereignty in 1999, local officials in the new SAR government dismantled Macau's 40-year-old gambling monopoly concession and opened the industry to foreign investment. The liberalization of the gaming industry coincided with a new PRC central government-administered exit visa policy, called the Individual Visit Scheme (IVS), which was introduced in 2003 and which allows mainland Chinese citizens from select cities and provinces to travel to the SARs of Macau and Hong Kong as individual tourists without having to join a state-sanctioned group tour. Foreign gaming operators from North America, Australia and Hong Kong who were awarded new casino concessions in Macau have invested tens of billions of dollars constructing integrated casino resorts in an effort to attract these tourists. As a result, the city has become the world's most lucrative site of casino gaming (Simpson 2014). Macau now boasts the second-highest per-capita GDP of any country or jurisdiction in the world, and the International Monetary Fund predicts that Macau will soon overtake Qatar to become the per capita wealthiest territory on the planet (Fraser 2018).

In addition, the construction of these megaresorts has essentially enclosed and privatized a significant portion of the former public space of the tiny city, and these new interiorized urban environments play a functional role in China's economic reforms (see Figure 8.2). Macau's post-colonial development has coincided with China's National New-Type Urbanization Plan, a set of nation-wide policies that the central government implemented in 2014 with the aim of rapidly urbanizing hundreds of millions of rural Chinese residents (Griffiths and Schiavone 2016). The plan's macroeconomic logic is based on the assumption that the residential and lifestyle purchases of these new urbanites will create a domestic consumer economy powerful enough to wean the PRC off the unsustainable production-for-export regime with which Deng jump-started economic reforms in 1978.

Key to this *macro economic* plan is a complementary *micro-physical* effort to enhance the "quality" (*suzhi*, 素质) of Chinese citizens. Since 1978, China's central government has introduced a series of policies whose intention has been to reverse the Mao-era pro-natal emphasis on building population *quantity* in order to promote citizen *quality*, with hopes to produce a population of educated, refined and self-enterprising citizens who are prepared to compete in the global marketplace.

"Quality" delineates both the "*physical and quantifiable features of the body*," which is conceived as a "material substance that can be physically shaped and administered" to a desired outcome, and personal conduct that may be "measured in terms of ethical, moral, and cultural value" (Sigley 2009: 547). That is, "quality" is conceived as an individual's palpable physical, intellectual and ethical characteristics, which may be molded and enhanced to conform to the goals of the state. Mobility itself is a state-certified mark of such distinction, and

FIGURE 8.2 Simulated Lisbon cityscape and privatized public space enclosed under glass atrium in the MGM Macau Resort. Valkyrie Octopus installation above the aquarium centerpiece by artist Joana Vasconcelos.

Source: Adam Lampton.

cross-border travel is a means for a citizen to amass levels of personal quality (Nyiri 2010). Therefore, as a popular destination for mainland tourists, Macau's megaresort environments are a prime site for cultivating the "quality" of Chinese tourists.

The Greater Bay Area Metropolis

One key focus of China's urbanization plan is the massive metropolitan environment that stretches across the GBA, which covers 50,000 km² and has a population of upwards of 120 million people, and which sociologist Manuel Castells describes as "the most representative urban face of the twenty-first century" (Castells 2000: 439). This metropolis is the epicenter of China's market reforms and the logistic heart of the country's post-socialist enterprise.

However, the GBA megaregion is not a conventional metropolis with an organic development and consistent composition. Rather, this space is a completely contrived "city," composed of a variety of distinct and differentiated locales, which have been assembled into a remarkably dynamic whole. These elements include economic zones, administrative regions, Coastal Open Cities, factory towns, urban villages and reclaimed islands. Each of these locales is designed to fulfill a specific function in regional economic activities and to articulate with global capitalist networks.

In 2001, architect and urbanist Rem Koolhaas, along with a group of post-graduate students enrolled in the Harvard Graduate School of Design, published a study of the GBA region entitled *Great Leap Forward* in which they refer to this entire megacity region as the "city of exacerbated differences" (COED). Whereas a "traditional city strives for a condition of balance, harmony, and a degree of homogeneity," they argue, the Chinese COED "is based on the greatest possible difference between its parts—complementary or competitive" (Chung et al. 2001: 704). These scholars suggest that Macau, along with China's other European colonial concessions, actually *inspired* the COED design of the region (Chung et al. 2001: 83). Today Macau's distinctive characteristic in the GBA, or its "exacerbated difference," lies in the city's casino gaming regime. The specific function of Macau's casino megaresorts in this metropolis becomes clear only when the resorts are considered within the context of this differential urban logic.

Scholars have coined the terms "megalopolis" and "megacity" to characterize expansive late-20th century urban developments such as the GBA (Gottman 1961; Perlman 1976). However, while both terms are relevant for describing this region, the Chinese case is distinct. The *megalopolis* is the urban product of a distinctly *post-Fordist* political economy, typified by the flexible accumulation that emerged in the United States after 1970; while the *megacity* is a *post-colonial* phenomenon common in the developing world and resulting from the demise of Europe's colonial project at the same time (McGrath and Shane 2012). Whereas the GBA metropolis today in some ways encapsulates both of these socio-economic conditions, it is also a *post-socialist* urban space, a *megacity with Chinese characteristics*, and for this reason, it is better understood as exemplary of what Lewis Mumford (1971), writing in a different context, called a *megamachine*.

As I will explain in the following, this megamachine concept clarifies the GBA's role in a *subjective economy* that is central to China's reform era. Viewing the GBA metropolis as a megamachine will allow us to understand Macau's function as an urban *laboratory of consumption* in which subjectivity itself becomes the object of experimental policies. Because of its unique colonial history, peripheral coastal location and immense popularity as a destination for mainland tourists, Macau is a unique *spatio-temporal nexus* of China's macro-economic program of urbanization and the micro-physical comportment of quality consumers, and the city's megaresorts exemplify this spatial subjectivation of urbane consumer citizens.

The Greater Bay Area Megamachine

Mumford described the megamachine in his three-volume *Technics and Civilization*, an exploration of humanity's historical relations to tools and technology (Mumford 1971: 308). In conceptualizing the megamachine, Mumford referred not to a city *per se* but to a machine-like social mechanism, a sort of biopolitical automaton that incorporates regimented human subjects into its component parts.

The prototype megamachine was the archaic human effort that constructed Egypt's pyramids with nothing more than the primitive technologies of the lever and inclined plane. In this *social machine*, "human beings themselves are constituent pieces of a machine they compose among themselves and with other things (animals, tools) under the control and direction of a higher unity" (Deleuze and Guattari 1987: 456–457). Mumford observed a contemporary megamachine operating in the post-war United States military-industrial complex, enabled by that era's "organization man" and symbolized by the Pentagon.

My appeal to the *megamachine*, rather than the *megacity*, to describe the GBA metropolis is indebted to Guattari's exploration of the role of urban subjectivation in contemporary capitalism (Gensoko 2016). Guattari calls subjectivity the "key commodity" of capitalism, and contends that the infrastructural and architectural "enunciations" of the city are formative of specifically urban capitalist subjects.

Therefore, the GBA metropolis is a massive machinic apparatus which functions in a *subjective economy* that cultivates contemporary market-socialist subjects to rival the "new man" of Maoism. If the pyramid and the Pentagon were Mumford's trans-historical architectonic archetypes of the megamachine, Macau's Venetian Resort is one model of the operations of the GBA megamachine today.

The Venetian Complex

> Bigness no longer needs the city: it competes with the city; it represents the city; it preempts the city; or better still, it is the city.
>
> *(Rem Koolhaas 1995)*

Macau's Venetian Resort was conceived and constructed by Sheldon Adelson, the Las Vegas casino mogul and profligate conservative political patron, who was awarded a gaming concession in Macau after the handover. When it opened in 2007, the Venetian was the world's sixth-largest building. With a total interior area of 980,000 m^2, the Venetian is nearly twice as big as the Pentagon, and perhaps the largest overtly themed structure on the planet. Constructed on the virgin territory of Macau's Cotai land-reclamation site, it was the first property in what Adelson named (and trademarked) the Cotai Strip.

The Venetian is an encapsulated city-within-the-city, which employs thousands of people and accommodates within its walls a remarkable collection of facilities: 3,000 hotel rooms, 350 retail shops, 100,000 m^2 of convention space, a 15,000-seat auditorium, an indoor canal network and the world's largest casino. It also features restaurants, a spa and gymnasium, swimming pools, a children's playground, private bus fleet and a training facility operated in cooperation with a local university. In addition, the Venetian's Malo Clinic, which provides dental implants, breast augmentation and other forms of cosmetic surgery, is the largest such facility in the region and the only one located inside a casino resort.

The Venetian is the anchor of Adelson's multi-resort Macau complex. This complex includes another of the world's largest buildings, the $4.4 billion Cotai Central Resort; the $2.7 billion Parisian Macau property, featuring a half-scale replica of the Eiffel Tower; and the five-star Four Seasons Resort. With his $10 billion stake in Macau, Adelson is China's largest foreign investor. The Venetian complex of buildings, which are each connected by enclosed and air-conditioned pedestrian walkways, collectively comprises what is perhaps the world's largest continuous interior space, a colossal enclosure with nearly 13,000 hotel rooms and 770 retail shops. The massive footprint of this edifice is all the more remarkable, given that at only 30.4 km^2, Macau is one of the world's smallest territories and, with a population of approximately 650,000, one of the world's most densely populated locales (Fraser 2018: A3).

Model City

Given its immense size, the construction of the Venetian Complex has privatized a significant portion of Macau's public space. The resort functions today as a sort of model urban environment for China's National New-Type Urbanization Plan and for a pedagogical program of "quality" consumption for tourists. As sociologist Borge Bakken demonstrates in *The Exemplary Society*, China has a long tradition of using educational models—such as model soldiers, workers, factories or villages—to guide ethical behavior (Bakken 2000). These exemplary models, which the Maoist government deployed to shape socialist China, inform my understanding of Macau as a *model city* for Chinese consumerism. The fact that Chinese tourists arrive in Macau well versed in such statist efforts of citizen education makes it useful to understand the city's attractions within the context of these Chinese educational techniques (see also McFarlane 2011).

As an interiorized *model city*, the Venetian foments an urban imaginary and maintains a normative mode of "urbanism as a way of life" which is consistent with the goals of China's urbanization plan and the country's economic reform regime. According to Louis Wirth, "urbanism as a way of life" is defined by a particular set of characteristics that include heterogeneity, density, anonymity, segmented roles and heightened mobility, as well as a mode of interpersonal contact with others that is superficial, impersonal and transitory (Wirth 1938). Wirth believed that these qualities shape a distinct urban personality.

Interestingly, each of these urban qualities was purposefully absent in the Chinese socialist city. Daily life for citizens in the socialist city was centered in the *danwei*, or work unit. The *danwei* combined work, accommodation, food, education, medical care, entertainment and all of the other components of the "iron rice bowl" provided by the socialist state. In essence, the *danwei* was a "spatial machine" for the (re)production of collectivist workers for the socialist economy (Bray 2005: 5). Given the encapsulated and insular nature of community

FIGURE 8.3 Interiorized urbanism in St. Mark's Square inside the Venetian Macao Resort; realistic cloud-flecked sky painted on the ceiling.

Source: Adam Lampton.

life, there was little use of urban public space outside of the *danwei*. Therefore, Chinese cities under socialism lacked the quality of "urbanism" which defined the modern European metropolis (Wu 2009). The interior urbanism modeled in the Venetian Complex, by contrast, reflects the logic of the post-socialist regime (see Figure 8.3).

Creating Quality Consumers

The Chinese central government uses tourism today to promote consumer spending, and the overriding goal of the tourist under this regime is to enhance individual "quality" as an urbane consumer. To that end, the retail offerings in the Venetian Resort are primarily focused on the refinement of the body: cosmetics, jewelry and fashion; spas, health clubs, foot massage, hair care and cosmetic surgery; and various other means of toning, refining and perfecting individual appearance. The resort activities participate in the literal practice of comporting consumer bodies and fashioning "quality" subjects.

In addition, shops in Macau's resorts stock such daily items as infant formula, diapers, shampoo, toothpaste and Chinese medicinal products, which are slightly cheaper than their mainland counterparts and whose compositional integrity and brand veracity are assured by their purchase in the city's relatively well-regulated retail environment. It is common to see Chinese tourists in Macau stuffing small suitcases with these quotidian items, or visiting tourist attractions while toting prepackaged plastic bags of promotional goods purchased at pharmacies or beauty product chains such as Watson's, Mannings or Sasa (see Figure 8.4).

FIGURE 8.4 Chinese tourists pack a suitcase with diapers and other everyday items purchased at shops in Macau.

Source: Adam Lampton.

FIGURE 8.5 Comportment of the quality tourist subject in the Venetian Macao Resort.

Source: Adam Lampton.

Such scenes demonstrate the ways in which Macau functions as a *laboratory of consumption* to cultivate those calculating consumers that China desires for its reform regime.

When contrasted with the socialist *danwei*, the Venetian model city ultimately naturalizes the privatization and commodification of public space, and normalizes the overarching conception of urban public life as a consumer realm.

Finally, on the Venetian's vast gaming floor, an innovative electronic baccarat game, which was designed by a Hong Kong biopharmaceutical company to appeal to Chinese tourists in Macau, functions to afford and enhance the calculative capacity of gamblers. This gaming machine translates baccarat, a simple game of chance, into a complex enterprise that requires each gambler to engage in forms of calculation and economic speculation that do not exist in conventional baccarat. This pedagogical gambling machine is a biopolitical apparatus of subjectivation and comports a calculating *homo economicus* characteristic of the post-socialist regime (Simpson 2019).

Therefore, the privatized public space and interior urbanism of the Venetian Complex, combined with the retail features and other consumption-oriented activities of the resorts, as well as the gaming machines in the casino, collectively function as spatial "enunciations" of Chinese consumer citizens (Simpson 2016). If China's SEZs transformed the country into the factory for the world, Macau's resorts and their post-socialist public spaces may be understood as factories for the "production of the self," a self that is understood as an "ability machine" of remunerative characteristics that maximize "quality" and competitive advantage (see Figure 8.5).

Macau's resorts complement other elements of China's consumer landscape that includes numerous public and private environments, such as mega shopping malls, gated communities, pedestrian shopping streets and theme parks, which collectively promote "urbanism as a way of life" (Wu 2005). While Macau's role in this process is not unique, in the Venetian Resort's massive interiorized model city, we may most clearly observe the logic of China's post-socialist urbanism and discern the consumer countenance of the country's post-socialist citizens. In short, this interiorized city exemplifies Macau's functional role in the GBA megamachine and in China's subjective economy.

Note

1. Most of the political leaders and academics I discuss in this chapter, including Deng Xiaoping, Manual Castells and Rem Koolhaas (and his colleagues), explicitly addressed the "Pearl River Delta" region in their commentary, but for the sake of convenience, I will adopt the more recent "Greater Bay Area" nomenclature.

References

Bakken, B. (2000) *The exemplary society: Human improvement, social control, and the dangers of modernity*. Oxford University Press.

Bray, D. (2005) *Social space and governance in urban China: The danwei system from origins to reform*. Stanford University Press.

Castells, M. (2000) *The rise of the network society* (2nd ed.). Blackwell.

Chung, C.H.J., Inaba, J., Koolhaas, R. and Leong, S.T. (Eds.) (2001) *Project on the city I: Great leap forward*. Taschen.

Deleuze, G. and Guattari, F. (1987) *A thousand plateaus*. University of Minnesota Press.

Fraser, N. (2018) "Macau 'set to be richest place on planet'." *South China Morning Post*, 8 August. P. A3.

Gensoko, G. (2016) "Postscript: for an urban machinic ecology." In: Frichot, H., Gabrielsson, C. and Metzger, J. (Eds.) *Deleuze and the city*. Manchester University Press. pp. 241–245.

Gottman, J. (1961) *Megalopolis: The urbanized northeastern seaboard of the United States*. Twentieth Century Fund.

Griffiths, M. and Schiavone, M. (2016) "China's new urbanization plan, 2014–20." *China Report* 52 (2). pp. 73–91.

Harvey, D. (2010) *The enigma of capital*. Oxford University Press.

Koolhaas, R. (1995) "Bigness or the problem of the large." In: *Small, medium, large, extra large*. Monticello Press. pp. 494–517.

Lazzarato, M. (2014) *Signs and machines: Capitalism and the production of subjectivity*. Semiotexte.

McFarlane, C. (2011) *Learning the city: Knowledge and translocal assemblage*. Wiley-Blackwell.

McGrath, B. and Shane, G. (2012) "Introduction: Metropolis, megalopolis, and metacity." In: Crysler, C.G., Cairns, S. and Heynen, H. (Eds.) *The Sage handbook of architectural theory*. Sage. pp. 641–656.

Mumford, L. (1971) *Technics and human development. Volume 1: The myth of the machine*. Mariner Press.

Newsdesk (2020) "Macau books 10.1% increase in tourists in 2019 to almost 40 million." *Inside Asian Gaming*, 22 January. At: www.asgam.com/index.php/2020/01/22/macau-books-10-1-increase-in-visitors-in-2019-to-almost-40-million/. Last accessed on 20 September 2020.

Nyiri, P. (2010) *Mobility and cultural authority in contemporary China*. University of Washington Press.

Perlman, J.R. (1976) *The myth of marginality: Urban poverty and politics in Rio de Janeiro*. University of California Press.

Sigley, G. (2009) "Suzhi, the body, and the fortunes of technoscientific reasoning in contemporary China." *Positions: East Asia Cultures Critique* 17 (3). pp. 537–566.

Simpson, T. (2014) "Macau metropolis and mental life: Interior urbanism and the Chinese imaginary." *International Journal of Urban and Regional Research* 38 (3). pp. 823–842.

Simpson, T. (2016) "Spatial machines of subjection: a materialist analysis of Macau's themed integrated casino resorts." In: Lukas, S.A. (Ed.) *A reader in themed spaces*. Carnegie Mellon University, ETC Press. pp. 183–193.

Simpson, T. (2018) "Neoliberal exception? The liberalization of Macau's casino gaming monopoly and the genealogy of the post-socialist Chinese subject." *Planning Theory* 17 (1). pp. 74–95.

Simpson, T. (2019) "LIVE baccarat calculations: Macau machine gaming and the production of the post-socialist subject." *Journal of Cultural Economy* 12 (6). pp. 521–538.

Wirth, L. (1938) "Urbanism as a way of life." *The American Journal of Sociology* 44 (1). pp. 1–24.

Wu, F. (2005) "Rediscovering the 'gate' under market transition: from work-unit compounds to commodity housing enclaves." *Housing Studies* 20 (2). pp. 235–254.

Wu, F. (2009) "Neo-urbanism in the making under China's market transition." *City* 13 (4). pp. 418–431.

9
A COMPARATIVE STUDY OF SPATIAL ANALYSIS AND RESIDENTS' PERCEPTION OF ACCESSIBILITY TO PUBLIC OPEN SPACE

Yang Xiaochun, Shi Ji, Pei Xiaochen, Li Jingsheng, Zhang Li

Introduction

Alexander defines public open space (POS) as "all open space of public value, including areas of water such as rivers, canals, lakes and reservoirs (not just land) which offer important opportunities for sport and recreation and also act as visual amenity" (Alexander 1977). POS is regarded as an essential part of the social infrastructure and the public welfare (Evert et al. 2010). It is "free for anyone to enter, where people are free to carry out various activities" (Nasution and Zahrah 2014). It is composed of "outdoor artificially developed places opened to all the citizens for free" (Yang and Hong 2009). Generally, streets are a very important POS in the urban context (UN-Habitat 2015), but in this study, streets were defined as the *paths to* POS for the users.

Well-planned POS with high spatial accessibility can encourage people to participate in outdoor activities to improve their health. Therefore, accessibility is an important indicator to represent the service capacity and equity of access to POS and other public service facilities (Nicholls 2001). Accessibility refers to the ease with which a site may be reached, being used as a measure that evaluates the relative opportunity for contact or use (Gregory et al. 1986). Miller (2007) asserts that evaluation methods for accessibility include space-based methods based on Hansen's work (Hansen 1959) and human-based methods based on Hägerstraand's work (Hägerstraand 1970). Similarly, the mechanical model and the empirical model (Sun et al. 2012) for evaluation of accessibility are also reported in the literature. The mechanical model is based on quantitative analysis of existing urban space structures and characteristics, such as supply ratios, distance to nearest POS or public service facility, cumulative opportunities-based measures and spatial interaction-based measures (Luo and Wang 2003; Guagliardo 2004; Chen et al. 2007; Song et al. 2010). The empirical model is based on the qualitative analysis of researchers' experiences and understandings and users' perceptions, mainly acquired by sociological methods of research. This classification is similar to that of Wang et al.'s geographic accessibility and perceived accessibility (2015). Based on a study by Miller (2007), Delafontaine et al. (2012) introduced a method to assess accessibility based on the combination of human and spatial methods.

Most research on POS has mainly considered the impacts of spatial factors (such as distance or time from POS to a residential area) and has applied spatial data of POS and streets as well as demographic data in mechanical models to evaluate accessibility of POS quantitatively. In practice, human motivation and perception of the environment also strongly affect people's willingness to go to POS. For instance, the previously cited study by Wang et al. indicates that perceived access is more important than geographic access or proximity in predicting park use (Wang et al. 2015). Curl et al. (2011) demonstrate that a discrepancy often arises between individuals' perception of access to POS and the evaluation results of the mechanical model, which only considers spatial factors. Therefore, it is necessary to articulate the concrete differences between the quantitative analysis of the mechanism model and the qualitative analysis of the empirical model to help urban planners configure adequate POS accessibility in relation to users' satisfaction.

The development of the cities of the Greater Bay Area, represented by Shenzhen, shows a typical high-density trend, and POS is increasingly becoming a scarce public resource in the urban built environment. From the perspective of space texture characteristics, high-intensity development has increased the difference between population densities in different areas. If the original simple planar distance index that ignores the weight of population density is still adopted to characterize accessibility, it will lead to neglecting the differences between different areas and bring about systemic imbalances in POS configuration at the meso-micro scale. From the point of view of post-use evaluation, different urban residents may feel differently about the same degree of quantitatively defined spatial accessibility; that is, there may be a significant deviation between spatial accessibility and perceived accessibility. The situation is particularly prominent in high-density development areas, in which residents' perception of the accessibility of POS may differ from its quantitatively measured accessibility, resulting in inefficient use or overcrowding. Therefore, in the situation of the Greater Bay Area's increasingly high-density urban development, based on the distribution of urban public space, we set out in this chapter to explore concise and effective accessibility evaluation methods for POS and then put forward research on strategies for the optimization of POS spatial patterns that can effectively reduce systemic imbalances and that are conducive to fair distribution of this public resource.

In the context of China's land use classification of POS, this study focuses on parks, squares and sports fields in the city of Shenzhen. This study took POS in the city's Nanshan District as a case study to make a comparison between quantitative spatial accessibility and perceived accessibility of POS in this district. It also explores the differences in spatial accessibility for people living in different residential buildings. For this purpose, this study selected two types of residential buildings to measure spatial accessibility of POS with a quantitative method and investigate the corresponding perceived accessibility qualitatively by traditional sociological methods of research. The research team then compared the results and concluded that the rationality and reliability of the quantitative spatial accessibility differed between different types of residential areas and that quantitative methods should be combined with a qualitative analysis to produce more reliable recommendations to be used in professional urban planning.

Spatial Accessibility of POS

Data Sources and Preprocessing

This study adopted the two-step floating catchment area method (2SFCA) model (Luo and Wang 2003) and made use of three kinds of data—spatial locations of POS, distribution of resident population in residential buildings and road network—to quantitatively calculate spatial accessibility from residential buildings to POS. In addition to several large country parks as non-built-up areas in the northern mountain areas (e.g. Tanglang Mountain) and several inner-city mountain parks (e.g. Dananshan and Xiaonanshan), there are 138 POSs in Nanshan's 187.17-km^2 total land area, including a municipal seashore park along the southern coastline (Shenzhen Bay Park) and several municipal parks in the inner built-up area (Figure 9.1). The total area of the POS is 7.98 km^2, which covers 4.25% of the total land area of Nanshan. The per-capita area of POS is 7 m^2, which is below the relevant standards of 10.4 m^2.[1] The entrances of POS were identified through Tencent street view (2015) and site survey.

There are two types of residential buildings distinguished in this study: general residential buildings (GRBs) and residential buildings as part of an urban village (UVRBs). GRBs are built by real estate developers, in accordance with building codes. Most are planned to have their own gardens or public green spaces, for residents of high socio-economic standing. UVRBs are built by local villagers with little consideration for POS. Also, the population density of UVRBs is much higher, while the living standards are lower than that in GRBs.

This study calculated spatial accessibility of POS based on the road network, including municipal roads, local roads inside residential areas walking paths between residential buildings and POS, sidewalks, pedestrian crossings, footbridges and underground passages.

Results of Spatial Accessibility Analysis

Figure 9.2 illustrates the results of spatial accessibility analysis of POS based on the buildings and kernel density of population in these buildings in Nanshan District. The values of spatial accessibility were classified into four levels with the method of nature breaks. The highest value of POS accessibility for a building was 179 m^2 per capita, and the lowest value was 0 m^2, which means there was no POS available within 10 minutes' walking distance. The following insights were revealed in this analysis:

1. The spatial accessibility to POS is relatively low in most areas with high-density population, especially in the UVRB areas shown in Figure 9.1.
2. The areas with good POS accessibility are concentrated in mature built-up areas. In addition to the current situation of villages, high-density development has reduced the available per-capita public resources.
3. Shenzhen Bay Park is a large municipal coastal park, and the population density of the adjacent areas is relatively low. However, the spatial accessibility of this POS is not high, due to an expressway between this park and residential areas, which necessitates the use of underground passages to access it.
4. The residential areas located in the northern area also have lower POS accessibility because of the low level of municipal service in this mountainous area.

Residents' Perceptions of POS Accessibility

Schema of Social Study

Parallel to the spatial accessibility study, an empirical study was conducted to gauge residents' perceptions of POS accessibility and their preference for using POS. This investigation

FIGURE 9.1 The distribution of the two types of residential buildings and their spatial relationships with POS.

Source: Authors.

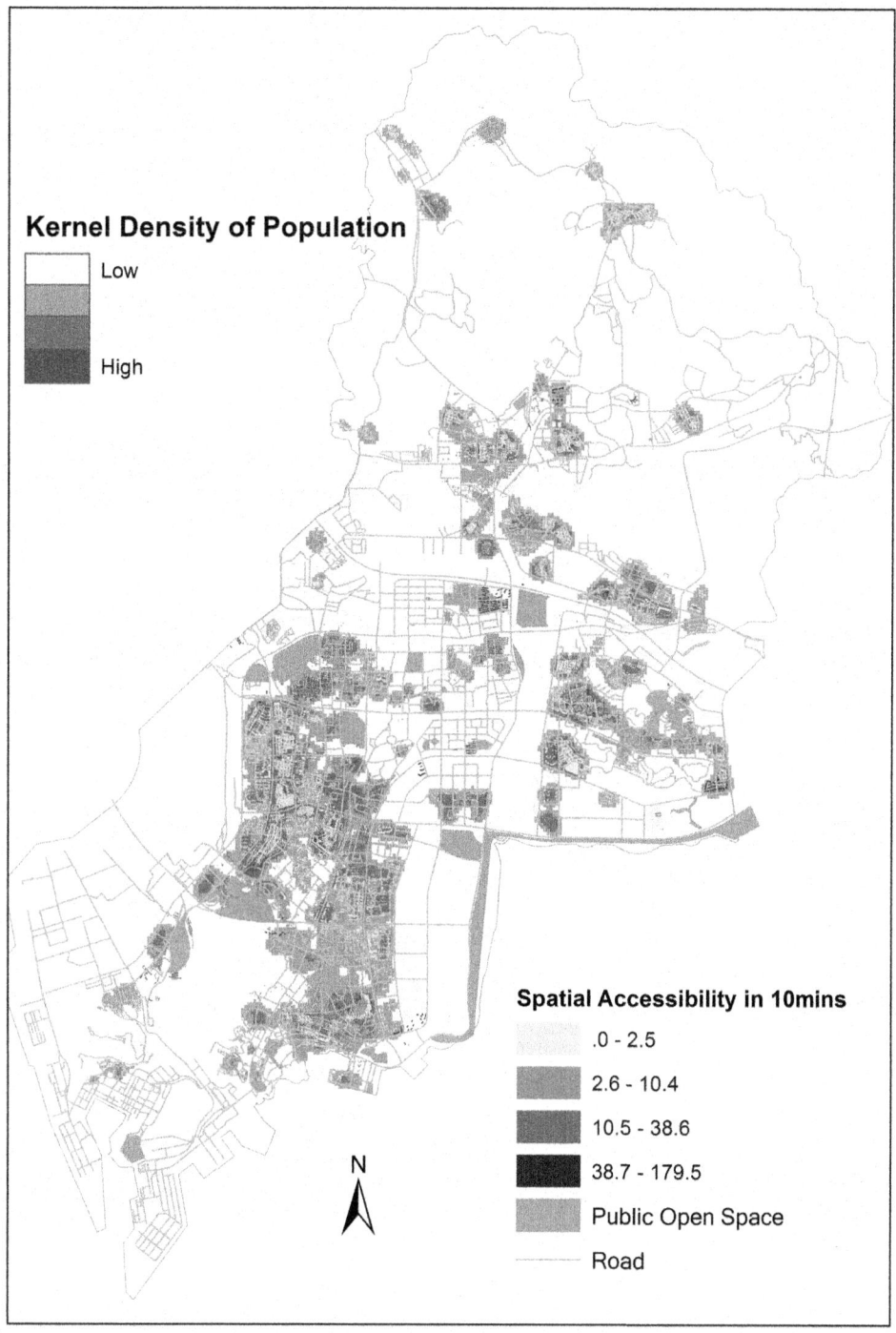

FIGURE 9.2 Estimated population kernel density and spatial accessibility to POS within 10-minute walking distance (2015).

Source: Authors.

included a site survey, interviews and a questionnaire in 29 selected areas. These areas were selected from the eight administrative sub-districts of Nanshan to include both UVRBs and GRBs and to include areas with different levels of spatial accessibility.

The purpose of the site survey was to analyze and understand the data on planning, investment, construction and administration of POS, while the interviews aimed to understand users' detailed preferences for using POS, as well as to verify the results of the site survey.

The questionnaire was used to collect users' personal information, perception of POS accessibility and preference for using POS. Table 9.1 lists the five questions posed on the latter two aspects.

Study Results

For Questions 2 and 3 in Table 9.1, 52% of respondents ($n = 409$) were able to access a POS within 10 minutes' walk of their residence, with 92% of them thinking that the distance was not far, and 46% ($n = 360$) of respondents were in the 10–30 minute range. Of these respondents, 67% found the distance acceptable. Only 2% ($n = 16$) respondents had over 30 minutes' walk to the nearest POS, with 63% of them thinking that it was far and 12% thinking very far.

With the increase of walking time from less than 10 minutes to over 30 minutes, the percentage of respondents who felt the distance to POS was far or very far increased from 8% to 75%. Only 2% of respondents spent over 30 minutes to access POS, but only 25% of this group thought that the distance was acceptable (not far). According to the answers to Question 1, the POSs to which respondents spend over 30 minutes to walk are Shenzhen Bay Park, Zhongshan Park, Sihai Park and Lixiang Park. All of these are large city parks with good facilities.

In response to Question 4, "How much time would you prefer to walk to POS from your home?" most respondents (64%) preferred to access POS in less than 10 minutes, while about 34% of respondents could accept 10–30 minutes, and only 2% found a walk to POS of more than 30 minutes acceptable.

The results indicate that a walking distance of up to 10 minutes is widely preferred by most residents; therefore, proximity is an important factor of usability for the daily use of POS. It is also to be expected that larger POS with better quality of facilities can attract people from further away.

TABLE 9.1 Questionnaire applied in this study.

Question	Alternative Items
Which POS do you often visit?	(specified by respondents)
How much time do you spend to get to POS generally?	Please specify the number of minutes: 0–10, 10–30, >30
Do you think it is far to walk from your home to nearby POS?	Very far, Far, Not far
How much time would you prefer to walk to POS from your home? (in minutes)	0–5, 5–10, 10–15, 15–20, 20–25, 25–30, 30–60, >60
Is the amount of POS nearby your home sufficient?	Abundant, Enough, Not enough, Absent

Comparison of Spatial Accessibility and People's Perceptions

Analyzing the relationship between accessibility as defined quantitatively and residents' perception of accessibility leads to a better understanding of the relationships between POS accessibility and resident satisfaction. This study adopted a one-way analysis of variance through Statistical Product and Service Solutions (SPSS) and revealed that residents of UVRBs were satisfied when the accessible POS area was more than 5.77 m^2 per capita. Residents of GRBs thought that 15.68 m^2 per capita was enough. This finding demonstrates that, although the actual per-capita accessible area is obviously different, residents' perceptions do not show the same degree of difference, as differentiated expectations for public amenities may be contingent on socio-economic status. Summarizing the upper and lower limits of 95% CI of UVRB/GRB residents' perception of POS and spatial accessibility in Table 9.2, it is obvious that there is a high degree of consistency in satisfaction with POS accessibility among UVRB

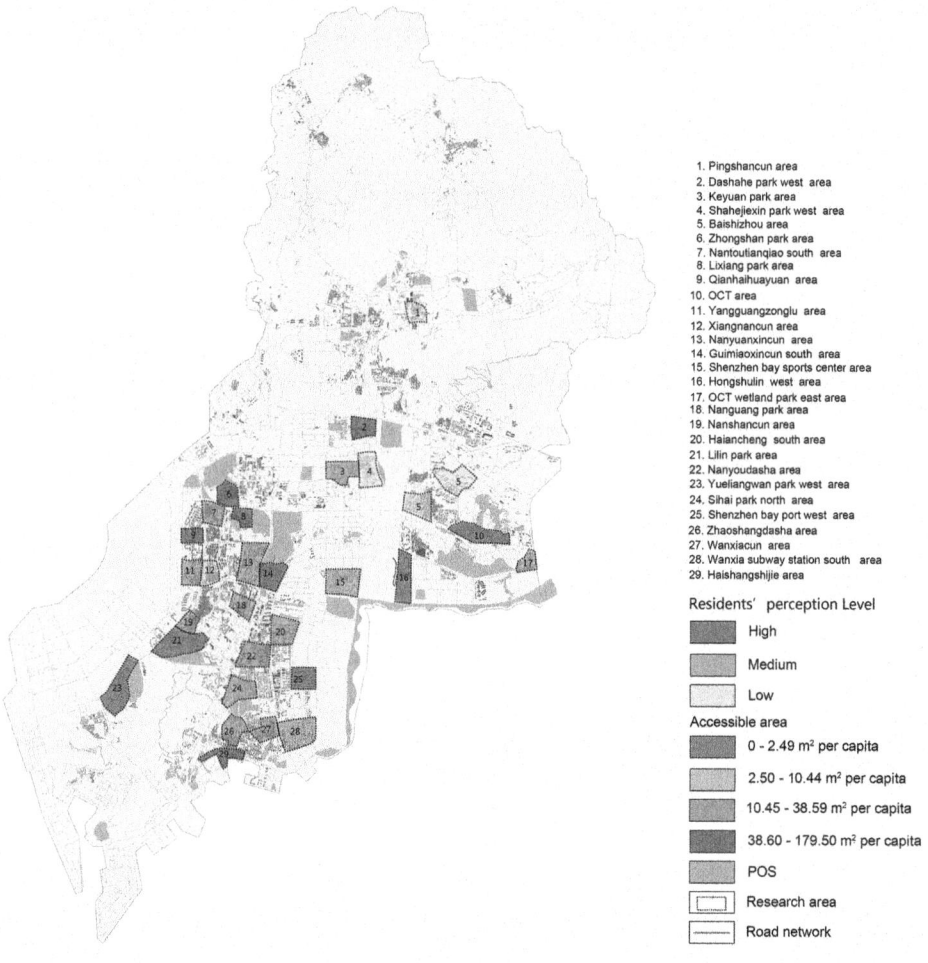

FIGURE 9.3 Comparison of spatial accessibility and residents' satisfaction by investigation area.
Source: Authors.

TABLE 9.2 Comparison of GRB and UVRB residents' perception of POS and spatial accessibility.

	Actual S.A. level	
	GRB	UVRB
Abundant	18–27	7–11
Enough	15–20	5–8
Not enough	13–19	3–4
Absent	5–18	0–3

TABLE 9.3 Residents' perception of accessible area of POS by investigation area.

ID	Investigation Area	Average Spatial Accessibility (m^2 per capita)	Residents' Perception		
			High	Medium	Low
17	OCT Wetland Park East Area (华侨城湿地公园东片区)	79.15		√	
2	Dashahe Park West Area (大沙河公园西侧片区)	70.50	√		
15	Shenzhen Bay Sports Center Area (深圳湾体育中心片区)	54.40		√	
28	Wanxia Subway Station South Area (湾厦地铁站南侧片区)	38.18		√	
23	Yueliangwan Park West Area (月亮湾公园西侧片区)	20.99	√		
14	Guimiaoxincun South Area (桂庙新村南片区)	19.11	√		
10	OCT Area (华侨城片区)	18.63	√		
13	Nanyuanxincun Area (南苑新村片区)	16.34		√	
21	Lilin Park Area (荔林公园片区)	14.98	√		
6	Zhongshan Park Area* (中山公园片区)	13.52	√		
16	Hongshulin West Area (红树林西片区)	10.45	√		
19	Nanshancun Area* (南山村片区)	9.81			√
4	Shahejiexin Park West Area (沙河街心公园西片区)	7.63			√
3	Keyuan Park Area (科苑公园片区)	5.31	√		
8	Lixiang Park Area (荔香公园片区)	4.80	√		
29	Haishangshijie Area (海上世界片区)	4.77	√		
24	Sihai Park North Area (四海公园北片区)	4.74		√	
26	Zhaoshangdasha Area (招商大厦片区)	3.68		√	
7	Nantoutianqiao South Area (南头天桥南片区)	2.26		√	
20	Haiancheng South Area (海岸城南侧片区)	2.07		√	
27	Wanxiacun Area* (湾厦村片区)	1.96		√	
1	Pingshancun Area* (平山村片区)	1.64			√
22	Nanyoudasha Area (南油大厦片区)	1.24			√
25	Shenzhen Bay Port West Area (深圳湾口岸西片区)	0.91	√		
18	Nanguang Park Area* (南光公园片区)	0.75		√	
5	Baishizhou Area (白石洲片区)	0.44			√
11	Yangguangzonglu Area (阳光棕榈园片区)	0.16		√	
9	Qianhaihuayuan Area (前海花园片区)	0.12		√	
12	Xiangnancun Area* (向南村片区)	0.03			√

residents, while there is more variation among residents of GRBs. The reason may be that resource constraints indicate higher sensitivity to the area of POS available, while when the POS area meets the basic demand, the residents' satisfaction with the accessibility of these areas is more affected by non-spatial factors. It may also suggest that in the case of insufficient land supply, a relatively lower level of POS area can be temporarily applied in low-income communities to ensure affordable public amenities.

Generally speaking, a comparison of the results of the two analyses reveals that:

1. Users with different socio-economic statuses may have different degrees of expectation for public space.
2. Broadly, the higher the quantitative level of spatial accessibility, the higher the satisfaction of residents. Basically, a medium level of satisfaction can be achieved when spatial accessibility is higher than 2 m^2 per capita. When the spatial accessibility is higher than 10 m^2 per capita, a high level of satisfaction is likely to be achieved.
3. Traffic conditions and administration of the POS can deeply impact residents' satisfaction with accessibility.
4. The quality and spatial organization of the POS can affect residents' satisfaction with accessibility.

Conclusion and Discussion

This study reveals that users' satisfaction with POS accessibility is not always consistent with quantitative spatial accessibility. In 72.4% of sample areas, residents' satisfaction with accessibility was consistent with quantitatively defined spatial accessibility, while in 27.6% of sample areas, the two were found to be divergent (the grey fields in Table 9.3). The consistent samples show that degree of spatial accessibility—which is confined by area and path distance—correlates with degree of perceived accessibility in a majority of the cases studied. However, the cases in which the two measures resulted in divergent assessments of accessibility indicate that other factors can intervene to disrupt this correlation. Qualitative aspects of the path via which the POS is accessed, the effectiveness of the management of the POS and the quality of POS and its spatial organization, for instance, might also be potential factors affecting users' perception. Therefore, while the provision of more POS, with attention given to its location *vis-à-vis* population distribution, could improve accessibility from the quantitative spatial analysis perspective, improving residents' satisfaction with POS accessibility must also rely on improving the quality the paths by which POS is accessed, the suitability of the design and provisions of these spaces for the community as well as reduction of management barriers that hinder the effective use of the space. Particularly in cases of limited land resources for the creation of new POS, such measures can optimize the perceived accessibility of existing public spaces in a city.

Another important finding is that people of different socio-economic status have different expectations towards POS accessibility. From the perspective of urban social equity, providing affordable housing in urban areas with high land prices can facilitate ease of physical access to employment in these urban areas for low-income people. The results of this study indicate that a lower level of POS accessibility in low-income communities can provide appropriate satisfaction with an affordable cost. This is an important insight in the endeavor to establish environments in which members of these communities can have access to both jobs and urban public spaces, requisite to their needs. Based on this study, a per-capita area of 5–8 m^2

POS can be recommended to be adopted in coming years as the accessibility configuration standard to ensure the basic quality of public space for low-income settlements in central Shenzhen, while POS exceeding 10.4 m² per capita could be considered surplus space. This criterion, and the insights into differential POS provisions offered by this study, could also inspire future studies to explore potential policy and governance strategies to promote quality of life for all, such as the potential of considering POS access in the taxation structure—for example, to be included in the higher-income housing tax—and using the excess tax obtained to subsidize POS and public amenities for low-income settlements. The study also leads to the conclusion that quantitative analysis accompanied with carefully designed qualitative analysis can help decision-makers to adopt appropriate measures to provide maximum accessibility to POS.

Acknowledgments

The research reported in this chapter was supported by the National Natural Science Foundation of China (NSFC) under the project: Research on Urban Public Open Space Accessibility Quantitative Analysis Based on Density Distribution, No.51478268

We are very grateful for Prof. Wenxiu Gao, Prof. Miodrag Mitrašinović and Prof. Timothy Jachna for insightful and constructive suggestions on the manuscript.

Note

1. In the Code for Classification of Urban Land Use and Planning Standards of Development Land GB50137–2011 (MOHURD 2011), the "per capita green space and square land area should not be less than 10.0 m²/person." In the Standard for Urban Public Service Facilities Planning (Draft for comments) (MOUHRD 2018), the provisions of the planning and construction land indicators for individual sports facilities in public sports facilities extrapolate that the area of urban public stadiums (sports spaces) is 0.22–0.42 m²/person. In Shenzhen, a higher level of 10.4 m²/person is adopted. Nanshan District has not yet reached these relevant standards.

References

Alexander, C. (1977) *A pattern language: Towns, buildings, construction*. Oxford University Press.
Chen, J., Liu, F. and Cheng, C. (2007) "Advance in accessibility evaluation approaches and applications." *Progress in Geography* 26. pp. 100–110.
Curl, A., Nelson, J.D. and Anable, J. (2011) "Does accessibility planning address what matters? A review of current practice and practitioner perspectives." *Research in Transportation Business & Management* 2. pp. 3–11.
Delafontaine, M., Neutens, T. and Van de Weghe, N. (2012) "A GIS toolkit for measuring and mapping space—time accessibility from a place-based perspective." *International Journal of Geographical Information Science* 26. pp. 1131–1154.
Evert, K.J., Ballard, E.B., Elsworth, D.J., Oquiñena, I., Schmerber, J.M. and Stipe, R.E. (2010) *Encyclopedic dictionary of landscape and urban planning: Multilingual reference book in English, Spanish, French and German*. Springer Science & Business Media.
Gregory, D., Johnston, R.J. and Smith, D.M. (1986) *The dictionary of human geography*. Blackwell Reference.
Guagliardo, M.F. (2004) "Spatial accessibility of primary care: Concepts, methods and challenges." *International Journal of Health Geographics* 3. p. 20.
Hägerstraand, T. (1970) "What about people in regional science?" *Papers in Regional Science* 24. pp. 7–24.

Hansen, W.G. (1959) "How accessibility shapes land use." *Journal of the American Institute of Planners* 25. pp. 73–76.

Luo, W. and Wang, F. (2003) "Measures of spatial accessibility to health care in a GIS environment: Synthesis and a case study in the Chicago region." *Environment and Planning B: Planning and Design* 30. pp. 865–884.

Miller, H. (2007) "Place-based versus people-based geographic information science." *Geography Compass* 1. pp. 503–535.

MOHURD (Ministry of Housing and Urban-Rural Development) (2011) *Code for classification of urban land use and planning standards of development land* (in Chinese). GB50137. At: www.mohurd.gov.cn/wjfb/201201/t20120104_208247.html. Last accessed on 20 September 2020.

MOHURD (Ministry of Housing and Urban-Rural Development) (2018) *Standard for urban public service facilities planning* (In Chinese, Draft for comments) GB 50442. At: www.mohurd.gov.cn/zqyj/201805/t20180522_236167.html. Last accessed on 20 September 2020.

Nasution, A.D. and Zahrah, W. (2014) "Community perception on public open space and quality of life in Medan, Indonesia." *Procedia-Social and Behavioral Sciences* 153. pp. 585–594.

Nicholls, S. (2001) "Measuring the accessibility and equity of public parks: A case study using GIS." *Managing Leisure* 6. pp. 201–219.

Song, Z., Chen, W., Zhang, G. and Zhang, L. (2010) "Spatial accessibility to public service facilities and its measurement approaches." *Progress in Geography* 29. pp. 1217–1224.

Sun, Z.R., Yin, H.W. and Kong, F.H. (2012) "Study on different calculation methods of park accessibility." *China Population, Resources and Environment* 5. pp. 162–165.

UN-Habitat (2015) *Global public space toolkit: From global principles to local policies and practice*. At: https://unhabitat.org/global-public-space-toolkit-from-global-principles-to-local-policies-and-practice. Last accessed on 22 September 2020.

Wang, D., Brown, G., Liu, Y. and Mateo-Babiano, I. (2015) "A comparison of perceived and geographic access to predict urban park use." *Cities* 42. pp. 85–96.

Yang, X.C. and Hong, T. (2009) "Rethinking for the systematic planning of urban public spaces—from Shenzhen to Hangzhou." *World Architecture Review* 世界建筑导报 24. pp. 100–103 (In Chinese).

10
RESPONSIBLE, REMOTE RESEARCH AND DESIGN OF THE PUBLIC REALM IN SHENZHEN

Georgeen Theodore

Schools of architecture, urban design and planning in the United States increasingly offer their students the opportunity to participate in international studios. Developing an understanding of different places and cultures is essential for the education of the next generation of global designers, and urbanism studios offer invaluable lessons towards developing this knowledge. However, there is a surprisingly limited academic debate on the best pedagogical practices for such studios.

Traveling abroad has a long tradition in the education of American architects (Ockman and Williamson 2012). In the United States, this tradition began in the 1800s when architects traveled to Paris to the *École des Beaux-Arts* to be trained in the classical European tradition. Today, many architecture students continue with this tradition by electing to study abroad for a semester in a school of architecture renowned for its design methodologies, that is, a particular school or style. Some schools of architecture work to bring this knowledge directly into their classrooms by inviting international practitioners as visiting professors. These cases—the early idea of going to Paris, attending a particular school, working with celebrated architects—all reflect an appreciation of "going to the source" of good design and learning "how it's done."

More recently, new research-based educational models enabling students to gain international perspectives have emerged. In many American schools of architecture, particularly in well-funded institutions, the so-called "travelling" studio or seminar has become a popular format. The sites and topics of these courses are not those that were typical in the Western "old world" of the *Beaux Arts* but instead are often located in dynamic metropolises in Asia and/or the Global South. In these courses, students benefit from being immersed in a completely different and foreign environment. This shift to non-Western cultures with a focus on urbanism as opposed to building traditions is exemplified by the Project on the City, an initiative started in the early 1990s and led by Rem Koolhaas at Harvard University's Graduate School of Design. Koolhaas and his students "[explored] the unstable urban conditions around the world at the turn of the 21st century, a tipping point at which the worlds' city-dwellers began to outnumber those in rural areas" (Chung et al. 2001). They focused on places such as Lagos and Beijing, among others, and famously published their work in

Mutations (2000) and *Great Leap Forward* (Chung et al. 2001). *Great Leap Forward* centered on the unprecedented growth and dynamism of China's Pearl River Delta, and this research served as a bellwether for the many studios and seminars focusing on this geographical area that have followed. Today, many American schools of architecture have ongoing studio and research initiatives in China, with the Pearl River Delta (PRD)/Greater Bay Area (GBA) a locus of much of this work. Indeed, as this volume demonstrates, this region continues to serve as the site of many different academic initiatives. Koolhaas' early urban research spotlighted the head-spinning pace of urbanization in this part of the world. His fascination with both the speed and extent of urban growth was expressed not through traditional architectural drawings of the city form but instead through statistics, bar and pie charts and aerial photography. As some critics have noted, this "view from above" did not interrogate the political histories of colonization or engage with "on the ground" everyday human experience (Gandy 2005). Koolhaas' Eurocentric perspective and infatuation with speed and size are reflected in other influential schools of urbanism, such as the work produced under the leadership of Richard Burdett at the London School of Economics' (LSE) Cities and Urban Age Program (Burdett and Sudjic 2010).

Koolhaas' impact remains significant. Indeed, many of the students who participated in the early years of Project on the City are active academics doing consequential work today. Yet the academic research mode of urban "exploration" (as practiced by Koolhaas and others) demands reconsideration as a method in architectural and urban education, particularly at the graduate level, due to significant demographic changes in student cohorts in the past twenty years. Today, the fastest-growing "ethnic" group in accredited programs in schools of architecture are international students. In 2009, international students accounted for 6% of the overall enrollment, while in 2018, the number increased to 21% (The National Architectural Accrediting Board 2018).[1] With these changing demographics, an internationally sited studio of an American school of architecture is likely to have students who identify as coming from the place or culture in which the studio is sited and which it interrogates, upending the critique that travelling studios are a form of "architectural tourism." Architectural education has become globalized, and therefore our understanding of what is foreign, exotic or "other" has changed and become more complex. The urban "explorer" of Koolhaas' 1990s model may no longer be relevant.

Given that architectural education and practice have become increasingly globalized in the past twenty years, the primary learning opportunities for international academic projects today are neither about "going to the source" of good design nor exploring exotic places but more broadly learning how to work in different contexts through careful observation and creative analysis. As an academic and a practitioner, over the course of my career, I have been mostly concerned about public space: what it is, who makes it, who uses it and the role and responsibility of the urban designer. I have interrogated these questions through teaching, writing and designing in the public realm at scales ranging from the object to the region. My methodology centers on techniques of observation, analysis, visualization and collaboration. I foreground the importance of lived experience, looking into the lives of others, generating multi-perspectival views of a place, learning from history and designing processes of collaboration.

This way of working has guided my teaching over the years. Over the course of fifteen years at New Jersey Institute of Technology (NJIT), I have iteratively developed and refined a studio curriculum around these principles. For this reason, in the first ten years of teaching,

I exclusively taught locally sited studios. With each course, I formulated exercises to ensure that students spent time at their site, talked to people, looked carefully at the physical environment and searched for clues about how people use space. In fall 2014, I decided for the first time to teach a non-local studio dealing with a site we could not visit. At that time, I had just completed three consecutive studios focused on rebuilding after Hurricane Sandy in the New York metropolitan region. These studios were conducted as part of the federally funded Rebuild by Design initiative for which I was leading an interdisciplinary, international team tackling sites and issues specific to New York and New Jersey. Our project sought to match local interests of public access to the river and bays with regional-scale water management measures. Working on the specific ways in which climate change played out in this region sparked my interest in looking at other delta cities. I found a great opportunity in an international urban design competition hosted by the Schindler Group and the *Eidgenössische Technische Hochschule* (ETH) Zürich that challenged students to create a district-scaled proposal in Shenzhen, China, in the Greater Bay Area.

The competition called for an urban design framework for future development in the Sungang Qingshuihe (SQ) District. The overall theme was mobility, which we interpreted broadly as including access to the public realm. At the time, city leaders had identified the district as an important, imminent redevelopment zone that would soon be connected to the rest of the city through a new metro line. In the documentation produced by the city government and consultants, the Planning Department envisioned a *"tabula rasa"* replacement of the existing warehousing and logistics of the district with new residential neighborhoods: a move considered necessary to house the exponentially increasing population. The site, a former important warehouse and logistics zone with significant rail infrastructure, had served as a key transfer zone for goods moving through Shenzhen from the mainland to Hong Kong. As the Shenzhen government opened up land north of the city for new industrial zones, SQ's warehouses and infrastructure were now viewed as obsolete vestiges of the early Special Economic Zone boom. The site was divided by an important east-west highway which provided excellent regional automobile connectivity but also created significant barriers to pedestrian circulation. Two lively and densely populated urban villages that served the migrant population marked the edge of a historic but degraded river system that had been channelized and covered up as the area was urbanized over the years. The site reflected a fascinating history specific to Shenzhen, yet at the same time, the site's challenges—the spatial and economic legacy of deindustrialization, lack of quality and safety in the pedestrian realm, housing insecurity and overcrowding, social exclusion and degradation of natural systems—represented the key urban design issues facing most global cities today. All in all, the competition offered a very interesting and challenging urban design problem for both the students and me.

However, given that I had always worked on sites that my students could visit, this particular project raised a set of pedagogical questions. I wanted the students to develop an understanding of local conditions and practices, yet since they were thousands of miles from Shenzhen, the types of on-site exercises I usually led were not possible. The primary pedagogical question for me was: how could I develop a studio process grounded in my foundation of close observation, looking and listening without visiting the site?

To begin to answer this question, for the first part of the semester, I created a series of exercises to encourage studio participants to develop a sense of lived experience on the site. My approach here was journalistic, rooted in cultural anthropology and ethnography. To start, the students and I read Leslie Chang's powerful *Factory Girls: From Village to City in a Changing*

China (2009). Chang's book describes the lives of young women who migrate from China's hinterland to places like Shenzhen in search of work and a more independent life. Her book strongly influenced my thinking about the project and established a particular human lens through which to see the city. I found Cheng's journalistic application of the social science research practice of longitudinal study—following and observing a subject through time— particularly inspiring. Following this reading, I asked each student to identify and research a person from Shenzhen and then to create a visualized portrait of that person that explained the reason for their selection. They had to research this person, through journalistic accounts, books, films and/or videos. Based on this research, students were challenged to use their visualization skills to illustrate the daily or weekly itinerary of their selected Shenzhen subject, looking for ways to reveal something about the city's organization. While some students interviewed friends or acquaintances (for example, one student had family in Shenzhen), the majority worked mostly online. Students read newspaper articles and personal blogs, watched films and YouTube videos and scoured social media for Shenzhen and SQ posts. This research also included countless hours reviewing publicly available satellite images, street maps and street and indoor view perspectives to become familiar with, and knowledgeable about, the built environment of the site.

With these visualized itineraries, many students examined the social and economic trajectories of migrants on the site who were arriving as factory workers and then growing into small-scale entrepreneurs. The portraits they developed helped cultivate an understanding of the aspirations of migrants and also the many challenges they faced, including high housing costs, disconnection from family support and limited mobility.

As the semester progressed, we developed a series of analytical thematic maps. We continued to hone these techniques of "seeing" the site from afar. For example, one student, Lauren Martin, spent hours "walking" the streets through Baidu Maps "Street View" to better understand pedestrian mobility.[2] Through this digital derive, she identified paths and passages but also barriers and blockages. She synthesized these careful and extensive observations into a pedestrian network map that ultimately informed our final proposal.

The studio created a collaborative digital map of all of the observations and data collected. This online, spatialized catalogue ultimately became the basis for our coded "clues" map. In the "clues" map, each color represented a different group of physical artifacts and conditions: black for transportation, purple for logistics and warehousing, pink for businesses, orange for housing and green for natural systems. In addition to representing what we found, we also included our own observations, which formed the beginnings of the studio's proposal.

In creating these illustrations, one of our earliest observations was that for what was considered an obsolete industrial zone, the site was extremely active. As the clues map indicates, there were clusters of businesses (seen in the map in the lower left) and of logistics (seen in the map in the upper right). We learned that because of the particularities of land ownership, many of the state-owned enterprises subdivided and leased their larger warehouses to microenterprises as they waited for the government's redevelopment plan for the district. These land-banking practices had incubated very specific agglomeration economies, particularly related to the home improvement and automotive retail sectors. The site had, under the radar, become a hothouse for start-up micro enterprises.

Through this observational process supplemented with historical research, we came to certain conclusions organized by theme. The growth of micro enterprises, which benefit small and mid-sized firms as opposed to big multinational companies, should be strengthened rather than displaced. The Urban Villages (城中村) had grown and evolved over time, offering affordable (albeit cramped and dark) housing and a vibrant quasi-public realm. The truck and train transportation infrastructure that makes this site so strategic for businesses does not serve workers' day-to-day mobility needs. At the time, there were no mass-transit options in the district. The site's natural systems had been either suppressed or destroyed: mountains had been leveled, wetlands destroyed and the river network altered beyond recognition. The Buji River and its tributaries have been channelized, polluted and sometimes run dry. With an incinerator plant just to the northwest of the site, air quality in the district was harmful.

Our project, "SEZ to EZX: Shenzhen Xrossroads," proposed that rather than starting again and remaking the site anew, 2Sungang-Qingshuihe should build on what it already had going for it: existing agglomerations of small and mid-sized firms, clusters of urban villages, incredible road and rail infrastructure and a nearly lost network of rivers. Our vision is the EZX, a next-generation economic zone that facilitates the growth of migrant business enterprises (MBEs) and offers a mix of housing options that will help retain the migrant population. The vision was shaped not by clearing the site and applying a known urban development model but through trying to understand what was already happening there and working to strengthen local dynamics. This endogenous approach began with visualizing the

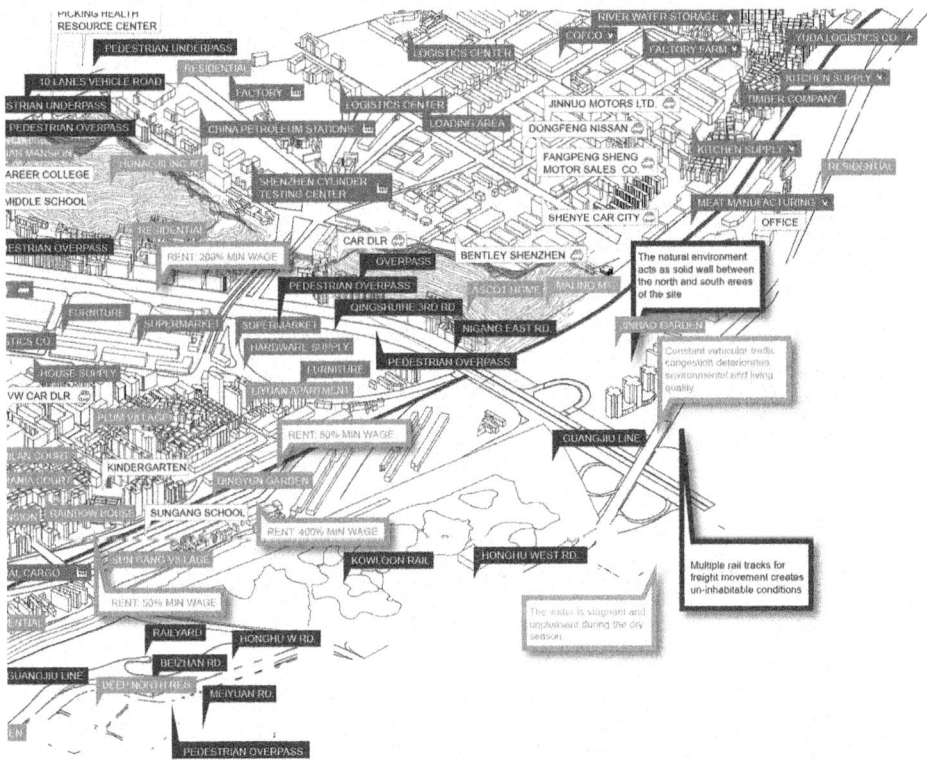

FIGURE 10.1 Detail of the "Clues" map. Each color represents a different thematic group of physical artifacts and conditions on the site. Also included are short narratives and data sets related to each group, shown in the larger white labels.

Source: Author.

Responsible Design of the Public Realm   125

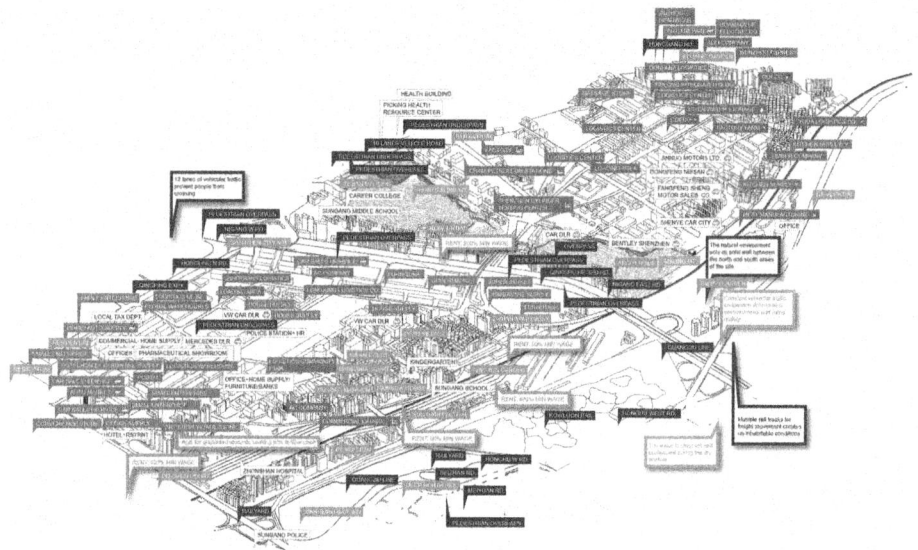

FIGURE 10.2   The "Clues" map was one of the drawings we developed early in the process, a cloud of color-coded observations that the students had collaboratively collected.

Source: Author.

existing conditions through a variety of drawings, including the "clues" map, and coming up with new models and policies that strengthened those existing conditions.

My students ultimately got to visit the site to make their own firsthand observations. Our team was selected as one of twelve winners, and I went together with my students to receive their award: fourth place in a field of around 250 entries. It was interesting how many of the students were surprised that their observations from afar were not that far off. They felt they knew the site intimately, and when they arrived, it felt eerily familiar.

Based on my first experiences of conceptualizing and teaching a remote studio, I have continued to develop this model in different locations around the world. Each academic year, I try to teach one local studio and one remote global studio, and I believe that this iterative practice of shifting perspectives is enriching. Since the Shenzhen studio, I have continued to develop and test this pedagogy in studios with sites in London, England (2016); Athens, Greece (2018); Mumbai, India (2018); and Lima, Peru (2020). I have continued with exercises that help students "see" from afar as I have described in the Shenzhen case. But I have also introduced new practices: in the Athens studio, I experimented with new ways of helping studio participants to "see" a place through a local peer. Here, we established local academic partnerships with the University of the Aegean and the National and Kapodistrian University of Athens, and each NJIT student was paired with an Athens-based student to collaborate on site observations.

I have learned that while some things become clearer through visiting, the mediated view from afar opens another specific window. I believe that my method of looking from these different perspectives, and of looking very carefully and intensively through a particular lens, has great value. One could call it an *oligoptic approach* in which we could "see a few things well"

(Latour 2007). The students were forced to be opportunistic in finding ways to see, and they had to look more carefully than they would have on a project close to home. I believe they honed and refined their observational skills.

As I am finalizing this chapter, we are enduring a global pandemic brought on by the novel coronavirus, COVID-19. As we practice social distancing and continue to quarantine, we have also been conducting our classes remotely. We continue to face a global ecological crisis, including the catastrophic sea level rise. International air travel has massively contributed to this via its massive carbon footprint and also by enabling the global mobility of pathogens. Designing remotely can help us understand places that are different from our own, and this makes us both better designers and better human beings. Developing ways to do this remotely and collaboratively is necessary and more urgent than ever.

Acknowledgments

The project SEZ to EZX: Shenzhen Xrossroads was produced in the fall 2014 Master of Infrastructure Planning (MIP) program at New Jersey Institute of Technology's College of Architecture and Design, by Gabriel Cañizo, Vincess Dimayuga, Grace Dong, Morgan Jones, Alexander LaFranco, Lauren Martin, Matthew McCabe, Monali Patel, Milena Popow, Matthew Potter, Eka Pramuditha and Esther Zipori, under the supervision of Professor Georgeen Theodore, AIA. I would like to thank NJIT's Maya Gervits, PhD, Director of the Littman Architecture Library, and Associate Dean John Cays for their support of research into the history and demographics of schools of architecture.

Notes

1. The demographics of graduate architectural education are likely to change in the wake of the COVID-19 pandemic.
2. Baidu Maps served as the primary source of this imagery. Baidu Maps is the mapping service of Baidu, the Chinese equivalent of Google (which is banned in mainland China), a desktop and mobile web mapping service application and technology offering satellite imagery, street maps, street view and indoor view perspectives, as well as functions such as a route planner for traveling by foot, car or with public transportation. See: http://map.baidu.com/. Last accessed on 14 July 2020.

References

Burdett, R. and Sudjic, D. (Eds.) (2010) *The endless city: The urban age project by the London school of economics and Deutsche bank's Alfred Herrhausen society*. Phaidon.
Chang, L. (2009) *Factory girls: From village to city in a changing China*. Random House.
Chung, C.H.J., Inaba, J., Koolhaas, R. and Leong, S.T. (Eds.) (2001) *Project on the city I: Great leap forward*. Taschen.
Gandy, M. (2005) "Learning from Lagos." *New Left Review* 33. pp. 37–53.
Koolhaas, R., Boeri, S., Kwinter, S., Tazi, N. and Obrist, H.U. (2000) *Mutations*. Actar.
Latour, B. (2007) *Reassembling the social: An introduction to actor-network-theory*. Oxford University Press.
The National Architectural Accrediting Board (2018) *2018 annual report on architecture education*. p. 11. At: www.naab.org/wp-content/uploads/2018_NAAB-Annual-Report.pdf. Last accessed on 14 July 2020.
Ockman, J. and Williamson, R. (2012) *Architecture school: Three centuries of educating architects in North America*. The MIT Press. pp. 80–81.

11
SOUL OF THE CITY: PUBLIC SPACE AND URBAN PLANNING IN HONG KONG

Bo-sin Tang and Siu Wai Wong

Introduction

Public space defines the essence of urbanity and can be seen as the "soul" of a city. Great cities are not just characterized by a concentration of high-rise buildings, population and activities. They are also the positive outcomes of urbanity arising from agglomeration, interdependence, sharing and experimentation of urban dwellers. These features are best exhibited in public space, which is owned by nobody but belongs to everybody in a city. Public space provides a useful lens to reveal the quality of life and the character of a city and its people. It can also exhibit many aspects of the dark side of urban living associated with neglect, exclusion, conflict and hazard. Public space is indeed fragile. It is by virtue of this fragility that the study of public space can reveal much about the underlying changes in urban society.

Urban planners have a key role to play in influencing the spatial order, nurturing the soul of a city and defending against the degeneration of its public space. This chapter illustrates how the planning, design and provision of public space have been influenced by the changing political economy of Hong Kong and its developmental trajectory from a colonial *entrepôt* to a global city. It will explore some emerging trends of public space provision and management in this place and advocate for the importance of urban planning in mitigating some undesirable consequences.

A City of Pragmatism

Hong Kong is internationally famous for its extremely high-density built environment. It had a colonial urban history of over 150 years from its founding in 1842 until its sovereignty was handed over by the British government back to China in July 1997. Population and economic growth have exerted enormous pressures on the efficient use of land in this city. With its strategic location as the southern gateway to China, Hong Kong was built initially as a trading port, then as an export-oriented manufacturing base and eventually as the international financial and business center that we see today. At present, only about 24% of its 1,100 km² of territory has been built up, housing a population of more than 7.4 million. Most of the remaining land area is either hilly terrain designated as green belts or country parks, ecologically sensitive areas or outlying sites.

All land in Hong Kong is ultimately owned by the government and is allocated to various land uses under leases or similar agreements. Not all public spaces have the same priority in land allocation, and in practice, particularly within the built-up areas, priority has been given to transport infrastructure in this pragmatic, land-starved city. Roads, highways, airport and transport facilities, for example, occupy more than 2.2 times more land than parks, stadiums, playgrounds and recreational facilities (HK Planning Department 2020). Outside of the primary built-up areas of the city, Hong Kong has reserved about 40% of its territory as country parks and another 13% as green belts, which can be used for passive public recreation. Country parks also play an important functional role in the urban ecosystem, as they were initially set up as water catchment areas. Many green belts are "transition zones" awaiting permanent urban development rather than being reserved for conservation or recreation in perpetuity (Tang et al. 2007).

Flexibility is the implicit guiding principle of public space planning and provision in Hong Kong. A substantial amount of proposed open space that appears on town plans has not actually been developed into public parks or playgrounds (Tang and Wong 2008). This often provides "solution space," which is badly needed in a profoundly congested urban environment to support development of new infrastructure such as metro station entrances. Furthermore, the Planning Authority has been rather flexible in allowing mixed uses in addition to recreation purposes in existing open space zones (Cheung and Tang 2016). This is perceived to facilitate a more "productive" use of public open space in this land-scarce city.

Ephemerality is another key characteristic of public space in Hong Kong and supports its rapidly changing urban landscape. Many public parks are still formally named by the government authority as "temporary" facilities despite having been in use as public spaces by the community for decades. It is not uncommon for parts of public parks and recreation grounds to be reclaimed by the government and converted into other urban uses. The dissolution of the two elected municipal councils in charge of public park management before 2000 has removed a major check preventing the bureaucracy from taking these steps whenever deemed necessary. Public recreation is only one of the many functions of public open space; enhancing public hygiene, promoting racial harmony and controlling social dissent were also some major purposes at different historical junctures in the development of Hong Kong (Cheung and Tang 2015; Tang 2017).

Hong Kong in the colonial era was once described as being characterized by "borrowed place, borrowed time" (Hughes 1968). This short-termism was reflected by the lack of commitment in its planning and provision of public open space. In the urban built-up areas, many public parks, playgrounds and recreation grounds are often small in size, boring and disconnected (Figure 11.1). Both quantity and quality of public open space are far from satisfactory. The fragmentation of open space has been reinforced by a pragmatic, pro-development urban planning discourse that defines neighborhood open space as a local facility and often allocates it in residual locations.

A Livable, Competitive and Sustainable "Asia's World City"

The reunification of Hong Kong with China in July 1997 brought an end to the colonial regime but not its pragmatism in urban planning. However, there is a need to reevaluate

FIGURE 11.1 Public sitting-out area before and after upgrading in an old urban district.
Source: Authors.

this approach to respond appropriately to the city's new circumstances. Hong Kong has to compete increasingly with other cities in providing a world-class urban environment that attracts international talent, companies and investment. The city is also facing the problems of "double-aging." Its aging building stock is in need of rehabilitation or redevelopment in order to curb the proliferation of urban decay. Additionally, the city's growing elderly population demands an age-friendly built environment to support healthy living and allow aging-in-place. Furthermore, a rising awareness in civil society about the threats of climate change has elevated the importance of green space in an urban setting. As a result, public space is now put under a different spotlight in the planning and development of Hong Kong.

The current vision of Hong Kong's strategic spatial plan, HK2030+, is to make it a livable, competitive and sustainable "Asia's World City" (Development Bureau and

Planning Department 2016). Three emerging trends in planning, developing and managing public space in Hong Kong are noticeable. First, the focus of urban planning strategy has shifted towards creating open space networks, such as waterfront promenades and interconnected public spaces at strategic locations and new development areas of the city. Second, the design and provision of public space have become major planning considerations in a district-based approach to urban renewal of old neighborhoods and in new private development. Third, innovative and collaborative initiatives have been generated from the bottom up to experiment with and reinvent the use and design of public space.

Networked Public Space

Both the quality and the quantity of public space are changing. To improve the livability of the high-density environment of Hong Kong, HK2030+ proposes to enrich the city's existing "green-blue" assets by forming "a 'Green and Blue System' network composed of parks, countryside, riverfronts, waterfronts, wetlands, green and blue infrastructure, and other water bodies" (Development Bureau and Planning Department 2016: 30). It also proposes to raise the open space provision target from a minimum 2 m^2 to 2.5 m^2 per person for the territory as a whole. The revised target is still low compared with international standards. Inequitable distribution of open space remains an issue, as some old urban districts continue to face a shortfall in public parks and accessible recreational facilities.

A lot of effort and resources have been put into redeveloping the harbor front and revitalizing the existing urban *nullahs* (open stormwater channels) for public enjoyment. Hong Kong, especially its metropolitan core, has grown up on both sides of Victoria Harbour. The strategic objective now is to transform such water-facing areas into iconic public spaces for leisure, recreation and relaxation by enhancing the land-water interface and strengthening a "water-friendly" environment for the community. The Harbourfront Commission, set up by the government and comprised of leaders and representatives from the professions, industry and community, serves advisory and advocacy functions in the formulation and implementation of a Harbourfront Plan. Constrained by its limited resources and authority, however, the Commission has to rely on the government bureaucracy, the private sector and other organizations to bring vision into action.

The creation of a public space network is gradually taking shape and is welcomed by the public. A fully connected harbor-front promenade is still far from complete, but the accessibility of public space at the waterfront has been greatly improved (Figure 11.2). Design, management and facility provision in different sections of the promenade are incongruent, as they are developed and operated by different authorities. For instance, located on a waterfront site of over 40 hectares, the West Kowloon Cultural District provides 23 hectares of public open space with a 2-km harbor-front promenade that links the many new museums and other arts and cultural facilities of the district. This public space is not only pet friendly but is also supportive to shared biking and open-air street performances. These activities are normally disallowed, for reasons of public safety, in the waterfront parks and public recreation grounds managed by the government's Leisure and Cultural Services Department.

FIGURE 11.2 New harbor-front promenade and public park network on Hong Kong Island.
Source: Authors.

Semi-Private Public Space

Qualitatively poor and quantitatively inadequate provision of public space is common in the urban districts of Hong Kong. Established in 2001 by the government, the Urban Renewal Authority (URA) is responsible for tackling the problem of urban decay, improving the living conditions of urban residents and enhancing the built environment of old districts through redevelopment, building rehabilitation, preservation and district revitalization. The small scale of the URA's projects has often restricted the opportunity of providing new public space in urban redevelopment schemes. Since 2015, the URA has shifted from a "project-led" model to a more holistic, district-based and integrated approach to urban renewal. This essentially means enlarging the scale of redevelopment schemes to enable rationalization of urban layout and land use disposition, under a comprehensive masterplan, in order to generate wider social benefits for neighborhoods. A recent example is the holistic planning of over 2 hectares of land in seven redevelopment projects in the old district of To Kwa Wan (Figure 11.3). By restructuring the existing road networks and providing a central carpark in future redevelopment, it helps maximize street-level shop frontage and create more integrated and organized open areas at ground level to improve the vibrancy and connectivity of public space (Urban Renewal Authority 2019).

More attention is also being paid to the urban design of public space in the development of strategic development areas. For instance, a whole new set of Urban Design Guidelines and Manuals has been promulgated by the government to inform and regulate the design

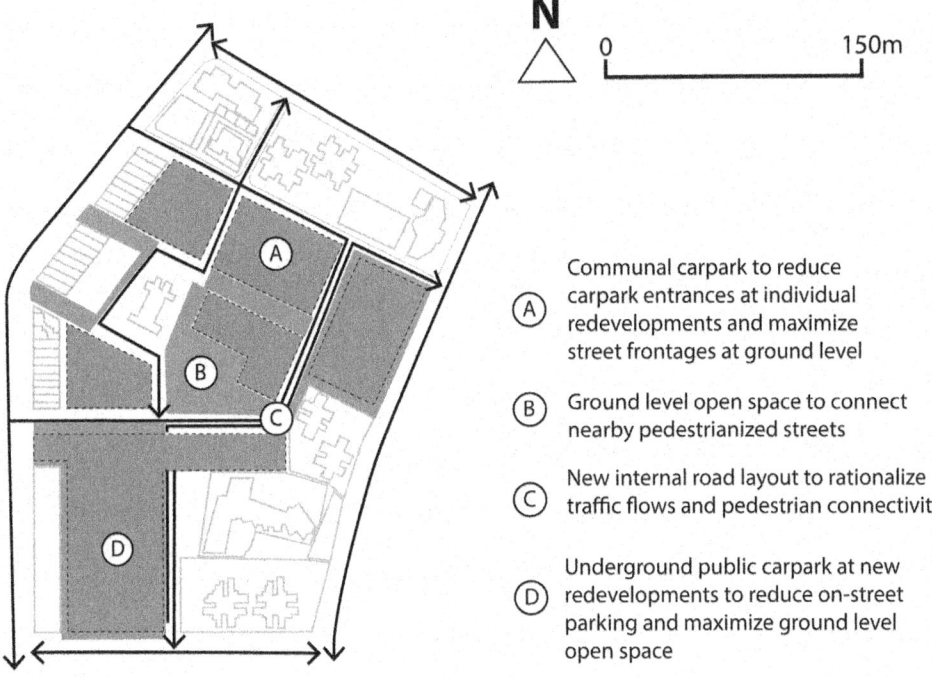

FIGURE 11.3 Holistic planning in urban redevelopment for public space enhancement.
Source: Authors.

of both private developments and public space in the disused former urban airport site of some 323 hectares at Kai Tak (Civil Engineering and Development Department 2020). The manuals cover both urban design control parameters, which are intended to be regulatory and enforceable, and urban design best practices on streetscape design, façade treatment, greening and so on for reference by professionals. The overall objective is to "achieve a coherent, high-quality urban design, of a consistent visual expression for the entire Kai Tak Development pedestrian realm." The role of urban planning is to incorporate these urban design parameters and considerations into statutory town plans, land leases and land allocation documents to govern their implementation in individual sites by public and private developers.

These high quality public spaces are expected to be better integrated with private property development, which may also encourage early implementation and completion of these public space provisions. Privately provided public spaces avoid the bureaucratic red tape of government funding. However, they do not come without a cost to developers, especially when they are required to continue managing and maintaining these public spaces. Privatization and expropriation of these public spaces by commercial capital are highly probable, unless an effective monitoring and enforcement mechanism is put in place to protect the public interest and prevent social exclusion in the use of these semi-public private spaces.

Reinvented Public Space

The rise of Hong Kong's civil society has generated a wide interest in public space and encouraged a range of bottom-up, innovative and collaborative approaches to its design, use and management. One example is the Hong Kong Public Space Initiative (HKPSI), founded in 2011 as a non-profit organization by a group of young professionals to promote the value of public space to the people of Hong Kong and encourage its effective use through research, education and community participation. In conjunction with public authorities and other institutions, HKPSI organizes regular public engagement activities in various districts to experiment with new ideas and approaches in the use, design and provision of public open spaces. Another example is the Jockey Club Design Institute for Social Innovation (DISI), which aims to improve the well-being of the people of Hong Kong and create social impact through transdisciplinary research and stakeholder collaboration. One of its current projects explores the future of intergenerational play space, which is expected to simultaneously accommodate the recreational needs of both the elderly and the younger generations.

A heightened public awareness has altered the government approach to public space. The Energizing Kowloon East Office (EKEO), inaugurated by the government as a multi-disciplinary professional team in 2012, has adopted a placemaking approach in developing and managing the public space in the Kowloon East area in order to facilitate its transformation into a second central business district (CBD) for Hong Kong. In collaboration with the public and other major stakeholders, EKEO not only coordinates government input and resources in physical improvement works—such as transforming an old public cargo working area into a waterfront promenade and turning the under-used space beneath a flyover into arts and cultural venues (Figure 11.4)—it also actively organizes many public events and community

FIGURE 11.4 Reinvented public space at the Kwun Tong waterfront by Energizing Kowloon East Office.

Source: Authors.

activities to encourage the use of these reinvented spaces and improve the vibrancy of the district. In another urban waterfront location, charitable organizations and social enterprises were invited by the government to operate a non-profit-making leisure farm of 2,000 m² on a temporary experimental basis, for the community to enjoy gardening activities and raise their awareness of urban greening. Urban farms and community gardens are regarded as part of the "community green networks" to enhance livability under HK2030+.

Apart from these organized efforts, reinvented public spaces have also arisen spontaneously from grassroots appropriation. A famous example in Hong Kong is the Western District Public Cargo Working Area, which is more popularly known as the "Instagram Pier" (Stone 2017). It is still an active seaside loading and unloading pier for cargo, especially construction materials, but it has also attracted a huge number of visitors from the neighborhood and afar to come for leisure and enjoyment. They come to shoot sunset photographs, take selfies, walk dogs, bike, fish, jog, exercise, skateboard, stroll, sunbathe or simply sit to enjoy the sea breeze (Figure 11.5). These visitors are technically breaking the law by trespassing into this working area and also potentially putting their personal safety at risk. However, so far, their unauthorized visits have been tolerated by the public authorities, hence making all these free, creative and informal uses of this public space possible. The continuing success of this reinvented and unregulated public space ultimately depends on the vigilance, self-restraint and mutual respect of all parties concerned. Indeed, these are all essences of urbanity.

FIGURE 11.5 Bottom-up reinvented public space at the Western District Public Cargo Working Area.

Source: Authors.

Conclusion

In Hong Kong, public space encompasses a range of regulated and unregulated spaces. In recent years, numerous strategic efforts and top-down interventions have been made to encourage the public use and enjoyment of regulated open spaces. The city has witnessed a facelift of its green and blue infrastructure. Many public parks, waterfront promenades, landscaped gardens, open streets, *nullahs* and other elements of public space have been upgraded by the authorities. Additionally, bottom-up initiatives from the community have continued to push beyond the current boundary of regulations and thinking and have experimented with unorthodox ways of using public spaces. New excitement, delight and inspiration may arise from the innovative use of these untidy, unregulated and even dangerous public spaces. Urban planners can play a key role in nurturing all these imaginative and innovative ideas and bring them into reality. Great cities are famous for the quality of their public space, and as the examples discussed in this chapter attest, this great public space is manifested not only in the built environment itself but also in the collective wisdom, co-creative spirit and civility of the people who make up the city's public.

Acknowledgments

The research published in this chapter was funded by the Research Grants Council of the Hong Kong Special Administrative Region (Projects No. 527910 and 17202617).

References

Cheung, D.M.W. and Tang, B.S. (2015) "Social order, leisure, or tourist attraction? The changing planning missions for waterfront space in Hong Kong." *Habitat International* 47. pp. 231–240.
Cheung, D.M.W. and Tang, B.S. (2016) "Recreation space or urban land reserve? Land-use zoning patterns and the transformation of open space in Hong Kong." *ASCE Journal of Urban Planning and Development* 142 (3).
Civil Engineering and Development Department (2020) *Kai Tak development: Urban design guidelines and manual.* At: www.ktd.gov.hk/udgm/en/. Last accessed on 20 September 2020.
Development Bureau and Planning Department (2016) *HK2030+ towards a planning vision and strategy transcending 2030.* At: www.hk2030plus.hk/index.htm. Last accessed on 20 September 2020.
Hughes, R. (1968) *Hong Kong: Borrowed place, borrowed time.* Deutsch.
Hong Kong Planning Department (2020) *Land utilization in Hong Kong 2018.* At: www.pland.gov.hk/pland_en/info_serv/statistic/landu.html. Last accessed on 20 September 2020.
Stone, D. (2017) "Welcome to Hong Kong's 'Instagram pier'." *National Geographic.* P. 19, October. At: www.nationalgeographic.com/photography/proof/2017/10/welcome-to-hong-kongs-instagram-pier/. Last accessed on 20 September 2020.
Tang, B.S. (2017) "Is the distribution of public open space in Hong Kong equitable, why not?" *Landscape and Urban Planning* 161. pp. 80–89.
Tang, B.S. and Wong, S.W. (2008) "A longitudinal study of open space zoning and development in Hong Kong." *Landscape and Urban Planning* 87 (4). pp. 258–268.
Tang, B.S., Wong, S.W. and Lee, A.K.W. (2007) "Green belt in a compact city: A zone for conservation or transition?" *Landscape and Urban Planning* 79 (3–4). pp. 358–373.
Urban Renewal Authority (2019) *Urban renewal authority annual report 2018/2019.* At: http://annualreport.ura.org.hk/2018-2019/en/. Last accessed on 20 September 2020.

12

WHERE 'CITY' MEETS 'VILLAGE': CONTESTING PUBLIC SPACES DURING SHENZHEN'S URBAN RENEWAL

Juan Du

Introduction

Simultaneously generic and complex, 'public space' is the most righteous designation on a city's masterplan: "This is Public Space." Yet the identification could also raise the most confrontational question *in-situ*: "This is Public Space?" The equivalent Chinese term, *Gonggong Kongjian* (公共空间), is similarly the most over-used and yet under-examined terminology in contemporary urban planning and design in China. Often state-led and monumental in scale, the production process of such public spaces is often pursued with good intentions but fraught with problematic outcomes. Adding to this complexity is the fact that some of the most vibrant urban spaces of public life in many Chinese cities are often not found in the formally planned and built squares but rather in the streets and communities. These two scales of public spaces often co-exist in parallel, each meeting its own purposes and hosting different population groups of the city. This is the case for Shenzhen, currently China's symbolic city of modern urban planning and design. The city hosts plenty of striking and modern public squares and parks, yet some of the city's most unique forms of public space are found in narrow pedestrian streets and open-air markets, most often found in Shenzhen's urban villages—informally developed neighborhoods that house the majority of the city's working-class residents. This chapter first examines the formation of Shenzhen's central business district (CBD) and its Civic Square, the city's most symbolic public space, as well as the development process of the nearby Huanggang urban village(皇岗城中村). The first is shaped through formal urban planning processes at the city scale and the other built by an influential urban village community at a neighborhood scale. Furthermore, through the analysis of a decade-long urban renewal project, Shenzhen CBD and Huanggang Urban Village Redevelopment, history and complexities are revealed through the research and design process of confronting demands for the demolition of an informal neighborhood in order to produce new large-scale public spaces in Shenzhen. The results may be surprising.

Shenzhen's 'Grand Urban Living Room'

> The 'Grand Urban Living Room' started construction last April, occupying 42.5 hectares, it is the largest and most important urban square and supersized public space in Shenzhen. It is also

the space where the central district transitions from administrative and cultural function areas to business areas. It is a new type of urban space that integrates functions such as large squares, green spaces, leisure and entertainment, tourism, transportation and traffic distribution.

Shenzhen Special Zone Daily, 1 October 2006 (Xu 2006)

Formally opened to the public on China's October First National Day in 2006, the Civic Square instantly became the most symbolic public space of the city and was dubbed Shenzhen's "Grand Urban Living Room" (Xu 2006). Paved in granite and accented by marble strips with fountains and greenery on either side, the large open plaza renders the adjacent colossal building with symmetrically undulating roof even more monumental. The building and square are made even more prominent by their location right at the center of a north-south urban axis. At the northern edge of the Civic Square is Lotus Hill Park, a beautiful sprawling public park accented by a statue of Deng Xiaoping on top of the hill. Adjacent to the park and symmetrically arranged to the east and west of the axis are the Children's Palace, Book City, Public Library and Shenzhen Museum of Contemporary Art and Urban Planning. To the south of the Civic Square are a series of large public green spaces flanked on both sides by some of Shenzhen's most prominent high-rise office towers. The 2-kilometer-long central axis ends at the southern edge marked by the massive Shenzhen Convention and Exhibition Center.

FIGURE 12.1 Shenzhen's Civic Square is the city's most symbolic public space and was dubbed the city's 'Grand Urban Living Room' since completion in 2006.

Source: Author

FIGURE 12.2 A left-over street corner in Huanggang urban village, the neighbourhood public space hosts the colourful everyday lives of its diverse residents.

Source: Author

Three built structures occupy the sacred axis: Shenzhen Convention Center, Civic Center and the bronze statue of Deng Xiaoping atop Lotus Hill. While Deng's statue was raised in 1997, completion of the two large building complexes was in the 2000s. Construction of the 210,000-m^2 Civic Center spanned five years and was finished in winter 2003. By 2005, over twenty municipal administrations, including the Mayor's Office, moved into the massive new building. Hosting most of the city's municipal administrative offices, including its City Hall, this is the new civic and political center of the new city. An important note to make here is that this is not Shenzhen's first planned political, civic and commercial center. When the City of Shenzhen was first established in 1979, the City Hall, along with the first group of civic buildings, were all planned and constructed in Luohu, a district 4 kilometers to the east of the new 2005 Civic Center.

Planning the New Civic Center

Located next to the Hong Kong border crossing checkpoint, Luohu District was the first urban epicenter of Shenzhen. In addition to the municipal buildings, all of the city's first-generation commercial high-rise towers were located in the area, per the city's first masterplan of 1982 (Du 2020a). However, Shenzhen's faster-than-planned development rate resulted in a space shortage for new construction and expansion within a decade of urbanization. This prompted

Shenzhen's decision to relocate its civic and commercial center to the adjacent Futian District, as drafted in the city's second and arguably most impactful city plan, the 1986 Shenzhen Masterplan. One important aspect of the 1986 Plan was to formalize a new central north-south axis in Futian District, to organize the city's most important administrative and cultural buildings. Throughout the ensuing decade, numerous design institutes in China were involved in drafting the Masterplan and Detailed Urban Plan of the new CBD.[1] There was also involvement of international architects and planners, such as the 1997 Eco-media Axis plan of the CBD's green public spaces by Japanese architect Kisho Kurokawa and the 1998 Double Dragon Urban Design Guidelines for the office building blocks flanking the central green space (Du 2020b).

These multiple urban plans and designs all further reinforced the central axis, and the activities also set a precedent for international urban planning and design consultations for Shenzhen. In 1999, the city's first detailed urban design plan was issued: The Statutory Plan of Shenzhen Futian Central Business District Area (Urban Planning, Land & Resource Commission of Shenzhen Municipality, 1999). It covers a land area of 600 hectares, including Lotus

FIGURE 12.3 1984 drawing of the planned Futian CBD, superimposed on survey mapping of the pre-existing village and industrial settlements. On the right, satellite image showing the same area 20 years later, where the former high-density rural village clusters developed into the higher density "urban villages".

Source: (Left) Shenzhen Planning and Land Resource Bureau, reproduced by author; (Right) Google Earth (2003)

FIGURE 12.4 Location of urban villages in inner-city Shenzhen - Huanggang urban village is located on central axis of the Futian CBD.

Source: Drawn by author

Hill Park and several modern urban blocks. Along the central axis from the north to the south, a series of public spaces with diverse characteristics were formally planned. The modern masterplan outlined road networks forming large urban blocks for civic, commercial and residential programs, all set within large green belts and parks. However, to implement this urban plan for Shenzhen's CBD, rural land had to be expropriated from agricultural villages in the area.

Prehistory of Shenzhen

The impacted villages on the land to become the new CBD were Gangxia and Huanggang, two villages whose inhabitants have cultivated these lands for centuries. Prior to the 1979 establishment of the City of Shenzhen and the 1980 Shenzhen Special Economic Zone designation, thousands of villages had cultivated, fished, traded and produced in the overall territory for centuries or longer. By 1980, the central government designated all land inside the Shenzhen Special Economic Zone, a zone set within the larger city territory, as 'urban' in order to expropriate land for urbanization and industrialization. Over the following decade, Shenzhen's municipal government conducted a process of negotiations with individual villages to purchase their farming, forestry and fishery fields. However, due to the limited financial resources of the government at that time, each village was left with land for self-industrialization and self-built village housing. These village lands became 'rural' enclaves inside the 'urban' city of Shenzhen and were given the name *chengzhongcun* (城中村), literally, "villages in the city" or "urban villages." Gangxia and Huanggang, similar to a number of other villages located in the new city's urban centers, experienced drastic transformations and unanticipated developments.

Superimposing the outlines of the 1999 CBD Statuary Urban Plan with a 1984 land survey map, it is possible to discern the two villages and other preexisting natural and human geographies. Indicated by the dashed boundary line, the eastern border of the CBD plan bisects Gangxia Village, the densest building clusters of the pre-urbanization area. The northern area of the CBD incorporated Lotus Hill, which later became the popular Lotus Hill Public Park. Just below the southern foot of the mountain are large urban blocks to be filled with Shenzhen's most important civic buildings. The central large square portion of the CBD plan is to become the Shenzhen Civic Square, which in the 1980s was occupied by existing industries such as a large furniture factory and an automobile plant, the land of which belonged to Gangxia Village. The large square and the entire CBD Plan is bisected east-west by an oval median and a wide roadway, which would become Shenzhen's most symbolic street and which remains the city's most important transportation thoroughfare today. However, as indicated by the 1984 survey map, the Shennan Avenue in fact was widened from a pre-existing country road that had been in place for decades prior to Shenzhen's establishment (Du 2020b). At the southern portion of the CBD is another large block with a geographical hill which belongs to Huanggang Village. The village maintained terraced fruit orchards on the hill and hosted electronics factory buildings at the foot. Just outside of the southernmost "dash-dot" boundary line, Huanggang Village's Home Base Land—the small square building footprints organized in a grid—marked the end of the new CBD masterplan.

Erasure, Urbanization and Demolition

Within five years of the Masterplan's release, Shenzhen's new urban center took shape through erasure, demolition, adaptation and construction. Other than the parcels of land reserved for the villages' self-housing and industry, village land was expropriated from Gangxia and Huanggang to make way for the new city center. Existing enterprises and factories were closed, buildings demolished, farming fields and orchards paved over and the entire Huanggang Hill flattened to make way for the Shenzhen Convention and Exhibition Center (Du 2016). With the 2005 inauguration of the Civic Center and Square, and the rise of a series of new office towers along the central axis occupied by large expanses of greenery, there was very little evidence left of what had existed on this land just a decade previously. The urban form and image of the Futian CBD helped to cement Shenzhen's status as China's new instant city, seemingly constructed overnight from *tabula rasa*.

With Shenzhen's rapid development and new city image, the urban villages became areas of exception in the city. While the city developed and intensified, so did the villages, turning the previously two-story village houses into structures with six floors or more of low-cost rental housing. In addition to unique residential building types, narrow streets and alleyways

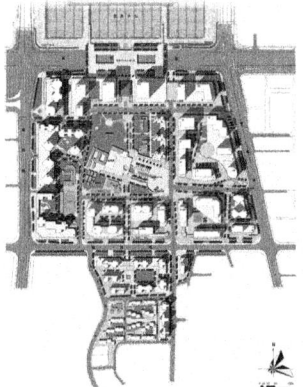 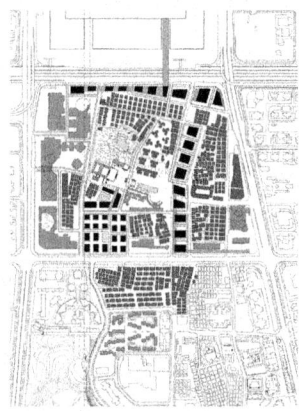 

FIGURE 12.5 2005 Huanggang Village Redevelopment Plan by CAUPD; 2007 Huanggang Redevelopment Plan by IDU that proposed to incrementally redevelop the neighbourhood following the existing street patterns and organizational logic; 2020 Satellite image of Huanggang.

Source: (Left) CAUPD Shenzhen Branch; (Middle) IDU, directed by author; (Right) Baidu Satellite Map

inside the urban villages were packed full of inexpensive restaurants, stores, workshops and street vending. Outside of the city's formal planning, the urban villages grew informally to provide Shenzhen's working class with affordable housing as well as physically and socially accessible public places in the city. However, the urban villages were mainly criticized, both by the government and the general public sentiment, as "backward" places with substandard building and environmental qualities. In 2004, the Interim Provision of Shenzhen Urban Village (Old Village) Redevelopment (Shenzhen Municipal Government 2004) was released, which directed to "demolish-rebuild" the urban villages. By 2005, a citywide campaign was launched to demolish all urban villages "within five years" (Du 2018). Having depleted most available land for construction, the year 2005 also marked the beginning of Shenzhen's urban renewal, seeking new land for urban development. As Shenzhen celebrated twenty-five years of establishment, "old" neighborhoods were to be demolished and redeveloped, including the first generation of industrial and residential compounds, but the majority of such designated sites were urban villages. Among the first targeted by the city's agenda were those located in the city centers, especially the two villages inside the CBD.

Dilemma of the Central Axis and Public Space

While the 1999 CBD Urban Plan ended the business district at the Convention Center, by the early 2000s, more space and land were needed for further expansion. Blocked by Lotus Hill to the north, the city center was to expand the CBD southward with similarly large public space along the central north-south axis (Chen 2015). However, there was one obstacle in the way: Huanggang Village, whose leaders did not agree to the city's CBD expansion plans. Across the six-lane Binhe Avenue from the Shenzhen Convention Center, by this time, Huanggang Village had grown from the small cluster of buildings surveyed on the 1984 map into a large urban neighborhood with a diverse range of buildings and spaces, from typical village rental housing to luxury residential and commercial hotel towers. Fully enveloped by urban developments of the CBD, Huanggang exemplified the difference between the formally planned city and the informally developed urban village, with intense density of buildings and diversity of residential as well as commercial activities.

Similar to other urban villages in Shenzhen, the vast majority of the approximately 70,000 residents of Huanggang are renting housing from the small group of indigenous villagers, which in Huanggang's case is a population of around 1,700. However, Huanggang Village is also exceptional even amongst other centrally located urban villages as among the best-developed urban villages in Shenzhen, with well-maintained buildings, streets and public spaces. While the Huanggang Village leadership understood the city's aim to extend the CBD, they rejected the plan to create a large public space through the central zone of the village neighborhood block to extend the axis. Huanggang in turn also proposed their own privately commissioned urban redevelopment plan, which marked the city's central axis with a set of twin towers, the renderings of which held a strong resemblance to the tallest twin towers in the world, Kuala Lumpur's Petronas Towers. Shenzhen's Urban Planning Bureau rejected the proposal.

With the two sides at a stalemate on how to redevelop, another round of international urban planning and design consultation was held in 2006. Covering 50 hectares of the CBD, including the 23 hectares managed by the Huanggang Village Collective, the Shenzhen CBD Huanggang Area Redevelopment called for the urban planning and design to extend the central axis and incorporates Huanggang Village's urban renewal. Invited to participate by the Shenzhen Planning Bureau, the Hong Kong-based practice IDU submitted a proposal to extend the ceremonial central axis with varying heights of buildings at the spatial scale of the urban block, thus enabling the contested ground space of Huanggang Village to remain active with bustling commercial activities and social life (Du 2016).

Research and Design

The IDU proposal was based on in-depth research into the historical, spatial, social and economic operations of Huanggang. Unlike the relatively well-documented development process of the CBD, the developmental history of Huanggang had to be assembled through diverse sources of information ranging from historic village records, formal spatial analysis and in-depth interviews to real estate finance and rental market analysis. The research revealed Huanggang's uniqueness not only from the formal CBD but its difference from other urban villages in terms of history, culture and management, resulting in unique qualities of spatial forms and multiple-scalar public spaces (Du 2020c). One of the findings was that all residential and commercial developments as well as public spaces of neighborhood parks and plazas are funded, developed and operated by its well-organized Village Corporation. In fact, the development-minded Huanggang leaders objected to the city's CBD extension not due to resistance to redevelopment but rather because they considered the city's plan not urban enough.

Huanggang's urbanization history demonstrated a track record of self-development and finance, with governmental agencies or private developers in limited capacities. Leveraging its centuries of cultural and social history of self-organization, the former rural village collective organization transformed into the well-run Huanggang Village Corporation in the 1980s and established a number of industries and enterprises as well as a series of large-scale residential and commercial developments. Huanggang Corporation also invested in and built various forms of public works such as tree-lined streets, open markets, shopping arcades and open squares with musical fountains named the Huanggang Cultural Plaza, as well as a publicly accessible 20,000-m^2 village park (Jinxiu Garden) with ornate pavilions, fruit trees and lush greenery, all surrounding a koi-filled lake in the center. Starting from an ornate village gate at the eastern edge of the Huanggang urban block, traversing the musical fountains of the Huanggang Cultural Plaza and ending at the Village Ancestral Hall, Huanggang's series of public spaces were all organized by the village's own east-west axis.

Learning from Huanggang Village's own incremental development history, IDU's Urban Redevelopment Plan advocated for long-term socially and economically sustainable self-development and operation of the Village Corporation that avoid total and all-at-once demolition. The entire process was designed as five stages of redevelopment that worked with the spatial forms of Huanggang's existing street patterns and blocks. In addition, the spatial scale of each stage's demolition and rebuilding was planned to be within the financial capacity of the village collective itself. Differing from a conventional masterplan composed of developmental phases, which normally is only considered complete and to have reached full operation at the end of all phases, each stage of the Huanggang Plan, composed of smaller existing blocks following the existing street pattern with minimal disruptions to buildings and public spaces, is a complete redevelopment cycle that allowed the neighborhood to function at every stage of the development.

Seven guiding principles organized the knowledge and concepts of the project as well as facilitated communication of the planning with various stakeholders: Connectivity Beyond Zoning, Porosity Beyond Inclusion, Flexibility Beyond Formality, Temporality Beyond Chronology, Topology Beyond Typology, Intensity Beyond Density and Continuity Beyond Renewal (Du 2016).

Advocacy and Contestation

In addition to incorporating Huanggang Village's cultural history and social operations, the research also revealed a fuller understanding of the overlooked renting population and the importance of the urban villages as a necessary supplier of affordable housing and accessible civic facilities of Shenzhen. With Shenzhen's growth into a megacity of 20 million in mere decades, it has been viewed as China's model case of the modern city created from *tabula rasa* (Du 2015). Less known, however, is that amongst many roles, the city's urban villages have played the indispensable role of providing affordable housing for over half of the city's total population (Guo 2018). The IDU's Huanggang Plan demonstrated an alternative to total demolition so that the urban village could continue to host the tens of thousands of residents and their pursuits to belong in Shenzhen. The Huanggang Plan intended to prolong the redevelopment process by operating more organically and over time, so that urban village residents could avoid the fate of sudden displacement. This was a risky proposal in 2006, for at the time, the position to advocate for the preservation and partial upgrades of the urban villages was against the governmental policy of demolition of all urban villages. It was therefore a surprise to many for the IDU Huanggang Plan to be selected as the winning proposal, for the project not only was counter to the newly launched governmental campaign, it was also against the grain of the general public opinion as well as conventional urban planning practices at the time. The competition's organizer viewed the IDU Huanggang Redevelopment Plan to have "helped the Shenzhen Urban Design Department to see alternatives to the preconceived notions of urban village planning and development," and the jury experts viewed the proposal's "planning as a logical and yet flexible developmental framework, so that complete demolition was not the only choice, and thus minimized the development's negative social impact on the urban village's role as a provider of affordable housing."[2]

The IDU Huanggang Redevelopment Plan was commissioned by the city to develop the project further over the following years; however, issues of transitional housing and affordable housing became sources of contention with the Huanggang Village Corporation. The proposal's advocacy for the new developments to continue to host as well as provide new affordable housing and accessible public spaces was against Huanggang Village's position. The Village Corporation leaders, while proud of Huanggang Village's cultural history, did not consider its role as an "urban village" particularly flattering in the context of the village's cultural history. While some aspects, such as new transitional housing, were not incorporated into the city's eventual urban plan for the area, many adaptations of the IDU Huanggang Plan did result in incremental development and partial demolition and upgrades. As the Huanggang Redevelopment Plan was further negotiated and developed from 2006 to 2008, the nearby Gangxia Village in the CBD underwent its Gangxia Redevelopment Project planning for total demolition and reconstruction. The entire urban block was cleared, displacing over 70,000 renters, and was redeveloped into a cluster of luxury commercial complexes and residential towers (Wang 2016).

Conclusion

A decade after the Shenzhen Civic Square's completion, the city's symbolic public space that was expected to be Shenzhen's "urban living room" did not live up to its grand expectations. An article in the *Shenzhen Evening News* summarized its status with the title: "The Front Square of Shenzhen Civic Center Lacks Entertainment Facilities and Almost No Citizen Usage." The reporting noted the quiet emptiness of the public space and quoted a Municipal People's Congress representative that

> since the opening of the front square of the Civic Center (the Civic Square), there has been a shortage of cultural and leisure facilities in the square. Such a situation of the Civic Square does not match Shenzhen's urban vitality,

and declared "the Civic Square needs to be developed into a true model of 'civic society,' and be a public space that encourages citizen participation and integration" (Yuan and Chen 2016).

Along the same central axis further south, Huanggang Village's public spaces' liveliness has also been frequently reported in the local news as public opinion on the urban villages has shifted during the last decade. The same newspaper, *Shenzhen Evening News*, carried an article titled "From Fishing Village to Back Garden of CBD, the Beautiful Huanggang Village" and reported that

> during days of good weather, by the evening there are always crowds of people on the Cultural Plaza (of Huanggang Village), either old Huanggang villagers or the migrant workers in the city, they sit down casually, chatting leisurely. Behind them, the 268-meter-high Huanggang Business Center stands and shines.
>
> *(Tong 2013)*

By 2016, the Shenzhen government started to release a series of urban planning policies that indicated "demolish-and-rebuild" is no longer the predominant treatment of the city's urban villages. The policy stated that while most of the urban villages in the Shenzhen's outer districts should be demolished and rebuilt, for the majority of the urban villages inside the city's urban center (the original special economic zone), the primary action should be one of "integrated rehabilitation" (*Zonghe Zhengzhi* 综合整治). The policy was extended to the entire city in March 2019 through the Shenzhen Urban Village (Old Village) Integrated Rehabilitation Master Plan (2019–2025) (Shenzhen Bureau of Planning & Natural Resource 2019). This new policy recommended a flexible and changeable strategy of "integrated rehabilitation" so as to maintain the spatial distribution of urban villages and guarantee the availability of low-cost residential areas in the city. However, the new policy release does not apply to the urban villages where redevelopment plans were already approved. Whether the Huanggang Urban Village follows the new policy remains to be seen. Clearly evident, however, is that by the writing of this chapter in 2020, the majority of housing, streets and public spaces that existed in Huanggang Village in 2008 still stand today, hosting the colorful everyday lives of its diverse residents.

The Shenzhen CBD development and redevelopment process reveals that the production of public space could be through the prevention of demolition, or a designed action of *not* building. In this case, the production of public space does not need to be the creation of something completely new by first demolishing what is already there. Furthermore, the drastic policy reversals and paradigm changes of public opinions in Shenzhen within the past two decades have been a powerful demonstration of how knowledge production and design advocacy contribute to and advocate for diversity of urban spaces as well as civic lives.

Notes

The author gratefully acknowledges research funding support provided by the General Research Fund (GRF) of the Research Grant Council, Hong Kong Special Administrative Region (Grant: No.: 17612918).
1. Main design institutes involved were the Shenzhen Branch of the China Urban Planning and Design Institute (CUPDI), Beijing Urban Infrastructure Design Institute, Shenzhen Urban Planning and Design Institute (SZUPDI) and the Architectural Design Institute of Tongji University.
2. 2006 statement from the competition jury experts and the former director of Urban Design Department and deputy chief planner at the Shenzhen Planning Bureau.

References

Chen, Y.X. (2015) *Shenzhen Futian CBD: A thirty-year history of urban planning and construction (1980–2010)* (深圳福田中心区（CBD）城市规划建设三十年历史研究 *(1980–2010)*). Southeast University Press.

Du, J. (2015) "The Shenzhen effect: The story behind Shenzhen's three-decade transformation from village to megacity." *Weapons of Reason, 2. Megacities: Bloom or Bust?* pp. 52–57.

Du, J. (2016) "Back to the future: Urban design informed by Shenzhen's hidden rural history." In: Vlassenrood, L. (Ed.) *Shenzhen: From factory of the world to world city*. NAI 010 Publishers. pp. 70–83.

Du, J. (2018) "Shenzhen 2005: Crisis amidst celebration." *Volume* 54. pp. 14–17.

Du, J. (2020a) "Towers by the Hong Kong border." In: Du, J. (Ed.) *The Shenzhen experiment: The story of China's instant city*. Harvard University Press. pp. 161–194.

Du, J. (2020b) "The 'Southern tours' that changed China." In: Du, J. (Ed.) *The Shenzhen experiment: The story of China's instant city*. Harvard University Press. pp. 50–87.

Du, J. (2020c) "Corporate village in the central business district." In: Du, J. (Ed.) *The Shenzhen experiment: The story of China's instant city*. Harvard University Press. pp. 235–264.

Guo, M. (2018) "Rent rises and the poor are evicted: 60% of the population in Shenzhen live in 1044 urban villages" ("Zujin shangzhang bizou qiongren, Shenzhen 1044 ge chengzhongcun li juzhu le 60% de chengshi renkou 租金上涨逼走穷人 深圳1044个城中村里居住了60%的城市人口"). *National Business Daily* (NBS) 每日经济新闻, 13 June.

Shenzhen Bureau of Planning & Natural Resource (2019) *Shenzhen Urban Village (Old Village) integrated rehabilitation Masterplan (2019–2025)* (深圳市城中村（旧村）综合整治总体规划 *(2019–2025)*). Shenguihua Ziyuan 深规划资源, No. 104.

Shenzhen Municipal Government (2004) *Interim provisions of Shenzhen Urban Village (Old Village) redevelopment* (深圳市城中村（旧村）改造暂行规定). Shenguihua Ziyuan 深规划资源, No. 177.

Tong, Y.T. (2013) "From fishing village to back garden of CBD, the beautiful Huanggang Village" ("Cong Yucun Dao CBD Houhuayuan, zuimei Huanggang Cun" 从渔村到CBD后花园最美皇岗村). *Shenzhen Evening News* 深圳晚报, D05, 19 February.

Urban Planning, Land & Resource Commission of Shenzhen Municipality (1999) *Statutory plan of Shenzhen Futian CBD area* (*Shenzhen Shi Zhongxinqu Fading Tuze* 深圳市中心区法定图则). Urban Planning, Land & Resource Commission of Shenzhen Municipality.

Wang, Y. (2016) "Shenzhen 'Gangxia Rashomon': How to study and treat urban villages" ("Shenzhen 'Gangxia Luoshengmen': Zenyang yanjiu yu Duidai Chengzhongcun" 深圳"岗厦罗生门"：怎样研究与对待城中村). *The Paper* 澎湃新闻, 16 February.

Xu, G.M. (2006) "The civic square opens today" ("Shimin Guangchang Jinri Qi Kaifang" 市民广场今日起开放). *Shenzhen Special Zone Daily* 深圳特区报, 1 October.

Yuan, L.Y. and Chen, Y.Z. (2016) "The front square of Shenzhen Civic Center lacks entertainment facilities and almost no citizen usage" ("Shenzhen Shimin Zhongxin Qianguangchang Quefa Xiuxian Sheshi, Jihu Wuren Guanggu" 深圳市民中心前广场缺乏休闲设施几乎无人光顾). *Shenzhen Evening News* 深圳晚报, 19 July.

13

THREE GENEALOGIES: THE SPATIAL PRODUCTION OF SOCIAL PUBLICS IN TSUEN WAN, HONG KONG

Brian McGrath and Paul Chu Hoi Shan

Introduction

This chapter weaves together three genealogies. The first maps an educational institution, the former Chu Hai University (CHU), now named Chu Hai College of Higher Education (CHCHE), adrift across the "Pearl Sea," as the Greater Bay Area (GBA) was formerly known. It follows the migration of an institutional enclave as it encounters various political regimes—nationalist, colonial, communist—even beyond the GBA megaregion. The second genealogy describes the development of a district-level governance model based on colonial notions of a "district citizen," which replaced a village-based Confucian clan lineage system in Tsuen Wan New Town in British Hong Kong. Finally, the third presents a pedagogical experiment in internationalizing a new generation of architects, coinciding with the introduction of One Country Two Systems in Hong Kong[1]—the International Design Program (IDP) developed at CHCHE in Tsuen Wan, Hong Kong, from 2005 to 2015. A genealogical method is capable of associating the disparate types of social publics at megaregion, metropolitan and civic scales. A genealogical method sees history not as a linear narrative but as the chance succession of accidental events. For Foucault, "effective history . . . shortens its vision to those things nearest to it—the body, the nervous system, nutrition, digestion, and energies" (Foucault 1971 in Bouchard 1977: 139). The biological and effective approach to genealogy fixes the locus of power relations within the body rather than in space. Genealogy traces human struggles against hostile foes and harsh environments in an "endlessly repeated play of force and dominations" (Foucault 1971 in Bouchard 1977: 150).

This approach serves to operationalize a "metacity" framework in an era of digital mediation (McGrath and Shane 2006, 2012) for an ethical urban praxis to counter the ideology of a unified metropolitan public or a megaregional imaginary with its state-led dependency on massive, physical infrastructure and autocratic informatic control of urban bodies. Public space is seen here as the spatial production of social publics, both prescribed and unintended. The layered public space infrastructures that were successively imposed in Tsuen Wan are situated atop a local clan system of lineage villages; a megacity condition of informal squatter urbanism; an industrial new town system of walk-to-work factory neighborhoods, markets

FIGURE 13.1 Map of the migration of Chu Hai University from its origins on the Pearl River in Guangzhou, to its temporary locations in Mong Kok and Tsuen Wan as Chu Hai College of Higher Education, to the new permanent campus of Chu Hai Hong Kong University in Tuen Mun.

Source: Paul Chu and Brian McGrath.

and open spaces; a metropolitan satellite system of commercial podiums around mass transit hubs; a megalopolitan system of high-speed train and car-based urbanism with green infrastructure; and a digital communication system collapsing the close-up and remote (McGrath and Shane 2005). The metacity, experienced both close up and remotely, offers urban imaginaries embedded in social processes and real-life worlds but is also capable of acting on new possibilities and capabilities of alternative forms of public life beyond the here-and-now. Based in part on metacommunity frameworks in ecology, metacity theory seeks to identify new forms of social publics in the gaps and fissures of the historical layers of spatial production (McGrath and Pickett 2011).

Chu Hai: A Genealogy of Institutional Exile

Chu Hai University was established by a group of Kuomintang (KMT) or Chinese Nationalists in Guangzhou in 1947.[2] The new university was named for the "Pearl Sea," the body of water the first campus faced along the Guangzhou waterfront. Following the declaration of the People's Republic of China (PRC) in 1949, CHU resettled in Hong Kong with the name of Chu Hai College, occupying various buildings in Mong Kok until 1992. Never recognized by the British Colonial Government of Hong Kong, the college prospered in Hong Kong as an educational enclave in exile. Chu Hai survived with recognition and support from the Nationalists' government, itself in exile in Taiwan. Its degrees were conferred by Taiwan Republic of China's Ministry of Education and recognized by universities in the United States when students sought post-graduate degrees abroad.

In 1992, Chu Hai established a less public presence when it moved from Mongkok in central Kowloon to the podium of Riviera Gardens, a middle-class private housing estate completed in 1988 in Hong Kong's Tsuen Wan New Town. Riviera Gardens was a massive brownfield redevelopment built on the headland south of Tsuen Wan Bay, once occupied by the Caltex Oil Company (Texaco). Riviera Gardens' podium marked a new era of multi-level public space housing in post-industrial Tsuen Wan. Its glossy sales brochure boasted of lavish public space amenities beyond the dense conditions and minimal provisions of the old satellite industrial city. The enormous housing estate was equipped with twenty residential towers, 30 to 41 stories high, containing 5,636 housing units, a public podium with nearly 100 shops, medical clinics, banks, clothing stores, a supermarket and an air-conditioned fresh food market. Residents are

> able to dine out in a variety of restaurants and food outlets. . . . Iceskating, bowling and cinemas [were provided] in addition to . . . many facilities available for sport, recreation and relaxation for persons of all ages; not forgetting the disabled and physically handicapped.
>
> *(Hayes 1993)*

Chu Hai's move to Tsuen Wan prefigured the imminent return of Hong Kong to China in 1997. While Chu Hai, as an enclave within an enclave, enjoyed its own entrance and an exterior court for sports in Riviera Gardens, it remained relatively isolated as an institutional enclave within the housing estate. While not a gated community, the housing development was certainly an isolated enclave itself, and the brochure emphasized that "security is closely monitored day and night—around the clock" (Hayes 1993: 165). While Riviera Gardens was designed as to be inward looking, in 1990, Tsuen Wan Riviera Park opened, indirectly connecting the campus to a public promenade extending along the entire length of Tsuen Wan Bay, giving Chu Hai at least adjacency to the megaregional imaginary and public realm of its namesake "Pearl Sea."

With the emergence of Taiwanese democracy and localism movements, and the approach of the handover of Hong Kong to China, Chu Hai began the process of attaining autonomy from Taiwanese support. Under the One Country Two Systems joint agreement, effective

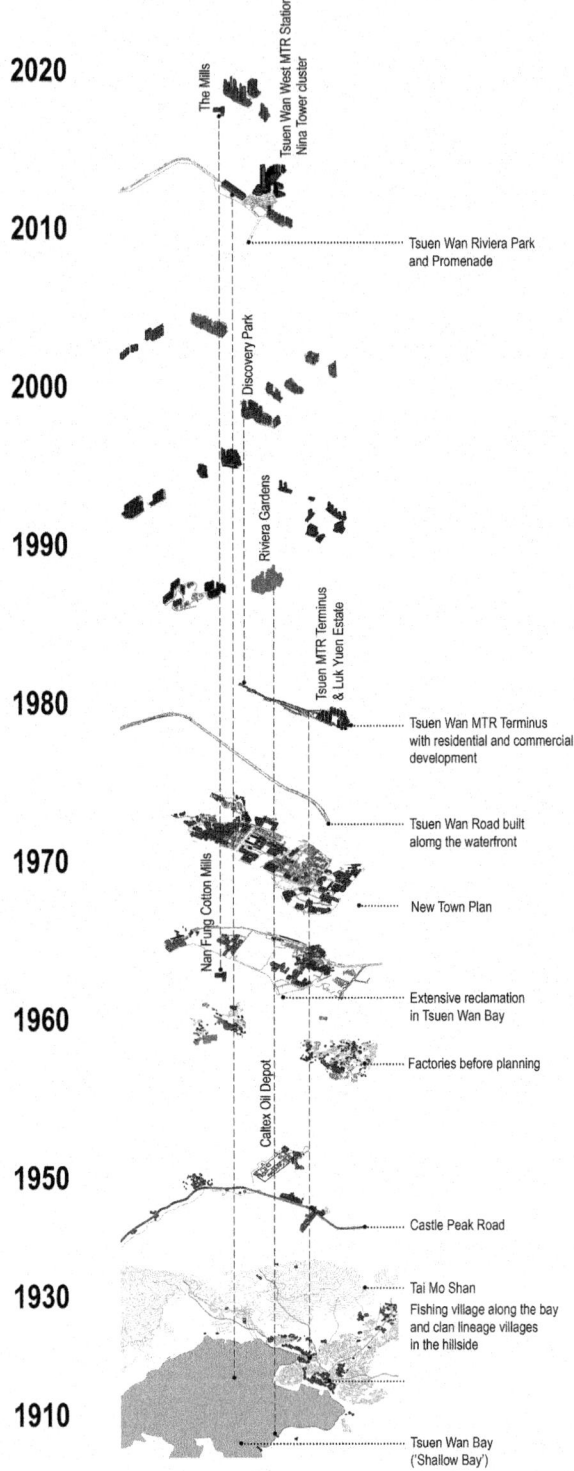

FIGURE 13.2 Layered model of Tsuen Wan, from fishing village to satellite new town, to commercial node in the Greater Bay megaregion.

Source: Paul Chu and Brian McGrath.

1 July 1997, Chu Hai was no longer under British control. In May 2004, the Hong Kong Education Bureau approved the renamed Chu Hai College of Higher Education to award post-secondary degrees and offer new programs, including a professionally accredited architecture department. Meanwhile, barely ten years after its opening, Riviera Gardens' podium was mostly vacant, as it could not compete with new residential and commercial complexes in Kowloon and Central Hong Kong. New college facilities, such as a library and classrooms, expanded into the empty shops in Riviera Gardens' commercial podium. The reformed Architecture and Civil Engineering programs also expanded to the underutilized adjacent commercial podium at Waterside Plaza. The joint agreement marked the end of Chu Hai being relegated as an institutional enclave unrecognized by the colonial government, and its expanded campus mixed academic facilities with the public podiums of Rivera Gardens and Waterside Plaza.

In 2016, amidst Beijing's rhetorical announcement of the Greater Bay Area of Guangdong, Hong Kong and Macau, Chu Hai again moved to its new custom-built waterfront campus in Tuen Mun designed by Rocco Design Architects, composed of two wings facing a lush public green space directly overlooking Castle Peak Bay. Relocated, the college initiated the process of reestablishing its full credentials as Hong Kong Chu Hai University. Chu Hai's genealogy encompasses the megaregional framework of this book, with the "Pearl Sea" as an imagined "public space," while adrift, Chu Hai encountered multiple political regimes and different notions of the spatial production of social publics: nationalist, laissez-faire, colonial, post-colonial, neo-liberal and communist.

Tsuen Wan: A Genealogy of a New Town

In the 1992 move, Chu Hai joined the "Chinese melting pot" (Johnson and Johnson 2019) in Tsuen Wan, a boom town populated by the exodus of unskilled migrants from Guangdong and industrialists and skilled workers from Shanghai following the establishment of the People's Republic of China. Hong Kong's British governors were overwhelmed by the huge influx of immigrant workers pouring into the coastal villages near Tsuen Wan Bay following the Chinese revolution, and Tsuen Wan remains distinct from other Hong Kong new towns in that it still contains vestiges of earlier unplanned urban developments under the previous colonial laissez-faire policy. Public space in such a quickly evolving urban environment was highly contested and provisional yet continues to be plural and overlapping. Ancient clan rituals for birth, marriage, death, appeasing ghosts and honoring ancestors collide with left and right political demonstrations. As market, industrial and consumer economies evolve, village hawkers compete with immigrant sports associations and, later, shopping mall patrons for the limited open space of hyper-dense Tsuen Wan.

Tsuen Wan New Town was overlaid in a rapid succession of infrastructural interventions atop a landscape formed over three centuries by farmers from the Hakka region of China who reoccupied coastal Southern China following the coastal regions forced evacuation during the Qing Dynasty's struggle to secure the island of Formosa (Taiwan) in the late 17th century. Through diking and reclamation work, migrants terraced the foothills of Tai Mo Shan along three streams that drained to the shallows of Tsuen Wan Bay, where a small market town thrived. In the 1950s, new cotton mills were built along the streams, and informal workshops occupied squatter structures or residential units within and around urbanized Hakka villages. In 1960, the first self-sufficient new town in Hong Kong was planned for the center of Tsuen Wan, which would comprise basic residential and factory facilities as well as public amenities such as a town hall, law court, hospital, police station, football pitches, markets and cemeteries. New streets were laid out in a grid and named after relocated villages.

Tsuen Wan was redeveloped as a metropolitan commercial and middle-class residential center at the terminus of the extended Mass Transit Railway (MTR) Tsuen Wan line in 1982. The station was integrated into a public podium, a long linear multi-level indoor shopping center, below seventeen 30-story residential buildings built above the station. Tsuen Wan West Station started to operate in 2003 on reclaimed land created with the MTR West Rail line. The luxurious Nina Tower and City Walk shopping and residential complex started operation in 2008. Together with the existing Tsuen Wan Plaza, they remade central Tsuen Wan as a cluster of luxury shopping malls and upper-middle-class residences between the two MTR stations. In 2015, the Tsuen Wan skybridge system was completed, with forty-three bridges allowing pedestrians to access twenty shopping malls while walking from the Tsuen Wan station to the waterfront Tsuen Wan West station without touching the ground.

Today, Tsuen Wan is emerging as a logistical and tourist hub of the GBA megaregion, situated adjacent to the container port of Kwai Chung and the Airport Express station at Tsing Yi. While Hong Kong's MTR Corporation and its joint ventures with property developers brought a new metropolitan Hong Kong sensibility, the spatial production of new bridges, highways and the tunnel to the other new town of Shatin signaled the anticipation of a megaregional network. The Airport Express, with its stop in Tsing Yi, and the new Hong Kong-Zhuhai-Macau Bridge have given Tsuen Wan a new centrality, with large traffic interchanges becoming public landmarks in a new GBA megaregion image. While the transition from spontaneous industrial city to commercial metropolis and logistical megalopolis marked the period up to the Handover in 1997, the 21st century also witnessed the emergence of a new urban forms and new more extensive and cosmopolitan social public that came with the proliferation of handheld cellular telephone devices in 2007.

With its opening in 2018, The Mills pioneered a new kind of public space for Hong Kong, which, according to its brochure, is a "destination." The Mills includes a business incubator, "experience retail" and a museum devoted to textile arts and the history of cotton spinning. The Nan Fung Group renovated several mid-20th-century cotton spinning factories in Tsuen Wan to curate its own Hong Kong lineage story: from exile Shanghainese textile business to global real estate and financial services company. Visiting The Mills, one can bring a used sweater and watch it be unraveled and repurposed into a new product, see exhibitions celebrating the many skilled women who had tied the threads in the factory who now and sip bubble tea in local brand stores that sell watercolor portraits of recent the Be Water protest movement. Meanwhile, upstairs in the fabrication labs, an emerging generation of design entrepreneurs is being "incubated." Matrilineal images can be traced from today's ethos of the Be Water movement to the mills' cotton spinners and the young female farmers of the Hakka villages of Tsuen Wan, who freed village men to work abroad, enter an educational system not available to women or succumb to opium or gambling addiction (Johnson and Johnson 2019).

Shortly following the construction of the first Nan Fung mills in 1954, Tsuen Wan became a separate administrative district with its own District Office in a hasty effort to introduce planning and management to the spontaneous industrial boomtown situated between a network of Hakka lineage villages radiating from a bayside market town. The eyewitness account of historian and British District Officer James Hayes provides insight in how these massive spatial changes can be understood in relation to the emergence of new forms of social publics

(Hayes 1993). We employ the term "social publics" in order to imply a more plural and diverse idea of public space 'alongside' rather than 'counter to' the colonial bourgeois civil servant model.[3] For Foucault, European genealogies reveal the enforcement of law repeated in scenes of violence as a system of rules proceeding from domination to domination (1971). In contrast, the Tsuen Wan experiment took advantage of the existing intervillage clan models of cooperation. Additionally, the cultural coherence, Feng Shui beliefs and Taoist theories of change were said to have ushered in "the smooth transition to a modern urban-industrial society" based on a culture of "forbearance, pragmatism and genius for self-management" (Boxer 1968).

Throughout, Tsuen Wan has been described as the "guinea pig" of first British Colonial and now of GBA megalopolitan planning logics (Hayes 1993). Each of these periods entailed a new mode of spatial production as well as new forms of social publics. According to Hayes, Tsuen Wan became the testing ground for the Colonial Government's relocation of both villagers and migrant squatters to create a "satellite town" based on the British new town movement, with Tsuen Wan Town Hall and the public square in front symbolizing a new civic identity. In addition to physically moving residents, Hayes also outlined the efforts to create a "new citizen" for the New Town's indigenous villagers and multilingual migrants that constituted a "Chinese Melting Pot" (Johnson and Johnson 2019). Although by 1975, Tsuen Wan was heralded as a New Town, for Hayes, its residents at that stage, "obsessed with seeking a livelihood or making a profit," had not yet developed a "public awareness or a community spirit." To his dismay, the new planned squares became repositories for the storage of vendor's stoves and other hawker equipment, chicken coops, wire-net and cardboard boxes, building materials, builders' debris and scrap metal and rubbish in general (Hayes 1993: 95).

This observation would come as a surprise to any visitor of clean, civil and efficient Tsuen Wan today, where many of the social public practices of Hong Kong were first developed by trial, error and improvisation. The commonly owned village lineage trusts were awarded Letters of Exchange for their land, which were accepted by development companies, creating a land market and profits for villagers. In parallel, migrant groups formed associations based on region of origin, dialect or occupation. Eighty area committees were soon established in all parts of Tsuen Wan. Villager leaders and migrant associations became involved in Clean Hong Kong and Clean Your Building campaigns, government-sponsored sports and recreation programs and efforts such as a public competition to create a town logo. For Hayes, this represented the transformation of the populace from obedient subjects in a clan system into 'righteous people' of a New Town, with a tremendous adaptability to the conditions imposed on them.

The British accelerated their efforts to nurture a district citizen in the shadow of the preparations for the signing of the Sino-British Joint Declaration. A District Advisory Board had previously merely conveyed the concerns of local leaders and associations, but a directly elected District Board was initiated in 1982. However, this resulted in the diminishing of the political importance, status and close involvement of the clan elders and migrant association leaders. Pro-government coalitions dominated the elections through 1994, but in anticipation of the Handover and during the "honeymoon period" thereafter, Pro-Beijing parties gained a consistent majority from 1994 to 2019. However, 2019 was a watershed year in district elections in Tsuen Wan. Following months of protests, as in many districts of Hong Kong, there was a decisive victory of the pro-democracy camp in district-level elections and the clear emergence of a cosmopolitan Hong Kong social public distinct from the British ideal of the district citizen and in defiance of control from Beijing.

International Design Program: A Genealogy of New Social Publics

We led ten annual academic workshops, called the International Design Program, at Chu Hai between 2005 and 2015. The IDP involved the entire student body of the Architecture Department working with faculty and students from Korea, Taiwan, Thailand and the United States. The IDP provided an opportunity to document both the legacy of spatial transformations of Tsuen Wan and the emergence of new social publics by an emerging generation of students who came of age not only during the transition to the One Country Two Systems policy but also the widespread assimilation of the internet, social media and handheld smartphones. The workshops engaged the observations of this new generation in surveying a rapidly changing urban environment and also in developing their own agency in socially mediated performances enacting new social publics.

The IDP served as a confidence-building workshop for Chu Hai's newest architecture students, descendants of Hon Kong's Melting Pot. Instead of training drafts-people for the offices of the graduates of more elite Hong Kong and international universities, the new accredited programs at Chu Hai endeavored to create a regionally focused curriculum based on social and ecological sustainability. We employed digital modeling, hand-held video recordings, social networking apps, drones and digital and analog "drawing machines" (Figures 13.3, 13.4 and 13.5) as tools to imaginatively model Tsuen Wan as an example of multiple layers of social occupations and adaptations of public infrastructures.[4] The students developed a digital database of the continued transformation of Tsuen Wan over the years that demonstrated the unique qualities of the layered public realms of Hong Kong's New Towns (Figure 13.2).

In the IDP, memories and artifacts from each generation of Tsuen Wan's ascendance populated the student's projects: uploaded filmed journeys and performative actions as spatially produced new social publics. These included a cross-dressing enactment of a Cantonese opera in Sam Tung Uk Hakka Walled Village Museum, a crime scene within the MTR station podium and elevated walkway system, a Cantonese love story in the narrow lanes of the first planned neighborhood of shop houses with its small lanes and intimate open space network, a chase scene in Tsuen Wan Town Hall and Plaza, a double-decker bus journey to Riviera Gardens coach terminal and a dramatic ghost story ending at the Tsuen Wan Chinese Permanent Cemetery. Their work matched Foucault's quip that genealogy is history in the form of a concerted carnival; they did not discover the roots of Tsuen Wan's identity but rather its dissipation. Much like the protestors in the Be Water protest movement that emerged in 2019, inherited public space was seen as a stage on which to perform socially mediated possible futures.

The 41st-floor sky-lobby of Nina Tower provides 360-degree views framed by a precious rock collection worthy of the Forbidden City's inner court. The sky lobby looks to Hong Kong's highest peak of Tai Mo Shan to the northeast, the Kwai Tsing Container Terminal to the southeast, the bridges to Tsing Yi and Chek Lap Kok Airport to the southwest and the Gold Coast Highway to Castle Peak and the skyscrapers of Shenzhen to the northwest. Originally planned to be the tallest building in the world, due to its proximity to the airport, Nina Tower was built instead as two spires connected by a glass-floored sky bridge, containing offices, a hotel and a retail base. It is from the aerie, atop a project that involved the removal of several blocks of the original New Town development, that the visiting faculty and students in the Chu Hai IDP, together with throngs of new tourists from mainland China, surveyed the most recent transformation of Tsuen Wan. The new L'Hotel in Nina Tower was an upgrade from our abode in previous years, the Panda Hotel, Tsuen Wan's first modern hotel

FIGURE 13.3 A field work "drawing machine" developed by Jose De Jesus, Parsons School of Design, as part of the Chu Hai International Design Program, Riviera Gardens, 2013.

Source: Brian McGrath.

built with over 1,000 rooms by the Hopewell Group in the 1960s, following one of the first removals of an old central village Kwan Mun Hau. The relocated Kwan Mun Hau clan were the subjects of Elizabeth Lominska Johnson's ethnographies described in *A Chinese Melting Pot* (Johnson and Johnson 2019). In ten short years, we travelled through the entire history of Tsuen Wan.

Tsuen Wan was our home as well as our object of research during the IDP, whose remarkable spatial transformation over the past two decades was not only breathtaking to witness; it indeed fundamentally transformed us. The Hong Kong government's massive investment in metropolitan and megaregional infrastructure seeded successive waves of taller residential towers and increasingly dense amenity-laden complexes. Yet the traces of Hakka villagers and migrant factory workers remain in the layered multiple open space networks of Tsuen Wan. The new generation of architecture students that participated in the decade of IDP workshops, tactically dispersing from the podium of Riviera Gardens, become the new social publics of the metacity, developing a growing confidence in their own agency to alter their environment within a logistical and systemic knowledge of the larger metropolis and megaregion yet culturally affiliated with their IDP peers from Korea, Taiwan, Thailand and the United States.

Conclusion

A genealogical method sees history not as a linear narrative but as the chance succession of accidental events. The method here operationalizes a metacity theory of public space that conceives of the spatial production of social publics, both physical and virtual, close up and remote. Our first genealogy traced an institution in exile as Chu Hai migrated from Guangzhou to its temporary home in Tsuen Wan's Riviera Gardens, before resettling into its new campus in Tuen Mun. The second traced the ancestry of "China's Melting Pot" in Tsuen Wan itself, as indigenous village clans made peace with new poor migrants after 1949, and whose children became cosmopolitan citizens, intent on a path to Hong Kong's self-determinacy. Finally, our last genealogy speculates on the emergence of a new generation of Hong Kong architects who learned important lessons from the collective knowledge of Tsuen Wan's multiple stories of exile, displacement and return. In retrospect, we can see that these lessons navigate not the politics of disappearance—as described by Ackbar Abbas at the moment of the 1997 Handover (Abbas 1997)—but the hyper-saturations of appearances of the dense collective social publics of a Hong Kong New Town, not in a megaregional imagination but as transnational citizens. Like the genealogical tablets in the Hakka village ancestral halls, Tsuen Wan is a palimpsest of all its lineages, a city of cities, reproducing images of itself, a metacity.

Both the metropolis and the megalopolis are diagrams of power, the former of European colonial authority, the latter of Cold War American hegemony usurped by a megaregional imagination directed from Beijing. That exertion of power has been put into crisis by a protracted political battle waged in Hong Kong with the closing of borders, trains and flights between Hong Kong and Guangdong in an attempt to contain the uncontrolled coronavirus. The spatial production of Hong Kong's evolved metropolitan efficiencies and the Greater Bay Area megaregion's infrastructure and propaganda looms over all three of our genealogies, but the freedom of information and the ability to peacefully gather in protest constitutes an empowered social public. Chu Hai's destiny as a Hong Kong university on the "Pearl Sea" prospered as an enclave in exile in the shallow reclaimed bay of Tsuen Wan. Hong Kong's newest school of architecture, now in its open new waterfront campus not far from the Shenzhen border, faces an uncertain future but will always look back towards its time as a Taiwanese-supported enclave in the melting pot of Tsuen Wan in order to imagine an alternative future for the Greater Pearl Sea Bay Area and beyond.

Notes

1. The Chinese/British joint agreement of 1997 maintains Hong Kong's semi-autonomy for fifty years under the One Country Two Systems policy.
2. The KMT is the Chinese Nationalist Party that moved to Taiwan after Mao's victory in the 1949 revolution and the founding of the People's Republic of China. The Nationalists established the Republic of China in 1912 with the downfall of the Qing dynasty and retained the name in their exodus to Taiwan.
3. This is in contrast to Nancy Fraser's notion of "counter-publics." For reference, see Fraser 1990.
4. The contemporary publication of two books became methodological references for the workshops. *Digital Modeling for Urban Design* (McGrath 2008) offered a critical method of computer aided design to layer, rescale and reposition urban spatial data (see Figure 13.2), while *Cinemetrics: Architectural Drawing Today* (McGrath and Gardner 2007) introduced the language of cinema as a sensorimotor instrument for framing and measuring urban flux (see Figure 13.3).

References

Abbas, A. (1997) *Hong Kong: Culture and the politics of disappearance*. University of Minnesota Press.
Boxer, B. (1968) "Space, change and Feng-Shui in Tsuen Wan's urbanization." *Journal of Asian and African Studies* 3 (3–4).
Fraser, N. (1990) "Rethinking the public sphere: A contribution to the critique of actually existing democracy." *Social Text* 25–26. pp. 56–80.
Foucault, M. (1971 [1977]) "Nietzsche, genealogy, history." In: Bouchard, D.F. (Ed.) *Language, counter-memory, practice: Selected essays and interviews*. Cornell University Press. p. 139.
Hayes, J. (1993) *Tsuen Wan: Growth of a new town and its people*. Oxford University Press.
Johnson, E.L. and Johnson, G.E. (2019) *A Chinese melting pot: Original people and immigrants in Hong Kong's first "new town"*. Hong Kong University Press.
McGrath, B. (2008) *Digital modelling for urban design*. John Wiley & Sons.
McGrath, B. and Gardner, J. (2007) *Cinemetrics: Architectural drawing today*. John Wiley & Sons.
McGrath, B. and Pickett, S.T.A. (2011) "The metacity: A conceptual framework for integrating ecology and urban design." *Challenges* 2(4). pp. 55–72.
McGrath, B. and Shane, D.G. (2005) *Sensing the 21st century city: Close-up and remote*. Architectural Digest (AD), John Wiley & Sons, December.
McGrath, B. and Shane, D.G. (2012) "Metropolis, megalopolis, metacity." In: Crysler, G., Cairns, S. and Heynen, H. (Eds.) *Sage handbook of architectural theory*. Sage. pp. 641–656.

14

HONG KONG'S CIVIC SQUARE: A SHORT HISTORY OF A PUBLIC SPACE

Mark W. Frazier

> . . . what makes a space *public*—a space in which the cry and demand for the right to the city can be seen and heard—is often not its preordained "publicness." Rather, it is when, to fulfil a pressing need, some group or another *takes* space and through its actions *makes* it public. The very act of representing one's group (or to some extent one's self) to a larger public creates a space for representation.
>
> Don Mitchell, *The Right to the City* (Mitchell 2003: 35)

> The CGO [Central Government Office, Hong Kong] is not a public place and access to it is permitted only with the prior consent of the Director of Administration. The Forecourt is used primarily as a vehicular circulation area for picking up/dropping off of passengers. It is not a public open space.
>
> *"Conditions of Use of the East Wing Forecourt of the Central Government Offices at Tamar," Director of Administration, Government of Hong Kong, December 2012 (High Court of the HKSAR, 2020)*

The emphatic tone of the Hong Kong government's Conditions of Use for an unassuming plaza and roundabout fronting the entrance to its office complex in Admiralty District belies the highly contentious nature of the space. The 1,000-m² stone-paved plaza and circular driveway, in whose center fly the flags of Hong Kong and the People's Republic of China (PRC), became the site of protests soon after its opening in 2011. Following large protests there in 2012 against "national education" reforms, it became known as "Civic Square."[1] In fall 2013, a retired photographer staged a months-long solo sit-in, followed by an extended legal challenge against official regulations governing the use of the plaza. In late September of 2014, protestors stormed fencing around the square that the government had erected as part of security-enhancement measures. When police took the unprecedented step to use tear gas and pepper spray on the protestors, the public outrage helped launch the 79-day Umbrella Movement. On 12 June 2019, a rally at the square to protest a measure that would have extradited Hong Kong citizens to face trial in mainland PRC courts triggered another highly coercive police response. Public reaction to that day's police brutality brought the historic protests that stretched across the summer and fall of 2019.

FIGURE 14.1 Students enter Civic Square, Hong Kong, on 28 September 2014.

Source: Photo Courtesy of VOA and Wikipedia Commons. Wikimedia Commons © Creative Commons

FIGURE 14.2 Hong Kong Civic Square on 18 October 2014.

Source: Ceeseven. Wikimedia Commons © Creative Commons.

160 Mark W. Frazier

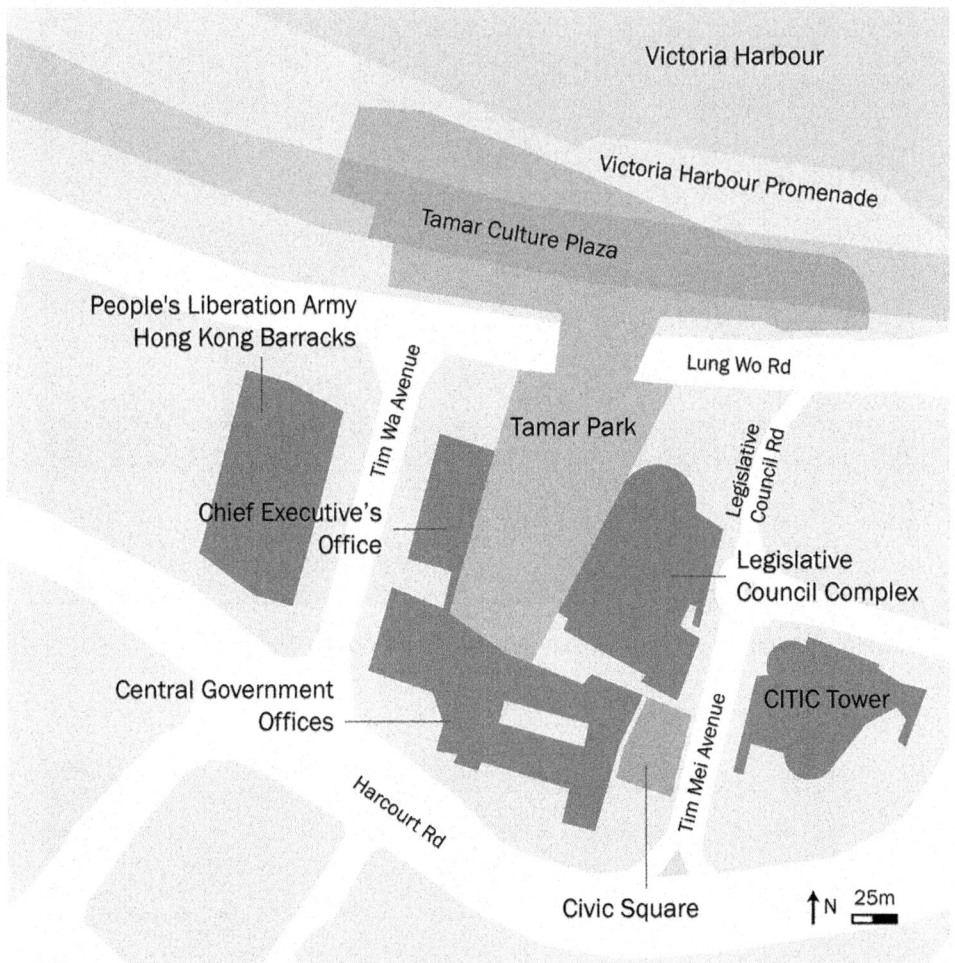

FIGURE 14.3 Map of the Civic Square district.
Source: Diagram by Blake Roberts.

Public spaces do not induce protests in the same sense that disputed territories might give rise to conflict among nation-states, but some public spaces can take on powerful symbolic meaning and regularly draw protestors to them to voice grievances and demands. The contested nature of urban public space has drawn a great deal of attention from scholars in recent years. These studies have asked how public space can catalyze a movement, including those that pose challenges to and at times succeed in taking down incumbent political regimes (Hou and Knierbein 2017; Batuman 2015; Kohn 2013; Nicholls et al. 2016; Said 2015; Beissinger 2011). Tahrir Square in Cairo, Taksim Square and Gezi Park in Istanbul, Maidan in Kiev and many others elsewhere served as staging grounds at which large groups of protestors voiced grievances and drew power from their occupation of prominent public spaces. In some ways, it's not surprising that an opposition movement would decide to concentrate its forces in highly visible civic squares of capital cities. When the civic squares are already imbued with historical meaning and symbols of the nation, a spatial appropriation to occupy civic squares can serve as a challenge to the legitimacy and even the patriotic credentials of an incumbent regime. A prominent example of this practice occurred in 1989, when students in Beijing occupied Tiananmen Square. The vast plaza, which had been designed in the early 1950s by the PRC state to display its power at official ceremonies, was quickly repurposed as a national and global protest stage from mid-April until the violent crackdown on 4 June 1989.

What makes the case of Hong Kong's Civic Square distinctive is its modest status as little more than a plaza entrance and pedestrian passage to a building housing government agencies. By all appearances, it hardly differs from the entrances to thousands of commercial office buildings in Hong Kong or any other city. Unlike Tahrir or Tiananmen Square, this is far from a monumental civic space to which protestors would be naturally drawn. Other venues in Hong Kong, including nearby Tamar Park or Victoria Park, still serve as venues for large public demonstrations. And there are other examples of urban spaces in Hong Kong that have become politically symbolic. Victoria Park is the site of an annual 4 June vigil to commemorate the victims of the crackdown in Beijing. Lion Rock became a prominent symbol of Hong Kong identity and assertion of autonomy against PRC encroachments. During the 2019 protests, numerous Lennon Walls (drawing on a practice that originated in Prague) sprang up for citizens to post messages of solidarity with the protestors. But Civic Square, more so than other protest sites in Hong Kong, illustrates the emergence of "spaces for representation" through contestation over access to and meanings of urban public space.

As implied in the work of classical theorists of the public sphere, such as Hannah Arendt (2018) and Jürgen Habermas (1989), public space is essential for the making of a meaningful public sphere. The latter is what Arendt (2018: 199–207) described as a "space of appearance," in which citizenship is produced through face-to-face communication and deliberation. As Hou and Knierbein (2017), Cassegård (2014) and many others have discussed, in line with earlier claims from Mitchell (2003), the making of a public space involves no small degree of contestation.

This chapter chronicles the short and curious history of the Hong Kong government's East Wing Forecourt and its transformation into Civic Square through political action over the past decade. It demonstrates the highly contingent process by which protestors and public authorities interact to produce a politically meaningful place from a quotidian urban space.

The Birth of Civic Square

The Central Government Office complex was designed, in the words of Rocco Yim, whose Rocco Design Architects received the commission in 2002, as a space with vast green belts and public access channels that symbolized the "effective dialogue" between government and citizens (Rocco Design Architects 2014). The site chosen for the Hong Kong Special Administrative Region's new Government Headquarters was the old dockyard area named Tamar. When it was opened in 2011, the complex housed the Legislative Council (LegCo), the Chief Executive Office and the Central Government offices, twelve-story twin towers connected to each other by a horizontal span of offices across the top three floors of each tower. The East Forecourt and its drive connected the Central Government Offices to Tin Mei Avenue. Rocco Design Architects made provision for plenty of public open space by locating what they described as a "Civic Park" or a "green carpet" stretching from the Legislative Council Garden and Sculpture Court toward the waterside promenade at Victoria

Harbor, which in Yim's words "gives Tamar back to the citizens and brings them right through the heart of the government." In a 2014 *ArchDaily* article, Rocco Yim listed the design concept themes as "Door always open," "Land always green," "Sky will be blue" and "People will be connected." Under the last concept, the two hectares of green space (which became Tamar Park) connected the ground-level gardens of the government buildings with a waterfront promenade, which he said demonstrated that "The essence of the design for people is on connectivity, dialogue and communication." In a now ironic claim, Yim said that "the unfolding architectonic planes [are] symbolizing the desire to make a better city where diversity flourishes with effective communication between people and Government" (Rocco Design Architects 2014). But when the new government office complex opened in 2011, tensions were already rising over the very lack of effective communication between Hong Kong citizens and their government.

In 2010, the Hong Kong authorities floated a plan for Moral and National Education for primary and secondary schools. The resistance to this proposal was not immediate. After all, for those claiming Chinese identity, it was not unreasonable for Chinese culture and history to be taught in the schools—something that had been inadequately covered under British colonial rule. The spark that mobilized the opposition and eventually led to the withdrawal of the proposal came from high school students, led by the 15-year-old Joshua Wong. The organization he founded, Scholarism, quickly framed the initiative as one of "brain-washing" in which Chinese Communist Party education and propaganda cadres would control the curriculum in Hong Kong schools. Scholarism, allied with other organizations, launched public opposition to the education reforms in spring 2011. Over two summers, large rallies and marches involving parents and children drew broad public attention to the national education measure.

As the schools prepared to reopen in late summer 2012, Wong embarked upon a strategic escalation. Scholarism called for students to head to the Hong Kong government offices in Admiralty and to rally at the East Forecourt, on 31 August 2012. That day, three secondary school students from Scholarism also announced that they were beginning a hunger strike at the site. Ten parents and retired teachers soon joined the hunger strike, followed by nine others, when the first group of hunger strikers ended their strike (Cai 2017: 33). The square became the site of a week-long open-air festival with speeches, performances and even a visit from the chief executive, C.Y. Leung, who, Wong notes, shook hands with the demonstrators but never checked in on the hunger strikers. At one point, the protestors brought in a Goddess of Democracy statue, an invocation of the statue of the same name that had been paraded in Tiananmen Square in 1989 (*Dongfang ribao* 2012b). In Wong's recent memoir, he says that he and the other Scholarism leaders "baptized the open space with a new, symbolic—and catchy—name: Civic Square" (Wong 2020: 32). At a large rally at the square on 7 September, Wong estimated that 120,000 students and others showed up after school and work, the largest unauthorized demonstration in the city's history (Wong 2020: 33). Other estimates put the crowd size at 36,000 (Cai 2017: 33). The next day, in a major victory for Scholarism and for the power of popular protest in Hong Kong, C.Y. Leung announced that he was suspending the national education reforms. Protests continued at university campuses, demanding the formal removal of the reforms from future consideration (Cai 2017: 33–35).

Soon after the failure of the national education campaign, a retired photographer named Cheung Tak Wing launched his sit-in at the square.[2] The year before, in October 2012, employees of Hong Kong Television had organized a large-scale protest at Civic Square to demand that a LegCo subcommittee reconsider its decision not to issue a license for a free television station (*Dongfang ribao* 2012a). There were only two such free stations in Hong Kong; the union that led the protest suspected that politics was involved in the regulatory decision. On 20 October 2013, Cheung began his sit-in over the same issue, building an encampment in one corner of the plaza, where he stayed until 3 December.

Following the Hong Kong government's issuance on 4 December of controversial nomination methods for the selection of candidates in the 2017 chief executive elections and the 2016 Legislative Council elections, Cheung switched the basis of his protest from the licensing dispute to the demand for "universal suffrage." Giving up his encampment, Cheung held a daily vigil within the plaza, from 9am to 9pm daily, from December 2013 until 16 July 2014, when the Hong Kong government closed the Forecourt in order to build fencing and security barriers. When the new security perimeter was established and the government's policy put into effect to allow access for public gatherings only on Sundays and holidays, Cheung put in an application to hold a public rally from 9am to 7pm on 19 September. His application was promptly turned down, since he had applied to hold the rally on a Friday. This action would become the subsequent basis for Cheung's appeals through the courts, a judicial review to challenge the regulations on the grounds that they violated rights to free speech and assembly (High Court of the HKSAR 2018). A week after Cheung's plan to hold a rally in Civic Square was rejected, the site became the birthplace of the 2014 Umbrella Movement.

The details of what happened on the evening of 26 September 2014 are mentioned in most accounts of the Umbrella Movement, but they are rarely examined in close detail for the ways in which the contested nature of the space helped to catalyze what became the broader movement. On 19 September, a week-long boycott of classes was called by the Hong Kong Federation of Students (HKFS) in response to the unsatisfactory electoral reforms that denied Hong Kong citizens the right to direct election of the chief executive. At the end of the boycott, on 26 September, Joshua Wong led Scholarism to join the university students in a march to the Hong Kong Government complex in Tamar. That evening, Wong led a group of some 200 protesters in an attempt to occupy Civic Square. The tactic had been discussed before in secret by Scholarism and HKFS (*Ming Pao* 2014; Chen and Szeto 2017: 75.) In Wong's recent memoir published in English, he describes a more spontaneous action: "We were sitting on a makeshift stage set up outside Civic Square. . . . My eyes were trained on the fence surrounding the square when an idea came to me. 'Tonight we reclaim Civic Square,' I said" (2020: 45). Whether it was more planned than spontaneous, the emphasis on "retaking" (*chongduo* in Mandarin) or "reclaiming" (in Wong's memoir) is significant. The connotation is that the space had been seized by the Hong Kong government and was now being retaken by those to whom it belonged—the citizens of Hong Kong. At about 10:15pm, according to a *Ming Pao* news report the next day, as that night's rally was coming to its conclusion, Wong ascended the podium and called out to the crowd "retake Civic Square!" In a sign that the operation wasn't really spontaneous, students proceeded in two groups to occupy the square. Some, including Wong, scaled the 3-meter fence, while others maneuvered from the direction of the LegCo Building. Wong and those scaling the fence were soon caught by the Hong Kong police, who pulled Wong off the fencing and placed him under arrest. But about 100 students coming from the other direction made their way inside Civic Square, where a dozen occupied the flag platform. They were soon trapped there by the police. Protestors outside the square used loudspeakers to rally their ranks and blocked the passages to the square to keep out police reinforcements (*Ming Pao* 2014). The standoff continued into the night of 26 September and throughout the day of 27 September.

As police set upon the ranks of the protestors outside the square with pepper spray, those at the front held up umbrellas to block it. Soon students in the back of the crowd were passing up their umbrellas to replace the umbrellas damaged in the fracas. From an overpass near the scene, protestors also hurled their umbrellas to their comrades below. As the news spread quickly on social media, it was termed "The Umbrella Movement." By 28 September, the crowds arriving at the scene were so large that as police blocked their access to Civic Square; they quickly covered the major arterial of Harcourt Road. At this point, the police took the unprecedented step to use tear gas on the crowds, a move that only attracted more outraged protestors and spread the occupations to two other locations in the city (to the main roads in Causeway Bay and to Mongkok in Kowloon, with peak estimates of protestors at the three venues put at 1.2 million).

The Umbrella Movement ended in late 2014, having failed to alter the proposed electoral system and having drawn opposition from a weary public inconvenienced from traveling through the busiest districts of the city. For their forced entrance into the East Wing Forecourt on 26 September, Joshua Wong, Alex Chow and Nathan Law would be convicted in July 2016 for taking part in an unlawful assembly and later sentenced to six to eight months in prison.

Civic Square Reopens as Regulated Public Space

Civic Square was closed to public access in September 2016, but in August 2017, the newly elected Chief Executive Carrie Lam commissioned a study on how to balance the rights of public assembly with the fact that the square served as a main entrance to government offices. In late December 2017, to the disappointment of many, Civic Square was reopened under guidelines that required all public assemblies to apply first for official permission, with the same provisions of older regulations that restricted public assemblies to Sundays and holidays. But the Hong Kong Civil Human Rights Front quickly applied for and received permission to hold a rally at the square.

The 1 January 2018 protest march followed an annual practice by the opposition to hold demonstrations on New Year's Day to call attention to the erosion of Hong Kong's autonomy. That year, the opposition decried the planned opening of a PRC border checkpoint in the West Kowloon railway station linking Hong Kong with Guangzhou by high-speed rail (the checkpoint was installed in September 2018). At the New Year's Day rally, an estimated 10,000 marchers proceeded toward the Tamar government compound, and 200 of them entered Civic Square. Scuffles soon broke out between demonstrators and the police when they made several attempts to access the flag platform (Zhao 2018). But the Square remained accessible under the new guidelines for properly approved "public order events."

As the protests were taking place in Civic Square, the High Court of Hong Kong, Court of First Instance, was hearing arguments in the Cheung case. Cheung's lawyers argued that government restrictions on the use of the space violated the Basic Law's Article 27 on freedom of expression and assembly, as well as two articles from the Hong Kong Bill of Rights that stipulated the same freedoms. The government's lawyers countered that the space was essentially regulated and protected as property—in this case, the Hong Kong government was the property owner and had the same rights to control access to the space as would a private property owner (High Court of the HKSAR 2018).

Justice Thomas Au, who issued his ruling on 19 November 2018, dismissed the Hong Kong government's contention that ownership rights trumped the rights of expression and assembly: "insofar as state-owned or government property is concerned, it is *wrong in principle* for the government to regard it as having an entitlement as property owner to have an unfettered choice to exclude the public or to grant access" (High Court of the HKSAR 2018). The government quickly appealed the ruling to the Court of Appeal of the High Court, with a hearing scheduled for August 2019.

This judicial review of the Hong Kong government's regulations on Civic Square transpired amidst the largest and most consequential protests in the city's history, which began over the Hong Kong government's rush to pass the extradition bill. The protests began in April, and a few months later, as pro-government legislators advanced the bill to a second reading on 12 June, protestors massed around LegCo Building entrances to prevent the members from entering the building. The evening before, at the other end of the complex, a group of protestors stood outside the fence of Civic Square, where some of them began singing a Christian folk song from the 1970s, in what some explained was an attempt to lower tensions among the police who stood on the other side in the square and who would be deployed the following day to remove the protestors at the LegCo Building. "Sing Hallelujah to the Lord" quickly became a protest anthem for the movement (along with "Glory to Hong Kong"). As the cultural geographer Justin Tse (2020) has noted,

> the 'people' were framed in that moment as a praying populace, and as such, like in the anti-national education curriculum protests and the beginning of the Umbrella Movement, the political action of this politicized public was to reclaim Civic Square with the song.

What happened on 12 June and in the following days and weeks is well known to those who followed the remarkable protests of 2019. Protestors blocking access to the LegCo Building on 12 June were set upon by riot police using pepper spray and tear gas, in quantities that in one day exceeded all the rounds fired in 2014 during the Umbrella Movement. On the following Sunday, the largest protest ever recorded in the city's history saw an estimated 2 million people take to the streets. As smaller but sustained protests continued in 2019, protestors chose not to occupy spaces for long periods but instead held marches and rallies at selected locations, only to disperse and reconvene at other venues around the territory days later. When the government suspended the extradition bill on 15 June and formally withdrew it in September, Civic Square became less important as a protest venue than were the streets and sites that symbolized PRC influence over Hong Kong: the PRC's Hong Kong Liaison Office, the West Kowloon railway station and hotels and shopping districts popular with mainland PRC tourists. Tamar Park continued to be the site of large rallies throughout 2019, but Civic Square remained guarded and off limits.

Conclusion

In February 2020, the three-judge panel of the Court of Appeal issued its ruling on Cheung Wak Ting's challenge to the Hong Kong government's regulations on public assemblies in

Civic Square. The Court of Appeal judges were far more sympathetic to the government's claims. Their ruling stated, "In order to be compatible with the use of the CGO [Central Government Offices] as a workplace and the Forecourt as the means of access, the permissible scale of public meetings and processions has to be duly limited." The judges, led by Chief Judge of the High Court Jeremy Poon, went on to discredit the very naming of the space. "It is a misnomer to call the Forecourt the Civic Square," he noted, "It is therefore wrong to perpetuate the self-improved but mistaken characterization of the primary function of the Forecourt by attributing symbolic significance to it as a special place for mass public protest under such misnomer" (High Court of the HKSAR 2020). The public, the ruling said, could freely and easily express opinions and hold demonstrations in the 85-square-meter "designated public activity area" outside the Forecourt on Tim Mei Avenue or, if they wished for a larger space, at the other side of the complex at Tamar Park. The ruling came while Hong Kong residents were confined to their residences under the government's stay-at-home orders to cope with the COVID-19 pandemic. The Court of Final Appeal was to make its determination on the case sometime in the second half of 2020.

This brief history of a public space in Hong Kong illustrates what I have called elsewhere "the power of place"—referring to the ways that political geographies of a city, whether a formal "civic space" or otherwise, can at times facilitate sustained challenges to public authority (Frazier 2019).[3] This is not a deterministic or probabilistic claim that some public spaces take on an aura that causes protestors to mobilize against public authorities. But it suggests a close view of the sort offered here for Hong Kong's Civic Square to see the mechanisms by which an ordinary urban space becomes what Mitchell (2003: 35) terms a "space for representation." The process of place-making is highly contingent—much depends on the interactions between protestors and authorities, the images and representations of the conflict and the audiences who view it at different scales (national and global). Authorities may, as the Hong Kong government did in 2014 in the case of Civic Square, wall off the space and regulate its use by the public. But the symbolic importance of the place remains, and with it the potential to use it as a resource in future protests. The words penned by the *Dongfang ribao* columnist Bi Riyao (2017) when Civic Square reopened in late 2017 remain all the truer today:

> Viewing this political treachery [strict public-use rules] with a cool detachment, the reopening of this piece of land still makes it the most raucous place in Hong Kong for politics and demonstrations. Here, one may feel the pulse of Hong Kong, hear the breath of Hong Kong, and ascertain Hong Kong's eras of flourishing and decline. Just like Victoria Harbor to its front, all the chaotic warfare and bastards of politics have, in the end, etched at this place the ebbs and flows of Hong Kong.

Notes

1. In simplified Chinese characters, the name is 公民广场 (pronounced *gongmin guangchang* in Mandarin). A literal translation is "Citizens' Square."
2. Details from this paragraph drawn from High Court of HKSAR 2018.
3. As this chapter was being written in early June 2020, the Trump White House extended a "security perimeter" around the seven acres of Lafayette Square, in Washington, DC, closing off the public space with fencing and Jersey barriers, on the false claim that protestors decrying racism posed a national security threat. The Square was reopened a week later, but the public memory of the extraordinary scene there on 1 June and in the days that followed is likely to endure.

References

Arendt, H. (2018) *The human condition* (2nd ed.). University of Chicago Press.

Batuman, B. (2015) "'Everywhere is Taksim': The politics of public space from nation-building to neoliberal Islamism and beyond." *Journal of Urban History* 41 (5). pp. 881–907.

Beissinger, M. (2011) "Mechanisms of Maidan: The structure of contingency in the making of the orange revolution." *Mobilization: An International Quarterly* 16 (1). pp. 25–43.

Bi, R. (2017) "Shizishan shang: Zhengzong tiandi hua cangsang" (狮子山上：政总前地话沧桑, "On Lion Rock: The ups and downs of the Government Office Forecourt"). *Dongfang Ribao* (東方日報), 29 December.

Cai, Y. (2017) *The Occupy movement in Hong Kong: Sustaining decentralized protest*. Routledge.

Cassegård, C. (2014) "Contestation and bracketing: The relation between public space and the public sphere." *Environment and Planning D: Society and Space* 32 (4). pp. 689–703.

Chen, Y.C. and Szeto, M.N. (2017) "Reclaiming public space movement in Hong Kong: From Occupy Queen's Pier to the Umbrella Movement." In: Hou, J. and Knierbein, S. (Eds.) *City unsilenced: Urban resistance and public space in the age of shrinking democracy*. Taylor & Francis Group. pp. 69–82.

Dongfang Ribao (东方日报) (2012a) "Lihui foujue tequanfa chafapai fengbo" (立会否决特权法查发牌风波, "LegCo Vetoes special powers law inspection for issuing broadcast license"), 26 October.

Dongfang Ribao (东方日报) (2012b) "Xingdong zhengzhihua—minzhu nüshenxiang 'zhanling zhenzong'" (行动政治化—民主女神像'占领政总', "The action gets political—the Goddess of Democracy 'occupies Central Government Offices'." 5 September.

Frazier, M.W. (2019) *The power of place: Contentious politics in twentieth-century Shanghai and Bombay*. Cambridge University Press.

Habermas, J. (1989) *The structural transformation of the public sphere*. MIT Press.

High Court of the Hong Kong Special Administrative Region (HKSAR) (2018) *Constitutional and administrative law list, no. 136 of 2014, between Cheung Tak Wing and director of administration*, 19 November. At: https://legalref.judiciary.hk/lrs/common/ju/ju_frame.jsp?DIS=118531&currpage=T. Last accessed on 4 June 2020.

High Court of the Hong Kong Special Administrative Region (HKSAR) (2020) *Civil appeal no. 577 of 2018 (on appeal from HCAL 136/2014), between Cheung Tak Wing and director of administration*, 14 February. At: https://legalref.judiciary.hk/lrs/common/search/search_result_detail_frame.jsp?DIS=126906 &QS=%28CACV%7C577%2F2018%29&TP=JU&ILAN=en. Last accessed on 4 June 2020.

Hou, J. and Knierbein, S. (Eds.) (2017) *City unsilenced: Urban resistance and public space in the age of shrinking democracy*. Taylor & Francis Group.

Kohn, M. (2013) "Privatization and protest: Occupy Wall Street, Occupy Toronto, and the occupation of public space in a democracy." *Perspectives on Politics* 11 (1). pp. 99–110.

Ming Pao (明報) (2014) "Duogongmin guangchang—Huang Zhifeng beibu" (夺公民广场—黄之锋被捕, "Seizure of Civic Square—Joshua Wong arrested." Vancouver Edition, 27 September.

Mitchell, D. (2003) *The right to the city: Social justice and the fight for public space*. The Guilford Press.

Nicholls, W., Miller, B. and Beaumont, J. (Eds.) (2016) *Spaces of contention: Spatialities and social movements*. Routledge.

Rocco Design Architects (2014) "HKSAR government headquarters." *ArchDaily.com*, 9 July. At: www.archdaily.com/481237/hksar-government-headquarters-rocco-design-architects. Last accessed on 4 June 2020.

Said, A. (2015) "We ought to be here: Historicizing space and mobilization in Tahrir Square." *International Sociology* 30 (4). pp. 348–366.

Tse, J. (2020) "Sing hallelujah to the lord: Secular Christianities on Hong Kong's Civic Square." *The Immanent Frame*, 15 April. At: https://tif.ssrc.org/2020/04/15/sing-hallelujah-to-the-lord/. Last accessed on 5 June 2020.

Wong, J. and Ng, J.Y. (2020) *Unfree speech: The threat to global democracy and why we must act, now*. Random House.

Zhao, S. (2018) "Showdown as police surround Hong Kong protesters at 'Civic Square' after New Year's Day March." *South China Morning Post*, 1 January.

15
REFLECTIONS ON EMERGING PUBLIC SPACE DESIGN APPROACHES IN HONG KONG

Hendrik Tieben and Chen Ying-Fen

Introduction

Since Hong Kong's development into an international hub of financial and service industries in the 1980s, it has also become a center for regional and international design firms capitalizing on Hong Kong's and Mainland China's rapid growth and opportunities in South East Asia. The main foci of these firms were large-scale urban masterplans, infrastructure, commercial and high-end residential projects. However, with the financial crises of 1997 and 2008, and the following local Occupy and Umbrella Movements, parts of the design community began to realize the limits of this development logic. New initiatives in the design field happened in tandem with these urban movements, which were energized through common causes of opposition to land reclamation (Ng 2011), loss of urban heritage (Lu 2016), lack of affordable housing (Lee 2019) and inappropriately designed public space (Xue and Manuel 2001), opening up imaginations of alternative design thinking.

A clear sign of this reorientation was the Refabricating City exhibition in the second Hong Kong/Shenzhen Bi-City Biennale of Urbanism/Architecture (UABB), which opened in December 2007. A range of alternative projects were exhibited, including one developed by the Community Group H15 with the help of local architects to save a cluster of traditional businesses related to wedding cards at Lee Tung Street from demolition in the context of the Urban Renewal Authority's redevelopment plan (Wang and Chung 2011). In addition to alternative co-design approaches for urban heritage areas such as Lee Tung Street and the Blue House (Chen and Szeto 2015), new design approaches were also developed for the city's public spaces reflecting on challenges including the insufficient amount and quality of public open space (Lai 2017; HKPSI 2018), lack of meaningful public participation and fragmented government planning. These alternative approaches emerged from a newly developing ecosystem of engaged citizens and communities, new university programs, young design practitioners, long-established religious charities, non-profit organizations and social enterprises.[1]

An International Trend of Emerging Public Space Design Approaches

Similar public space design approaches have been emerging in other parts of the world. Mitrašinović (2016) examined similar developments in Western contexts as responses to uneven urban development caused by neo-liberal policies. The private sector, urban activists, the third sector and communities began to initiate such urban design approaches, aiming to reclaim and create public spaces through new tactical and participatory methods. His observations overlap with similar interpretations by other scholars focusing on insurgent approaches to public spaces and community design in the Pacific Rim (Hou 2010). In this chapter, we examine the previous phenomena in Hong Kong by deploying Mitrašinović's analytical framework while reflecting on Hong Kong's specific political and economic conditions.

Hong Kong and most other East Asian cities seem not to fall into the narrow definition of neo-liberalism (Harvey 2005) due to the strong involvement of state power in the market economy. However, to better comprehend the contemporary urban development of East-Asian cities, scholars expanded the definition of neo-liberalism. For instance, neo-liberalism was interpreted here as an approach for economic reforms in developing cities in order to participate in the global economic system (Kim and Ward 2007) and also as an ideology hybridized with developmentalism to assist in the formation of urban policies and practices in the East-Asian context (Hill et al. 2012). Based on the work of these scholars, studies of Hong Kong vis-à-vis neo-liberal policies have examined its health policy (Chiu et al. 2012) and housing planning (Huang 2019). Following the Asian Financial Crisis and Hong Kong's Handover to the People's Republic of China in 1997, the high involvement of the private sector and a wave of privatizations contributed to the formation of neo-liberal conditions for urban development processes in Hong Kong. These have in turn created the grounds for the development of new, creative design approaches and responses to the state of crisis and transition.

In the following section, to explicate responses to the specific circumstances of Hong Kong, three examples of emerging design approaches for public space are discussed. Because these more recent cases have been less analyzed, our research is based on the methodologies of participatory observation, first-hand experience (in the case of Magic Carpet) and secondary sources. The cases will be analyzed with reference to Mitrašinović's five design domains of new urban practices (Mitrašinović 2016: 182).[2] The aim is to go beyond locating these global trends of emerging design approaches in Hong Kong to consider their particular potential to address Hong Kong's current urban crisis.

Case 1: Magic Carpet Community Re-Envisioning

Initiated by the School of Architecture at the Chinese University of Hong Kong (CUHK)[3] to develop more process-oriented and cross-sectoral approaches to public space, the Magic Carpet project assisted NGOs and residents in Sai Ying Pun, Hong Kong Island, in building their capacity to co-create public spaces and strengthen a sense of belonging and engagement in the community. The project has been developed in stages—Magic Carpet Project (2013), Magic Tables (2014), Magic Spaces (2015) and Magic Lanes (2016–ongoing)—and has organized various community activities in relation to spatial designs, for instance, by reclaiming the underused Centre Street[4] of Sai Ying Pun to become again a more vibrant and inclusive public space. This has also been done as a part of the district's ongoing transformation motivated by the extension of the Mass Transit Railway (MTR) West Island Line and urban renewal initiatives in the district (Kang and Tieben 2017). According to Mitrašinović's five design domains, the series of Magic Carpet projects moved step by step from short-term tactical events to the second domain of self-organization, a regularized pattern of tactical activities, and to the third domain in which innovative value propositions are created from these activities.

The Magic Carpet project was launched in 2013 to pursue an inclusive design process[5] by incorporating the methods of community documentary filming and screening and public open space design as means to empower the residents through retelling the neighborhood's history, establishing community identity and creating a space for communal activities. A key step in this process was to invite students of a long-established secondary school in Sai Ying Pun, King's College, to join the project—using the techniques they learned from a series of video-production workshops—aimed at interviewing community members and collecting their stories as well as their reflections on the current land development. These short films were screened at a community gathering event during the traditional Moon Festival, reclaiming Centre Street's role as central meeting place by covering it with artificial grass as a green "magic carpet" and inviting residents and visitors to take off their shoes and recline on soft pillows and cushions.[6] At the lower end of the street, a screen was fixed to a large truck upon

FIGURE 15.1 Magic Carpet Community Re-Envisioning event in Sai Ying Pun at Moon Festival 2013 (Magic Carpet, 2013).

Source: MAD. Courtesy of Ada Wong.

which films documenting the individual stories of residents and shopkeepers in the district were projected and scaled up as a means of community empowerment.

In the following project stages, the capacity of this community was further built by shifting the responsibility to the third-sector organization Caritas as well as to the residents by regulating tactical activities with value propositions. For instance, the Magic Lanes project moved from temporary interventions to more long-term changes, with the opening of a community studio, employment of two place makers with backgrounds in architectural design and social policy and the co-creation of a design project for Sheung Fung Lane with a newly formed residents group (Friends of Sheung Fung Lane).[7] While according to a social impact assessment conducted by the Magic Lanes team in 2019, the project is generally positively received by the community, it still faces hurdles in securing permission to manage the public space beyond the project funding phase. Despite these limitations, a combination of short-term tactical design interventions at Centre Street and the longer-term capacity building for co-creation at Magic Lanes has begun to create a stronger sense of belonging, followed by a range of design and placemaking initiatives by community members, NGOs and more recently also the formation of alternative political claims and voices.

Case 2: Make a Difference Social Lab

The second case is the third-sector organization Make a Difference (MaD) in Hong Kong, founded in 2009. It is one of several organizations that emerged after the Financial Crisis (2007–08), together with the Hong Kong Public Space Initiative (2008) and Very Hong Kong (2012). What distinguishes MaD from the Magic Carpet is its setup as a non-profit organization and its background. The founder and chairperson, Ada Wong,[8] originally studied law and education before becoming renowned as an influential district councilor for Hong Kong's Wan Chai District. The organization could leverage Ada Wong's ample experience in local politics and her connections to Hong Kong's business world and community organizations.

According to its mission statement, "MaD believes in the social potential of creativity. Through participatory programs, we inspire and empower young people all over Asia to come up with innovative responses to our time's challenges." It was set up as a non-profit organization with the "long term goal [of] building a creative civil society." Following this goal, MaD uses different platforms and reaches out to a wide range of community and educational organizations, as well as corporations and government departments and authorities. Its core values are defined as creating for sustainable causes, value diversity and coexistence, focusing on constructive actions and promoting a creative ecology. Activities are not limited to Hong Kong and extend to other Asian countries and also include large-scale events such as the annual MaD Festival.

MaD has launched a range of design-related projects with different partners and funding programs. One of the signature programs is its Jockey Club Make a Difference Social Lab, "where citizens and civil servants co-design and experiment on services and policies for a better public life." So far, the Social Lab has developed four projects organized on its New Model of Public Participation: the LIBoratory Lab, Market Lab, Park Lab and Healthy Street Lab. Each of these projects is related to a different aspect of public space.[9] As the main strategy to push for change in Hong Kong's planning practice, the Social Lab involves representatives of Hong Kong's Transport Department. The project is funded by the Hong Kong Jockey

FIGURE 15.2   Public space prototyping and co-design of the MaD "Health Street Lab" at Sham Shui Po, Hong Kong, 2019.

Source: MAD. Courtesy of Ada Wong.

Club Charities Club Trust. Through cross-sectoral cooperation with a state actor (Transportation Department) and funding by a market actor (Hong Kong Jockey Club Charities Club Trust), MaD focused its efforts on developing new, emerging design approaches beyond the community domain, thus reaching out to the level of political and economic systems.

Case 3: Self-Build Bishop Hill Community

The so-called "morning exercise park" located on Bishop Hill, or, under its Cantonese name, Wo Chai Hill (窩仔山), was initiated by the residents of the Shek Kip Mei district as an informal, even illegal public open space. It differs fundamentally from the previous two cases in that "design" was deployed here under grassroots circumstances as a catalyst, on the one hand to assist the residents in opening a long-term abandoned but fenced infrastructure location for public use and on the other to develop the residents' capacities for self-organization through forming and continuously maintaining a community that was born along with this public open space.

In the 1950s, the site had acquired historic significance when a water reservoir was built there after a fire at a large squatter settlement in Shek Kip Mei, one of the oldest and densest neighborhoods in Hong Kong. The event led the colonial government to build Hong Kong's first large-scale public housing resettlement estate. After losing its role as an emergency water supply reservoir, the area remained fenced in until residents entered the area and created a self-initiated outdoor gym in the aftermath of the 2003 SARS epidemic (Chen 2019). The main initiator was Mr. So, a mechanical engineer who survived SARS. Based on his knowledge as a craftsman of lathe techniques, he started to reassemble and refine exercise equipment used in hospital rehabilitation and brought it to the hill to create an exercise park. By doing so, he intended to find meaning in his post-SARS life and also to contribute to the healthier life of the community and neighbors. Since then, more local residents and also people from other areas of Hong Kong have participated in this process, helping Mr. So in producing new equipment as well as in maintaining the environment (Huang 2017). The District Council furthermore built a small pavilion providing a table and seating for these community activities. Today, the government basically accepts the residents' informal use of this area, while the community organizes the shifts of maintenance work and holds gatherings and activities based on volunteerism, communication software and independent finance.[10] Such novel capabilities for a self-organized community have been gradually developing in the community-initiated design practice at Bishop Hill.

Even though the development of Bishop Hill's public space only starts as the first level of Mitrašinović's five domains and doesn't more widely affect the civil society, economy and institutional regulations, it demonstrates a possibility that indicates the potentials of processes of empowering communities, which demonstrates how a successful design practice can be cultivated without governmental planning and professional intervention, here simply starting with the action of a resident and his neighbors' participation.

FIGURE 15.3 "Morning exercise park" at Bishop Hill established by residents of Shek Kip Mei in the aftermath of the 2003 SARS epidemic.

Source: Hendrik Tieben.

FIGURE 15.4 "Morning exercise park" at Bishop Hill established by residents of Shek Kip Mei in the aftermath of the 2003 SARS epidemic.

Source: Hendrik Tieben.

Discussion

In all three cases, members of the civil society initiated the projects with different resources and backgrounds, representing different design domains, combinations of team members and degrees of community involvement, with or without the engagement of state actors and the market. In the first example, Magic Carpet was initiated by an academic team collaborating with a local secondary school and heritage organization to re-imagine specific public spaces

Emerging Public Space Design Approaches 175

FIGURE 15.5 "Morning exercise park" at Bishop Hill established by residents of Shek Kip Mei in the aftermath of the 2003 SARS epidemic.

Source: Hendrik Tieben.

and to build the capacity of the community. Later, in a series of follow-up projects, the main work shifted to an NGO (Caritas Hong Kong), while the role of residents in the co-creation process increased.[11] Decisions here were made largely independently from market and state actors (apart from the project's support by a government fund). During the process, design approaches varied from tactical space interventions in the beginning to co-creation processes with residents based on regular interactions to strengthen the sense of community and permanently improve the physical environment.

The MaD Social Lab, the second example, mostly worked with similar tactical design interventions to those used in Magic Carpet. As a difference, MaD included state actors (the Transportation Department) in the project team. This has been a key feature of MaD to reach solutions with higher chances of implementation and to build capacity for more innovative approaches within the governmental sector. With this approach, MaD aims to overcome key hurdles within Hong Kong's planning practice. Based on the particular background of MaD's founder, Ada Wong, as former Wan Chai district councilor, this NPO is able to significantly scale up activities, engage parallelly on a variety of well-staffed programs and reach a wider audience.

In the case of Bishop Hill, residents started with an insurgent intervention by opening up a fenced-in government owned space. Design elements were ready-mades such as play equipment, which was sourced by the residents and adapted to their specific needs and aspirations. This self-initiated DIY approach circumvented long and costly procurement and approval processes, leading to immediately visible results, which attracted further users and supporters. The intervention was tolerated by the authorities due to its well-grounded cause and the selected space being largely hidden from public view and with no immediate other competing users. Later, some district councilors from nearby neighborhoods began to support the project, facilitating needed construction work and appealing for legalization of the informal public space (Lu 2019). This leads to further considerations about the role of the state under the circumstance of current emerging design approaches, as well as post-disaster redevelopment, since the Bishop Hill community was formed in response to the SARS epidemic.

What Will Be the Future for Such Initiatives in View of Hong Kong's Recent Crises?

The three cases discussed previously demonstrate how designing has been employed in Hong Kong in recent years to co-design and co-develop public spaces. It also demonstrates how local residents and community organizations found ways to create hope and rebuild communities through design-centered propositions. Similarly, during the 2020 Chinese New Year, a group of newly elected district councilors, some of whom began their political careers in the 2019 Anti-Extradition Law Amendment Bill Movement, organized a two-day New Year Market on Sai Ying Pun's Centre Street in which numerous store owners of Sai Ying Pun participated, demonstrating new community initiatives and a sense of community (Chen 2020).

On the one hand, these examples illustrate the potential of newly emerging public space approaches in Hong Kong to cultivate not only communities' capacity for self-organization and design but also the resilience to evolve through repeated crises. Moreover, they indicate a strong grassroots contribution to the process, which seems linked to Hong Kong's unique political condition and will likely further affect the development of new design approaches. Specifically, comparing Hong Kong with its counterparts in the Western context vis-à-vis the neo-liberal condition, the strong state power and the continuing lack of effective mechanisms for civil society to influence political and planning decisions are two crucial differences from Western democratic societies. These further create space for the development of organizations specialized in mediating between the government sector and communities, such as Collaborate Hong Kong (CollaborateHK 2018), and its mission to assist community initiatives in finding the right matches of policies, funding and cooperative institutions to achieve their goals. In 2020, MaD founder Ada Wong wrote:

> It is now ten years since MaD's beginning. Hong Kong has become divided and this generation of young people feels helpless, and the "can do" spirit has turned into anger and frustration. The sphere for social innovation has also somewhat narrowed, and social experiments are difficult to push. However, if we still hope to bring more justice to society, this is not just a matter for the government: change happens when each person who loves this place participates vigorously and co-create ideas and experiments to solve social issues.

Potentially, the severity of the current crises, exacerbated by political protests and followed by the COVID-19 pandemic, could lead to a rethinking of how public spaces can be realized through community initiatives in Hong Kong. Moreover, through such new design-led approaches, the process of public space construction could be further synchronized with the development of a domain "of organized social and political activity commonly synonymous with the notion of civil society" (Mitrašinović 2016: 182) that currently seems still lacking in Hong Kong.

Notes

1. As part of the awareness of the shortcomings of Hong Kong's established planning practice, new university programs were created such as the Urban Studies programs in CUHK and HKU and CUHK's Urban Design program. Design educators developed pilot projects (such as the Magic Carpet project) in close collaboration with the third-sector organizations. After graduating, former students have started their own non-profit organizations and practices (e.g. Hong Kong Public Space Initiative and DOMAT). Other new non-profit organizations such as Very Hong Kong, Walk Des Voeux Road Central (Walk DVRC) and Collaborate Hong Kong were created by well-established and resourced individuals from the design profession and business community with the aim to mediate between urban activists and civil-society and state actors.
2. Mitrašinović's five design domains of new urban practices are: (1) an "insurgent" domain where most of the activity is of an ad hoc type and often does not translate into more complex forms of socio-spatial praxis, (2) a domain where modalities of self-organization begin to emerge as patterns of fairly regular tactical activity, (3) a domain where forms of socio-spatial activity are deliberately configured to produce value propositions for specific urban communities of practice which often translate into forms of alternative economic exchange with links to the market place, (4) a domain "of organized social and political activity commonly synonymous with the notion of civil society," and (5) a domain which is institutional and intentionally links the previous with institutions and agencies of the state and also that of the market (Mitrašinović 2016: 181–183).
3. The cooperation between CUHK and the community had started in 2008 after several years of background research funded by General Research Funds of the University Grants Committee; it was followed by an invitation of the Conservancy Association Centre for Heritage (CACHe) and Caritas Hong Kong to participate in joint exhibitions and community activities.
4. Centre Street used to be an open-air market until hawkers were moved to a new indoor market in the 1980s.
5. By that time, larger numbers of urban projects in Hong Kong already included forms of public participation; however, they were often limited to collecting residents' agreements to predefined options rather than offering more inclusive processes.
6. On the other hand, in the first project, the initiative and most design decisions for the temporary transformation of Centre Street were made by the CUHK project team with funding of two Knowledge Transfer Funds and the Kwang Hwa Information and Culture Center.
7. These projects did not include a direct project collaboration with government departments, which would potentially bring more institutional change, even though for the most recent project, Magic Lanes, a more substantial Urban Renewal Fund was secured. These projects also remained independent from Hong Kong's dominant private sector and the established processes of producing public spaces in private development.
8. Ada Wong is a lawyer, educator, politician, radio host and social activist. From 1995 to 2008, she was elected multiple times as urban councilor (before 1999) and district councilor, which has developed her influence in Hong Kong politics. She has been active in different social movements (including the preservation movements of Lee Tung Street and Blue House, both in the Wan Chai District) and later in 2010 established MaD and in 2012 The Good Lab (an office-sharing space), intending to influence society through innovative thinking, social enterprise and youth participation. For reference, see: www.mad.asia/about?lang=en; and, www.mad.asia/programmes/mad-social-lab/517. Last accessed on 20 September 2020.
9. For instance, the Healthy Street Lab focuses on the enhancement of street spaces in grass-roots district Sham Shui Po, which, similarly to Sai Ying Pun, is undergoing urban renewal. The project included the NGO Clean Air Network as research partner and the Yu Mak Yuen Integrated Services Centre and Tung Wah Group of Hospitals as community partners. The project was developed with similar steps to the Magic Carpet project, using workshops and on-site testing of co-created prototypes.

10. The spatial observation and community information was collected during a CUHK students' visit to Bishop Hill and interview with Mr. So on 14 January 2020.
11. During this period, the academics—who were originally the main actors in the projects—stepped back and took on a consulting role.

References

Chen, X. (2020) "'Mountain City Lunar New Year Festival' was rejected by district councilors and changed to street station crowded with crowds." *Inmediahk*, 19 January. At: www.inmediahk.net/node/1070073. Last accessed on 20 September 2020.

Chen, Y.C. and Szeto, M.M. (2015) "The forgotten road of progressive localism: New preservation movement in Hong Kong." *Inter-Asia Cultural Studies* 16 (3).

Chen, Z. (2019) "Sham Shui Po Bishop Hill: Mieshan water supplies department plans to withdraw after leveling, whether it will remain open." *Inmediahk*, 25 January. At: www.inmediahk.net/node/1061988. Last accessed on 20 September 2020.

Chiu, S.W.K., Ho, K.C. and Lui, T.L. (2012) "Reforming health: Contrasting trajectories of neoliberal restructuring in the city-states." In: Hill, R.C., Park, B.G. and Saito, A. (Eds.) *Locating neoliberalism in East Asia: Neoliberalizing spaces in developmental states*. Blackwell Publishing Ltd.

CollaborateHK (2018) *CollaborateHK: A new approach to community initiatives* [Report]. At: https://b30bad3f-6f7f-4350-828a-afaa2c239d24.filesusr.com/ugd/5d142c_a971dc81639349538288694bae026134.pdf. Last accessed on 20 September 2020.

Harvey, D. (2005) *A brief history of neoliberalism*. Oxford University Press.

Hill, R.C., Park, B.G. and Saito, A. (2012) "Introduction: Locating neoliberalism in East Asia." In: Hill, R.C., Park, B.G. and Saito, A. (Eds.) *Locating neoliberalism in East Asia: Neoliberalizing spaces in developmental states*. Blackwell Publishing Ltd.

Hong Kong Public Space Initiative (2018) *Privately owned public space—Audit report*. HKPSI. At: www.hkpsi.org/chi/main/. Last accessed on 20 September 2020.

Hou, J. (Ed.) (2010) *Insurgent public space: Guerrilla urbanism and the remaking of contemporary cities*. Routledge.

Huang, S.M. (2019) "Displacement by neoliberalism: Addressing the housing crisis of Hong Kong in the restructuring of Pearl River Delta region." In: Chen, Y.L. and Shin, H.B. (Eds.) *Neoliberal urbanism, contested cities and housing in Asia*. Palgrave Macmillan.

Huang, Y. (2017) "Yugong builds a mountain: SARS ex-patients go to level 800 daily and spend 10 years to build Bishop Mountain Morning Fortune Park." *hk01*, 17 August. At: https://tinyurl.com/y89n3rus. Last accessed on 20 September 2020.

Kang, M.J. and Tieben, H. (2017) *Magic carpet: Towards community benefit plans for regeneration in Taipei and Hong Kong* [妙想毡开：展开台北与香港都市再生的社区共利计画]. Tonshan [唐山].

Kim, E. and Ward, K. (2007) "Introduction: Reading neoliberalization." In: Kim, E. and Ward, K. (Eds.) *Neoliberalization: States, networks, people*. Blackwell Publishing Ltd.

Lai, C. (2017) *Unopened space: Mapping equitable availability of open space in Hong Kong* [Report]. Civic Exchange. At: http://civic-exchange.org/report/unopened-space-mapping-equitable-availability-of-open-space-in-hong-kong/. Last accessed on 20 September 2020.

Lee, J. (2019) *Housing, home ownership and social change in Hong Kong*. Routledge.

Lu, N. (2019) "[Morning paradise] Bishop Hill is expected to officially open the neighborhood to promote the addition of lighting systems." *hk01*, 18 March. At: https://tinyurl.com/y7catcqx. Last accessed on 20 September 2020.

Lu, T.L.D. (2016) "Empowerment, transformation and the construction of 'urban heritage' in postcolonial Hong Kong." *International Journal of Heritage Studies* 22 (4).

Magic Carpet Project (2013) At: www.magiccarpet.hk/. Last accessed on 20 September 2020.

Mitrašinović, M. (Ed.) (2016) *Concurrent urbanities: Designing infrastructures of inclusion*. Routledge.

Ng, M.K. (2011) "Power and rationality: The politics of harbour reclamation in Hong Kong." *Environment and Planning C: Government and Policy* 29 (4).

Very Hong Kong (2012) At: www.veryhk.org/en/. Last accessed on 20 September 2020.

Wang, W. and Chung, T. (Eds.) (2011) *Refabricating city: A reflection. Hong Kong-Shenzhen Bi-City Biennale of urbanism/architecture*. Oxford University Press.

Wong, A. (2020) "Make a difference: Social innovators are accumulators." In: *Journeys of change: Piloting social innovation*. The Hong Kong Jockey Club Charity Trust, Make a Difference School. At: https://issuu.com/mad.asia/docs/journeys_of_change_for_web. Last accessed on 20 September 2020.

Xue, C.Q.L. and Manuel, K.K.K. (2001) "The quest for better public space: A critical review of urban Hong Kong." In: Miao, P. (Ed.) *Public places in Asia Pacific cities*. The GeoJournal Library. p. 60.

16
RELEARNING THE CITY AND PUBLIC SPACE IN THE GREATER BAY AREA

Merve Bedir and Jason Hilgefort

Introduction

The Greater Bay Area (GBA) has been one of the main geographical foci of the accelerating modernization that has swept China. Interventions along the four pillars of modernization (Liu 1996)—agriculture, industry, national defense and science and technology—have radically transformed the landscape in the region with incredible speed and at an enormous scale. This acceleration was afforded by the "Gai Ge Kai Fang" (改革开放, reform and opening-up) policy, which brought increased contact between this region and the West starting in the 1980s (Zhao 1993) and more recently also the export of the Chinese model of modernization to other urban territories around the world.

Processes of modernization in the GBA can be observed across expanding spaces of production, infrastructure and urbanization. Shenzhen was constituted as a city from an agglomeration of villages (Huang 2017), and the principle of urbanization and growth in this region was one of the "exception becoming the rule" (Bach 2017), based in part on the designation of parts of the region as Special Economic Zones (SEZs) or Open Coastal Cities (OCCs). Koolhaas (1998) framed Shenzhen as a "generic city" (a term he originally coined to refer to Tokyo) characterized by "urban enclaves" to draw attention to the increasingly formulaic and repetitive methods and tools applied to the production of architecture and urbanism. Spaces of exception—factories, special economic zones, urban villages and natural reserves—in Shenzhen and the GBA exemplify the succession of different processes of mass production and infrastructural expansion and urbanization that Bach, Huang and Koolhaas describe.

In this context, one of the main considerations of this chapter is the significance of public space in relation to the previously described urban transformation. Based in the position that the city and public space are produced through public life—as a site of collaboration, negotiation and compromise among different agencies and interests—this chapter asks: what do physical and digital spaces of spectacle and gathering tell us about the city and the public space in the GBA, and what ways of practicing design can support their performative production and knowledge about them by those who have a stake in the city, who occupy it and use it?

The second consideration of this chapter is design education, which parallels and complements the role of design practice in producing cities and public space and shares the same fate. With standardized formal learning in the design fields (design, architecture, landscape and urbanism), site-specific learning has been losing ground to the implementation of more abstract forms of professional expertise related to the built environment (Deamer 2015; Okofu 2015; Axel et al. 2019). The pedagogical discourse has to respond to the critique of modernization and re-imagine the agency of learning and design beyond disciplinary boundaries in order to situate the creative work in the larger context of the city and the planet (Rendell 2004; Dewey 2015). More specifically, thus, this chapter will consider the ways of engaging in design-centered learning in order to discover ways of practicing that actively focus on producing public space.

Betsky et al. (2016) talked about "re-living the city," re-imagining, repurposing and remaking existing urban spaces and architecture, in Shenzhen and the GBA, and exploring the ways in which designers can work with people to make the city more useful, just and sustainable. Thinking along the same lines, we call for "re-learning the city" as part of and in order to re-live the city. This chapter explains the methods and tools employed in the program called Aformal Academy, which critically engages with the learning of design within the city. It is invested in understanding social relationships in and around things, spaces and infrastructures; labor and technologies of making; how these relations and economies create public space; and where the position of design is or could be among these. The core hypothesis of the program—learning by actively being, making and intervening in the city—means that the program is actively engaged in the creation of public space as well.

This ongoing program started in 2015 in Shenzhen and the GBA. It was initiated with an attitude of unlearning the city of Shenzhen in order to re-learn it, each workshop adding to the knowledge produced from the one before, remaining on-site and living in the locality in order to learn and produce living knowledge from within. The context-specific principles of this approach were derived in the course of more than twenty workshops, some of which are exemplified in the following sections: Shennan Avenue, Maozhou River, Trash to Treasure, Baishizhou Village and Melbourne University visiting school workshops. Subsequent sections in this chapter aim to accomplish the following: (1) introduce and explain the principles of unlearning and "re-learning the city" and its theoretical background based on Shenzhen, (2) articulate one of the sites of re-learning the city and public space in Shenzhen based on these principles and (3) discuss the capacity and potential futures of such attitudes and initiatives of learning in relation to the design and production of public space and the built environment.

On "Aformality" and Re-Learning the City

Re-learning the city is presented as an attitude of understanding Shenzhen and its public spaces based on experience and embeddedness, embracing its complexity, collectivity and representation, as well as critical observation and empathy. This attitude is concerned with the processes and the participation of the agents (human and nonhuman) that create a certain space and considers spatial form as an outcome of these processes. "Aformality" in Aformal Academy is proposed as an approach to learning urban space outside a dichotomy of formality vs. informality. Aformality refers to the ways in which distributed (human and nonhuman) agencies interact in the city and public space, how this interaction creates the rules of the network and the ways in which these rules and the network transform dynamically and continuously. Second, aformality refers to a fluidity within the learning program—without a definite set of expectations but continuously self-generating and reflecting where the next step is iterated and changed based on the step before—therefore slowly evolving and articulating its direction. Aformality enables the revealing of the nuanced complexities of a certain space and site, where learning experience assumes taking an active part in the production of public space.

Un-Learning

The Campus in Camps program, initiated in the West Bank, Palestine, was one of the main inspirations for Aformal Academy. There, un-learning was defined as creating a language that fits the context and the situation of the inhabitants' lives and "a process of producing knowledge that comes from the inside, not from outside, where we (participants of the program) look to ourselves as sources of meaning, and from this meaning create and define according to our experience and our lives" (Racco 2014). From this perspective, un-learning is meant to be a slow and cautious practice, and trust in one's own intuitions is by nature built up through trial-and-error. If the aim is to "re-learn" the city, then the first step is un-learning. This entails abandoning assumptions, the language, and canonical discourse created on typologies and fixed terminologies related to the city (Shenzhen) and creating space for learning from within. The knowledge produced from the local situation challenges dominant disciplinary canon in design and urbanism. This attitude was particularly important in urban villages.

FIGURE 16.1 Discussion at Hubei metro stop during Shennan Avenue workshop on the public transportation infrastructure system of Shenzhen. All sessions of the workshop took place during different times of day over ten days in the Hubei metro stop on Shennan Avenue.

Source: Aformal Academy.

Floating School: Learning Is for Everyone

Re-learning also refers to a horizontal mode of learning in which each participant shares their knowledge and learns from others. The classroom transforms from a place of instruction to a node of exchange that suspends the authority/hierarchy relationship that establishes the master/expert as the one who knows and who communicates knowledge to participants who supposedly don't know (Dpr Barcelona 2015). By reducing the assumption of "superiority" of the master/expert, the logic of a learning system based on explanations is reversed; intelligence is shared and manifested in experience through which an incremental acquisition of knowledge is made possible by self-instruction.

Agency, Perspective and Medium

Learning happens through imagination, which is always shaped by the participants' perspective. The two aspects of learning, as perspective and as medium, complement each other and enable a space of imagination for the participant experiencing the context. Different attempts to exercise perspective and medium supported embedded critical observation in Shenzhen, which was essential for un-learning the assumption that this city is a quickly produced, copy/paste urban environment with no history.

Collective Intelligence

On the rural front, Ou Ning (in Mai 2020) emphasized revealing the potential of people's intelligence. Based on participatory decision-making and consensus democracy, a bookstore

FIGURE 16.2 Gathering at an urban park in Shenzhen during an Aformal Academy workshop.
Source: Aformal Academy.

FIGURE 16.3 Collage made during the Melbourne University visiting-school workshop. Participants from Melbourne University collaborated with students from Shenzhen and the Greater Bay Area to produce a mural collage using several section drawings of real and imaginary buildings of Shenzhen.

Source: Aformal Academy.

in the rural village of Bishan in China's Anhui Province became the common space of an unfinished utopia, referencing alternative communities, architectural utopias, collectivity, rurality and a different relationship between city and countryside. On the urban front, Mattern (2019) stressed the need to find ways of accommodating temporal entanglement and epistemological plurality and developing more capacious and historically attuned ways of generating and operationalizing urban intelligences in order to create cities that are wiser than the sum of their intelligent parts. Ning and Mattern have been inspirations of Aformal Academy's methodological construction in terms of a collective intelligence of the city and of the public space.

Collective intelligence is then claimed as the capacity for critical thinking and observation, an awareness of collectivity, emotional knowledge and creativity. Collective intelligence encompasses not only the intelligence of humans but also the diverse array of nonhumans, thus decentering human intelligence. How can we re-learn and produce living knowledge differently and then use it to design/live the spaces shared by all beings?

Making: Craft and Design

The rise of design pedagogy as a response to industrial production required designers to be proficient not only in craft but in the art of instruction, that is, in trans-coding the artwork into a procedural method capable of integrating different modes of labor (Norwood et al. 2019). In Shenzhen, design had belonged to common knowledge instead of intellectual property, and this is what Aformal Academy has been interested in: re-learning design and public space as part of daily life—making, iterating, collectivizing, learning and re-iterating.

Sites of Aformal Academy

In many ways, Shenzhen is a microcosm of the world, with physical, digital and financial infrastructures that efficiently connect the city to the globe. The city itself is simultaneously segregated physically and socially through those very infrastructures but then is recreated by its residents who actively engage in public space. This is the type of context in which designers increasingly operate. In this sense, selected sites of Aformal Academy are specific while seeming generic, meaning that these sites are points of departure for a critical evaluation of the present by which we can begin to introduce critical ways of learning.

Public space takes on specific forms in different contexts, and the aim of Aformal Academy is to engage in each of these sites, seeking to unearth the multiple histories and contemporaneities of labor, domesticity, financialization and environmental concerns and how they produce public space. In *Other Ways of Doing Architecture*, Awan et al. (2011) discuss the problem of defining the practice of architecture—commonly based on the short-term priorities of those involved—which hence depends to a significant extent on habits in the profession, which hinder the possibility of self-reflection. The aim of re-learning sites and public spaces

FIGURE 16.4 Shangmeilin Village workshop.

Source: Aformal Academy.

FIGURE 16.5 Baishizhou village workshop.

Source: Aformal Academy.

FIGURE 16.6 Maozhou River walk.

Source: Aformal Academy.

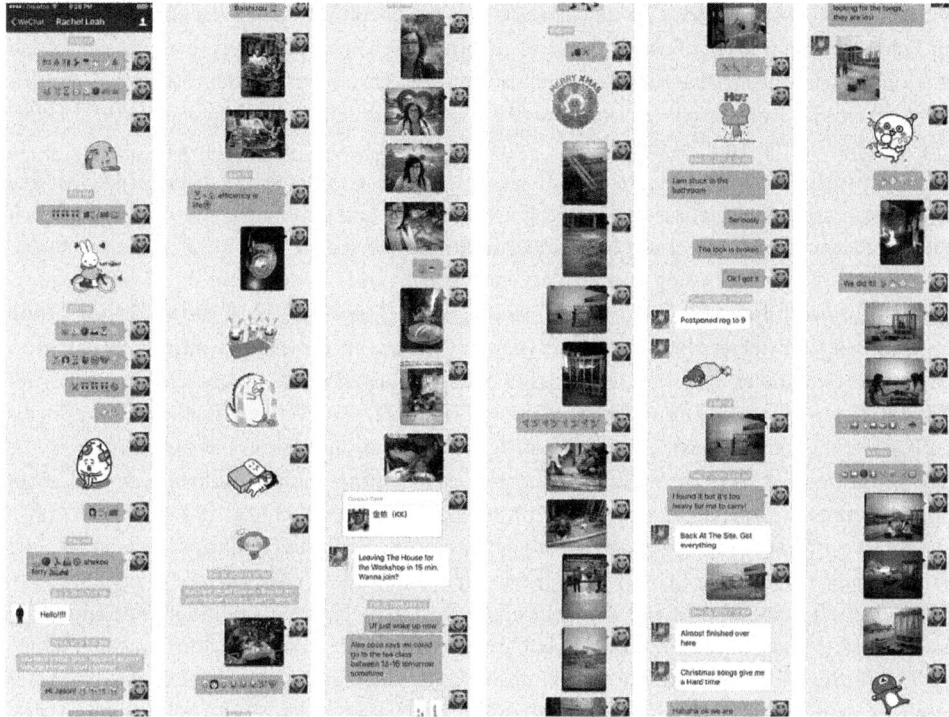

FIGURE 16.7 Wechat newspaper made during Mobile Spa + Tea House workshop.
Source: Rachel Leah Cohn and Aformal Academy.

in Shenzhen is not only to understand their present conditions but also to raise the possibility of re-imagining them through re-learning.

Aformal Academy started with a call for participants, who later took other participants back to their neighborhoods (sites) for lengthy programs, including tours, visits, conversations and discussions. These activities were followed up with other programs about design interventions, workshops and focused investigations and symposia.

Public Space in the Village

What defines an "urban village" (*chengzhongcun*, 城中村)? Is the word "urban village" the most accurate and productive analytical term to characterize "the village in the city" (城中村)? Is the village in the city a type of informal settlement? If so, how is it distinct from other types of informal settlement? What condition does this urbanism imply regarding access to public space? What can be discovered by taking the public space in the village in the city as an inspiration against gentrification processes at the hands of the government?

One of the motivations of taking Baishizhou, Hubei and Shangmeilin as sites comes from the term "the village in the city" used to designate such neighborhoods in the Chinese language. While the term "urban village" is used in English to refer to informal settlements which were rapidly urbanized in the global South and in China (Perlman 2010; Webster et al. 2015), the story of Shenzhen is more that of a city that grew amongst villages, in which these villages remained embedded in the urban fabric as exceptional states, retaining their rights of land ownership and collective decision-making mechanisms granted to them since Mao Zedong. These villages have transformed in ways that have been parallel to the changes that have taken place in the city at large but have also exhibited distinct characteristics of self-organization in the built environment, as well as in the creation of public space.

What is the best way to learn the village in the city, its indigenous characteristics, plural urban living practices, people, diversity of environments and public spaces; its social processes and protocols; and the legal and historical conditions that spawn it?

The Baishizhou workshop started with several walks and conversations in the village, initiated by the workshop participants who lived in Baishizhou. They took the workshop group around and told stories about their everyday experience in the village; introduced them to their friends, families and shop renters; and brought them to different public spaces, corner hangouts, playgrounds, gaming spots, wells and other sites of everyday public life. Residents of Baishizhou conversed with them about their understanding of time and public space in the village, notions of work and rest, hanging out and chatting, eating and drinking and other such practices.

Based on these initial interactions and observations, Erik Rietveld joined the workshop and brought forth the notions of "familiarity and trust" and "affordances" (Rietveld 2008). He suggested that everyday use of public space forms the basis for building familiarity with certain places and gaining the trust of people from other societal groups. Without such "public familiarity," fear of the unknown often prevails, which can cause the sharing of a space with strangers to be experienced as threatening. In the conversations, he posed the question of whether smooth interaction with strangers is a special embodied skill that people can develop.

The term "affordances" was proposed as a way to understand these action-oriented possibilities (Gibson 1977; Rietveld 2008; Norman 2013; Still and Dark 2013; Masoudi et al. 2019), to denote the way that a frequently used object becomes a familiar object and invites people to interact with the object, and also with other people, as social affordances can imply the possibility and even the imperative for social interaction: "The sight of a sad friend impels the desire to comfort them, a neighbor at the barbecue invites one to have a chat, and seeing an outstretched hand immediately evokes an impulse to shake it" (Rietveld 2008).

The idea for the workshop evolved to acknowledge and preserve the spontaneous character of use (instead of programming it in advance) and to better understand the apparent contradiction in the conscious design of casual interactions. It is possible to create multiple affordances through one single physical intervention. The designed artifact is thus ambiguous because it invites and encourages people with different backgrounds to different interactions. Rietveld (2008) suggests that thanks to this variety of pre-reflexive lived affordances, design provides a certain kind of freedom, the kind of freedom that is characteristic of our actions without reflection.

The conversations, insights, walks and observations enabled a re-living of the village, developing an understanding of the things, relations and spaces that create it. Based on the previous, different propositions emerged: some participants made posters, others set up Wechat newspapers and yet others proposed physical interventions in public space. Bauder and Cohn, two participants in the program, facilitated the design of a mobile spa + tea house inspired by the urban village but also intended to be inserted into other sites in order to explore the affordances for generation of public space and public interaction that it may create. This mobile

FIGURE 16.8   "Maozhou River." Collage made during the Maozhou River workshop.
Source: Jung In Kim and Aformal Academy. Courtesy of Jung In Kim.

spa + tea house was a hybrid of two elements in the village—spa and tea house—produced from recycled materials into a mobile design that demonstrates the fluidity and continuity of the dynamic character of public space in the village and the possibility of exploring this elsewhere in Shenzhen as a provocation.

Conclusion

Public space is produced by intense encounters between different ways of living. Philosophical, historical and critical reasoning need to be brought together to comprehend and learn from patterns of public spatial practices. At the same time, knowledge production is not an abstract matter but constructed from the ground. A self-conscious position benefits from both theory and practicing/performing in context for learning and production of knowledge related to the city and the public space. Human and nonhuman agents act and interact in public space, together with existing power structures and decision-making mechanisms, articulating and altering them. Public space relates to self-organization and indigenousness and cannot be reduced to formal/informal dichotomies.

Aformal Academy focuses on sites as thresholds that situate design within the diversity and complexity of urban space and the built environment. The principles and sites discussed in this chapter are not intended to set deterministic boundaries of an alternative learning method but rather to open up ways in which different practices, experiences and ways of learning can be related. We have attempted to avoid universalization or essentialization and recognize that design and learning can take on different forms than those that have been canonized in practice. The "canon" in living, practice and learning exists in relation to what it excludes. Even though indigenous voices do not falsify "the canon," including them allows us to rethink the scope of approaches and agencies that can contribute to the production and design of public space.

Acknowledgments

Aformal Academy: Re-learning the City was initiated during the Bi-City Biennale of Urbanism and Architecture, Shenzhen and Hong Kong, edition 2015–2016, curated by Aaron Betsky, Urban Think Tank and Doreen Heng Liu. The river site project was conducted with the invited collaboration of Antje Steinmuller California College of the Arts, San Francisco,

USA; Jung In Kim, Soongsil University, Seoul, South Korea; and Pnina Avidar, Fontys School of Fine and Performing Arts, Tilburg, the Netherlands. The urban village site project was conducted with the invited collaboration of Erik Rietveld, RAAAF, Amsterdam, the Netherlands; Clemens Bauder, Linz, Austria; and Rachel Leah Cohn, from VCU Qatar, Doha. Other collaborators include Superuse Studio and Melbourne University, as mentioned.

References

Awan, N., Schneider, T. and Till, J. (2011) *Other ways of doing architecture*. Routledge.
Axel, N., Bedford, J. and Hirsch, N. (2019) "Theory's curriculum." *eflux Architecture*. At: www.e-flux.com/architecture/curriculum/. Last accessed on 20 July 2020.
Bach, J. (2017) "From exception to rule." In: O'Donnell, M., Wong, M. and Bach, J. (Eds.) *Learning from Shenzhen: China's post-Mao experiment from special zone to model city*. University of Chicago Press. pp. 23–39.
Betsky, A., Shapiro, G.F. and Liu, D.H. (2016) *Re-living the city: UABB catalogue*. Actar.
Deamer, P. (2015) "Letter to the editors." *Learning* 45. pp. 6–7.
Dewey, J. (2015) *Experience and education*. Free Press.
Dpr Barcelona (2015) "Alchemy of the classroom." *Volume* 45. pp. 66–72.
Gibson, J.J. (1977) "The theory of affordances." In: Shaw, R.E. and Bransford, J. (Eds.) *Perceiving, acting, and knowing*. Lawrence Erlbaum Associates.
Huang, W.W. (2017) "The tripartite origins of Shenzhen: Beijing, Hong Kong, and Bao'an." In: O'Donnell, M., Wong, M. and Bach, J. (Eds.) *Learning from Shenzhen: China's post-Mao experiment from special zone to model city*. University of Chicago Press. pp. 65–86.
Koolhaas, R. (1998) *Generic city*. Monacelli Press.
Liu, K. (1996) "Is there an alternative to (capitalist) globalization? The debate about modernity in China." *Boundary 2* 23 (3). pp. 193–218.
Mai, C. (2020) "Trojan horses in the Chinese countryside: Ou Ning and the Bishan commune in dialogue and practice." *Field Journal, a Journal of Socially Engaged Art Criticism*. At: http://field-journal.com/issue-9/trojan-horses-in-the-chinese-countryside-ou-ning-and-the-bishan-commune-in-dialogue-and-practice. Last accessed on 20 April 2020.
Masoudi, N., Fadel, G.M., Pagano, C.C. and Elena, M.V. (2019) "A review of affordances and affordance-based design to address usability." *Design Methods and Tools* 1 (1). pp. 1353–1362.
Mattern, S. (2019) "Ether and ore: An archaeology of urban intelligences." In: Kurgan, L. and Brawley, D. (Eds.) *Ways of knowing cities*. Columbia Books. At: www.arch.columbia.edu/books/reader/483-ways-of-knowing-cities?fbclid=IwAR3mJKYBwK8-BgmCB9rBQHHD4S0DG1MAeU5vpJakbMOqciYPeKkWRARa_DI#reader-anchor-11. Last accessed on 20 April 2020.
Norman, D.A. (2013) *The design of everyday things* (revised and expanded ed.). Doubleday.
Norwood, B.E., Nolan, G. and Dainese, E. (2019) "Architecture unbound." *E-flux Architecture, Theory's Curriculum*. At: www.e-flux.com/architecture/curriculum/260414/architecture-unbound/. Last accessed on 20 April 2020.
Okofu, N.P. (2015) "Architecture at the edge of practice: A pedagogical approach to social architectural education." In: *Future of architectural research*. pp. 565–571. Building Research Information Database. At: www.brikbase.org/sites/default/files/ARCC2015_77_okofu.pdf. Last accessed on 20 July 2020.
Perlman, J. (2010) *Favela: Four decades of living on the edge in Rio de Janeiro*. Oxford University Press.
Racco, G. (2014) "Cross-section of an unlearning process." In: *Campus in camps*. At: www.campusincamps.ps/wp-content/uploads/2014/03/section-of-unlearning-giuliana.pdf. Last accessed on 20 April 2020.
Rendell, J. (2004) "Architectural research and disciplinarity." *Architectural Research Quarterly* 8 (2). pp. 141–147.
Rietveld, E. (2008) "The skillful body as a concernful system of possible actions: Phenomena and neurodynamics." *Theory and Psychology* 18 (3). pp. 341–363.

Still, J.D. and Dark, V.J. (2013) "Cognitively describing and designing affordances." *Design Studies* 34 (3). pp. 285–301.

Webster, C., Wu, F., Zhang, F. and Sarkar, C. (2015) "Informality, property rights, and poverty in China's 'favelas'." *World Development* 78. pp. 461–476.

Zhao, S.S. (1993) "Deng Xiaoping's southern tour: Elite politics in post-Tiananmen China." *Asian Survey* 33 (8). pp. 739–756.

17

THE GBA PUBLIC REALM AND THE MEGAREGIONAL DIALECTIC: THE PUBLIC SPACE OF THE MEGAREGION, PUBLIC SPACES IN THE MEGAREGION

Miodrag Mitrašinović

Researchers of public space in China, both Chinese and foreign, have largely replaced "public space" as the object of analysis with "open space" because "in the Chinese context, the definition of public space is not simple" and lacks clarity (Wiethoff 2014: 338). As Du also indicates (in this volume), public space as a zoning category employed in the practice of urban planning in China is a commonplace yet unexamined designation. Li and Genovese suggest that the Chinese term *gong gong kong jian* (公共空间) embodies subtle distinctions between "public" and "official" spaces; it frequently denotes a normative space while connoting varied degrees of public accessibility. This confusing semantic classification results in few Chinese studies on public space as such (Li and Genovese 2017), except in the context of "senior-urbanism" (Huang 2020: 32) and the "degrees of care" that negotiate socio-spatial distinctions between "the inside" (*neibu*) and "the outside" (*waibu*) (Li 2014).

The definition of "public space" is analytically unclear nowadays not because there are no plausible definitions but because multiple and often contradictory definitions simultaneously hold true; hence, it ought to be framed as a "cluster concept" (Kohn 2004). The complex processes of geopolitical and socio-spatial production of public spaces can hardly be confined by analytical concerns over clarity and simplicity. At stake here is less the question of space than of how "public" is constituted by/through public space. In a massive society experiencing enormous transition—with a centralized, single-party political system and with limited civil liberties, free press or other means of autonomous opinion formation and public debate (arguably all Western concerns)—it is difficult to overestimate the significance of this distinction. Whereas replacing "public" with "open" does facilitate the expediency (and often the very possibility) of research, it also leaves untouched the relations and conditions of production of public space.

This volume is structured around a few central ideas: first, public space is a significant, timely subject for scholars and professionals working in China today; second, public space has been an important catalyst for the emergence of the Greater Bay Area (GBA) public realm; third, public space is a proper analytical unit, albeit with somewhat porous boundaries, a fact embraced with enthusiasm by the authors in this volume rather than reluctance; fourth, public space must be studied across the differentiated scales and organizational levels of the GBA megaregion; and, finally, public space should be considered inseparable from other arenas in which 'public' is simultaneously constituted. They include (1) the public realm, as sites and spaces of collectivization and symbolic practices often demarcated by the built environment; (2) the the public sphere, a domain of discursive social relations centered on communication; and (3) the public domain, a regulatory arena where legal and policy dimensions of public sites and gatherings are determined and debated. Assuming that public space enables manifestations of 'public encounter,' some authors in this volume focus on the urban-spatial form, some on normativity and function of public space, and yet others on the socio-spatial, economic and political processes of the production and consumption of public spaces and the public realm.

In discussing public space as a medium for production of the public realm in the GBA megaregion, I heuristically bring together the dialectical framework (Schafran 2014) discussed in Chapter 1—a confluence of 'megaregional space,' 'spaces in/of the megaregion' and 'tactical sub-regionalism' with Madanipour's (2019) distinction between 'the public space' (an epitome driving the rhetoric of economic development and political homogenization) and 'public spaces' (lived urban places with differentiated yet negotiated layers of meaning and everyday practice). Accordingly, I will structure the following discussion by distinguishing between *the megaregional public space* (**tmps**) and *public spaces in the megaregion* (**psmr**). The theoretical and practical focus here is not on prioritizing either one but on the strategies, tactics and processes that constitute and operationalize both and ultimately on the courses of action that transform them.

The GBA Megaregional Public Space

tmps is integral to the GBA public realm and the megaregional imaginary—a strategic vehicle produced by government agencies, global economic and political organizations, economic planners and the finance industry, together with engineers, urban planners, urban designers and architects, and in close collaboration with the transportation, entertainment, gaming, tourism and leisure industries. Its totalizing effect manifests in treatment of "the public" as a standardized, governable entity operationalized in the production of a homogeneous narrative across the public sphere, standardized protocols across the public realm and policies across the public domain and a coherent symbolic language (e.g., urbanization, internationalization) deployed across the design and planning domains. What follows is an examination of four instances where protocols and mechanisms for the production of **tmps** are evident—where megaregionalism is experienced "in the flesh" (Ellul 1967).

tmps as Infrastructure of Mobility

Megaregionalism in the GBA implies reorganization and integration of its multiple urban systems. As outlined in Chapter 1, establishing consistency across geographic scales—and thus integration of the fragmented, polycentric GBA units—is a major challenge inherent in the megaregional space. Hence a massive communication and mobility infrastructure connecting the units (hubs)—by Intercity Commute Railway (ICR), High Speed Railway (HSR), subways, trams, airports and highways—is planned and increasingly coordinated to facilitate the movement of 80 million GBA denizens and hundreds of millions of travelers targeted by the Belt and Road Initiative (BRI) global strategy. This vast infrastructure follows a centrally

FIGURE 17.1 West Kowloon Station, Hong Kong. Images from top down depict the West Kowloon Cultural District under construction in 2018, the interior of the West Kowloon Station, the Mainland Port Area, and hi-speed CR train on Platform 8 of the Hong Kong West Kowloon Station.

Source: Adapted from the photos by baycrest (panorama and platform © CC BY-SA 2.5), s22tse (interior © CC BY 2.0) and wpcpey (port area © CC BY-SA 4.0). Source: Wikimedia Commons.

established set of standards and normative expectations, such as viewing regional distances in temporal terms that acknowledge the pivotal role of high-speed mobility (Mitrašinović 2006).

No organization has the capacity to develop a megaregional system individually, so public-private partnerships—as well as global partnerships, external funders and municipal collaborations—expedite both funding and management. The restructuring of land-use laws in Guangdong since 1986 (see Chapter 1) has also supported the development of **tmps** and its infrastructure. As a process driven by land development, infrastructure creation has fast-tracked new hubs and public spaces in the "spillover" areas between urban centers. Blackwell (in this volume) argues that in the emerging public realm of the GBA, interaction between urban mobility infrastructures and "high-value urban centers" formed around the nodes and hubs of the transportation networks produces new "networks of value." Both the magnitude of infrastructure development and the rise of social and physical mobilities place railways at the heart of the GBA public realm. Train stations, both transitory hubs and destinations, act as ideological symbols, political arenas, centers of economic exchange and "influential new public spaces" that reinforce new consumerist and urban lifestyle imaginaries through advertising and public service announcements (Lewis 2006: 275).

Built in 2018, Hong Kong's West Kowloon Station was designed as a terminus of a high-speed Guangzhou–Shenzhen–Hong Kong rail network.[1] Yet the station also transforms a transactional stop along the intercity commute into a dramatized performance of urban mobility at a novel, scale, volume and speed and a spectacle of public encounter. It is a landmark of the West Kowloon Cultural District, an up-and-coming arts district built on the reclaimed waterfront, with a master plan by Foster and Partners, and buildings designed by global firms including Herzog & de Meuron and UNStudio. The station building was designed by Aedas, the firm responsible (along with Rogers Stirk Harbour + Partners) for designing the Hong Kong Port Passenger Clearance Building of the Hong Kong–Zhuhai–Macau Bridge. The building represents a symbiosis of the national and regional governments with the support of private capital invested in the Cultural District—typical of "grand theater urbanism" (Xue 2019). Concealed in its lower levels, however, is the border crossing and customs apparatus that signals one's entrance into PRC territory in Hong Kong proper. Thus, an edifice that represents travel comfort to outsiders signifies to many Hong Kongers instead a departure from pre-2018 border protocols and a source of political discomfort.

tmps as Open Space System

Uniting ecological systems, topography, parks, land use patterns and material infrastructure (such as streets), open space systems[2] are abstract, rational, calculable and governable—an ideal vehicle for the production of **tmps**. In China, the volume of open space is calculated per capita, as a total sum of "green" open spaces within the designated geographic area of the megaregion divided by the combined total number of urban and transient residents (UN-Habitat 2012 [2013]: 88). Like most researchers and scholars, Yang et al. (in this volume) define public open space (POS) as the entirety of constructed outdoor places in Shenzhen that are open to "all citizens for free." Recognizing accessibility as an indicator of both service capacity and social equity, they conclude that public agencies must pay attention not only to equitable spatial distribution of POS but to improved accessibility, quality of public provisions, effective management, satisfaction among residents and funding. Their findings align with UN-Habitat's report claiming that the overall "quality of life could be enhanced by increasing accessibility" and quality of public spaces in Shenzhen (Lang and Shi 2019).

Sustaining concerns of public interest, including health and well-being, outdoor recreation and environmental preservation, is a discernible priority in open space planning in the GBA megaregion. As Zhao (2014: 293) indicates, a "system of urban green spaces" was first integrated into The Comprehensive Plan (SMG 1996) and later elaborated in the Planning of the Green Space System (SMG 2004) with the implementation of the three-level park system: forest/suburban landscape park (*senlin/jiaoye gongyuan*), comprehensive park (*zonghe gongyuan*) and community park (*shequ gongyuan*). The "urban green system" of parks and recreational areas—together with the Shenzhen Ecological Control Line, designed to protect nearly half of Shenzhen's available land from urban development—indicate a continuous effort by urban planners to clearly delineate ecoregions and establish growth boundaries as environmental protection measures (Barnett 2020). Hong Kong, for its part, has reserved more than half of its overall landmass as parks and green belts (Tang and Wong in this volume). However, as "continuous urbanity" (Pickett and Zhou 2015) expands, it alters the environment and affects ecological balance, increasing the risk of floods, wildfires and a warming climate, all reported in recent years by climatologists working in the Pearl River Delta (PRD). Within the framework of megaregionalism, however, open space systems are ultimately assessed in relation to the economic value of regional ecosystems (Zhang et al. 2019), particularly as a conduit to achieving profit-oriented outcomes—for example, the ecological tourism well under way in the GBA.

tmps as Economic Engine

The instrumentalization of public space in economic development has infiltrated policies of governments and corporations the world over (Madanipour 2019). The World Bank has long framed public space as a "hidden wealth of cities"—an "asset" within urban development and economic growth paradigms (Kaw et al. 2020). UN-Habitat has repeatedly asserted "quality" and "connective matrix of public space"—both supposedly managed by governments (United Nations 2020: 46)—as conditions for "urban prosperity" (UN-Habitat 2016) and an engine of economic growth (UN-Habitat 2015: 4; Rudd and Mutai 2019).[3]

In the GBA megaregion, homogenization of the economic space and development of mobility infrastructure imply assignment of economic functions to specific space-time locales both regionally and in alignment with the global urban system (GBA Gov 2019). Accordingly, the GBA's major function nodes have specific allocations: government, global financial markets and trade in Hong Kong; economic productivity and technological innovation in Shenzhen and Zhuhai; "ludic space" in Macau. Simpson argues (in this volume) that Macau has been relegated to the role of an "experimental laboratory of consumption for market-socialism," a heterotopian reflection of the GBA's productivist economic zones. Indeed, the Chinese government has liberalized the gaming industry in Macau, invited transnational capital and foreign gaming operators, devised financial policies which limit the flow of capital across the Special Administrative Region's borders and implemented new policies and routes to bring masses of Chinese tourists. Macau is thus both a scholastic program and a "model city" for Chinese consumerist society, the world's most lucrative gaming destination and the largest integrated interior space designed to produce a commodified, urban-themed **tmps**.

FIGURE 17.2 The megaregional public space of Macau contrasted with exchange and negotiation in everyday public spaces of the old city. Images from top down depict: view of the Grand Lisboa casino from St. Paul's Cathedral in the old city of Macau, the UNESCO World Heritage site; The Venetian in Cotai, exterior and the interior canal; and local market street in downtown Macau off Avenida Almeida Riberio. Elsewhere, I have discussed the mechanisms through which the 'outside' of what Simpson calls "interiorized urbanity," the real colonial buildings and public spaces of Macau complete the **tmps** scenography as "the post-colonial cityscape" (Simpson in this volume) backdrop to be visited as an open-air museum, the ethno-village of Macau's colonial past (Mitrašinović 2006).

Source: Author.

Since **tmps** is framed as an economic engine and key ingredient of "high-quality" urban environments (United Nations 2020), systemic waterfront revitalization in the GBA has been put forth as a parallel strategy for producing it. This approach not only attracts global prestige and investment but also satisfies the leisure and recreation demands of China's new upper and middle classes. As Tong and Wong (in this volume) point out, the goal of Hong Kong's Harbourfront Commission is the creation of a "fully connected harbor front promenade" that links fragmented parcels of land in an "iconic" public space network. The larger HK2030+ plan proposes to enhance the city's "green-blue assets" (e.g., parks, waterfronts, land-water interfaces) through the Green and Blue System, connecting transportation hubs with publicly owned lands and private property development such as luxury housing, retail and entertainment facilities and leisure spaces. This is **tmps** system in the making.

tmps and Political Homogenization

Using public space in China to propagate and disseminate political ideology dates back to 1949, with the construction of massive, Soviet Union-inspired public squares, the most symbolic of which was Beijing's Tian'anmen Square (Wu and Gaubatz 2012: 248), "big enough to hold an assembly of one billion" (Wu 2005: 23).

In China today, urban planning and design, landscape architecture and architecture are coordinated to manifest new political imaginaries. Simpson (in this volume) describes Macau as a social and political "megamachine" for the production of consumerist subjects. Shane and Al (in this volume) illustrate how specific organizational logic and spatial tropes—including monumentality and the inscription of economic and political power in urban form—have been mobilized across the GBA. Du (in this volume) discusses how the Statutory Plan of Shenzhen Futian CBD (SMG 1999) instituted a powerful central north-south axis in the Futian District in order to organize the new seat of administrative and cultural power, connecting the Shenzhen Convention Center, the Shenzhen Civic Center and the bronze statue of Deng Xiaoping in Lianhuashan Park. The core of this "sacred axis" is Civic Square (2006)—the "Grand Urban Living Room" at the heart of government buildings and cultural institutions designed by an international cast of "starchitects," often chosen through international competitions. Its formal and symbolic features, and the way it institutionalizes urbanization as a particular kind of urban governmentality that establishes a new public domain of the GBA—and thereby reorders the logic of territory, land and property (Roy 2016: 818)—make Civic Square the **tmps** prototype. Its attributes include the forceful expropriation of land, new state designations and administrative classifications, land parcellation and zoning, novel forms of taxation and socio-spatial totalization aimed at erasing "undecidability" and historical specificity and excluding contestation (Roy 2016: 821). As Du asserts, political homogenization is identifiable not only in newly constructed public space but also in new regulations applied to old public spaces in urban villages and elsewhere.

Akin to Simpson's notion of Macau as "model city" and Roy's proposition of "urban" as a particular type of governing, O'Donnell frames Shenzhen as an instrument of public policy (in this volume), where "the public" is constituted through government actions—an administrative category that produces a distinct governed population—with explicit and measurable outcomes. The urban organization of Shenzhen—in which **tmps** plays a significant role—is supposed to regulate the delivery of policy-defined "public goods." However, given the city's dual role as a major node in both the GBA megaregion's polycentric organization and in the global value chain, neither its "urban form" nor its "spatial means" of delivery have been evenly advanced (Johnson and Davis 2019). Cities conceived this way always produce 'the public space' as a strategic vehicle that enables power to be strategically inscribed in specific locations. After all, the political public space is only one aspect of larger urban political geographies (Frazier 2019) of Chinese cities. O'Donnell posits that eventually establishing "critical public spaces" would enable a more equitable urban distribution of social and public resources.

Public Spaces in the GBA Megaregion (psmr)

Such "critical public spaces" demand that government steps in not only to redistribute public resources but also to foster cross-sector collaboration and networked governance (not yet characteristic of the GBA megaregion) and to allow the domain of civil society (likewise not well developed outside of Hong Kong) to mobilize. Currently, **psmr** are by and large experienced as fragmented, incoherent, uneven spaces where denizens experience the impact of shifting GBA geographies and often find ways of thinking and acting otherwise: spaces of struggle and resistance, appropriation and contestation, but also spaces of everyday life such as market streets, local parks, community gardens and neighborhood playgrounds. This is where possibilities for tactical sub-regionalism emerge.

As described in Chapter 1, the explosive growth of the PRD between 1980 and 2010 obliterated or fragmented existing public spaces through pragmatic, pro-development urban planning policies that preferred to conceptualize public spaces as "open spaces" allocated to individual neighborhoods and residential locations as local recreational resources (Tang and Wong in this volume). Since the 2008 financial crisis, GBA has experienced a significant slowdown in urban growth. As Tieben and Chen suggest (in this volume), facing the new context and inspired by the Occupy and Umbrella movements, parts of Hong Kong's design community saw an opportunity in developing a critique of the pro-development logic in design and planning and began to develop "alternative design thinking." The introduction of design as an instrumental medium is indispensable: on the one hand, design functions as a means for organizing associational activities in the social space of civil society to expedite the emergence of new subjectivities, shared meanings and novel civic and social imaginaries. On the other hand, it works as a catalyst for urban coalitions and communities, as well as third-sector organizations, to define and represent their needs, desires, expectations and demands to others in the public sphere—as they contest and negotiate desired outcomes in their interactions with institutions and systems of power (Mitrašinović 2016: 182).

Finally, design also demonstrates the potential of new, cross-sectoral, multi-disciplinary approaches to the production of **psmr**, which not only provide more responsive environments for recreation and enjoyment (or for negotiation and contestation) but also re-introduce the critical need to re-establish connective spatial tissue for civic life: a new public realm. Namely, as Li and Genovese suggest, the gap between family structures, evolving social needs and organization of public spaces in China is significant because public spaces currently do not represent the social and civic needs of the people but rather the structure and needs of the government (2017: 117). So how can the connections between family structure, social fabric and public spaces in the GBA megaregion be reimagined?

Participation

Citizen and community participation in the GBA is a complex topic; although it has existed in Hong Kong in various forms, participation in urban planning and design processes in mainland China is a very recent phenomenon. Shenzhen was among the first Chinese cities to incorporate public participation in the planning process in the late 1990s, but to this day, the city lacks clear protocols for its implementation and assessment (Li 2016: 118). Instead of empowering civil society to work within communities to build and distribute public resources (Li 2016)—including **psmr**—the government typically provides "community services" in a top-down manner by establishing community-based "service stations" (Fu 2016: 116). After being frequently used in China between 1990 and 2011, the very concept of "civil society" (*gongmin shehui*, 公民社会) has all but disappeared (Kuhn 2018), and government instead uses "social organizations" (*shehui zuzhi*, 社会组织) and "civil organizations" (*minjian zuzhi*, 民间组织).[4]

One of the biggest challenges with participation in the GBA is land tenure. In Shenzhen, for example, only 20% of all inhabitants have residents permits (*hukou*), up to 40% have permanent residence and the rest belong to the "floating population" of renters in urban villages, living mostly in sub-standard conditions (Vlassenrood 2016: 6). Land ownership conveys relative autonomy in local decision-making, bestowing on long-term residents an important role in processes of participation, and thereby also in supplying affordable housing, civic services and public spaces for the overlooked renting population in the urban villages of Shenzhen (Du 2020). In Huanggang, Huanggang Village Corporation funds, develops and operates all residential and commercial developments as well as public spaces such as neighborhood parks and plazas (Du in this volume). The corporation is self-organized and self-funded through commercial real estate sales and rentals; the proceeds have built tree-lined streets, open markets and squares, shopping arcades and the village centerpiece: Huanggang Cultural Plaza. Robust forms of local participation and self-organization are also behind the redevelopment of Liede Village, in Tianhe District, Guangzhou (Tan and Schoon 2014), since 2007, including design and construction of public spaces that serve both the community's existing needs and its newly framed aspirations.[5]

Civil society in Hong Kong has generated widespread interest in **psmr** and encouraged a range of bottom-up, collaborative innovations in its design, use and management (Tang and Wong in this volume). One example is the ongoing work of the Hong Kong Public Space Initiative (HKPSI), founded in 2011, which has boosted citizen participation across its many successful projects and initiatives. Tieben and Chen (in this volume) discuss the Magic Carpet and Make a Difference (MaD) initiatives, which promote different modalities of emerging, design-led activist practices in Hong Kong. Magic Carpet started in 2013 as a collaboration between the Chinese University of Hong Kong (CUHK), various NGOs and residents of Sai Ying Pun district. The overarching goal was to develop process-oriented, cross-sectoral, participatory approaches to **psmr** and to build communities' capacity to co-create public spaces and thereby strengthen its sense of belonging and engagement.

Appropriations, Occupations, Contestations

Highly differentiated theoretical and practical approaches to the appropriation of **psmr** exist in Hong Kong. In the tactical domain of everyday urbanism, the fascination with the "messiness" of street life (Siu and Zhu 2016), the countless forms of urban social life (Chalana and Hou 2016; Hou 2010), informal and mobile street vendors (Guiterrez and Portefaix 2000), appropriation of the Central Business District by foreign domestic helpers (香港外籍家庭佣工), with aspects of material urbanity (Frampton et al. 2012; Kvan et al. 2013; Shane in this volume) and the liquid public realm (Gutierrez and Portefaix in this volume) have all inspired a large body of literature. Political contestation, however, occurs through the appropriation and occupation of both **tmps** and **psmr**. Frazier discusses (in this volume) Hong Kong's Civic Square, an unassuming, normative symbol of **tmps** that has catalyzed civic protests since opening in 2011. This "space of representation" of governmental authority has hosted ongoing contestation of the GBA's political geography. In 2014, the appropriation and subsequent contestation of the space sparked the Umbrella Movement, which then engulfed the city. Even after the protests ended and Civic Square was walled off, it continued to represent civil society's sustained challenge to public authority (Frazier 2019).

Contemporary examples of appropriation and contestation on the scale of the Occupy and Umbrella movements are rare in the GBA outside of Hong Kong. As Shane argues (in this volume), the power of "strategic micro-urbanism," where citizens' capabilities are enriched by handheld devices and digital networks "in the augmented reality of the metacity" (Shane 2014), has propelled these civic practices. Moreover, social media and networking, digital communities and evolving communication platforms vis-à-vis appropriation of public space

FIGURE 17.3 Appropriations of GBA public spaces (in clockwise order): singing in Central Park, Guangzhou; parallel traders at work in Macau; villain hitters of Causeway Bay, Hong Kong; and tai chi practice in Kowloon Park, Hong Kong.

Sources (in clockwise order): Adapted from the photos by Dr. Meierhofer (Wikimedia Commons © CC BY-SA 3.0); author; author; Jakub Hałun (Wikimedia Commons © CC BY-SA 3.0).

FIGURE 17.4 Hong Kong Umbrella Revolution, October 2014. Images from top down depict occupations of the Hong Kong International Airport; Admiralty, central Hong Kong; and Harcourt Road (Admiralty) in front of the Central Government Offices.

Source: Adapted from the photos by Pasu Au Yeung. Wikimedia Commons © CC BY 2.0.

have enabled numerous self-organized, community-based groups across the GBA to appropriate parks and conduct successful programming of leisure activities such as group dancing, singing or matchmaking (Li 2016: 118). Li suggests that even the nominal diversity in these "informal" endeavors to organize multiple existing publics produces an imbalance of power and influence at the municipal level: a more assertive local government, together with a robust civil society, would result in more equitable access to public parks and more adequate geographic distribution of public services. Tieben and Chen (in this volume) describe the grassroots insurgence of a local resident in the Shek Kip Mei district in Hong Kong who, after refurbishing physical therapy equipment abandoned by hospitals, launched a recreational "morning exercise park" on Bishop Hill for appreciative local residents. As this act of appropriation grew in popularity, local politicians provided funds for additional construction and appealed for legal recognition of this informal public space.

Borders, political boundaries and spatial thresholds are fundamental in understanding the complex political ecologies and "territorial exceptionalism" of the PRD's border regions (Blackwell and Ma 2017).[6] Hasdell (this volume) discusses the Hong Kong–Shenzhen border as a contested threshold between **tmps** (the power of the state to regulate cross-border flows) and **psmr** (transient public spaces that emerge where the border is porous), resulting in myriad tactical practices by "liminal operators" such as parallel traders and smugglers but also communities whose schoolchildren and family members cross the border on their daily commute. As Hasdell argues, border practices produce "invisible," non-sanctioned forms of "proto-urban" public encounter as well as specific dispositions that could be institutionalized at a later time.

FIGURE 17.5   Foreign domestic helpers gathering on Sunday morning in the entryway of the HSBC headquarters building, between Queen's Road and Des Voeux Road in the Central District of Hong Kong, 13 January 2019.

Source: Author.

Urban Pedagogy and Education

Urban pedagogy and education build both the dispositions and the capabilities of individuals and organizations—be it in the civil society, government or market based—to conceptualize, design, develop, steward and sustain public spaces. They also build capacities and conditions for cross-sectoral collaboration, public-private partnerships and the resources to sustain them. The most relevant examples are found in Hong Kong—due to a working civil society—yet more formalized educational practices are surfacing elsewhere in the GBA both within and outside of existing academic institutions, often in partnership with civil society organizations.

The Magic Carpet project led by CUHK mentioned previously is one example. The Jockey Club Design Institute for Social Innovation (DISI) at Hong Kong Polytechnic University has assembled educators, government entities and representatives of the market and civil society sectors through its numerous initiatives. Shenzhen University's Department of Urban Planning continuously collaborates with urban village cooperatives and regularly organizes co-design workshops with urban villagers. McGrath and Chu (in this volume) discuss how Chu Hai College of Higher Education has produced "social publics" on the

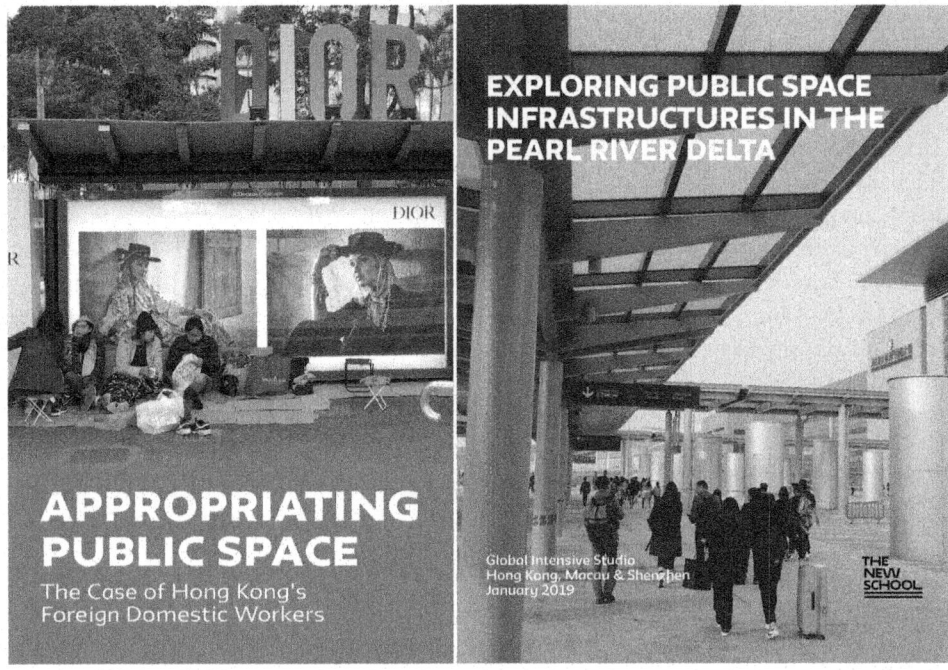

FIGURE 17.6   Global Urban Studio books 2018 and 2019, Parsons School of Design. A series of design workshops organized by Parsons School of Design (2015–2019) in collaboration with Hong Kong Polytechnic University's School of Design, Chinese University of Hong Kong (CUHK)'s School of Architecture, Shenzhen University's School of Architecture and Urban Planning, and St. Joseph University's (in Macau) Department of Architecture explored the new public realm of the GBA, focusing on public spaces and infrastructures. The New School students worked in teams with students from these regional universities and configured a series of planning, design and policy proposals. The design workshops are a part of the Global Urban Intensive Studio offered as part of the Urban@Parsons curriculum, and they always produce a studio book documenting research and proposals. More info at: http://sds.parsons.edu/urban/. Last accessed on 20 September 2020.

Source: Depicted are covers of the 2018 (designed by Isela Lopez) and 2019 (designed by Danni Peng) studio books. Courtesy of Parsons School of Design.

megaregional, metropolitan and municipal scale—in direct contrast to the state-led megaregional imaginary. They argue that the College, now located in the Tsuen Wan district, has evolved as a place of ethical design practice that positions public space as a vehicle for the spatial production of social publics. Theodore (in this volume) describes her innovative methodology of working remotely on a studio assignment in Shenzhen with students at the New Jersey Institute of Technology, through techniques of long-distance observation, analysis, visualization and collaboration; she stresses the importance of conceptualizing "lived experience" by generating multi-perspectival views of a place, learning from history and designing processes of collaboration. Employing longitudinal studies of actual residents and creating analytical thematic maps allowed the students to organize and systematize clues in response to the conditions observed. Aformal Academy (Bedir and Hilgefort in this volume) is a series of knowledge exchange workshops in Shenzhen's urban villages that has enhanced cooperation and multi-layered learning across disciplines, engendering research and action by participants, urban villagers and instructors. Ultimately, the workshop methodology suitably preserves the informal conceptualizations of public space and the spontaneous character of use and casual daily interactions and includes the villagers in the production and design of the **psmr**.

The Hong Kong government has produced and disseminated urban design guidelines and public space manuals to both inform the public and regulate the design of public spaces (Tang and Wong in this volume). Meanwhile, organizations like the HKPSI and MaD engage in different forms of urban pedagogy, teaching citizens how to read policy documents but also how to build capabilities and capacities of individuals and communities for co-producing the public realm. Finally, in Macau, the Center for Architecture and Urbanism was established in 2014 as a platform for knowledge exchange between academia, civil society and the government.

Approaches, Assumptions, Possibilities

Such learning partnerships, and the grounded knowledge they produce through engagement, collaboration and exchange, confirm the main trust of this book. As Timothy Jachna outlines in the introductory chapter, the ambition of this book was neither to arrive at a single definition of public space nor to predict its future development. The idea is to recognize public space as a critical and timely subject in the context of the GBA, represent current approaches and practices, and theorize it in order to delineate new territories for scholarly research, design education and professional practice.

This chapter focused on *the megaregional public space* as a catalyst for the realignment of governance, economic development and infrastructure in the GBA and on *public spaces in the GBA megaregion* as a medium of resistance to the twin meta-narratives of globalization and urbanization but also as a vehicle for organizing (community, social and civic) through increasingly design-led tactical sub-regionalism. Together, they configure what we have called *the emerging public realm of the GBA megaregion*. Studying public space in this context, it has been argued, transgresses limitations inherent in the methodological privileging of "the city" (Angelo and Wachsmuth 2011) as a unique analytical lens for examining urbanization of the PRD. The megaregional heuristics enables us to extend the inquiry across the differentiated megaregional scales and study how public space has been constitutive of the new geographies of the public realm and public sphere in the PRD and inseparable from the domains in which the politics and policy of megaregionalism in China have been defined and operationalized since 2016.

The megaregional perspectives point both to the totalizing forces of megaregionalism (and its corollary, **tmps**) as well as to the promising possibilities embedded in public spaces of the megaregion (**psmr**) and in the practice of tactical sub-regionalism alike. Their dialectical relations—evident through the strategies, tactics, processes and forms examined previously—ultimately render public space a critical medium for future socio-spatial transformations in the GBA. Needless to point out, the only confident thing in the above conjecture is that nothing will happen as suggested, but there is a possibility that it might (Hart 1954: 139).

Notes

1. The new rail line reduced travel time from Hong Kong to Shenzhen to twenty minutes and to Guangzhou to forty-seven minutes.
2. "Open space systems" are commonly defined as the sum of open, functionally *integrated* "surfaces of the city" that permit public access, whereas "open space networks" are defined as an *integrative* geography of locations, activities and flows (lines and nodes). Neither approach typically discriminates between private land, public property, government property and the commons, as long as there is a "possibility of public access." In the literature on this subject principally concerned with democracy, social justice and the right to the city (as in Brazil, for example), the public dimension of open space systems plays a fundamental role (Tângari 2018). In China, however, where all land is state owned, this is a moot point.
3. "Good public spaces play a decisive role in attracting investment, uses and activities, thus enhancing safety; increasing property values, generating municipal revenue; providing opportunities for economic interaction and enhancing livelihood opportunities. A good connective matrix of public space has impact on economic productivity as it improves the efficiency of the supply chain, reducing production costs and promoting the mobility of goods and people. Public space provides important benefits to all forms of business, both formal and informal" (UN-Habitat 2015: 4). UN Sustainable Development Goal 11 (Target 11.7) outlines the role of governments in providing safe and inclusive public spaces (United Nations 2020: 46).
4. In 2016 and 2017, China's State Council adopted two laws intended to frame the development of civil society: the Charity Law established regulatory framework for "social organizations" (over 1 million domestic NGOs), while the Foreign NGO Law was intended to regulate the operations of international organizations in China (Kuhn 2018).
5. Tan and Schoon observe that clan ties, family structures and intra-collective social relations and networks of social power (*guanxi*) play important roles the decision-making elements at the grassroots level (2014: 264–265).
6. The co-called "First Line" (the Sino-British border) was established in 1842; the "Second Line" (the administrative boundary between Shenzhen SEZ and the rest of China) was established in 1982 and decommissioned in 2010 (Blackwell and Ma 2017: 124–125). Today, the geography of exceptionalism is further configured by the border between Macau Special Administrative Region (SAR) and Zhuhai Special Economic Zone (SEZ), with two points of crossing (Gongbei Port and the Lotus Bridge) and the Hong Kong–Zhuhai–Macau Bridge, completed in 2018.

References

Angelo, H. and Wachsmuth, D. (2011 [2014]) "Urbanizing urban political ecology: A critique of methodological cityism." In: Brenner, N. (Ed.) *Implosions/explosions: Towards a study of planetary urbanization*. Jovis. pp. 372–385.
Barnett, J. (2020) *Designing the megaregion: Meeting urban challenges at a new scale*. Island Press.
Blackwell, A. and Ma, E.X. (2017) "The political architecture of the first and second lines." In: Bach, J., O'Donnell, M.A. and Wong, W. (Eds.) *Learning from Shenzhen: China's post-Mao experiment from special zone to model city*. University of Chicago Press. pp. 124–137.
Chalana, M. and Hou, J. (Eds.) (2016) *Messy urbanism: Understanding the "other" cities of Asia*. Routledge.
Du, J. (2020) *The Shenzhen experiment: The story of China's instant city*. Harvard University Press.
Ellul, J. (1967) *The technological society*. Random House.
Frampton, A., Solomon, J.D. and Wong, C. (2012) *Cities without ground: A Hong Kong guidebook*. ORO Editions.
Frazier, M. (2019) *The power of place: Contentious politics in twentieth-century Shanghai and Bombay*. Cambridge University Press.
Fu, N. (2016) "Community building: Releasing the pressure: Interview with Li Jinkui." In: Vlassenrood, L. (Ed.) *Shenzhen: From factory of the world to world city*. International New Town Institute (INTI) and The Netherlands Architecture Institute (NAI). pp. 114–117.
GBA Gov. (2019) *Outline development plan for the Guangdong-Hong Kong-Macao Greater Bay Area*, 18 February. At: www.bayarea.gov.hk/en/about/overview.html. Last accessed on 20 September 2020.

Guiterrez, L. and Portefaix, V. (2000) *Mapping Hong Kong*. Map Book.
Hart, L.B. (1954) Strategy. New York: Praeger.
Hou, J. (Ed.) (2010) *Insurgent public space: Guerrilla urbanism and the remaking of contemporary cities*. Routledge.
Huang, Y. (Ed.) (2020) *Chinese cities in the 21st century*. Palgrave Macmillan.
Johnson, C. and Davis, L.C. (Eds.) (2019) *The story of Shenzhen: Its economic, social and environmental transformation*. United Nations Human Settlements Programme (UN-Habitat).
Kaw, J.K., Lee, H. and Wahba, S. (Eds.) (2020) *The hidden wealth of cities: Creating, financing, and managing public spaces*. The World Bank, International Bank for Reconstruction and Development.
Kohn, M. (2004) *Brave new neighborhoods: The privatization of public space*. Routledge.
Kuhn, B. (2018) "Changing spaces for civil society organisations in China." *Open Journal of Political Science* 8. pp. 467–494.
Kvan, T., Shelton, B. and Karakiewicz, J. (2013) *The making of Hong Kong: From vertical to volumetric*. Routledge.
Lang, W. and Shi, Y. (2019) "Basic services and local infrastructure." In: Johnson, C. and Davis, L.C. (Eds.) *The story of Shenzhen: Its economic, social and environmental transformation*. United Nations Human Settlements Programme (UN-Habitat). pp. 66–85.
Lewis, S.W. (2006) "Political and economic implications of new public spaces in Chinese and Asian global cities." In: Wu, F. (Ed.) *Globalization and the Chinese city*. Routledge. pp. 271–291.
Li, D. (2016) "Self-organized groups in Shenzhen's parks." In: Vlassenrood, L. (Ed.) *Shenzhen: From factory of the world to world city*. International New Town Institute (INTI) and The Netherlands Architecture Institute (NAI). pp. 118–121.
Li, P. and Genovese, P.V. (2017) "The identity of Chinese public space from ancient times to contemporary society: The sociology of public behaviours in Chinese cities." *L'Architettura delle Città, The Journal of the Scientific Society Ludovico Quaroni*. pp. 2281–8731, UNESCO-Chair, "Sustainable Urban Quality", Series, #2, November.
Li, S. (2014) "Degrees of care." In: *Understanding the Chinese city*. Sage. pp. 98–116.
Madanipour, A. (2019) "Rethinking public space: Between rhetoric and reality." *Urban Design International* 24. pp. 38–46.
Mitrašinović, M. (2006) *Total landscape, theme parks, public space*. Routledge.
Mitrašinović, M. (Ed.) (2016) *Concurrent urbanities: Designing infrastructures of inclusion*. Routledge.
National New-Type Urbanization Plan (2014–2020). *Released in March 2014*. At: www.gov.cn/zhuanti/xxczh/. Last accessed on 20 September 2020.
Pickett, S.T.A. and Zhou, W. (2015) "Global urbanization as a shifting context for applying ecological science toward the sustainable city." *Ecosystem Health and Sustainability* 1 (1). pp. 1–15.
Roy, A. (2016) "What is urban about critical urban theory?" *Urban Geography* 37 (6). pp. 810–823.
Rudd, A. and Mutai, J. (2019) *City-wide public space strategies: A compendium of inspiring practices*. United Nations Human Settlements Programme (UN-Habitat).
Schafran, A. (2014) "Rethinking mega-regions: Sub-regional politics in a fragmented metropolis." *Regional Studies* 48 (4). pp. 587–602.
Shane, D.G. (2014) "Metacity: Origins and implications." In: Contin, A. and Salerno, R. (Eds.) *Innovative technologies in urban mapping*. Springer. pp. 59–72.
Shenzhen Municipal Government (SMG) (1996) *Comprehensive plan for Shenzhen 1996–2010*. Shenzhen Municipal People's Government, posted online on 18 May 2018 (in Chinese, with English translation). At: http://pnr.sz.gov.cn/ywzy/ghzs/ztgh/index.htm. Last accessed on 20 September 2020.
Shenzhen Municipal Government (SMG) (1999) *Statutory plan of Shenzhen Futian CBD area (Shenzhen Shi Zhongxinqu Fading Tuze (*深圳市中心区法定图则*)*. Urban Planning, Land & Resource Commission of Shenzhen Municipality.
Shenzhen Municipal Government (SMG) (2004) *Planning of the green space system in Shenzhen, 2004–2020*. Shenzhen Municipal Government (in Chinese).

Siu, K.W.M. and Zhu, M. (2016) "Neutral equilibrium in public space: Mong Kok Flower Market, Hong Kong." In: Chalana, M. and Hou, J. (Eds.) *Messy urbanism: Understanding the "other" cities of Asia*. Hong Kong University Press. pp. 136–153.

Tan, X. and Schoon, S. (2014) "Villagers' participation in mega-urban upgrading. Liede Village: Guangzhou's pioneer." In: Altrock, U. and Schoon, S. (Eds.) *Maturing megacities: The Pearl River Delta in progressive transformation*. Springer. pp. 247–266.

Tângari, V.R. (2018) "Open space systems in Rio de Janeiro: The public and private spheres reflected in the urban landscape." In: Alvares, L.C. and Barbosa, J.L. (Eds.) *Urban public spaces: From planned policies to everyday politics*. Springer. pp. 109–126.

UN-Habitat (2012 [2013]) *The state of China's cities, 2012/2013*. UN-Habitat and Foreign Languages Press.

UN-Habitat (2015) *HABITAT III issue papers, # 11: Public space*, 31 May. At: http://habitat3.org/wp-content/uploads/Habitat-III-Issue-Paper-11_Public-Space-2.0.compressed.pdf. Last accessed on 20 September 2020.

UN-Habitat (2016) *City prosperity index*. At: https://cpi.unhabitat.org/. Last accessed on 20 September 2020.

United Nations (2020) *The sustainable development goals report 2020*. United Nations.

Vlassenrood, L. (Ed.) (2016) *Shenzhen: From factory of the world to world city*. International New Town Institute (INTI) and The Netherlands Architecture Institute (NAI).

Wiethoff, K. (2014) "The role of public space in the upgrading of urbanized villages." In: Altrock, U. and Schoon, S. (Eds.) *Maturing megacities: The Pearl River Delta in progressive transformation*. Springer. pp. 335–358.

Wu, H. (2005) *Remaking Beijing: Tiananmen Square and the creation of a political space*. University of Chicago Press.

Wu, W. and Gaubatz, P. (2012) *The Chinese city*. Routledge.

Xue, C.Q. (Ed.) (2019) *Grand theater urbanism: Chinese cities in the 21st century*. Springer.

Zhang, F., Chung, C.K.L. and Yin, Z. (2019) "Green infrastructure for China's new urbanisation: A case study of greenway development in Maanshan." *Urban Studies* 57 (3). pp. 508–524, 1 February.

Zhao, J. (2014) "Parks as soft location factors." In: Altrock, U. and Schoon, S. (Eds.) *Maturing megacities: The Pearl River Delta in progressive transformation*. Springer. pp. 289–310.

INDEX

Page numbers in *italics* indicate a figure and page numbers in **bold** indicate a table on the corresponding page. Page numbers followed by "n" indicate a note.

1986 Shenzhen Masterplan 31, 139
1994 Guangzhou-Shenzhen (Guangshen) Expressway 31
1998 Double Dragon Urban Design Guidelines 139
1999 CBD Statuary Urban Plan 140
2017 Framework Agreement 18
2019 Anti-Extradition Law Amendment Bill Movement 176
2019 Outline Development Plan 18

Abbas, A. 84, 156
Abercrombie 31, 37n5, 66
accessibility 109
activist public policy 92
Adelson, S. 103
affordances 188
Aformal Academy 181, 189; sites of 185–187; workshop 183
aformality and re-learning the city 181–185
Alexander, C. 109
American schools of architecture 120–121
analytical thematic maps 123, 204
Anti-Extradition Law Amendment Bill Movement 176
appropriation 4, 6, 20, 134, 161, 199–201, 203
architectural tourism 121
architecture 95, 120–121, 151, 154, 156, 169, 185, 198; built environment 18–20
Arendt, H. 161
"Asia's World City" 128–130
Au, T. 165
Awan, N. 185

Baishizhou village workshop 181, *186*
Bakken, B. 104
Bauder, C. 188
Belt and Road Initiative (BRI) 9; global strategy 193
Betsky, A. 181
Be Water protest movement 154
big mothers (*damas*) 86–87
Bishop Hill Community 172–174
boat dwellers 91
border crossings *12*
Brenner, N. 81
Burdett, R. 121

Caltex Oil Company 149
Canton River 41
Canton Sea Route 40
Canton system 45, 64
Cassegård, C. 161
Castells, M. 15, 27, 29, 30, 81, 84, 107n1
central business district (CBD) 66, 201; Hong Kong 133; Shenzhen 136
Central Government Office complex (CGO) 158, 161, 166
Chang, L. 122–123
Chek Lap Kok Island 42
Chen, L. 37n5
Chen, Y.-F. 199, 202
Cheung, S. N. S. 37n3
Chilajiao Island of Hong Kong 43
China Academy of Urban Planning and Design (CAUPD) 37n5
China Urban Planning and Design Institute (CUPDI) 146n1

Chinese Melting Pot 153
Chinese Revolution of 1949 17–18
Chinese tourists in Macau 99–101
Chinese University of Hong Kong (CUHK) 169, 177n1
Chow, A. 164
Chu Hai, a genealogy of institutional exile 149–151, 154
Chu Hai College of Higher Education (CHCHE) *141*, 147, *148*, 151, 156, 203
Chu Hai International Design Program (IDP) 154, *155*, 156
Chu Hai University *see* Chu Hai College of Higher Education (CHCHE)
Chung Ying Street Market 85
city 1–2, 5–7, 32, 62–65, 103–105, 127–128
"City Machine" 62, 64–67
City of Exacerbated Differences (COED) 101–102
City of Faith 62–65
City of Pragmatism 127–128
Civic Square, Hong Kong's 158–166, *159*; birth of 161–164; map of *160*; reopens as regulated public space 164–165
civil organizations (*minjian zuzhi*) 200
civil society (*gongmin shehui*) 145, 200
Clos, J. 13
cluster concept 192
Coase, R. 37n4
Cohn, R. L. 188
community park (*shequ gongyuan*) 196
comprehensive park (*zonghe gongyuan*) 196
core cities 10
COVID-19 pandemic 68, 126, 126n1, 166, 176
cross-border and transient public space in GBA 77–87; loopholes and liminal bodies 85–87; transient public space 83–85; Umbrella Movement Hong Kong 77, *78*; *see also* Hong Kong-Shenzhen border
Cruz, T. 82
Curl, A. 110
Cuthbert, A. 82–83

Dachan Islands of Shenzhen 43
danwei (factory) 66, 67, 69, 72, 104–105, 107
Dapeng Peninsula 33
Davis, M. 82
Daya Bay 33
Dayu Islands of Hong Kong 43
Decoding Shenzhen: The Huaqiangbei Backstory 95
Delafontaine, M. 109
Delisle, G. 94, 95
design 62, 69, 95–96, 122, 130, 143–144, 154, 169, 184–185
Design Institute for Social Innovation (DISI) 133, 203
DIY approach 175
Dong'ao 43
Dongguan 10, *51*, 80
Dongxing-Mon Cai border zone 81

Easterling, K. 81
East Wing Forecourt, Hong Kong Central Government Offices 161, 164
"ecocity" 62, 68
ecology/ecological 17, 41, 43–44, 72, *79*, 84, 126, 171, 195–196, 203
Eleventh Five-Year Plan (2006–2010) 10
Energizing Kowloon East Office (EKEO) 133
ephemerality 128
Euro-American hegemony 22
exclusion zones 82

Factory Girls: From Village to City in a Changing China 122–123
Feng, J. 72
Fishing Village (渔民村) 91
Five Connections One Leveling Policy (五通一平) 90
floating school 183
Florida, R. 10
fluid mythology 45–48
Forbidden City 154
Forbidden Palace 63–64
forest/suburban landscape park (*senlin/jiaoye gongyuan*) 196
Foshan/Fuoshan 10, *50*, 80
Foucault, M. 153
Franklin, B. 93
Fraser, N. 157n3
Fuhai, W. 37n5
Fulong, W. 31

Ganzhi, Z. 38n6
Gaolan 43
gardens as public space 62–73; central business district (CBD) 66; Central Statue Square garden 66; Disneyland theme park 68; Futian CBD and Tianhe, Gangzhou, comparison *70*; grand theater urbanism 68; Litchi Park 67, 69; performative urbanism 69; *see also* metacity heterotopic systems
general residential buildings (GRBs) 111
Genovese, P. V. 199
global-city regions 22n5, 23n6
globalization 82
global urban system 23n6
Gottmann, J. 22n5, 27
Grand Urban Living Room 6, 136–138, 198
Great Leap Forward 121
Greater Bay Area (GBA) 1–8; 2017 Framework Agreement 18; 2019 Outline Development Plan 18; Aggregate Rail Transit Network *16*; analytical work, challenges in 22; change in 1920–2020 62–73; defined 1; as megaregion 1–8; megaregionalism of 13–14; megaregionality in 13–14; spatial form of 17; *see also* gardens as public space; re-learning the city in GBA
Greater Bay Bridge 68

Green and Blue System 130, 198
Guangzhou 10, 44–45, *50*, 63–64, *65*, 80
Guangzhou-Shenzhen Expressway (Guangshen) 10
Guangzhou–Shenzhen–Hong Kong rail network 195
Guattari, F. 98
guerrilla policy style 30

Habermas, J. 93
Hägerstraand, T. 109
Hai, C. 149, 151, 154
Hakka clan villages 66
Hansen, W. G. 109
Harrison, J. 13, 14, 22n4, 23n6
Harvey, D. 99
Hebao Islands of Zhuhai 43
Heilmann, S. 30
Hengqin 43
High Speed Railway (HSR) 18, 193
Ho, O. H. 46, 47
holistic planning, in urban redevelopment 131, *132*
Hong Kong 17–18, 20, 29, 31, 34, 40–43, 46–47, 64–65, 67–69, 72–73, 77–80; British-designed 18; colonial urbanization in 18; *see also* Special Administrative Regions (SARs)
Hong Kong, emerging public space design in 168–178; future for 176–177; international trend of 169–174; magic carpet community re-envisioning (Case 1) 169–171; Make a Difference (MaD) social lab (Case 2) 171–172, *172*; reflections on 168–178; Self-Build Bishop Hill Community (Case 3) 172–174, 173–176; Special Administrative Region (SAR) 1, 9–10, 80, 100, 161, 196
Hong Kong Federation of Students (HKFS) 163
Hong Kong Mass Transit Railway (MTR) 34
Hong Kong Public Space Initiative (HKPSI) 133
Hong Kong, public space and urban planning in 127–135; "Asia's World City" 128–130; borrowed place, borrowed time 128; City of Pragmatism 127–128; community green networks 134; harbor-front promenade and public park network *131*; Harbourfront Commission 130; holistic planning in urban redevelopment *132*; Instagram Pier 134; networked public space 130; public sitting-out area *129*; reinvented public space 132–134; *133–134*; semi-private public space 131–132; solution space 128; transition zones 128; urban renewal authority (URA) 131
Hong Kong/Shenzhen Bi-City Biennale of Urbanism/Architecture (UABB) 168
Hong Kong-Shenzhen border 78–83; border ecologies *79*; delineating Hong Kong 80; exogenous border conditions 78–83; logistics mapping *83*; parallel trading mapping *86*; schoolchildren at *79, 81*

Hong Kong Task Force for Land Supply 43
Hong Kong–Zhuhai–Macau Bridge 43, 80
horizontal metropolis 68–69
Hou, J. 161
Hoyler, M. 13, 14, 22n4, 23n6
Huanggang Urban Village Redevelopment (皇岗城中村) 136, 142; advocacy and contestation 144; public space 136, *138*; research and design 143–144
Huangpu Port 45
Huaqiangbei, Chimerica 94–96
hub-to-hub networking 18
Huizhou 10
hyper-collage city of PRD 49–61, *52–59*; Dongguan *51*; Foshan *50*; Grand Emperor *60*; Guangzhou Islands *50*; Shenzhen *51*; Venetian *61*; Zhongshan *50*

IDU Huanggang Redevelopment Plan 144
Imperial Treasury 63
infrastructure 1–3, 9–10, 17–18, 27–30, 37, 40, 193–195
Individual Visit Scheme (IVS) 100
Instagram Pier 134
integrated rehabilitation (*Zonghe Zhengzhi*) 145
inter-city and inner-city express trains 34
Intercity Commute Railway (ICR) 18, 193
International Design Program (IDP) 147, 154–156
International Financial Center (IFC) 68
island network 43–45; Chilajiao island of Hong Kong 43; Dachan islands of Shenzhen 43; Dayu islands of Hong Kong 43; Dong'ao 43; Gaolan 43; Guangzhou Islands 44–45; Hebao islands of Zhuhai 43; Hengqin 43; Jiu'ao island of Macao 43; Lintin Island/Nei Lingding (Shenzhen) 45; Nansha area *44*; Neilingdin island of Shenzhen 43; Qi'ao 43; Sanzao 43; timeline, realities and fictions 43–45; Whampoa Island/The Canton System (Guangzhou) 45

Jiangmen 10
Jinping, X. 43
Jiu'ao Island of Macao 43
Jockey Club Design Institute for Social Innovation (DISI) 133
Johnson, E. L. 156

Kai Tak 132
Karatani, K. 37n1
key node cities 10
Knierbein, S. 161
Koetter, F. 49
Koolhaas, R. 68, 101, 107n1, 120, 121, 180
Korean War 78
Kowloon–Canton Railway Corporation (KCRC) 23n11
Kwai Chung Container Port 67
Kwan Mun Hau 156

Lam, C. 164
Lane, S. F. 171
Lantau Island *42*; Lantau Tomorrow Vision 42–43; Lo Tin in 45–48, *47*
Law, N. 164
Lefebvre, H. 29, 30
Legislative Council (LegCo) Building, Hong Kong 165
Lennon Walls 161
Leung, C. Y. 162
Li, D. 202
Li, P. 199
Lianhuashan Park, Shenzhen *19*
Lintin Island/Nei Lingding (Shenzhen) 45
Lion Rock 161
liquid stories 40–48; built *vs.* non-built of PRD *41*; from 1980 to 2002 42; liquid geography 40–43; maritime cultures in PRD 40–48; sand and other fluid grounds 40–43; sediments 40–43; *see also* fluid mythology; island network
Litchi Gardens 72
Litchi Park 67
London School of Economics' (LSE) 121
Lo Tin in Lantau 45–48, *47*
Lotus Hill Park 140
Luohu District 138
Lynch, K. 62, 63

Macartney, G. 45
Macau 18, 20, 43, 80, 99–107, 151, 196, 198, 205; colonial urbanization in 18; Macau SAR 10; Portuguese-Chinese urban-spatial configuration 18
Macau, interiorized urbanism in 98–107; Chinese tourists in Macau 99–101; Cotai Central Resort 103; Four Seasons Resort 103; Macau complex 103; macro-economic plan 100; megamachine, GBA 102–103; metropolis, GBA 101–102; MGM Macau Resort *101*; micro-physical effort 100; model city 103–105; National New-Type Urbanization Plan 100; Parisian Macau property 103; quality consumers creating 105–107; Venetian Complex 103, *104*, *106*; Venetian Macao Resort *99*
macro-economic plan 100
Madanipour, A. 193
Magic Carpet Project 169–170, *170*
Magic Lanes 169, 171
Make a Difference (MaD) social lab 171–172, *172*, 176
"Maozhou River" *186*, 188, *189*
Mar, P. 82
market economies 31
Mass Transit Railway (MTR), Hong Kong 23n11, 34, 67; Tsuen Wan line 152; West Island Line 170
Mattern, S. 184

McGee, T. 66
megacity 15, 23n5, 102
mega-city regions 22n5, 23n6
megalopolis 15, 22n5, 102
megamachine 15, 102–103, 198
megapolitan areas 22n5
megaregion: built environment 18–20; concept 10–13; emerging public realm of 17–22; land-infrastructure nexus 17–18; open space systems 18–20; public spaces 18–20; spaces in 13; spatial form of 14–17; theoretical terms 14–15; weak publics of 20–22
megaregional dialectic, GBA public realm and 192–206, *197*; *see also* megaregional public space, the (**tmps**); public spaces in the megaregion (**psmr**)
megaregionalism of GBA 13–14, 17–18, 23n9, 193
megaregionality in GBA 13–14, 17, 20–22, 23n8
megaregional public space, the (**tmps**) 193; as economic engine 196–198; as infrastructure of mobility 193–195; as open space system 195–196; political homogenization and 198–199
megaregional space 13
metacity 15, *50*; heterotopic systems 68–70; public space in 70–73; *see also* third space and gardens
metapolis 15
metropolis 15, 22n5
Metropolis, GBA 101–102
metropolitan region 23n6
MGM Macau Resort *101*
micro-physical effort 100
migrant business enterprises (MBEs) 124
Miller, H. 109
Mitchell, D. 158, 161, 166
model city 103–105
Mumford, L. 102
Mutations 120–121

National New-Type Urbanization Plan (2014–2020) 10, 80
national urbanization strategy 10
"*neibu*" (inside) 192
Neilingdin Island of Shenzhen 43, 45
neo-liberal commercial developments 77
neo-liberalism 169
neo-liberal policies 81
nested networks and systems 1–3
networked public space 130
networked urbanism *see* Shenzhen, value networks creation in
New China Land Reform 66
New Civic Center planning 138–140
New Jersey Institute of Technology (NJIT) 121
Ng, M. K. 83
Ning, O. 183, 184
non-governmental organizations (NGOs) 20
non-transparent territorial strategies 22

oligoptic approach 125–126
One Band and Three Axes plan 34
One Belt One Road (OBOR) strategy 22n2
One Country Two Systems 80
On Rural Work 91
Open Coastal Cities (OCCs) 180
open space system 18–20, 206n2
Orff, K. 9
organic decentralization 37n5
Other Ways of Doing Architecture 185
Overseas Chinese Town (OCT), Shenzhen 68

Pain, K. 22n4
Peak Funicular 66
Pearl River (*Zhu Jiang*) 41
Pearl River Delta (PRD) 4; Castells' network diagram of *15*; public space in 49–61; rapid urbanization of 9; urbanization of *11*; *see also* hyper-collage city of PRD; liquid stories
Pearl River Delta (PRD) estuary to GBA megaregion 9–23; chronology of transformation 9–10; social organizations 14; urban governmentality 14
Pei Tao (*Beidu Chanshi*) 48n5
People's Republic of China (PRC) 9, 80, 94, 98, 149, 158
performative/performativity 4, 7, 69, 72, 154, 180
planetary urbanization 23n6
Portuguese-Chinese urban-spatial configuration 18
public open space (POS) accessibility 109–118, 195; data sources and preprocessing 110–111; residential buildings 111, *112*; residents' perceptions 111–114, **114**; social study schema 111–114; spatial accessibility and people's perceptions, comparison 115–117, *115*, **116**; spatial accessibility of 110–111, *113*
public realm 2–3, 4, 7, 9–23, 37, 120–126, 149, 154, 192–206
public realm in Shenzhen 120–126; "Clues" map *124–125*; Sungang-Qingshuihe 124; migrant business enterprises (MBEs) 124; oligoptic approach 125–126; responsible, remote research and design of 120–126; Urban Villages 124
public space 18–20; "aformal" approach to 7; in the Imperial City of Faith 63–65; pedagogical approach to 5; in the PRD City Machine 65–67; theorizations of 3; in the village 187–189; *see also* gardens as public space
public space, Shenzhen city as 89–97; access to public goods 90–92; English-language media 95; Huaqiangbei, Chimerica 94–96; Luohu-Shangbu companies 90; nets-to-riches 90–92; Shekou Industrial Zone 93; significance 90–92
public spaces in the megaregion (**psmr**) 193, 199–205; approaches 206; appropriations 200–203, *201*; assumptions 206; contestations 200–203; occupations 200–203; participation 200; possibilities 206; urban pedagogy and education 203–205; *see also* megaregional public space, the (**tmps**)
Pun Tong Village 69

Qi'ao 43

rail connections, grades of 34; inter-city and inner-city express trains 34; local lines 34; trunk lines 34
reinvented public space 132–134
re-learning the city in GBA 180–190; "Aformality" and 181–185; Aformal Academy workshop *183*; agency, perspective and medium 183; Baishizhou village workshop *186*; floating school 183; Maozhou River walk *186*; public space in the village 187–189; Shangmeilin Village workshop *185*; un-learning 182
residential buildings as part of an urban village (UVRBs) 111–114
Rietveld, E. 188
Rise of the Network Society, The (Castells) 15, 27
Riviera Gardens 149
Riyao, B. 166
Rowe, C. 49
Roy, A. 22

Saarinen, E. 31, 37n5
Sai Kwan Literary Pagoda Tower 69
Sam Tung Uk Hakka Walled Village Museum 154
Sands Casino 68
Sanzao 43
SARS epidemic 173–174
Sassen, S. 81
Schafran, A. 23n8
Schmitt, C. 47, 48
Schoon, S. 206n5
Scott, J. C. 48n1
Secret of the Shenzhen Sphinx, The 90
sediments 40–43
Self-Build Bishop Hill Community 172–174
semi-private public space 131–132
Sen, S. Y. 66
Shamian Island 64
Shan, P. C. H. 6
Shantou 1, 9
Sha Tau Kok 85
Shek Kip Mei 172
Shekou Industrial Zone 93
Shenzhen 1, 17–20, 27–37, 45, *51*, 68, 77, 80, 84, 85, 89–97, 99, 110–111, 114, 122–126, 136–141, 180–189; Special Economic Zone (SEZ) 1, 9–10, 31, 40, 68, 90, 140, 180
Shenzhen Convention and Exhibition Center 141
Shenzhen Qianhai Eco City 69
Shenzhen's urban renewal 136–146; advocacy and contestation 144; Civic Square *137*;

dilemma of the central axis and public space 142–143; erasure, urbanization and demolition 141–142; Futian CBD planning *139*; 'Grand Urban Living Room' 136–138; Huanggang urban village *138*; inner-city Shenzhen *140*; operational strategy *141*; planning 138–140; prehistory of Shenzhen 140–141; public spaces during 136–146; research and design 143–144; Shenzhen Futian Central Business District Area 139

Shenzhen: The Silicon Valley of Hardware 95
Shenzhen Urban Planning and Design Institute (SZUPDI) 146n1
Shenzhen, value networks creation in 27–38; 1980–2020, infrastructures and centers *28*; 1986 Shenzhen Masterplan 31; 2010–2020 plan 32–36; exacerbating differences in value, machines for 27–30; in the 2000s 31; infrastructures and centers in 27–38; planning 31; spatialized economic strategy, planning as 30–31; urban networks 27–30; value networks in motion 36–37, 37n1; ways of 30; *see also* Three-Axis Two-Band Multi-Center
Shimao Shenzhen-Hong Kong International Center 36
Sicheng, L. 31, 37n5
Simmel, G. 2, 87
Singapore-Johore border zone 81
Sino-British Joint Declaration of 1984 22n1, 23n7, 153
Sino-Portuguese Joint Declaration of 1987 22n1
social machine 102
social organizations (*shehui zuzhi*) 200
socio-materiality 2
spatial accessibility and people's perceptions, comparison 115–117, *115*, **116**
spatialized economic strategy, planning as 30–31
Special Administrative Regions (SARs) 1, 5, 6, 9, 10, 23n7, 80, 100, 206n6
Special Economic Zones (SEZs) 1; Shenzhen 1, 31; Zhuhai 1
Starling Inlet 85
Statistical Product and Service Solutions (SPSS) 115
Statue Square garden 66–67
Story of Shenzhen, The 92
Sungang Qingshuihe (SQ) District 122
Swan, W. 66
systems 1–3
systems theory 2

tactical sub-regionalism 13
Tahrir Square 160
Taksim Square 160
Tan, X. 206n5
Tang, B. 6
Taylor, P. J. 22n5
Tenth Five-Year Plan (2001–2005) 10

third space 62, 65–66, 68, 82
third space and gardens 70–73; city living room *71*; community plaza *71*; roof playground *71*; sky garden *71*
Thirteenth Five-Year Plan (2016–2020) 10
Three-Axis Two-Band Multi-Center 32–36; 1986 plan of Shenzhen SEZ *32*; 1996–2010 plan of Shenzhen *32*; by August, 2020 *34*; investment intensity in Shenzhen, 1997–2018 *35*; Shenzhen urban design plan *33*; *see also* rail connections, grades of
Three Olds Regeneration Policy 21
Tiananmen Square 161
Tijuana-San Diego border zone 81
Tin, S. 66
Tin Mei Avenue 161
Tolo Harbour, Hong Kong *46*
transient public space 83–85
transport networks 4, 86
trunk lines 34
Tse, J. 165
Tsuen Wan Bay 149
Tsuen Wan, Hong Kong 147–157; Chu Hai University migration *148*; Chu Hai, a genealogy of institutional exile 149–151; drawing machine *155*; a genealogy of a new town 151–153; International Design Program 154–156; layered model of *150*; metacommunity frameworks 148–149; Nan Fung Mills 152; spatial production of social publics in 147–157
Tsuen Wan New Town 149
Tsuen Wan Riviera Park 149
two-step floating catchment area method (2SFCA) model 110–111

Umbrella Movement 20, *78*, 163–164, *202*
un-learning 182
Urban Age Program 121
urban green system 196
urbanization 141–142
urban metrofitting 6
urban planning 9, 18, 27, 31, 110, 128–132, 136, 139, 142–145, 192, 198–200; between 1949 and 1978 18; first wave (1980 to 2010) 20; from 1980 18, 20; of Shenzhen 18–20; in the 21st century 20; urban post-planning 6
Urban Planning and Design Institute of Shenzhen (UPDIS) 32
Urban Renewal Authority (URA) 131
urban tinkering 6
Urban Villages (*chengzhongcun*, 城中村) 124, *140*, 187
Urbanus 69, *71*

value networks in motion 36–37, 37n1
Venetian Casino 68
Venetian Complex 103

Venetian Macao Resort *99*
Victoria Park 161
villages in the city (*chengzhongcun*) 1
Vlassenrood, L. 9

waibu (outside) 192
Wan, T. 67, 153–155
Wang, X. 37, 38n9
Wanshan Archipelago 42
Weizman, E. 84
West Kowloon Station 68, *194*
Whampoa Anchorage 45
Whampoa Island/The Canton System (Guangzhou) 45
Wing, C. T. 162
Wirth, L. 104
Wong, A. 171, 172, 176

Wong, J. 163, 164
Wong, S. W. 6
Woo, E. S. W. 29
world city network 22n5
Wu, G. 10, 34

Yim, R. 162

Zaha Hadid (Guangzhou Opera House) 69
Zhang, X. 22
Zhanxiang, C. 31, 37n5
Zhao, J. 196
Zhaoqing 10
Zheng, T. 29
Zongheng, X. 34
Zhongshan 10, *50*
Zhuhai SEZ 9–10, 80